Lecture Notes in Computer Science   13998

Founding Editors

Gerhard Goos
Juris Hartmanis

The series Lecture Notes in Computer Science (LNCS), including its subseries Lecture Notes in Artificial Intelligence (LNAI) and Lecture Notes in Bioinformatics (LNBI), has established itself as a medium for the publication of new developments in computer science and information technology research, teaching, and education.

LNCS enjoys close cooperation with the computer science R & D community, the series counts many renowned academics among its volume editors and paper authors, and collaborates with prestigious societies. Its mission is to serve this international community by providing an invaluable service, mainly focused on the publication of conference and workshop proceedings and postproceedings. LNCS commenced publication in 1973.

Catia Pesquita · Hala Skaf-Molli ·
Vasilis Efthymiou · Sabrina Kirrane ·
Axel Ngonga · Diego Collarana ·
Renato Cerqueira · Mehwish Alam ·
Cassia Trojahn · Sven Hertling
Editors

The Semantic Web: ESWC 2023 Satellite Events

Hersonissos, Crete, Greece, May 28 – June 1, 2023
Proceedings

Editors

Catia Pesquita (iD)
University of Lisbon
Lisbon, Portugal

Vasilis Efthymiou (iD)
Foundation for Research and Technology
Heraklion, Greece

Axel Ngonga (iD)
University of Paderborn
Paderborn, Germany

Renato Cerqueira (iD)
IBM Research
Rio de Janeiro, Brazil

Cassia Trojahn (iD)
Institut de Recherche en Informatique de
Toulouse
Toulouse, France

Hala Skaf-Molli (iD)
University of Nantes
Nantes, France

Sabrina Kirrane (iD)
Vienna University of Economics
and Business
Vienna, Austria

Diego Collarana (iD)
Fraunhofer IAIS
Sankt Augustin, Germany

Mehwish Alam (iD)
Institut Polytechnique de Paris
Palaiseau, France

Sven Hertling (iD)
University of Mannheim
Mannheim, Germany

ISSN 0302-9743   ISSN 1611-3349 (electronic)
Lecture Notes in Computer Science
ISBN 978-3-031-43457-0   ISBN 978-3-031-43458-7 (eBook)
https://doi.org/10.1007/978-3-031-43458-7

This Springer imprint is published by the registered company Springer Nature Switzerland AG
The registered company address is: Gewerbestrasse 11, 6330 Cham, Switzerland

Paper in this product is recyclable.

Preface

This volume contains the satellite proceedings of the 20th edition of the Extended Semantic Web Conference (ESWC 2023). ESWC is a major venue for discussing the latest in scientific results and innovations related to the Semantic Web, knowledge graphs, and Web data. The satellite events are an important aspect of facilitating this discussion. The satellite events at ESWC 2023 included the poster and demo session, the PhD symposium, the industry track, and project networking, as well as workshops and tutorials. Due to scheduling, the papers from these events are published as post-proceedings. The poster and demo track received 71 submissions of which 12 posters and 19 demos were accepted. All submissions received 2 to 3 reviews. Posters and demos highlight new research trajectories and ideas within the community and allow for discussions of the latest results. Here, we see topics such as semantics and multi-modality (e.g. video, audio), the importance of Wikidata, methods for dealing with tabular data, and advances in semantic technologies and machine learning. The PhD symposium is an important venue for doctoral students to present and receive feedback on their research. In total, 24 submissions were received, of which 12 papers were accepted. Both the review and guidance processes were intensive and tailored to helping the students improve their research plans. This included two-three reviews for each paper as well as peer review by the students themselves. Additionally, all papers were guided by mentors who are senior members of the community. Importantly, senior members of the community attended each presentation to give in-depth feedback. The symposium also featured a keynote by John Domingue, Professor of Computer Science, Knowledge Media Institute, The Open University, United Kingdom. The industry track features papers that discuss the adoption and usage of semantic technologies within organisations. Importantly, papers must have a co-author with a non-academic affiliation. We received 14 submissions of which 7 were accepted. All papers received 3. The industry track featured papers from a wide variety of organisations including Bosch, eBay, Fraunhofer, TALES, and Yext. Topics included scalability of semantic technologies in real-world cases, the application of knowledge graphs to empower eCommerce sites, ontologies for smart buildings, hybrid AI solutions for supplier optimization, knowledge base systems in critical systems, and combining knowledge graphs with large language models. ESWC 2023 featured a strong collection of 10 workshops and 2 tutorials covering different topics revolving around knowledge graphs, such as natural language processing, biomedical data, and web of things. An addition to this year's program was a main conference presentation of the outcomes of the workshops and tutorials, quickly bringing the learning and observations to the entire community. Later in this volume you will find a more detailed review of the workshops and tutorials. While not formally part of the proceedings, ESWC has a history of providing network opportunities for projects and in particular EU projects.

We would like to thank Armando Stellato and Maria Poveda-Villalon for organising this part of the program for this year.

July 2023

Catia Pesquita
Hala Skaf-Molli
Vasilis Efthymiou
Sabrina Kirrane
Axel Ngonga
Diego Collarana
Renato Cerqueira
Mehwish Alam
Cassia Trojahn
Sven Hertling

Organization

General Chair

Catia Pesquita   LASIGE, Faculdade de Ciências, Universidade de
                                        Lisboa, Portugal

Research Track Program Chairs

Ernesto Jimenez-Ruiz   City, University of London, UKSIRIUS, Norway
Jamie McCusker   Rensselaer Polytechnic Institute, USA

Resource Track Program Chairs

Anastasia Dimou   KU Leuven, Belgium
Raphael Troncy   EURECOM, France

In-Use Track Program Chairs

Daniel Faria   INESC-IDInstituto Superior Técnico,
                                        Universidade de Lisboa, Portugal
Mauro Dragoni   Fondazione Bruno Kessler, Trento, Italy

Workshops and Tutorials Chairs

Mehwish Alam   Télécom Paris, Institut Polytechnique de Paris,
                                        France
Cassia Trojahn   IRIT, France

Poster and Demo Chairs

Hala Skaf-Moli   University of Nantes, France
Vasilis Efthymiou   FORTH-ICS, Greece

Symposium Chairs

Sabrina Kirrane   Technische Universität Dresden, Germany
Axel Ngonga   Universität Paderborn, Germany

Industry Track Program Chairs

Diego Collarana   Fraunhofer IAIS, Germany
Renato Cerqueira   IBM Research, Brazil

Sponsorship

Albert Meroño   King's College London, UK
Joe Raad   University of Paris-Saclay, France

Project Networking

Armando Stellato   University of Rome Tor Vergata, Italy
Maria Poveda-Villalon   Universidad Politécnica de Madrid, Spain

Web and Publicity

Eleni Ilkou   L3S Research Center, Leibniz Universität
                                             Hannover, Germany
Romana Pernisch   Vrije Universiteit Amsterdam, the Netherlands

Proceedings

Sven Hertling   University of Mannheim, Germany

ESWC: The Next 20 years

Heiko Paulheim   University of Mannheim, Germany
Irene Celino   Cefriel, Italy

ESWC: 20th Anniversary

John Domingue   Knowledge Media Institute, The Open University,
                                 UK

Program Committee

Ibrahim Abdelaziz	IBM, USA
Maribel Acosta	Ruhr University Bochum, Germany
Nitish Aggarwal	Roku Inc., USA
Shqiponja Ahmetaj	Vienna University of Technology, Austria
Mehwish Alam	Télécom Paris, France
Céline Alec	Université de Caen-Normandie, France
Vladimir Alexiev	Ontotext Corp, Bulgaria
Panos Alexopoulos	Textkernel B.V., The Netherlands
Alsayed Algergawy	University of Jena, Germany
José Luis Ambite	University of Southern California, USA
Vito Walter Anelli	Politecnico di Bari, Italy
Grigoris Antoniou	University of Huddersfield, UK
Julián Arenas-Guerrero	Universidad Politécnica de Madrid, Spain
Natanael Arndt	eccenca GmbH, Germany
Luigi Asprino	University of Bologna, Italy
Ghislain Auguste Atemezing	Mondeca, France
Maurizio Atzori	University of Cagliari, Italy
Sören Auer	TIB Leibniz Information Centre for Science & Technology and University of Hannover, Germany
Nathalie Aussenac-Gilles	IRIT CNRS, France
Amr Azzam	Vienna University of Business and Economics, Austria
Carlos Badenes-Olmedo	Universidad Politécnica de Madrid, Spain
Ratan Bahadur Thapa	University of Oslo, Norway
Booma Sowkarthiga Balasubramani	University of Illinois at Chicago, USA
Rafael Berlanga	Universitat Jaume I, Spain
Nikos Bikakis	ATHENA Research Center, Greece
Russa Biswas	Hasso Plattner Institute, Germany
Christian Bizer	University of Mannheim, Germany
Peter Bloem	Vrije Universiteit Amsterdam, The Netherlands
Eva Blomqvist	Linköping University, Sweden
Carlos Bobed	University of Zaragoza, Spain

Fernando Bobillo   University of Zaragoza, Spain
Iovka Boneva   University of Lille, France
Georgeta Bordea   Université de Bordeaux, France
Alex Borgida   Rutgers University, USA
Paolo Bouquet   University of Trento, Italy
Zied Bouraoui   CRIL - CNRS & University of Artois, France
Loris Bozzato   Fondazione Bruno Kessler, Italy
Janez Brank   Jožef Stefan Institute, Slovenia
Anna Breit   Semantic Web Company, Austria
Carlos Buil Aranda   Universidad Técnica Federico Santa Mara, Chile
Davide Buscaldi   LIPN, Université Sorbonne Paris Nord, France
Jean-Paul Calbimonte   University of Applied Sciences and Arts Western
    Switzerland, Switzerland
Pablo Calleja   Universidad Polytécnica de Madrid, Spain
Antonella Carbonaro   University of Bologna, Italy
Leyla Jael Castro   ZB MED Information Centre for Life Sciences,
    Germany
Sylvie Cazalens   LIRIS - INSA de Lyon, France
Irene Celino   Cefriel, Italy
Renato Cerqueira   IBM Research Brazil, Brazil
Yoan Chabot   Orange Labs, France
Pierre-Antoine Champin   LIRIS, Université Claude Bernard Lyon 1, France
Vinay Chaudhri   Self-Employed
David Chaves-Fraga   Universidad Politécnica de Madrid, Spain
Jiaoyan Chen   University of Oxford, UK
Gong Cheng   Nanjing University, China
Sijin Cheng   Linköping University, Sweden
Philipp Cimiano   Bielefeld University, Germany
Andrea Cimmino Arriaga   Universidad Politécnica de Madrid, Spain
Michael Cochez   Vrije Universiteit Amsterdam, The Netherlands
Diego Collarana Vargas   Fraunhofer IAIS, Germany
Pieter Colpaert   Ghent University imec, Belgium
Oscar Corcho   Universidad Politécnica de Madrid, Spain
Francesco Corcoglioniti   Free University of Bozen/Bolzano, Italy
Julien Corman   Free University of Bozen-Bolzano, Italy
Marco Cremaschi   Università di Milano-Bicocca, Italy
Vincenzo Cutrona   University of Applied Sciences and Arts of
    Southern Switzerland, Switzerland
Claudia d'Amato   University of Bari, Italy
Enrico Daga   Open University, UK
Jérôme David   Inria, France
Victor de Boer   Vrije Universiteit Amsterdam, The Netherlands

Daniele Dell'Aglio	Aalborg University, Denmark
Elena Demidova	University of Bonn, Germany
Ronald Denaux	Amazon, Spain
Gayo Diallo	ISPED & LABRI, University of Bordeaux, France
Stefan Dietze	GESIS - Leibniz Institute for the Social Sciences, Germany
Anastasia Dimou	KU Leuven, Belgium
Milan Dojchinovski	Czech Technical University in Prague, Czech Republic
John Domingue	Open University, UK
Elvira Domínguez	Universidad Politécnica de Madrid, Spain
Ivan Donadello	Free University of Bozen-Bolzano, Italy
Hang Dong	University of Oxford, UK
Mauro Dragoni	Fondazione Bruno Kessler, Italy
Vasilis Efthymiou	FORTH-ICS, Greece
Shusaku Egami	National Institute of Advanced Industrial Science and Technology, Japan
Fajar J. Ekaputra	Vienna University of Economic and Business, Austria
Vadim Ermolayev	Ukrainian Catholic University, Ukraine
Paola Espinoza Arias	Universidad Politécnica de Madrid, Spain
Lorena Etcheverry	Universidad de la República, Uruguay
Pavlos Fafalios	Institute of Computer Science, FORTH-ICS, Greece
Alessandro Faraotti	IBM, Italy
Daniel Faria	INESC-ID, Universidade de Lisboa, Portugal
Catherine Faron	Université Côte d'Azur, France
Anna Fensel	Wageningen University and Research, The Netherlands
Alba Fernandez-Izquierdo	BASF Digital Solutions, Spain
Javier D. Fernández	F. Hoffmann-La Roche AG, Switzerland
Mariano Fernández López	Universidad San Pablo CEU, Spain
Jesualdo Tomás Fernández-Breis	Universidad de Murcia, Spain
Sebastián Ferrada	Linköping University, Sweden
Sebastien Ferre	University of Rennes, CNRS, IRISA, France
Erwin Filtz	Siemens AG Österreich, Austria
Giorgos Flouris	FORTH-ICS, Greece
Flavius Frasincar	Erasmus University Rotterdam, The Netherlands
Naoki Fukuta	Shizuoka University, Japan
Adam Funk	University of Sheffield, UK
Michael Färber	Karlsruhe Institute of Technology, Germany
Roghaiyeh Ramisa Gachpaz Hamed	Trinity College Dublin, Ireland

Mohamed H. Gad-Elrab	Bosch Center for Artificial Intelligence, Germany
Alban Gaignard	CNRS, France
Luis Galárraga	Inria, France
Fabien Gandon	Inria, France
Aldo Gangemi	Università di Bologna & CNR-ISTC, Italy
Raúl García-Castro	Universidad Polytécnica de Madrid, Spain
Andrés García-Silva	Expert.ai, Spain
Daniel Garijo	Universidad Politécnica de Madrid, Spain
Yuxia Geng	Zhejiang University, China
Gerhard Wohlgenannt	LGT, Liechtenstein
Genet Asefa Gesese	FIZ Karlsruhe Leibniz-Institut für Informationsinfrastruktur, Germany
Pouya Ghiasnezhad Omran	Australian National University, Australia
Shrestha Ghosh	Max Planck Institute for Informatics, Germany
Martin Giese	University of Oslo, Norway
Eleonora Giunchiglia	University of Oxford, UK
Birte Glimm	Universität Ulm, Germany
Jose Manuel Gomez-Perez	Expert.ai, Spain
Jorge Gracia	University of Zaragoza, Spain
Irlan Grangel	Bosch Corporate Research, Germany
Alasdair Gray	Heriot-Watt University, UK
Dagmar Gromann	University of Vienna, Austria
Paul Groth	University of Amsterdam, The Netherlands
Claudio Gutierrez	Universidad de Chile, Chile
Christophe Guéret	Accenture Labs, Ireland
Peter Haase	metaphacts GmbH, Germany
Mohad-Saïd Hacid	Université Lyon 1, France
Lavdim Halilaj	Bosch Research, Germany
Armin Haller	Australian National University, Australia
Harry Halpin	American University of Beirut, Lebanon
Andreas Harth	University of Erlangen-Nuremberg, Fraunhofer IISSCS, Germany
Olaf Hartig	Linköping University, Sweden
Mounira Harzallah	LS2N, University of Nantes, France
Oktie Hassanzadeh	IBM, USA
Janna Hastings	University of Zurich, Switzerland
Maria M. Hedblom	Jönköping University, Sweden
Ivan Heibi	University of Bologna, Italy
Nicolas Heist	University of Mannheim, Germany
Lars Heling	Stardog Union, Germany
Daniel Hernandez	University of Stuttgart, Germany
Nathalie Hernandez	IRIT, France

Tobias Käfer   Karlsruhe Institute of Technology, Germany
Jose Emilio Labra Gayo   Universidad de Oviedo, Spain
Frederique Laforest   Laboratoire d'Informatique en Image et Systéme
                                       d'Information UMR CNRS 5205, France
Sarasi Lalithsena   IBM Watson, USA
Patrick Lambrix   Linköping University, Sweden
André Lamúrias   NOVA School of Science and Technology,
                                       Portugal
Danh Le Phuoc   TU Berlin, Germany
Maxime Lefrançois   MINES Saint-Étienne, France
Huanyu Li   Linköping University, Sweden
Sven Lieber   Royal Library of Belgium, Belgium
Pasquale Lisena   EURECOM, France
Wenqiang Liu   Xi'an Jiaotong University, China
Jun Ma   Amazon, USA
Maria Maleshkova   University of Siegen, Germany
Claudia Marinica   Polytech Nantes, LS2N, France
Beatrice Markhoff   Université de Tours, France
Maria Vanina Martinez   IIIA - CSIC, Spain
Miguel A. Martinez-Prieto   University of Valladolid, Spain
Jose L. Martinez-Rodriguez   Autonomous University of Tamaulipas, Mexico
Jamie McCusker   Rensselaer Polytechnic Institute, USA
Lionel Medini   CNRS, France
Albert Meroño-Peñuela   King's College London, UK
Nandana Mihindukulasooriya   IBM Research AI, USA
Daniel Miranker   University of Texas at Austin, USA
Pascal Molli   University of Nantes - LS2N, France
Gabriela Montoya   Aalborg University, Denmark
Jose Mora   Universidad Politécnica de Madrid, Spain
Boris Motik   University of Oxford, UK
Enrico Motta   Open University, UK
Diego Moussallem   Paderborn University, Germany
Summaya Mumtaz   University of Oslo, Norway
Raghava Mutharaju   IIIT-Delhi, India
Ralf Möller   University of Lübeck, Germany
Hubert Naacke   Sorbonne Université, LIP6, France
Shinichi Nagano   Toshiba Corporation, Japan
Natthawut Kertkeidkachorn   Japan Advanced Institute of Science and
                                       Technology, Japan
María Navas-Loro   Universidad Politécnica de Madrid, Spain
Axel Ngonga   Universität Paterborn, Germany
Tuan-Phong Nguyen   Max Planck Institute for Informatics, Germany

Vinh Nguyen	National Library of Medicine, NIH, USA
Andriy Nikolov	AstraZeneca, UK
Andrea Giovanni Nuzzolese	University of Bologna, Italy
Cliff O'Reilly	City, University of London, UK
Femke Ongenae	Ghent University – imec, Belgium
Andreas L. Opdahl	University of Bergen, Norway
Fabrizio Orlandi	ADAPT, Trinity College Dublin, Ireland
Francesco Osborne	Open University, UK
Ankur Padia	Liberty Mutual Insurance, USA
Matteo Palmonari	University of Milano-Bicocca, Italy
Jeff Z. Pan	University of Edinburgh, UK
George Papadakis	National Technical University of Athens, Greece
Pierre-Henri	Paris Télcom Paris, France
Heiko Paulheim	University of Mannheim, Germany
Terry Payne	University of Liverpool, UK
Tassilo Pellegrini	St. Pölten University of Applied Sciences, Austria
Maria Angela Pellegrino	Università degli Studi di Salerno, Italy
Bernardo Pereira Nunes	Australian National University, Australia
Sujan Perera	IBM Watson, USA
Nathalie Pernelle	LIPN, Université Sorbonne Paris Nord, France
Romana Pernisch	Vrije Universiteit Amsterdam, The Netherlands
Catia Pesquita	Universidade de Lisboa, Portugal
Alina Petrova	University of Oxford, UK
Rafael Peñaloza	University of Milano-Bicocca, Italy
Patrick Philipp	KIT (AIFB), Germany
Guangyuan Piao	National University of Ireland, Ireland
Francesco Piccialli	University of Naples Federico II, Italy
Lydia Pintscher	Wikimedia Deutschland, Germany
Alessandro Piscopo	BBC, UK
Dimitris Plexousakis	Institute of Computer Science, FORTH, Greece
Axel Polleres	Vienna University of Economics and Business, Austria
María Poveda-Villalón	Universidad Politécnica de Madrid, Spain
Nicoleta Preda	Université Paris-Saclay (Versailles), France
Valentina Presutti	University of Bologna, Italy
Cédric Pruski	Luxembourg Institute of Science and Technology, Luxembourg
Guilin Qi	Southeast University, China
Joe Raad	Vrije Universiteit Amsterdam, The Netherlands
Alexandre Rademaker	IBM Research and EMAp/FGV, Brazil
Sandro Rama Fiorini	IBM Research Brazil, Brazil
David Ratcliffe	Microsoft, Australia

Simon Razniewski	Bosch Center for AI, Germany
Diego Reforgiato	Università degli studi di Cagliari, Italy
Achim Rettinger	Trier University, Germany
Juan L. Reutter	Pontificia Universidad Católica de Chile, Chile
Artem Revenko	Semantic Web Company GmbH, Austria
Mariano Rico	Universidad Politécnica de Madrid, Spain
Petar Ristoski	eBay Inc., USA
Giuseppe Rizzo	LINKS Foundation, Italy
Sergio José Rodríguez Méndez	Australian National University, Australia
Edelweis Rohrer	Universidad de la República, Uruguay
Julian Rojas	Ghent University, Belgium
Maria Del Mar Roldan-Garcia	Universidad de Málaga, Spain
Julien Romero	Samovar, Télécom SudParis, France
Oscar Romero	Universitat Politécnica de Catalunya, Spain
Miguel Romero Orth	Universidad Adolfo Ibáñez, Chile
Henry Rosales-Méndez	University of Chile, Chile
Catherine Roussey	INRAE, France
Jože Rožanec Jožef	Stefan Institute, Slovenia
Sebastian Rudolph	TU Dresden, Germany
Anisa Rula	University of Brescia, Italy
Marta Sabou	Vienna University of Economics and Business, Austria
Harald Sack	FIZ Karlsruhe, Leibniz Institute for Information Infrastructure & KIT Karlsruhe, Germany
Angelo Antonio Salatino	Open University, UK
Muhammad Saleem	University of Leizpig, Germany
Emanuel Sallinger	TU Wien, Austria
Uli Sattler	University of Manchester, UK
Fatiha Saïs	LRI (Paris Sud University & CNRS8623), Paris-Saclay University, France
Ralf Schenkel	Trier University, Germany
Stefan Schlobach	Vrije Universiteit Amsterdam, The Netherlands
Jodi Schneider	University of Illinois at Urbana-Champaign, USA
Daniel Schwabe	Pontificia Universidade Católica, Brazil
Jetzabel Maritza Serna Olvera	Universitat Politécnica de Catalunya, Spain
Patricia Serrano-Alvarado	LS2N - University of Nantes, France
Bariş Sertkaya	Frankfurt University of Applied Sciences, Germany
Cogan Shimizu	Wright State University, USA
Pavel Shvaiko	Informatica Trentina SpA, Italy
Lucia Siciliani	University of Bari Aldo Moro, Italy

Gerardo Simari	Universidad Nacional del Sur and CONICET, Argentina
Kuldeep Singh	Cerence GmbH and Zerotha Research, Germany
Sneha Singhania	Max Planck Institute for Informatics, Germany
Hala Skaf-Molli	University of Nantes - LS2N, France
Xingyi Song	University of Sheffield, UK
Rita Sousa	Universidade de Lisboa, Portugal
Blerina Spahiu	Università degli Studi di Milano-Bicocca, Italy
Marc Spaniol	Université de Caen–Normandie, France
Kavitha Srinivas	IBM, USA
Steffen Staab	Universität Stuttgart, Germany and University of Southampton, UK
Kostas Stefanidis	Tampere University, Finland
Nadine Steinmetz	TU Ilmenau, Germany
Armando Stellato	University of Rome Tor Vergata, Italy
Lise Stork	Vrije Universiteit Amsterdam, The Netherlands
Umberto Straccia	ISTI-CNR, Italy
Zequn Sun	Nanjing University, China
Vojtěch Svátek	Prague University of Economics and Business, Czech Republic
Danai Symeonidou	INRAE, France
Ruben Taelman	Ghent University imec, Belgium
Valentina Tamma	University of Liverpool, UK
David Tena Cucala	University of Oxford, UK
Andrea Tettamanzi	Université Côte d'Azur, France
Andreas Thalhammer	Roche Diagnostics, Switzerland
Krishnaprasad Thirunarayan	Wright State University, USA
Steffen Thoma	FZI Research Center for Information Technology, Germany
Ilaria Tiddi	Vrije Universiteit Amsterdam, The Netherlands
Konstantin Todorov	LIRMM/University of Montpellier, France
Riccardo Tommasini	INSA Lyon – LIRIS, France
Sebastian Tramp	eccenca GmbH, Germany
Cassia Trojahn	IRIT, France
Raphael Troncy	EURECOM, France
Yannis Tzitzikas	University of Crete and FORTH-ICS, Greece
Katerina Tzompanaki	CY Cergy Paris University, France
Takanori Ugai	Fujitsu Limited, Japan
Ricardo Usbeck	Hamburg University, Germany
Sahar Vahdati	InfAI, Germany
Edlira Vakaj	Birmingham City University, UK
Ludger van Elst	DFKI, Germany

Marieke van Erp	KNAW Humanities Cluster, The Netherlands
Frank van Harmelen	Vrije Universiteit Amsterdam, The Netherlands
Guillermo Vega-Gorgojo	Universidad de Valladolid, Spain
Ruben Verborgh	Ghent University imec, Belgium
Maria-Esther Vidal	TIB, Germany
Serena Villata	CNRS - Laboratoire d'Informatique, Signaux et Systémes de Sophia-Antipolis, France
Fabio Vitali	University of Bologna, Italy
Domagoj Vrgoc	Pontificia Universidad Católica de Chile, Chile
Kewen Wang	Griffith University, Australia
Meng Wang	Tongji University, China
Peng Wang	Southeast University, China
Ruijie Wang	University of Zurich, Switzerland
Zhe Wang	Griffith University, Australia
Xander Wilcke	Vrije Universiteit Amsterdam, The Netherlands
Cord Wiljes	Nationale Forschungsdateninfrastruktur (NFDI) e.V., Germany
Honghan Wu	King's College London, UK
Josiane Xavier Parreira	Siemens AG Österreich, Austria
Yanghua Xiao	Fudan University, China
Fouad Zablith	American University of Beirut, Lebanon
Hamada Zahera	Paderborn University, Germany
Ondřej Zamazal	Prague University of Economics and Business, Czech Republic
Songmao Zhang	Chinese Academy of Sciences, China
Xiaowang Zhang	Tianjin University, China
Ziqi Zhang	Sheffield University, UK
Yizheng Zhao	Nanjing University, China
Lu Zhou	Flatfee Corp., USA
Rui Zhu	University of Bristol, UK
Antoine Zimmermann	École des Mines de Saint-Étienne, France
Hanna Ćwiek-Kupczyńska	University of Luxembourg, Luxembourg
Umutcan Şimşek	University of Innsbruck, Austria

Additional Reviewers

Aghaei, Sare
Akaichi, Ines
Badenes-Olmedo, Carlos
Bento, Alexandre
Bernardy, Laura
Biancofiore, Giovanni Maria

Blin, Inès
Braun, Christoph
Calbimonte, Jean-Paul
Chen, Jiaoyan
Chhetri, Tek Raj
Darnala, Baptiste

Domínguez, Elvira
Dsouza, Alishiba
Emamirad, Ehsan
Ilkou
Jain, Monika
Jradeh, Khadija
Khajeh Nassiri, Armita
Lamprecht, David
Liu, Xiangyu
Majumdar, Abhishek
Markwald, Marco
Marx, Edgard
Massimino, Giulia
Mehrotra, Shubham
Mohammadi, Hossein
Morales Tirado, Alba Catalina
Moro, Gianluca
Möller, Cedric
Nararatwong, Rungsiman
Nayyeri, Mojtaba
Noullet, Kristian

Porena, Margherita
Quercini, Gianluca
Reyero Lobo, Paula
Rovetto, Robert
Sain, Joy
Sanguinetti, Manuela
Shen, Zhejun
Simonne, Lucas
Singh, Gunjan
Tan, Yiming
Tauqeer, Amar
Tian, Xiaobin
Tounsi Dhouib, Molka
Troullinou, Georgia
Werner, Simon
Westphal, Patrick
Wu, Hong
Xiong, Bo
Yacoubi Ayadi, Nadia
Zeginis, Chrysostomos
Zhao, Tianzhe

Sponsors

Gold Sponsors

metaphacts is a German software company that empowers customers to drive knowledge democratization and decision intelligence using knowledge graphs. Built entirely on open standards and technologies, our product metaphactory delivers a low-code, FAIR Data platform that supports collaborative knowledge modeling and knowledge generation and enables on-demand citizen access to consumable, contextual, and actionable knowledge. metaphacts serves customers in areas such as life sciences and pharma, engineering and manufacturing, finance and insurance, retail, cultural heritage, and more. For more information about metaphacts and its products and solutions please visit www.metaphacts.com.

VideoLectures.NET is an award-winning free and open access educational video lectures repository. The lectures are given by distinguished scholars and scientists at the most important and prominent events like conferences, summer schools, workshops and science promotional events from many fields of Science. The portal is aimed at promoting science, exchanging ideas and fostering knowledge sharing by providing high-quality didactic contents not only to the scientific community but also to the general public. All lectures, accompanying documents, information and links are systematically selected and classified through the editorial process taking into account also users' comments.

Silver Sponsors

Ontotext is a global leader in enterprise knowledge graph technology and semantic database engines. Ontotext employs big knowledge graphs to enable unified data access and cognitive analytics via text mining and integration of data across multiple sources. Ontotext GraphDBᴛᴍ engine and Ontotext Platform power business critical systems in the biggest banks, media, market intelligence agencies, car and aerospace manufacturers. Ontotext technology and solutions are spread wide across the value chain of the most knowledge intensive enterprises in financial services, publishing, healthcare, pharma, manufacturing and public sectors. Leveraging AI and cognitive technologies, Ontotext helps enterprises get competitive advantage, by connecting the dots of their proprietary knowledge and putting it in the context of global intelligence.

Semantic Technology Institute (STI) Innsbruck is a leading research group in semantic technology at the Department of Computer Science at the University of Innsbruck, Austria, engaged in research and development to bring information and communication technologies of the future into today's world.

Springer is part of Springer Nature, a leading global research, educational and professional publisher, home to an array of respected and trusted brands providing quality content through a range of innovative products and services. Springer Nature is the world's largest academic book publisher, publisher of the world's most influential journals and a pioneer in the field of open research. The company numbers almost 13,000 staff in over 50 countries and has a turnover of approximately €1.5 billion. Springer Nature was formed in 2015 through the merger of Nature Publishing Group, Palgrave Macmillan, Macmillan Education and Springer Science+Business Media.

In parallel with the 20th anniversary of ESWC this year, **eccenca** is proud to announce the launch of the Community Edition Sandbox. Through eccenca.my you can register and evaluate the creation of Knowledge Graphs easily and intuitively. No code. No bugs. No time.

eccenca Corporate Memory is cutting-edge Knowledge Graph technology. It digitally captures the expertise of knowledge workers so that it can be accessed and processed by machines. The fusion of human knowledge with large amounts of data, coupled with the computing power of machines, results in powerful artificial intelligence that enables companies to execute existing processes as well as innovation projects of all kinds at high speed and low cost. And it creates an impressive competitive advantage.

Join pioneers like BOSCH, SIEMENS, Astra Zeneca and many other global market leaders - our world-class team of Linked Data Experts is ready when you are.

Bronze Sponsors

IOS Press is an independent, international STM publishing house established in 1987 in Amsterdam. One of our guiding principles is to embrace the benefits a lean organization offers. While our goal is to keep things simple, we strive to meet the highest professional standards. Our business practices are straightforward, transparent and ethical. IOS Press serves the information needs of scientific and medical communities worldwide. IOS Press now publishes more than 100 international journals and approximately 75 book titles each year on subjects ranging from computer sciences and mathematics to medicine and the natural sciences. Please visit iospress.com to find out more.

R²A GmbH & Co. KG
https://r2a.link/

R²A is a dynamic startup that offers comprehensive support for software projects. Our team of experts specializes in agile software development, full stack web development, mobile development, and data engineering. We understand the importance of a well-structured data model, sustainable software development, and integrating data from different sources. With our combined expertise, we can guide you through the entire software development process, from idea to implementation. Trust us to build software that is both functional and sustainable. Contact us today to learn more.

Contents

Industry

PhD Symposium

Summary of Workshops and Tutorials at European Semantic Web Conference 2023

Mehwish Alam[1](✉) and Cassia Trojahn[2](✉)

[1] Telecom Paris, Institut Polytechnique de Paris France, Paris, France
`mehwish.alam@telecom-paris.fr`
[2] Institut de Recherche en Informatique de Toulouse, Toulouse, France
`cassia.trojahn@irit.fr`

Abstract. This document summarizes the workshops and tutorials of the Extended Semantic Web Conference 2023. This edition accepted 10 workshops on different topics revolving around knowledge graphs, such as natural language processing, biomedical data, etc. Moreover, 2 tutorials were accepted which included building scientific knowledge graphs and a beginner's guide to reasoning.

Keywords: Semantic Technologies · Knowledge Graphs · Natural Language Processing · Knowledge Graph Construction

1 Tutorials

1.1 SciKG: Tutorial on Building Scientific Knowledge Graphs from Data, Data Dictionaries, and Codebooks

Data from scientific studies are published in datasets, typically accompanied by data dictionaries and codebooks to support data understanding. The data acquisition methods may also be described in additional documentation to support reproducibility. To conduct rigorous analysis, data users need to leverage this documentation to correctly interpret the data. While this process can be burdensome for new data users, it is also prone to errors even for seasoned users. A computational formal model of the knowledge that was used to create the study can facilitate better understanding and thus improved usage of the study data. Knowledge graphs can be used effectively to capture this study knowledge.

This tutorial[1] introduced the basics of knowledge graph construction using data, data dictionaries, and codebooks from scientific studies. It has used the Center for Disease Control and Prevention's (CDC) National Health and Nutrition Examination Surveys (NHANES) data as a testbed and introduced standardized terminology, novel and established techniques, and resources such as scientific/biomedical ontologies, semantic data dictionaries, and knowledge graph

---

[1] https://tetherless-world.github.io/scikg-eswc-2023/.

C. Pesquita et al. (Eds.): ESWC 2023, LNCS 13998, pp. 1–7, 2023.
https://doi.org/10.1007/978-3-031-43458-7_1

frameworks in both lecture and practical sessions. By the end of the tutorial, participants created a small knowledge graph that can be accessed to retrieve study knowledge and data.

1.2 A Beginner's Guide to Reasoning: How to Reason Your Way to Better Data

Reasoning has become an increasingly valued tool in the semantic web space, and yet to many, it's still a black-box solution. Perhaps more tragically, despite the explosion of its development in recent years, many in the space still perceive it as a slow, cumbersome, and ultimately impractical technology, which is far from true today.

This tutorial provided a hands-on with a reasoning engine in this interactive walkthrough: A Beginner's Guide to Reasoning[2]. The participants were exposed to the power of reasoning, what it can add to the data, and the fundamentals of how to apply it. With technology in this space running away, there's never been a better time to learn! This tutorial touched upon the basics of SPARQL, OWL, and Datalog, before diving into reasoning at a technical level.

2 Workshops

2.1 Trusting Decentralised Knowledge Graphs and Web Data (TrusDeKW)

Knowledge Graphs have become a foundation for sharing data on the web and building intelligent services across many sectors and within some of the most successful corporations in the world. The over centralisation of data on the web, however, has been raised as a concern by several prominent researchers in the field. Data centralisation can lead to a number of problems including lock-in/siloing effects; lack of user control over their personal data; limited incentives and opportunities for interoperability and openness; and the resulting detrimental effects on privacy and innovation. A number of diverse approaches and technologies exist for decentralising data, such as federated querying and distributed ledgers.

This workshop[3] brought together researchers and stakeholders to explore how we can decentralise data on the web and come to a common understanding of the benefits and issues associated with decentralised KGs. The format of the workshop was engineered to facilitate a cross-flow of ideas amongst the participants to generate a post-workshop white paper. Thus, the workshop was structured to incorporate the views of workshop participants by covering several key stakeholder areas.

---

[2] https://www.oxfordsemantic.tech/events/eswc-2023-a-beginners-guide-to-reasoning-how-to-reason-your-way-to-better-data.

[3] https://events.kmi.open.ac.uk/trusting-decentralised-knowledge-graphs-and-web-data/#eswc.

2.2 Knowledge Graph Construction

More and more knowledge graphs (KGs) are constructed for private use, e.g., Google, or public use, e.g., DBpedia, and Wikidata. While many solutions were proposed to construct KGs from existing data on the Web, there is still no systematic evaluation to compare the performance and resource usage of the different systems independently of the mapping language they use or the way they construct the knowledge graph (materialization or virtualization). Addressing the challenges related to KG construction requires both the investigation of theoretical concepts and the development of systems and methods for their evaluation.

This workshop[4] had a special focus on the efficiency of the systems during the construction of knowledge graphs, exploring the trade-offs between different approaches (e.g., planification VS physical operators). It included a keynote and a panel, as well as (research, in-use, experience, position, tools) paper presentations, demo jam, and break-out discussions. In particular this year, the workshop provided an evaluation setup to the workshop participants to compare the different tools for KG construction. The goal was to provide a venue for scientific discourse, systematic analysis, and rigorous evaluation of languages, techniques, and tools, as well as practical and applied experiences and lessons learned for constructing knowledge graphs from academia and industry. The workshop complements and aligns with the activities of the W3C Community Group on KG construction.

2.3 Linked Data-Driven Resilience Research

Recent crises like the COVID-19 pandemic wave and the Russia-Ukraine War have not only tested supply chains and economic value networks to their limits but revealed the need to increase the flexibility of technical infrastructures, energy supply, health systems, and social textures alike. Currently, many economic and social spheres are continuously challenged by recession fear, political ploys, and weather disasters to unfold capacities to withstand as well as refine and transform themselves to stay ahead of changes. Semantically represented data can play a crucial role in increasing the transparency of value chains and understanding the complex mechanisms of crisis factors on a global level. The systematic integration, KI-based modeling, and analysis of huge amounts of data from various sources can build a new basis for situational awareness and decision-making as well as for the elaboration of advanced resilience strategies.

This workshop[5], organized by the CoyPu project, provided an open forum to exchange current issues, ideas, and trends in the area of Data-driven Resilience Research. The workshop brought together scientists, software engineers, resilience practitioners, and domain experts to approach the topic from a multi-disciplinary perspective. Ongoing technological developments, current research approaches as well as use case scenarios, and field reports were presented and discussed with a broad specialist audience.

---

[4] https://kg-construct.github.io/workshop/2023/.
[5] https://d2r2.aksw.org/.

2.4   Metadata and Research Management for Linked Open Science

Scientific research involves various digital objects including publications, software, data, workflows, and tutorials, all key to FAIRness, reproducibility, and transparency. The research lifecycle, from questions and hypotheses to results and conclusions, requires data production, collection, and transformation, a process commonly supported by software and workflows. For this cycle to prosper, we require Research Data and Software Management Plans (DMPs and SMPs), Research Objects packing things together, and metadata supporting the FAIR (data) principles and its extensions (e.g., software, and workflows) as well as coverage for reproducibility, transparency, trustability, and explainability. Furthermore, despite playing an important role, data on its own is not enough to establish Linked Open Science, i.e., Open Science plus Linked Open Data (LOD). LOD principles, aka LOD 5 stars, follow objectives overlapping with FAIR and Open Science (e.g., LOD includes "openness" and usage of "non-proprietary open formats").

In this workshop[6] workshop, requirements for research digital objects and their corresponding management plans were explored to effectively instantiate an integrated layer supporting Linked Open Science. The contributions were focused on the following topics: machine-actionable DMPs and SMPs; machine/deep learning approaches around rich metadata; FAIRification; FAIR by design; FAIR tooling; recognition, publication, and citation for data, software, and other research digital objects, and scientometrics beyond the scholarly publication (i.e., combining the different digital objects playing a role in the research cycle).

2.5   Semantic Technologies for Scientific, Technical and Legal Data

The rapid growth of online available scientific, technical, and legal data such as patents, technical reports, articles, etc. has made the large-scale analysis and processing of such documents a crucial task. Today, scientists, patent experts, inventors, and other information professionals contribute to this data every day by publishing articles or writing patent applications. In order to benefit from the scientific-technical knowledge present in such documents, it has become critical that the communities related to Semantic Technologies, NLP, and Deep Learning join forces to provide more effective and efficient solutions.

This workshop[7] aimed at providing a venue for researchers and practitioners to foster inter-disciplinary research in the areas of Semantic Technologies, NLP, and Deep Learning. It received contributions ranging from new tools and systems for capturing scientific, technical, and legal data including patents, to novel semantic technologies and ontologies and annotation schema to model scientific, technical and legal data.

---

[6] https://zbmed.github.io/damalos/.
[7] https://rima-turker.github.io/SemTech4STLD/.

2.6   Semantic Web on Constrained Things

The combination of the Internet of Things (IoT), Semantics, and Web of Things (SWoT) has been more and more popular to collect sensing data according to the semantic web stack and build smart services and applications. One momentum is the release of a W3C recommendation for WoT architecture along with a formal specification of Thing Descriptions. The Web of Things (WoT) allows describing device semantics, bridging the gap between device and service descriptions. At the same time, decentralized infrastructures able to capture and transform data at the edge have gained attraction over centralized ones, due to both the constant attempts to reduce industrial costs and the real necessity to reduce global carbon emissions. However, fulfilling the SWoT promises using such infrastructures poses new challenges as these small devices are constrained in terms of computing capabilities and memory, and wireless network communications are also energy-consuming and can hinder the battery life of autonomous devices. Deploying SWoT standards on such devices requires controlling and monitoring the consumption of these resources, whereas semantic technologies are known to be verbose and computationally intensive.

This workshop[8] brought together research and industry communities working on the different aspects of embedding data semantics and standards-based solutions into edge and/or constrained Internet and Web of Things setups, as well as reducing the carbon footprint of semantic technologies. It provided a venue for scientific presentations, systematic analysis and evaluation of semantic WoT architectures, ontologies and tools, as well as practical and applied experiences and lessons-learned applied to constrained devices.

2.7   Semantic Web Solutions for Large-Scale Biomedical Data Analytics

The life sciences domain has been an early adopter of linked data and, a considerable portion of the Linked Open Data cloud is composed of life sciences data sets. The deluge of inflowing biomedical data, partially driven by high-throughput gene sequencing technologies, is a key contributor and motor to these developments. The available data sets require integration according to international standards, large-scale distributed infrastructures, specific techniques for data access, and offer data analytics benefits for decision support. Especially in combination with Semantic Web and Linked Data technologies, these promise to enable the processing of large as well as semantically heterogeneous data sources and the capturing of new knowledge from those.

This workshop[9] aimed at seeking original contributions describing theoretical and practical methods and techniques that present the anatomy of large-scale linked data infrastructure, which covers: the distributed infrastructure to consume, store and query large volumes of heterogeneous linked data; using indexes

---

[8] https://mondecalabs.github.io/SWoCoT23/.
[9] https://sites.google.com/view/sewebmeda-2023/home.

and graph aggregation to better understand large linked data graphs, query federation to mix internal and external data sources, and linked data visualisation tools for health care and life sciences. It aimed at providing researchers in biomedical and life science, insight and awareness about large-scale data technologies for linked data, which are becoming increasingly important for knowledge discovery in the life sciences domain.

2.8   Knowledge Graph Generation from Text

Knowledge Graphs are getting traction in both academia and the industry as one of the key elements of AI applications. They are being recognized as an important and essential resource in many downstream tasks such as question answering, recommendation, personal assistants, business analytics, business automation, etc. Even though there are large knowledge graphs built with crowdsourcing such as Wikidata or using semi-structured data such as DBpedia or Yago or from structured data such as relational databases, building knowledge graphs from text corpora still remains an open challenge.

This workshop[10] brought together researchers from multiple focus areas such as Natural Language Processing (NLP), Entity Linking (EL), Relation Extraction (RE), Knowledge Representation and Reasoning (KRR), Deep Learning (DL), Knowledge Base Construction (KBC), Semantic Web, Linked Data, and other related fields to foster a discussion and enhance the state-of-the-art in knowledge graph generation from text. It welcomed a broad range of papers including full research papers, negative results, position papers, datasets, and system demos examining the wide range of issues and processes related to knowledge graphs generation from text corpora including entity linking, relation extraction, knowledge representation, and Semantic Web.

2.9   Data Management for Knowledge Graphs

The rapid increase in the adoption of knowledge graphs over the past years, both in the open data domain as well as the industry, means that data management solutions for knowledge graphs today have to support ever increasing amounts of data. The continuously growing KGs resulting from the increasing popularity of semantic technologies highlight the necessity for scalable and efficient solutions for the management of knowledge graphs in distributed, federated, and centralized environments.

---

[10] https://aiisc.ai/text2kg2023/.

The DMKG workshop[11], therefore, focused on novel research and advances in scalable data management solutions for large-scale knowledge graphs. Such data management solutions include techniques for storage and indexing, partitioning for decentralized/centralized systems, archiving and versioning, validation with SHACL/shEx, or federated data management. The main goal of the workshop was to bring together both early-stage and established researchers as well as industrial partners in order to facilitate communication and collaboration between partners in different domains on the issues relating to scalable data management techniques for large-scale knowledge graphs.

2.10   Semantic Methods for Events and Stories

An important part of human history and knowledge is made of events, which can be aggregated and connected to create stories, be they real or fictional. These events as well as the stories created from them can typically be inherently complex, reflect societal or political stances, and be perceived differently across the world population. The Semantic Web offers technologies and methods to represent these events and stories, as well as to interpret the knowledge encoded into graphs and use it for different applications, spanning from narrative understanding and generation to fact-checking.

The aim of SEMMES[12] was to offer an opportunity to discuss the challenges related to events and stories, and how we can use semantic methods to tackle them. The submissions were revolving around combining data, methods, and technologies coming from the Semantic Web with methods from other fields, including machine learning, narratology, or information extraction. This workshop brought together researchers working on complementary topics, in order to foster collaboration and sharing of expertise in the context of events and stories.

---

[11] https://dmkg-workshop.github.io/.
[12] https://anr-kflow.github.io/semmes/.

Posters and Demos

Sparnatural: A Visual Knowledge Graph Exploration Tool

Thomas Francart[(✉)] [iD]

Sparna, 5 Rue Georges Courteline, 37540 Saint-Cyr-Sur-Loire, France
thomas.francart@sparna.fr

Abstract. Knowledge Graphs are often relying on conceptual models with a high level of abstraction, making them hard to understand for nonexpert users, and are often hidden behind search forms, losing the flexibility to interact with the graph as a graph. In order to leverage knowledge graphs there is a need to propose end-user-oriented interactions demonstrating how they can allow to discover a knowledge domain. Sparnatural was designed and developed as a visual, configurable, easily deployable, open-source, client-side SPARQL query builder, allowing users to query any RDF knowledge graph. We describe here how Sparnatural works, how it can be configured, and we show how it was deployed in two demonstrators for the Archives Nationales de France and Bibliothèque Nationale de France. We show how Sparnatural has made it possible to give access to nonexpert users, with little effort, to these two large graphs. Workshops conducted with end-users showed they were enthusiastic about the possibility offered. They also revealed that this novel search paradigm is surprising and could benefit from user onboarding. The configuration of Sparnatural is key in providing efficient access to the graph and can be done through the specification of a search-oriented ontology.

Keywords: SPARQL · query builder · UI · Typescript · Knowledge Graph

1 Introduction

The requirement for data interoperability has driven the development of conceptual models used for structuring knowledge graphs, like CIDOC-CRM [1] for cultural heritage, LRM [2] for libraries, or RIC-O [3] for archives. Knowledge graphs based on these ontologies are accessible either using a developer-oriented service (SPARQL endpoint), or sometimes they underly other search systems, typically multicriteria query forms or faceted search engines.

Data interoperability and data aggregation from silos in a homogeneous graph require a lot of effort, at the intellectual, business process and technical levels. These efforts are hard to demonstrate, because no good solution exists to make the graph tangible for managers and accessible for end-users: SPARQL endpoints are too technical, and search systems don't make the underlying graph tangible.

C. Pesquita et al. (Eds.): ESWC 2023, LNCS 13998, pp. 11–15, 2023.
https://doi.org/10.1007/978-3-031-43458-7_2

2   Sparnatural: an intuitive visual SPARQL query builder

Sparnatural [4] provides an innovative search paradigm to explore and discover these knowledge graphs. A presentation video [5] demonstrates its features. Technically speaking, Sparnatural is a visual SPARQL query builder, written in Typescript, operating purely on the client. Its only requirement is a SPARQL endpoint to which the queries can be sent. Sparnatural is open source, under a LGPL license (Fig. 1).

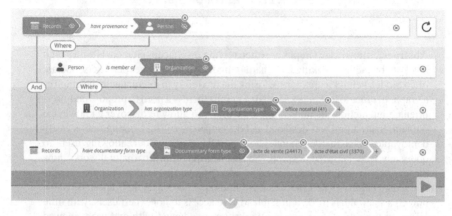

Fig. 1. A query edited in Sparnatural: "Archive records that have as provenance a Person who is a member of an organization of type 'Notarial Office', and that are of type 'bill of sale' or 'civil status document.'"

Each line in the query mimics the structure of an RDF triple pattern with a subject type, a predicate, an object type and, optionally, some values. At each step, dropdown lists enable the user to directly see the classes and predicates available.

Values of a criterion can be selected with different widgets (dropdown lists, autocompleted search fields, calendars, etc.) and the set of columns in the result set can be controlled by activating the "eye" icon on the arrows in the query pattern.

Sparnatural also offers the ability to load predefined queries, enabling data publishers to propose sample queries that can be loaded in one click. This can serve as query templates that the users can modify.

While OPTIONAL and FILTER NOT EXISTS are supported, Sparnatural does not have the objective of covering 100% of SPARQL keywords; currently it does not support UNION, FROM, or Aggregate functions like COUNT.

3   Demonstrators

The French National Archives (ANF) and the French National Library (BNF) conducted a project to add features to Sparnatural and to build two demonstrators to test its deployment on their respective knowledge graphs. The project was successfully concluded in June 2022 by a presentation at the ANF [6].

The demonstrator of the ANF [7] allows exploring a dataset based on RIC-O [3], of about 50 million triples describing notarial archives. The demonstrator proposes two configurations of Sparnatural to navigate the same data: a generic one, that could be used for any RIC-O-based knowledge graph, and a more precise, showing specific criteria for notarial archives.

The demonstrator of the BNF [8] allows querying the data already accessible in the data.bnf.fr portal, of about 600 million triples, and based on an LRM-like [2] ontology. The performance of the SPARQL endpoint was sufficient to allow to deploy Sparnatural without further performance tuning.

The project included three workshops to confront end-users with the tool and gather feedback. Users were mostly enthusiastic, but some were lost by this new search paradigm. Some feedback was considered, such as the inclusion of the query execution button, or the "reset" button.

4 Ontology-Driven Configuration of Sparnatural

Sparnatural is configured by an OWL ontology, defining which classes and relationships are shown in the interface. The ontology defines the (multilingual) labels and tooltips, icons, or which value selection widget should be used for each predicate. The dropdown list and autocomplete widgets are also associated with a SPARQL query that populates the list or the autocomplete suggestions.

A key aspect of that configuration ontology is that it does not need to be the same as the ontology of the underlying knowledge graph. Classes or properties can be removed or labelled differently; shortcuts can be proposed: a single link in the search interface can correspond to a property path in the underlying graph; classes presented to users can be subsets of the (in general relatively abstract) classes of the underlying ontology.

The configuration ontology can be edited in the Protégé OWL editor, by importing two configuration ontologies [9] that provides base classes for the configuration.

The decoupling of the search ontology from the graph structure enables to show the same graph in different ways for different users. The configuration ontologies can also be shared, such as the generic configuration for the ANF demonstrator [9].

This has been a design choice that this configuration must be defined manually. We believe it is a key aspect of any knowledge graph publishing work. It does require additional work but allows to decouple the user search configuration from the actual graph structure. Work is ongoing to facilitate this process by generating a base configuration from the actual dataset, that can be further edited to produce the actual Sparnatural configuration.

5 Related Work

Sparnatural builds on the visual paradigm of ResearchSpace semantic search component [10], but improves the user experience and is more expressive, with support for OPTIONAL and NOT EXISTS.

RDFExplorer [11] is another graph based SPARQL builder. Sparnatural is less expressive than RDFExplorer (it can generate only tree-shaped queries, not complete basic graph pattern), but we believe more end-user-friendly. The presentation of RDF-Explorer [11] cites Bhowmick et al. [12] to summarize the challenges of visual graph querying paradigm: (1) development of graph queries requires a considerable cognitive effort; (2) users need to be able to express their goal in a systematic and correct manner, which is antagonistic with the goal of catering to lay users; (3) it is more intuitive to "draw" graph queries than to write them, which implies the need for intuitive visual interfaces. In the same family of tools, Visual SPARQL Builder [13] proposes a visual query building pane like RDFExplorer, while A-QuB [14] is more form-based. Sparnatural addresses the challenges of visual graph querying by providing the following set of features: UX is intuitive and "gamifies" the query experience; dynamic results can be provided on-the-fly; example queries can be loaded; some level of non-emptiness guarantee are provided.

6 Summary

Sparnatural offers an easy way to leverage knowledge graphs. Users with no technical knowledge of SPARQL and no a priori knowledge of the graph structure can query the data. Its client-side only deployment allows to easily include it in a webpage, replacing or complementing existing SPARQL endpoint forms.

Future work on Sparnatural includes addition of geographical and numerical search widgets; and on the configuration side, the ability to automatically derive a configuration ontology from the underlying graph structure, that can be manually tuned to be presented to end-users. SHACL-based configuration is also considered.

References

1. Le Bœuf, P., Doerr, M., Emil Ore, C., Stead, S.: CIDOC Conceptual Reference Model. https://cidoc-crm.org. Accessed 18 Apr 2023
2. Riva, P., Le Boeuf, P., Žumer, M.: IFLA Library Reference Model: A Conceptual Model for Bibliographic Information (2018). https://repository.ifla.org/handle/123456789/40
3. Records In Contexts Ontology. https://www.ica.org/en/records-in-contexts-ontology. Accessed 18 Apr 2023
4. Sparnatural https://sparnatural.eu. Accessed 18 Apr 2023
5. Sparnatural presentation video. https://youtu.be/jcfldxjsBkk. Accessed 18 Apr 2023
6. Sparnatural project presentation (French). https://sparnatural.eu#restitution-an-bnf. Accessed 18 Apr 2023
7. Sparnatural ANF demonstrator. https://sparna-git.github.io/sparnatural-demonstrateur-an/. Accessed 18 Apr 2023
8. Sparnatural BNF demonstrator. https://data.bnf.fr/sparnatural. Accessed 18 Apr 2023
9. Sparnatural configuration ontologies: http://data.sparna.fr/ontologies/sparnatural-config-core-and-data.sparna.fr/ontologies/sparnatural-config-datasources. Accessed 18 Apr 2023
10. Sparnatural configuration for ANBF demonstrator A. https://github.com/sparna-git/sparnatural-demonstrateur-an/blob/main/sparnatural-config-A.ttl. Accessed 18 Apr 2023

11. Oldman, D., Tanase, D.: Reshaping the knowledge graph by connecting researchers, data and practices in ResearchSpace. In: Vrandečić, D. (ed.) ISWC 2018. LNCS, vol. 11137, pp. 325–340. Springer, Cham (2018). https://doi.org/10.1007/978-3-030-00668-6_20
12. Vargas, H., Buil-Aranda, C., Hogan, A., López, C.: RDF explorer: a visual SPARQL query builder. In: International Joint Conference on Aritificial Intelligence (IJCAI–PRICAI) (2020)
13. Bhowmick, S.S., Byron, C., Li, C.: Graph querying meets HCI: state of the art and future directions. In: ACM International Conference on Management of Data, pp. 1731–1736. ACM (2017)
14. Eipert, L.: Visual SPARQL Builder. https://leipert.github.io/vsb/. Accessed 18 Apr 2023
15. Assistive Query Building for Semantic Data. In: SEMANTICS Posters & Demos (2018)

Integrating Faceted Search with Data Analytic Tools in the User Interface of ParliamentSampo – Parliament of Finland on the Semantic Web

Eero Hyvönen[1,2](✉), Petri Leskinen[1,2], and Heikki Rantala[1]

[1] Semantic Computing Research Group (SeCo), Aalto University, Espoo, Finland
eero.hyvonen@aalto.fi
[2] Helsinki Centre for Digital Humanities (HELDIG), University of Helsinki, Helsinki, Finland

Abstract. This paper presents the idea and implementation of integrating faceted search and browsing with data-analytic tools in the user interface design of the new in-use semantic portal PARLIAMENTSAMPO.

Keywords: Parliamentary Studies · Linked Data · User Interfaces · Portals

1 Parliamentary FAIR Linked Data for Problem Solving

PARLIAMENTSAMPO – *Parliament of Finland on the Semantic Web* [8] is a new Linked Open Data (LOD) service[1] and an in-use semantic portal[2] on top of its SPARQL endpoint. Its main knowledge graph (KG) includes nearly million speeches of the plenary sessions of the Parliament of Finland (PoF) since its foundation in 1907 [7,13], interlinked with another KG and ontology about the 2800 Members of Parliament (MP) and other speakers, parties, and other organizations in PoF [12]. The LOD has been enriched with data from several external sources and by reasoning. Both KGs are published and are available on the Linked Data Finland [9] platform[3], including a SPARQL endpoint and other LOD services, such as content negotiation and RDF browsing. The RDF data is also openly available (CC BY 4.0) at Zenodo.org, and in Parla-CLARIN and CSV form [7]. The CSV data is updated on a daily basis.

The minutes of the plenary speeches of PoF have been available as scanned books (1907–1999), HTML pages (2000–2014), or as XML documents (2015–), but not as Findable, Accessible, Interoperable, and Re-usable FAIR data[4]. If the user knows during which parliament a speech was given, he could download the corresponding document for close-reading. But if one wants, for example, to find

---

[1] LOD service available at: https://ldf.fi/dataset/semparl.
[2] Portal available at: https://parlamenttisampo.fi.
[3] Linked Data Finland platform: https://ldf.fi.
[4] Cf. the FAIR Data initiative: https://www.go-fair.org/.

C. Pesquita et al. (Eds.): ESWC 2023, LNCS 13998, pp. 16–21, 2023.
https://doi.org/10.1007/978-3-031-43458-7_3

out the answers to the following questions, this kind of web service and research method is not a viable solution:

1. **Question**: Who has given most regular speeches and when? **Answer**: Mr. Veikko Vennamo, SMP Party, over 12 600 speeches in 1945–1987 in total. Their distribution can be visualized on a timeline.
2. **Question**: Who was the first to speak about "NATO" in the PoF plenary sessions? **Answer**: Mr. Yrjö Enne, SKDL communist party, May 27, 1959
3. **Question**: What places are most often mentioned by the current MPs of the Swedish People's Party of Finland"? **Answer**: Can be visualized as a table or on heat maps and markers on maps.
4. **How are the MPs of the current Parliament referring to each other in their speeches** : **Answer**: Can be studied using network analysis.

PARLIAMENTSAMPO makes it possible to study parliamentary discussions and networks of politicians easily using methods Digital Humanities (DH), and find answers to questions, such as those above. Furthermore, applications can be created using LOD services, such as the PARLIAMENTSAMPO portal. It is based on the Sampo model [5] and was created using a new declarative version of the Sampo-UI framework [10] for user interface (UI) design.

2 Using the PARLIAMENTSAMPO Portal

Based on the Sampo-UI framework, the landing page of the portal contains *application perspectives* through which instances of the major classes of the underlying KG can be searched [10]. In this case, there are perspectives for speeches and people. Their instances can be searched and browsed using faceted search, and after filtering out a subset of interest 1) its individual instances can be studied by looking at their *instance pages* by browsing or 2) the whole result set can be analyzed as a whole. In both cases, a set of tabs are available for visualizing or analyzing the instance (a speech or person) or a set of them (say the speeches of MPs belonging to a party during a certain time period).

For example, in Fig. 1, the user has selected the Speeches perspective with facets Content, Speaker, Party, (Speech) Type, and others on the left. The search result, i.e., the speeches found, be visualized on the right in five ways by selecting tabs: 1) in tabular form (by default), 2) on a timeline (this tab is selected in the figure), 3) using histograms and pie charts, 4) on a map based on places mentioned in the speeches, or 5) using a heatmap. In the figure, the user has written a query "NATO*" in the Content text facet, the speech type is set to regular speeches, and then 3622 regular speeches that mention the word "NATO" in its various inflectional forms have been filtered into the search result starting from 1959. By clicking on the pie chart visualization button on the Party facet, the distribution of NATO speeches in terms of parties is shown: the most active party with 722 speeches has been the right-wing National Coalition Party Kokoomus.

In Fig. 2 the People perspective is seen, and the user has found all 507 members of the Centre Party, the active supporter of farming in the countryside, by

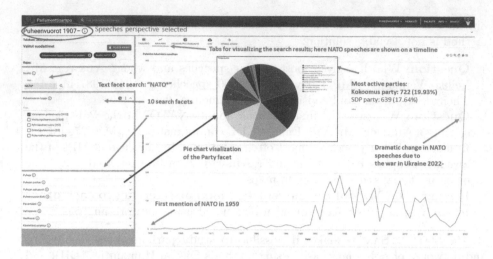

Fig. 1. Using faceted search to filter out and analyze speeches about NATO.

a selection on the Party facet. For analyzing and visualizing the result, seven tabs (e.g., table, pie chart, ages, etc.) can be used. Here the Life chart visualization is chosen where the MPs are shown as arcs from their places of birth (blue end) to places of death (red end). The width of the arc illustrates the number of MPs related to the arc. By clicking on an arc, links to the instance pages of the corresponding MPs are shown. The graph shows strong movement from the countryside to the capital area of Helsinki.

3   Easy Declarative Implementation Using Sampo-UI

The UI was implemented using a new declarative version of the Sampo-UI framework[5]. Here the UI with its components can be created with little programming by using a set of configuration files in JSON format in three main directories: 1) `configs`. JSON files configuring the portal and its perspectives. 2) `sparql`. SPARQL queries referred to in the `configs` files. 3) `translations`. Translations of things like menu items and labels for different locales. When creating a new UI configuration, existing UI components, such as those for the facets and visualization tabs, can be re-used, and the system can also be extended with new components. Sampo-UI has been found handy to use in practise, and it has been used to create some 15 portals in the Sampo series[6] [5] of LOD systems.

4   Related Works and Contributions

Parliamentary debate datasets have been created from the both historical and contemporary parliaments [11]. The data is typically modelled as documents

---

[5] Open code and documentation: https://github.com/SemanticComputing/sampo-ui.
[6] For a full list of Sampo systems see: https://seco.cs.aalto.fi/applications/sampo/.

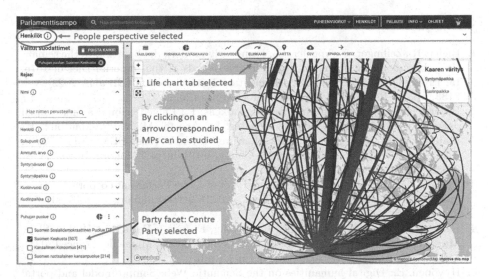

Fig. 2. Using the People perspective of PARLIAMENTSAMPO to study the movement of 507 MPs of the Centre Party from their place of birth to place of death. (Color figure online)

using XML-based formats, such as parla-CLARIN [4] and ParlaMint [3]. Linked data has been used before for modelling and publishing speeches of the European Parliament (LinkedEP) [14], the Latvian parliament [2], the Italian Parliament[7], and in the historical Imperial Diet of Regensburg of 1576 project [1]. The contribution of our paper is to demonstrate novel ideas in the UI design for parliamentary DH research: 1) seamless integration of faceted search with data analytic tools for DH problem solving and 2) easy implementation of the UI based on declarative configurations and re-use of existing components. Published on February 14, 2023, the portal was used by some 3000 users in ten days. More information, links, videos, and publications related to PARLIAMENTSAMPO data services and the portal can be found on the project homepage[8]. PARLIAMENTSAMPO is based on and is part of the Finnish Linked Open Data infrastructure LODI4DH[9] [6].

Acknowledgements. Esko Ikkala, Mikko Koho, many others contributed to our research, funded by the Academy of Finland. Computing resources of the CSC – IT Center for Science were used.

---

[7] http://data.camera.it.
[8] https://seco.cs.aalto.fi/projects/semparl/en/.
[9] https://seco.cs.aalto.fi/projects/lodi4dh/.

References

1. Bleier, R., Zeilinger, F., Vogeler, G.: From early modern deliberation to the semantic web: annotating communications in the records of the Imperial Diet of 1576. In: Proceedings of the Digital Parliamentary Data in Action (DiPaDA 2022), vol. 3133, pp. 86–100. CEUR Workshop Proceedings (2022)
2. Bojārs, U., Dargis, R., Lavrinovičs, U., Paikens, P.: LinkedSaeima: a linked open dataset of Latvia's parliamentary debates. In: Acosta, M., Cudré-Mauroux, P., Maleshkova, M., Pellegrini, T., Sack, H., Sure-Vetter, Y. (eds.) SEMANTiCS 2019. LNCS, vol. 11702, pp. 50–56. Springer, Cham (2019). https://doi.org/10.1007/978-3-030-33220-4_4
3. Erjavec, T., Ogrodniczuk, M., Osenova, P., et al.: The ParlaMint corpora of parliamentary proceedings. Lang. Resour. Eval. (2022). https://doi.org/10.1007/s10579-021-09574-0
4. Fišer, D., Eskevich, M., Lenardič, J., de Jong, F. (eds.): ParlaMint II: The Show Must Go On. European Language Resources Association, Marseille, France (2022). https://aclanthology.org/2022.parlaclarin-1.1.pdf
5. Hyvönen, E.: Digital humanities on the Semantic Web: Sampo model and portal series. Semantic Web - Interoperability, Usability, Applicability (2022, accepted). https://seco.cs.aalto.fi/publications/2021/hyvonen-sampo-model-2021.pdf
6. Hyvönen, E.: How to create a national cross-domain ontology and linked data infrastructure and use it on the semantic web. Semantic Web - Interoperability, Usability, Applicability (2022, under review). https://seco.cs.aalto.fi/publications/2022/hyvonen-infra-2022.pdf
7. Hyvönen, E., et al.: ParliamentSampo infrastructure for publishing the plenary speeches and networks of politicians of the Parliament of Finland as open data services. In: Proceeding: International Workshop on Knowledge Graph Generation from Text (TEXT2KG), co-located with ESWC 2023 Conference. CEUR Workshop Proceedings (2023, forth-coming). https://seco.cs.aalto.fi/publications/2023/hyvonen-et-al-ps-data-2023.pdf
8. Hyvönen, E., Sinikallio, L., Leskinen, P., et al.: Finnish parliament on the semantic web: using ParliamentSampo data service and semantic portal for studying political culture and language. In: Digital Parliamentary data in Action (DiPaDA 2022), Workshop at the 6th Digital Humanities in Nordic and Baltic Countries Conference, long paper, pp. 69–85. CEUR Workshop Proceedings, vol. 3133 (2022)
9. Hyvönen, E., Tuominen, J., Alonen, M., Mäkelä, E.: Linked data Finland: a 7-star model and platform for publishing and re-using linked datasets. In: Presutti, V., Blomqvist, E., Troncy, R., Sack, H., Papadakis, I., Tordai, A. (eds.) ESWC 2014. LNCS, vol. 8798, pp. 226–230. Springer, Cham (2014). https://doi.org/10.1007/978-3-319-11955-7_24
10. Ikkala, E., Hyvönen, E., Rantala, H., Koho, M.: Sampo-UI: a full stack JavaScript framework for developing semantic portal user interfaces. Semant. Web 13(1), 69–84 (2022)
11. La Mela, M., Norén, F., Hyvönen, E. (eds.): Digital Parliamentary Data in Action (DiPaDA 2022): Introduction, vol. 3133. CEUR WS (2022)
12. Leskinen, P., Hyvönen, E., Tuominen, J.: Members of parliament in Finland knowledge graph and its linked open data service. In: Further with Knowledge Graphs. Proceedings of the 17th International Conference on Semantic Systems, 6–9 September 2021, Amsterdam, The Netherlands, pp. 255–269 (2021)

13. Sinikallio, L., et al.: Plenary debates of the Parliament of Finland as linked open data and in Parla-CLARIN markup. In: 3rd Conference on Language, Data and Knowledge, LDK 2021, pp. 1–17. Schloss Dagstuhl- Leibniz-Zentrum fur Informatik GmbH, Dagstuhl Publishing (2021)
14. Van Aggelen, A., Hollink, L., Kemman, M., Kleppe, M., Beunders, H.: The debates of the European Parliament as Linked Open Data. Semant. Web 8(2), 271–281 (2017)

SHACL-ACL: Access Control with SHACL

Philipp D. Rohde[1,2,3]($\boxtimes$) (iD), Enrique Iglesias[2] (iD), and Maria-Esther Vidal[1,2,3] (iD)

[1] TIB Leibniz Information Centre for Science and Technology, Hannover, Germany
{philipp.rohde,maria.vidal}@tib.eu
[2] L3S Research Center, Hannover, Germany
iglesias@l3s.de
[3] Leibniz University of Hannover, Hannover, Germany

Abstract. The number of publicly accessible knowledge graphs is increasing and so are their applications. Knowledge graphs may contain private data and need to be protected against unauthorized access. There are different approaches for access control to knowledge graphs, e.g., user-based or policy-based. User-based access control can be hard to maintain in systems with hundreds or even thousands of users. In contrast, policy-based approaches use rules to decide whether the access should be granted or denied. ODRL is designed for licensing but also used for policy-based access control. Hence, the evaluation of access policies is not defined and no external data can be considered during the decision-making process. Policies can be seen as integrity constraints and, hence, it is natural to specify them in SHACL; the semantics of SHACL validation are well-defined. SHACL-ACL demonstrates how SHACL can be utilized in a policy-based access control approach. Furthermore, utilizing RML mappings, SHACL-ACL is capable of considering data from various heterogeneous sources for the policy evaluation, e.g., JSON data from Web APIs. The demo is available as an interactive Jupyter notebook.

Keywords: Access Control · Privacy · SHACL

1 Introduction

Knowledge graphs are used more and more to publish data on the Web [7]. The data of a knowledge graph is commonly expressed in the *Resource Description Framework* (RDF) [11,12]. When it comes to sharing private data over the Web, security comes into play. *Solid Pods* [1] are one possibility to control the access to one's private data. Solid relies on OpenID [15] and usually grants access to a resource on a per-user basis, i.e., for each resource, the access rights of each user need to be set. In contrast, access policies define conditions for the access, e.g., access is granted during the night or on rainy days. The *Open Digital Rights Language* (ODRL) [8] is designed with licensing in mind but also used for access control in some projects [4,5]. Since the access is granted when all access policies are fulfilled, access policies can be seen as integrity constraints for access control.

C. Pesquita et al. (Eds.): ESWC 2023, LNCS 13998, pp. 22–26, 2023.
https://doi.org/10.1007/978-3-031-43458-7_4

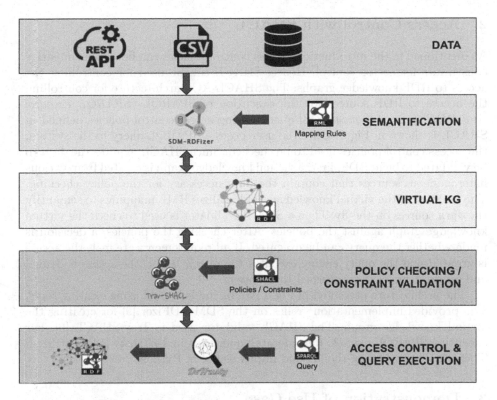

Fig. 1. The SHACL-ACL Architecture. With the use of RML mappings, data from various heterogeneous sources are semantified into a virtual knowledge graph (KG). The virtual knowledge graph is then validated against the access control policies specified in SHACL. If all requirements are met, the SPARQL query is executed. After the execution of the query, the query result is presented to the user.

This paper demonstrates *SHACL Access Control Lists* (SHACL-ACL), a framework able to grant access to RDF knowledge graphs based on access control policies defined in the *Shapes Constraint Language* (SHACL) [10]. While the evaluation of ODRL policies is not explicitly explained in the specification, the semantics of SHACL validation are well-defined [2]. Since ODRL is designed for licensing instead of access control, only data from the policy or known to the evaluation system can be considered during the evaluation of ODRL policies. SHACL-ACL overcomes this limitation by utilizing the *RDF Mapping Language* (RML) [3] to create a virtual RDF knowledge graph on the fly. This allows the consideration of external data, e.g., JSON data from a Web API, during the decision-making process. Hence, decisions can be based on up-to-date data. The virtual knowledge graph is then evaluated by a SHACL validator; following the known semantics for SHACL validation. If all requirements are fulfilled, the access to the resource is granted. Once the access is granted, a SPARQL query posed by the user can be executed and the results presented.

2   Access Control with SHACL

As mentioned in the introduction, access control policies can be seen as integrity constraints for access control. Hence, SHACL can be used for controlling the access to RDF knowledge graphs. The SHACL-ACL architecture for controlling the access to RDF sources for the execution of SPARQL (*SPARQL Protocol And RDF Query Language*) [13] queries using access control policies defined in SHACL is shown in Fig. 1. Once the user poses a SPARQL query to the system, the access control policies need to be checked. Since SHACL requires the data to be validated to be in RDF, first, a virtual knowledge graph is created from various heterogeneous sources that contain the data necessary for the policy checking. The creation of the virtual knowledge graph utilizes RML mappings to semantify the data sources on-the-fly. Then a SHACL validator is used to check the virtual knowledge graph against the policies. After checking the policies, a decision is made whether the query can be executed. If all requirements are met, the access is granted and the query engine executes the query. If not, the access is denied and an error message is returned to the user.

The architecture presented in Fig. 1 can be implemented using existing tools. The provided implementation[1] relies on the SDM-RDFizer [9] for creating the virtual knowledge graph. The SHACL validator used is Trav-SHACL [6]. For executing SPARQL queries, the federated query engine DeTrusty [14] is utilized. These tools are state-of-the-art and implemented in Python.

3   Demonstration of Use Case

To demonstrate the application of SHACL-ACL[2], an access control policy is defined in SHACL as well as a SPARQL query over the data from the World Bank. The World Bank knowledge graph comprises 250,097,215 RDF triples stating per year and country the value of several indicators, e.g., life expectancy, population, inflation, and age distribution. The knowledge graph contains the data for 1,436 different indicators for 265 countries covering the years 1960 to 2021. The average number of indicators per country per year is 711.225 which implies that not all indicators are recorded for all countries for all years. One reason is that some indicators are not yet available for 2021, e.g., the life expectancy in Germany. The query for the demonstration retrieves the life expectancy in Germany for the last three years available, i.e., 2018 to 2020. The access control policy considers local conditions, i.e., conditions of the machine of the user like CPU usage, available RAM, and local time. Additionally, the weather conditions in Hannover (Germany) are considered. *i* the CPU usage is below 30%, *ii* at least 80% of RAM are available, *iii* it is night time, i.e., 7 pm to 6 am, *iv* the temperature in Hannover (Germany) is below 25 °C, and *v* the humidity in Hannover (Germany) is at least 75% (see Table 1).

---

[1] The code is available at https://github.com/SDM-TIB/SHACL-ACL.
[2] The live demo is available at https://mybinder.org/v2/gh/SDM-TIB/SHACL-ACL/HEAD?labpath=SHACL-ACL.ipynb.

Table 1. Access Control Policy and Simulated Data Overview. Data values for the *current conditions* use case are omitted since they depend on the time of execution.

	Policy	Invalid Conditions	Valid Conditions
Time	19:00:00 to 06:00:00	09:09:09	20:15:36
CPU Usage	<30%	0.4%	20.5%
RAM Available	≥80%	50.50%	86.21%
Temperature	<25 °C	0.6 °C	9.1 °C
Humidity	≥75%	99%	87%

Current Conditions. The first use case collects the current conditions of the machine executing the demonstration and gathers the current weather data of Hannover (Germany) via a Web API. For this, a modified version of the SDM-RDFizer [9] is used. The modifications include data collection from Web APIs as well as returning a virtual knowledge graph instead of a file containing the RDF triples. The virtual knowledge graph is validated against the access control policies mentioned above using Trav-SHACL [6]. This use case demonstrates the capability of gathering live and external data for the policy evaluation. Since the result of the decision-making process cannot be guaranteed, two additional use cases with static data are presented.

Invalid Conditions. This use case uses static data for the policy evaluation that is known to violate the access control policy (see Table 1). More precisely, the time in the data is 9 am and only about 50% of the RAM are available. Hence, the time and memory policy are violated. All other conditions are met. Due to the violations, the access is denied and the query is not executed. An error is returned stating that the access was denied.

Valid Conditions. The static data for this use case ensures that the policy evaluation succeeds without any violations, i.e., all the constraints are fulfilled (see Table 1); it is night time, the machine is under a low load, and it is cold and humid in Hannover (Germany). Since no violations are detected, SHACL-ACL grants access to the World Bank knowledge graph and the SPARQL query is executed. After the execution of the query, the query result is shown to the user presenting the life expectancy in Germany for the last three years (in the data).

4   Conclusion

SHACL-ACL demonstrates the use of SHACL as a language to define access control policies which can be seen as integrity constraints. In contrast to ODRL, SHACL is defined for validating constraints over KGs. Additionally, the use of RML mappings allows to generate a virtual KG from various heterogeneous sources, i.e., local and external. SHACL-ACL relies on widespread concepts that are well-known in the Semantic Web community and is capable of controlling the access to resources on the Web, e.g., a SPARQL endpoint with private data.

Acknowledgements. This work has been partially supported by the EU H2020 RIA funded project CLARIFY (grant agreement No 875160) and the Federal Ministry for Economic Affairs and Energy of Germany (BMWK) in the project CoyPu (project number 01MK21007[A-L]).

References

1. Capadisli, S., Berners-Lee, T., Verborgh, R., Kjernsmo, K.: Solid Protocol. W3C Solid Community Group Submission (2021). https://solidproject.org/TR/2021/protocol-20211217
2. Corman, J., Reutter, J.L., Savković, O.: Semantics and Validation of Recursive SHACL. In: The Semantic Web - ISWC 2018 (2018). https://doi.org/10.1007/978-3-030-00671-6_19
3. Dimou, A., Vander Sande, M., Colpaert, P., Verborgh, R., Mannens, E., Van de Walle, R.: RML: a generic language for integrated RDF mappings of heterogeneous data. In: Proceedings of the Workshop on Linked Data on the Web co-located with WWW (2014). https://ceur-ws.org/Vol-1184/ldow2014_paper_01.pdf
4. Esteves, B., Pandit, H.J., Rodríguez-Doncel, V.: ODRL Profile for Access Control. Working Draft (2022). https://protect.oeg.fi.upm.es/odrl-access-control-profile/oac.html
5. Esteves, B., Rodríguez-Doncel, V., Pandit, H.J., Mondada, N., McBennett, P.: Using the ODRL profile for access control for solid pod resource governance. In: Groth, P., et al. (eds.) ESWC 2022. LNCS, vol. 13384, pp. 16–20. Springer, Cham (2022). https://doi.org/10.1007/978-3-031-11609-4_3
6. Figuera, M., Rohde, P.D., Vidal, M.E.: Trav-SHACL: efficiently validating networks of SHACL constraints. In: The Web Conference (2021). https://doi.org/10.1145/3442381.3449877
7. Hogan, A., et al.: Knowledge graphs. ACM Comput. Surv. **54**(4), 1–37 (2021). https://doi.org/10.1145/3447772
8. Ianella, R., Villata, S.: ODRL Information Model 2.2. W3C Recommendation (2018). https://www.w3.org/TR/2018/REC-odrl-model-20180215/
9. Iglesias, E., Jozashoori, S., Chaves-Fraga, D., Collarana, D., Vidal, M.E.: SDM-RDFizer: an RML interpreter for the efficient creation of RDF knowledge graphs. In: CIKM 2020: The 29th ACM International Conference on Information and Knowledge Management, Virtual Event, Ireland, 19–23 October 2020 (2020). https://doi.org/10.1145/3340531.3412881
10. Knublauch, H., Kontokostas, D.: Shapes Constraint Language (SHACL). W3C Recommendation (2017). https://www.w3.org/TR/2017/REC-shacl-20170720/
11. Lassila, O., Swick, R.R.: Resource Description Framework (RDF) Model and Syntax Specification. W3C Recommendation (1999). https://www.w3.org/TR/1999/REC-rdf-syntax-19990222/
12. Manola, F., Miller, E.: RDF Primer. W3C Recommendation (2004). https://www.w3.org/TR/2004/REC-rdf-primer-20040210/
13. Prud'hommeaux, E., Seaborne, A.: Shapes Constraint Language (SHACL). W3C Recommendation (2008). https://www.w3.org/TR/rdf-sparql-query/
14. Rohde, P.D.: DeTrusty v0.11.2 (2023). https://doi.org/10.5281/zenodo.7670670
15. Sakimura, N., Bradley, J., Jones, M., de Medeiros, B., Mortimore, C.: OpenID Connect Core 1.0 incorporating errata set 1. OpenID (2014). https://openid.net/specs/openid-connect-core-1_0.html

A Hybrid Knowledge Graph and Bayesian Network Approach for Analyzing Supply Chain Resilience

Naouel Karam[✉], Shirkouh Matini, Roman Laas, and Thomas Hoppe

Fraunhofer FOKUS, Berlin, Germany
{naouel.karam,shirkouh.matini,roman.laas,
thomas.hoppe}@fokus.fraunhofer.de

Abstract. Supply Chain Risk Management focuses on the identification, assessment and management of disruptive events that can affect companies, transport routes and resources involved in critical goods supply chains. Modern supply chains consist of interconnected components that can be complex and dynamic in nature. In this demo, we present our system for analysing the resilience of supply chains for crisis relevant products. A dependency Bayesian Network is automatically generated from relevant information about the supply chain maintained in a Knowledge Graph. The main objective of the proposed approach is the early identification of bottlenecks and timely prediction of the consequences of probable disruptions of the network.

Keywords: Supply chain resilience · Knowledge Graph · Bayesian Network · Crisis management · Automatic bottleneck identification

1 Context and Motivation

Recent disruptive events like COVID-19 or the Suez canal obstruction in 2021 showed how vulnerable our society and economy are to unforeseen disruptions of supply chains [1]. Due to a strong globalisation, modern supply chains became very complex, spanning multiple countries or even continents, involving longer transport distances and globally distributed suppliers. They depend highly on interconnected and tightly synchronized networks of a dynamic nature. Disruptions from an event affecting one subnetwork of the system can have costly and sometimes disastrous cascading effects on the whole supply chain.

Together with critical public safety organisations, we are developing ResKriVer[1], a crisis management platform and services offering relevant, interconnected and high-quality information for a wide range of crisis scenarios. The main aim of the platform is to provide crisis teams with the best possible overview for assessing the current situation and communicating it to the population. The demonstrator "Supply with substitutable Goods and Resources" focuses on the reliability of supply networks for crisis relevant goods and resources. The central objective is the assessment and management of threats

---

[1] reskriver.de.

C. Pesquita et al. (Eds.): ESWC 2023, LNCS 13998, pp. 27–31, 2023.
https://doi.org/10.1007/978-3-031-43458-7_5

and events that can affect the network and the early identification of bottlenecks. The platform is constantly enriched with necessary information about supply chains of crisis goods, such as manufacturers, production capacities, importers and transport routes. If a supply shortage is predicted by the system, suggestions for possible product substitutes, transport routes, or alternative manufacturers will be generated.

In ResKriVer knowledge is captured semantically based on an ontology we developed using a modular approach. As upper-level ontology we use the PROV Ontology (PROV-O) [3] and the Basic Formal Ontology (BFO) [2] and for the mid-level the Common Core Ontologies (CCO) [8], a suite of ontologies describing generic classes across all domains of interest. In addition to the knowledge graph (KG), we developed an extended Bayesian Network approach (BN) to analyze supply chain disruptions, this network is automatically generated from the KG. Bayesian Networks have proven to be a powerful tool to model and analyze supply chain disruptions under uncertainty conditions [5,6]. Approaches combining KGs and BNs have been proposed recently for Knowledge Graph inference [10,11] and collaborative recommendation [7]. In order to take advantages of both worlds, we propose a new approach and tool called ReSCA (Resilience of Supply Chain Analyzer) combining the flexibility of Knowledge Graphs with the computation power of Bayesian Networks. Our knowledge on supply network can be continuously extended and adapted by new findings through the KG, the Bayesian Network structure can then be extracted from the KG in order to make timely predictions.

2   ReSCA Knowledge Graph Representation

A supply chain is the network of individuals, organizations, activities and resources involved in the production and transport of goods from a supplier to an end customer. A disruption will affect a specific supply chain if it affects one of the activities and components involved in it. Based on this definition, we consolidated a set of high-level entities and their relations for describing supply chains of crisis goods and their disruptions and shown in Fig. 1.

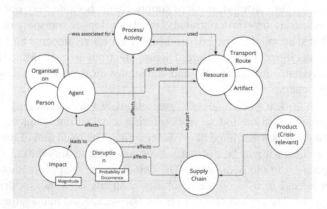

Fig. 1. High-level entities and relations for supply chains and their disruptions

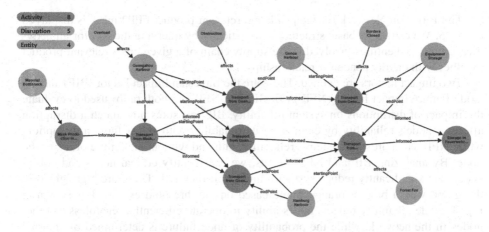

Fig. 2. A subset of the Knowledge Graph describing the supply chain of FFP2 masks

Our basis for the knowledge representation was the consolidated high-level entities and their counterpart PROV-O Starting Point classes: prov:Entity, prov:Activity and prov:Agent [3]. We mapped those through BFO to a useful set of the CCO ontologies, namely: the Event, the Agent and the Artifact ontologies. For the mapping, we extended the alignment between PROV-O and BFO proposed in [4] for core classes.

Figure 2 shows a subset of the Knowledge Graph describing activities and entities involved in the supply chain of the pandemic relevant product FFP2 mask. Disruptions can affect any element of the subgraph. For instance, a material bottleneck can affect a production activity and the closing of borders a transport one. We show in the next section how information from the KG can be used to generate the corresponding Bayesian Network.

3 Bayesian Network Extraction and Impact Factor Calculation

In order to enable a dynamic extraction of the Bayesian Network from the KG, we defined a set of object properties expressing the notion of dependency. We extended the PROV-O properties under prov:influenced as follows:

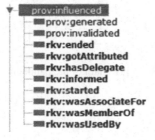

The Bayesian Network for the pandemic relevant product FFP2 mask is displayed in Fig. 3. We extract its basic structure automatically by querying the KG for all activities, agents and entities involved in the supply chain of a given crisis relevant product together with their dependency relationships.

Two impact factors are defined. These are the Bayesian Impact Factor (BIF) and the Node Failure Impact Factor (NFIF) [9]. BIF and NFIF are both ratios used to evaluate the impact of disruptions on system reliability. BIF measures how much a disruption affects a node's reliability by comparing its reliability with and without a disruption, while NFIF compares the system's reliability with and without the failure of a specific node. By analyzing BIF and NFIF results, we can identify critical nodes and bottlenecks that significantly reduce system reliability if they fail. Those are highlighted in the graph with a blue or orange frame based on the threshold exceeded as shown in Fig. 3. Node reliability reflects nodes ability to operate efficiently, regardless of other nodes in the network, while the probability of node failure is determined by internal failures, disruptions, and parent node failures. In the graph, the probability of the last node is the most important as it represents the probability of the entire system operating well. Node reliability is initially obtained from the knowledge graph, and the probability of disruptions is randomly generated within a range of 0.0 to 0.05.

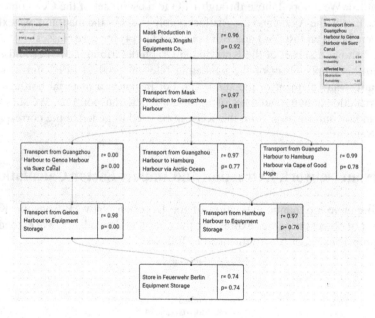

Fig. 3. Bayesian Network for the supply chain of the pandemic relevant product FFP2 mask

4   Demonstration

In this demonstration, visitors will be able to use the interface to enter disruptions, the system will compute the network's overall score and point out bottleneck nodes. We will provide guidance and example scenarios. A demo video can be found at: https://owncloud.fokus.fraunhofer.de/index.php/s/4ux8YvusxrA2gqx. For users interested in the models and RDF data behind the demo, we will provide access to the SPARQL endpoint and the Knowledge Graph visualisation.

Acknowledgements. This work was funded by the German Federal Ministry for Economic Affairs and Climate Protection (BMWK) as part of the AI Innovation Competition under contract 01MK21006A.

References

1. Alexander, A., Blome, C., Schleper, M.C., Roscoe, S.: Managing "the new normal": the future of operations and supply chain management in unprecedented times. Int. J. Oper. Prod. Manag. (2022)
2. Arp, R., Smith, B., Spear, A.D.: Building Ontologies with Basic Formal Ontology. The MIT Press, Cambridge (2015)
3. Belhajjame, K., et al.: Prov-o: the prov ontology. Technical report (2012)
4. Cox, S.: PROV ontology supports alignment of observational data (models) (2017)
5. Soberanis, I.E.D.: An extended Bayesian network approach for analyzing supply chain disruptions. Doctor of Philosophy, University of Iowa (2010)
6. Hosseini, S., Ivanov, D.: Bayesian networks for supply chain risk, resilience and ripple effect analysis: a literature review. Expert Syst. Appl. **161**, 113649 (2020)
7. Pan, H., Yang, X.: Intelligent recommendation method integrating knowledge graph and Bayesian network. Soft. Comput. **27**(1), 483–492 (2023)
8. Rudnicki, R.: An Overview of the Common Core Ontologies, p. 27. CUBRC Inc. (2019)
9. Soberanis, I.E.D.: An extended Bayesian network approach for analyzing supply chain disruptions. Ph.D. thesis, University of Iowa (2010)
10. Wan, G., Du, B.: Gaussianpath: a Bayesian multi-hop reasoning framework for knowledge graph reasoning. In: AAAI Conference on Artificial Intelligence (2021)
11. Luo, W., Cai, F., Wu, C., Meng, X.: Bayesian network-based knowledge graph inference for highway transportation safety risks. Adv. Civil Eng. **2021**, 6624579 (2021)

More Power to SPARQL: From Paths to Trees

Angelos Christos Anadiotis[1] , Ioana Manolescu[2] ,
and Madhulika Mohanty[2(✉)]

[1] Oracle, Zürich, Switzerland
angelos.anadiotis@oracle.com
[2] Inria and Institut Polytechnique de Paris, Palaiseau, France
{ioana.manolescu, madhulika.mohanty}@inria.fr

Abstract. Exploring Knowledge Graphs (KGs, in short) to discover facts and links is tedious even for experts with knowledge of SPARQL due to their unfamiliarity with the structure and labels of entities, classes and relations. Some KG applications require finding the connections between groups of nodes, even if users ignore the shape of these connections. However, SPARQL only allows checking if paths exist, not returning them. A recent property graph query language, GPML, allows also returning connecting paths, but not connections between three or more nodes.

We propose to demonstrate RELSEARCH, a system supporting *extended* SPARQL queries, featuring standard Basic Graph Patterns (BGPs) as well as novel Connecting Tree Patterns (CTPs); each CTP requests *the connections* (paths, or trees) between nodes bound to variables. RELSEARCH evaluates such extended queries using novel algorithms [2] which, unlike prior keyword search methods, return connections regardless of the edge directions and are independent of how we measure the quality (score) of each connection. We will demonstrate RELSEARCH's expressivity and efficiency using a variety of RDF graphs, user-selected score functions, and search exploration orders.

Keywords: Graph Queries · Keyword Search · Exploratory Search

1 Introduction

Knowledge Graphs (KGs) like Yago, DBPedia and Freebase form the backbone of many applications ranging from search engines, business intelligence to question answering. The RDF data model is the most common way to represent the KGs. They comprise subject-predicate-object (SPO) triples where subjects and predicates are resources, while objects are either resources, e.g., ElvisPresley, or literal values like strings, numbers, and dates. Thus, a KG has subjects and objects as its nodes, connected by relations as directed edges. KGs can be queried using SPARQL, with Basic Graph Patterns (BGPs) at its core. As RDF graphs typically lack a prescriptive schema, their structure may be complex. This makes

C. Pesquita et al. (Eds.): ESWC 2023, LNCS 13998, pp. 32–36, 2023.
https://doi.org/10.1007/978-3-031-43458-7_6

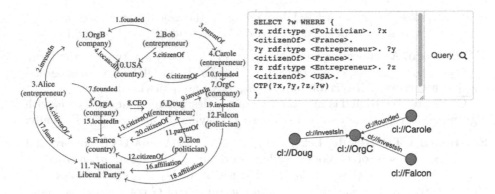

Fig. 1. Sample KG (left), and RELSEARCH demo screenshot (right).

it difficult for users to query KGs when they ignore the structure of the relationships between node groups that interest them. For example, consider the KG in Fig. 1. A journalist may be interested in finding the connections between three groups of nodes: (*i*) US entrepreneurs, (*ii*) French entrepreneurs and (*iii*) French politicians, regardless of the structure and directionality of these connections. Current graph query languages, e.g., SPARQL, do not support expressing such a query, which is however useful when combining some criteria users have in mind ("US entrepreneurs", etc.) with graph structure discovery.

We propose to demonstrate the RELSEARCH system, enabling users to explore a KG, even when they cannot specify the exact labels or structure of these connections. RELSEARCH (*i*) extends the SPARQL syntax to support Connecting Tree Patterns (CTPs) alongside BGPs, (*ii*) efficiently executes the extended queries, and (*iii*) allows users to customize results by freely choosing the scoring function to use for ranking CTP results (thus, the extended query results), and several filters on their results. Scoring is important, because some paths are much more interesting than others, e.g., the journalist asking the above query is more interested to find that "Elon" is a parent of "Doug", than to find both are French (which was specified in the query). Being orthogonal wrt the score function is important, since it has been shown [4] that different applications and information needs are best served by different functions. These may privilege: node closeness, semantic coherence (or, on the contrary, diversity) on the edge labels in the connection, ranks of nodes along the connections, etc.

2   Framework: Extending SPARQL for Connection Search

SPARQL queries may contain BGPs and/or Property Path Queries (PPQs). A BGP is a set of triple patterns, each of whose components may be a variable or a constant (URI or literal); BGP triples are connected by shared variables. A PPQ is a regular path query over the RDF graph; it allows checking (only) the presence of paths whose labels (property) match a regular expression, between query variables. Note that a PPQ does not allow the *any* regular expression, and can only combine user-specified properties. We extend SPARQL as follows:

CT Pattern. A connecting tree pattern (CTP, in short) is a tuple of the form: $g = (g_1, g_2, \ldots, g_m, v_{m+1})$ where each g_i, $1 \leq i \leq m$ is an URI or a variable and v_{m+1} is a variable. All variables $g_1, \ldots, g_m, v_{m+1}$ are pairwise distinct.

CTPs are used to find connections among nodes: when replacing each g_i with a graph node, v_{m+1} is bound to a *subtree* of G, having the g_is as leaves. Formally:

Set-Based CTP Result. Let $g = (g_1, \ldots, g_m, v_{m+1})$ be a CTP pattern and $S_1, \ldots, S_m$ be sets of G nodes, called **seed sets**. The *result of g based on* $S_1, \ldots, S_m$, denoted $g(S_1, \ldots, S_m)$, is the set of all $(s_1, \ldots, s_m, t)$ tuples such that $s_1 \in S_1$, ..., $s_m \in S_m$ and t is a *minimal* subtree of G containing the nodes $s_1, \ldots, s_m$. Here, minimal means: (i) removing any edge from t disconnects it and/or removes some s_i from t, and (ii) t contains only one node from each S_i.

Extended Query. An extended query (EQ) consists of SPARQL BGPs, PPQs and/or CTPs. Its semantics is as follows. (i) When a g_i variable from a CTP appears also in some BGPs and/or PPQs, the respective seed set S_i is formed of all the nodes that (as per SPARQL semantics) match, simultaneously, the respective BGPs and PPQs. If a CTP variable g_j does not appear in any other place in the query, S_j consists of all the nodes in the KG. (ii) The EQ result is obtained by joining the BGP/PPQ results (seen as a table, binding variable to nodes) with the set-based results of all the CTPs in the EQ.

For example, Fig. 1 shows the EQ seeking the connections between US entrepreneurs, French entrepreneurs and French politicians (at the top right). On the KG shown at left, the RELSEARCH screenshot in Fig. 1 also shows a sample connecting tree, matching the variable ?w.

Our CTPs consider the graph *undirected*. This ensures that we do not miss any connections just because edge directions are not aligned. In our example, the CTP result connecting "Alice", "Falcon" and "Carole" via "National Liberal Party" and "OrgC" can only be found by considering edges in both directions.

CTP Filters. A CTP can have a very large number of results. Consider a KG of $2N$ triples over $N+1$ nodes (labeled 1, 2, and so on). Each node i is connected to $i+1$ by a triple whose property is a, and to the node $i-1$ through a property b. If v_1 is bound to 1 and v_2 to N+1, the CTP $(v_1, v_2, \underline{v_3})$, asking for all the connections between the end nodes, has 2^N solutions, or $2^{|E|/2}$, which grows exponentially in $|E| = 2N$, the number of KG triples. Observe that if we allowed only unidirectional paths, there would be only $N+1$ results, rooted at each node. Thus, matching CTPs regardless of the edge direction may drastically increase the number of CTP results; in some cases, computing all the CTP results may be **unfeasible**. To control the amount of effort spent evaluating CTPs, we also provide a set of orthogonal filters which allow to restrict set-based CTP results. Specifically, adding UNI for a CTP indicates that only *unidirectional* trees are sought, that is: a tree t, as in Definition 2, must have a *root* node, from which a *directed path* goes to each seed node in t. Specifying a set of labels $\{l_1, l_2, \ldots, l_k\}$ for a CTP indicates that the edges in any result of that CTP must have labels from the given set. Indicating a MAX n for a CTP indicates that only trees of at most n edges are sought. Further, a **score function** σ can be used to assign a real number $\sigma(t)$ (the higher, the better) to each connecting tree, measuring their interestingness to users. Using TOP k, one can restrict the CTP result to those having the k-highest σ scores. Finally, a practical way to limit the evaluation of a CTP is to specify a timeout T, that is, a maximum allowed evaluation time.

3   System and Demonstration Scenario

RELSEARCH relies on the ConnectionLens [3] system for storing the KG in a PostgreSQL table graph(gID, s, p, o), heavily indexed. RELSEARCH extends a SPARQL parser to incorporate the CTP atoms. The query execution engine is implemented in Java 11; the CTP evaluation algorithms [2] are integrated within ConnectionLens; BGPs are evaluated within Postgres.

We demonstrate RELSEARCH over two real-world datasets, a 6M edges subset of YAGO3, and a 18M edges subset of DBPedia. Users write their own queries and inspect the results, including connections shown as trees in the GUI. They can also select multiple filters for the CTPs – changing the number of results shown, the score function to be used to rank the trees, any specifications of permitted labels, direction of edges in the results and also limit the size of the results. https://team.inria.fr/cedar/projects/relsearch/ outlines our demo.

4   Related Work

Many works address KG exploration; a recent categorization can be found in [7]. Such works have focused on: graph summarization, query by example, query suggestion and refinement, etc. Keyword search systems over KGs [8,9] return trees connecting nodes matching user-specified keywords. However, users cannot specify more conditions on nodes to be connected, e.g., "is of type Person, has age <20, and their name matches *Jane*". Symmetrically, query languages do not currently support searching for connecting trees. SPARQL allows checking for (but not returning) paths connecting nodes; property graph languages such as GPML (not implemented) [5] and Neo4j's Cypher return paths, however, the latter does not scale [2]. RPQProv [6] uses recursive SQL to return path labels; JEDI [1] returns unidirectional paths (only). Going beyond paths, RELSEARCH combines SPARQL's expressive power with the ability to return trees connecting an arbitrary number of node sets, traversing edges in any direction, independent of a scoring function.

Acknowledgments. This work has been funded by the AI Chair SourcesSay (ANR-20-CHIA-0015-01) project.

References

1. Aebeloe, C., Setty, V., Montoya, G., Hose, K.: Top-K diversification for path queries in knowledge graphs. In: ISWC (2018)

2. Anadiotis, A., Manolescu, I., Mohanty, M.: Integrating connection search in graph queries. In: ICDE (2023)
3. Chanial, C., Dziri, R., Galhardas, H., et al.: ConnectionLens: finding connections across heterogeneous data sources (demonstration). PVLDB **11**(12), 4 (2018)
4. Coffman, J., Weaver, A.C.: An empirical performance evaluation of relational keyword search techniques. IEEE TKDE **26**(1), 30–42 (2014)
5. Deutsch, A., Francis, N., Green, A., Hare, K., Li, B., Libkin, L., et al.: Graph pattern matching in GQL and SQL/PGQ. In: SIGMOD (2022)
6. Dey, S.C., Cuevas-Vicenttín, V., Köhler, S., et al.: On implementing provenance-aware regular path queries with relational query engines. In: EDBT (2013)
7. Lissandrini, M., Mottin, D., Hose, K., Pedersen, T.B.: Knowledge graph exploration systems: are we lost? In: CIDR (2022)
8. Wang, H., Aggarwal, C.C.: A survey of algorithms for keyword search on graph data. In: Aggarwal, C., Wang, H. (eds.) Managing and Mining Graph Data, vol. 40. Springer, Cham (2010). https://doi.org/10.1007/978-1-4419-6045-0_8
9. Yang, J., Yao, W., Zhang, W.: Keyword search on large graphs: a survey. Data Sci. Eng. **6**(2), 142–162 (2021)

Assessing Knowledge Graphs Accountability

Jennie Andersen[(✉)], Sylvie Cazalens, and Philippe Lamarre

Univ Lyon, INSA Lyon, CNRS, UCBL, LIRIS, UMR5205, 69621 Villeurbanne, France
{jennie.andersen,sylvie.cazalens,philippe.lamarre}@insa-lyon.fr

Abstract. Demand for accountability is increasing, driven by the growth of open data and e-governments. Accountability requires specific and fairly accurate information about people's responsibilities and actions. Studies on data quality or FAIRness do not have a specific focus on that aspect. Therefore, we describe our approach to evaluate the accountability of several knowledge graphs of the LOD cloud and the results obtained.

Keywords: Knowledge graphs · RDF graphs · Accountability

1 Introduction

Designing systems enabling individuals and institutions to be held accountable is increasingly important [6], especially as it enhances trust in the data. Dataset accountability means that "there is sufficient information to justify and explain the actions" on the dataset, "in addition to descriptive information and information on the people responsible for it" [4]. Concerning Knowledge Graphs (KGs), many works look for meta-information, either for evaluating some quality aspects [2,7] or conformance to recommendations, such as FAIRness [1,5]. None of them focuses specifically on accountability as a whole. They consider some elements of accountability but do not take into account all the elements required by it. For example, FAIRness requires meta-information such as creators but accountability goes further requiring affiliation and contact information of creators for instance.

Therefore, in this paper, we aim to conduct an evaluation of the accountability of KGs. For datasets in general, precise requirements are expressed as questions by the LiQuID metadata model [4]. It has been validated based on a real-world workload that relies on existing regulations and an expert survey. The use of this model and questions to evaluate KGs requires (i) adapting the hierarchical model and questions to KGs, (ii) expressing the questions into SPARQL queries, (iii) querying the KGs, (iv) computing accountability scores that can be detailed according to different levels of the hierarchy. These steps are illustrated by Fig. 1 and detailed in the next sections. Notice that we use the IndeGx framework [3]. This SPARQL-based test suite proposes several functionalities.

C. Pesquita et al. (Eds.): ESWC 2023, LNCS 13998, pp. 37–42, 2023.
https://doi.org/10.1007/978-3-031-43458-7_7

We only use it as an engine to submit multiple queries to many KGs, and to store the results in RDF, without querying its index. For further information, all our evaluation material and results are available on Github[1].

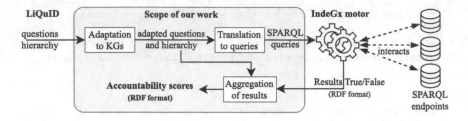

Fig. 1. Process to Define and Measure Knowledge Graph Accountability

2 Adaptation of LiQuID and Translation into Queries

LiQuID relies on a hierarchical structure: first, the steps of a dataset's life cycle, then the different question types (who, when, etc.) and finally the types of information (description, justifications, etc.). The authors provide an exhaustive and explicit list of questions to describe each leaf of this hierarchy, and so, what must be provided to be considered accountable.

Adaptation. Ideally, to assess the accountability of a KG, all this hierarchy and associated questions should be considered. However, not all of them can be adapted to KGs and translated into SPARQL queries, as shown by the comparison between LiQuID and the two metadata models Dublin Core and PROV [4]. Indeed, a lack of expressivity of the vocabularies prevents many questions from being translated into queries or often induces a loss of precision (e.g. inability to distinguish between data collection and data processing steps). Faced with these difficulties, we decide to consider only questions that are compatible with the current vocabularies of semantic web. For instance, we only keep the field "description" of the last level of LiQuID, removing too specific questions such as "Why is it ethical to create a dataset for this cause?". Therefore, we only keep a part of the LiQuID hierarchy, shown in Fig. 2, which leads us to consider a core set of 25 LiQuID questions (out of 207). These questions are adapted, as faithfully as possible, to the context of KGs, and made more precise. For instance, "Who has used/can use the published data set?" splits into "Who has the right to use the KG?" and "Who is intended to use the KG?". It results into 30 questions: 5 for Data Collection, 5 for Data Maintenance and 20 for Data Usage.

---

[1] https://github.com/Jendersen/KG_accountability.

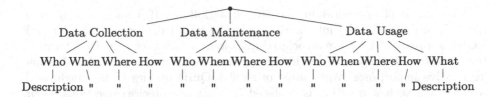

Fig. 2. Hierarchy Classifying Accountability Questions Adapted from LiQuID [4]

Translation. Finally, all the questions are translated into SPARQL queries. Ten vocabularies of reference are chosen regarding their pertinence, let them be specific to describe datasets (VoID, DCAT, SPARQL-SD, DataID and DQV), more general (the Dublin Core, FOAF and schema.org), or focusing on provenance (PROV-O and PAV). Each query uses all coherent properties and classes of these vocabularies to be as complete as possible. For instance, a query asking for a publisher accepts all publisher-like properties (using the Dublin Core, schema and PROV), see Listing 1.1. An important point about our approach is a strict interpretation and translation of questions into queries. This leads us to be very demanding as for the way KGs express metadata: we look for metadata explicitly linked to the IRI of the KG to ensure that the information is actually about the KG. To identify it, queries look for an entity of class Dataset which is linked to the URL of the endpoint interrogated. If the KG does not provide such an IRI, it will not answer any of our queries.

Listing 1.1. Query Associated with "Who publishes this dataset?"

```
PREFIX dct: <http://purl.org/dc/terms/>
PREFIX dce: <http://purl.org/dc/elements/1.1/>
PREFIX schema: <http://schema.org/>
PREFIX prov: <http://www.w3.org/ns/prov#>
ASK { # <kg> is the KG IRI obtained by a preliminary query.
    {<kg> dct:publisher ?publisher .}
    UNION {<kg> dce:publisher ?publisher .}
    UNION {<kg> schema:publisher ?publisher .}
    UNION {<kg> schema:sdPublisher ?publisher .}
    UNION {<kg> prov:wasGeneratedBy ?act .
        ?act a prov:Publish .
        ?act prov:wasAssociatedWith ?publisher .} }
```

3 Querying KGs and Aggregating Accountability Scores

To query numerous KGs, the framework IndeGx is used. To determine whether a KG contains the necessary information for accountability, we use ASK queries, ensuring that we get a True result if the information is present and a False otherwise. We embed the set of queries previously defined into the framework and configure the format of the results to be Data Quality Vocabulary (DQV).

The metric of accountability is defined as follows. If a query obtains the result True (meaning the information is in the knowledge graph), the queried KG gets a score of 1 for the associated question, and 0 otherwise. To determine the score on each aspect of the hierarchy, each question has a weight, showing its relative importance. We assume original LiQuID queries to be weightened to 1. When such a question is replaced by n (more precise) questions, their respective weights is set to $\frac{1}{n}$. Therefore, for a leaf of the hierarchy, the score of accountability on that aspect is the weighted average of the score obtained on each question. For the other elements of the hierarchy, we determine their score by recursively computing the (non-weighted) average of the score on the elements underneath. A fine analysis is possible as all the scores are available, including those obtained for each question and the intermediate ones.

4   Experiments

Each knowledge graph is queried at three different time points. Only the results of the last experiment for which it was available are kept. Among the 670 queried knowledge graphs, we keep those which have answered and provided their own IRI. We only get 29 KGs. This result is in line with [3]: only a few KGs provide their own IRI and thus a self-description.

Considering these 29 KGs, Fig. 3 shows their overall accountability with the scores detailed on the three lifecycle steps. Our evaluation of accountability allows to discriminate between them, with values distributed between 2.2% and 44%, with a mean and median of 22%. On average, KGs are more accountable on Data Usage than on Data Collection, than on Data Maintenance. In addition, the results enable to compare KGs in more detail using a radar chart[2].

Regarding our evaluation, one must keep in mind that some meta-information may be provided by KG producers outside of the KG itself, for instance on its web page. It can also be inside the KG, but in such a way we did not identify the IRI of the KG: if it is not related to the URL of the endpoint nor to an entity of type Dataset. In any case, the meta-information is not detected and therefore not considered. While this may penalize some KGs, it points out the fact that they are less accountable because information is less accessible.

Concerning the measure itself, it is important to notice that some queries never succeed, 9 out of 30. A part of them is due to some strict choices we made that resulted in over-constrained queries. The rest is due to a lack of information provided by the KGs.

---

[2] https://github.com/Jendersen/KG_accountability/tree/main/results.

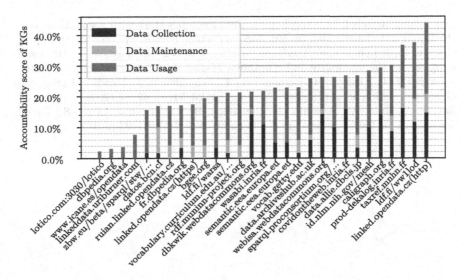

Fig. 3. Accountability of Knowledge Graphs

5 Conclusion

Our assessment of knowledge graphs accountability highlights the weaknesses of many KGs regarding accountability, even if the requests for certain information is very common. The obtained low or no scores show that there is room for improvement, and the presence of good ones shows that linked data is very suitable for accountability. Our measurement is detailed enough to help any KG producer to precisely identify missing information and therefore to improve on these aspects. Having started with a strict interpretation of the questions, we plan to relax some queries and introduce gradations in the definition of accountability requirements.

Acknowledgments. This work is supported by the ANR DeKaloG (Decentralized Knowledge Graphs) project, ANR-19-CE23-0014, CE23 - Intelligence artificielle.

References

1. Amdouni, E., Bouazzouni, S., Jonquet, C.: O'FAIRe: Ontology FAIRness evaluator in the agroportal semantic resource repository. In: Groth, P., et al. (eds.) ESWC 2022–19th Extended Semantic Web Conference, Poster and Demonstration. Springer, Cham (2022). https://doi.org/10.1007/978-3-031-11609-4_17
2. Färber, M., Bartscherer, F., Menne, C., Rettinger, A.: Linked data quality of DBpedia, Freebase, OpenCYC, Wikidata, and YAGO. Semant. Web 9(1), 77–129 (2018)
3. Maillot, P., Corby, O., Faron, C., Gandon, F., Michel, F.: IndeGx: a model and a framework for indexing RDF knowledge graphs with SPARQL-based test suits. J. Web Semant. **76**, 100775 (2023)

4. Oppold, S., Herschel, M.: Accountable data analytics start with accountable data: the liquid metadata model. In: ER Forum/Posters/Demos, pp. 59–72 (2020)
5. Rosnet, T., de Lamotte, F., Devignes, M.D., Lefort, V., Gaignard, A.: FAIR-checker - supporting the findability and reusability of digital life science resources (2021)
6. Weitzner, D.J., Abelson, H., Berners-Lee, T., Feigenbaum, J., Hendler, J., Sussman, G.J.: Information accountability. Commun. ACM **51**(6), 82–87 (2008)
7. Zaveri, A., Rula, A., Maurino, A., Pietrobon, R., Lehmann, J., Auer, S.: Quality assessment for linked data: a survey. Semant. Web **7**(1), 63–93 (2016)

Reinforcement Learning-Based SPARQL Join Ordering Optimizer

Ruben Eschauzier[1]([envelope]) [iD], Ruben Taelman[1] [iD], Meike Morren[2] [iD],
and Ruben Verborgh[1] [iD]

[1] IDLab, Department of Electronics and Information Systems, Ghent University -
imec, Ghent, Belgium
`ruben.eschauzier@ugent.be`
[2] Marketing, School of Business and Economics, Vrije Universiteit Amsterdam,
Amsterdam, The Netherlands

Abstract. In recent years, relational databases successfully leverage reinforcement learning to optimize query plans. For graph databases and RDF quad stores, such research has been limited, so there is a need to understand the impact of reinforcement learning techniques. We explore a reinforcement learning-based join plan optimizer that we design specifically for optimizing join plans during SPARQL query planning. This paper presents key aspects of this method and highlights open research problems. We argue that while we can reuse aspects of relational database optimization, SPARQL query optimization presents unique challenges not encountered in relational databases. Nevertheless, initial benchmarks show promising results that warrant further exploration.

Keywords: SPARQL · Join Order Optimization · Reinforcement learning · Machine Learning

1 Introduction

Optimizing the order in which database management systems execute joins is a well-studied topic in database literature because it heavily influences the performance characteristics of queries [11]. SPARQL endpoints over consistently evolving datasets, like Wikidata, can benefit from an algorithm that optimizes queries based on previous experiences. Different signals exist to inform an appropriate choice of join order, such as cardinalities. One such signal is *previous experiences*. We use previous experiences as a predictor to produce better join plans for future queries.

In recent literature, reinforcement learning(RL)-based optimizers that use *greedy search procedures*, guided by a learned *value function*, achieve impressive results in relational databases. Neo [5] shows that learned optimizers can match and surpass state-of-the-art commercial optimizers.

In SPARQL, machine learning is primarily used to predict query performance. These approaches [2,3,12] use supervised machine learning with a static

C. Pesquita et al. (Eds.): ESWC 2023, LNCS 13998, pp. 43–47, 2023.
https://doi.org/10.1007/978-3-031-43458-7_8

dataset of query executions. Learned query optimizers use reinforcement learning to dynamically generate training data, complicating the use of existing query performance prediction methods. The April [10] optimizer uses reinforcement learning for query optimization, with a one-hot encoded [6] feature vector denoting the presence of RDF terms in joins. However, the paper does not report any performance characteristics.

We fill this gap in the literature by exploring a fully-fledged RL-based query optimizer for SPARQL join order optimization on SPARQL endpoints. Endpoints query over the same dataset, likely making the previous experience signal stronger for join order optimization. We model our approach after the RTOS [11] optimizer for relational queries, which uses Tree-LSTM neural networks [9] to predict the expected latency of a join plan.

2   Method

To iteratively build up an optimized join plan, the RL-based optimizer greedily adds the join that minimizes the estimated query execution time at each iteration. For the first iteration, we have the result sets of all triple patterns, and in each subsequent iteration, we join two result sets. We estimate the execution time of the query using a neural network, which we train to minimize the mean squared error between predicted and actual query execution time. We feed a numerical representation of the current join plan as an input to the neural network.

Join Plan Representation. Like in the optimizer RTOS [11], we represent join plans as a tree that we build from the bottom up. Each leaf node represents the result set of a triple pattern, and internal nodes represent join result sets. We represent result sets using their cardinality, the presence and location of variables, named nodes and literals, and a vector representation of the predicate. We learn the predicate representation vectors by applying the RDF2Vec [7] algorithm to the RDF graph.

RDF2Vec generates learned vector representations of RDF terms that encode information on what RDF terms co-occur often. RDF2Vec first generates random walks on the input RDF graph, then for each random walk, it randomly removes an RDF term and trains a neural network to predict the missing term. The weights obtained during the model training are the feature vectors of the RDF terms in the graph. RDF2Vec does not learn variable representations because an RDF graph has no variables. The subject and object of triple patterns are often variables, so we do not encode named nodes in these positions. We obtain the representations for intermediate joins by applying an N-ary Tree-LSTM [9] neural network on the result sets representations involved in the join. These representations are optimized during training, thus allowing the model to determine which features of the result sets involved in the join are important. Finally, at the (partial) join plan root node, we apply the Child-Sum Tree-LSTM network [9] to all unjoined result sets to obtain the numerical join plan representation.

Data Efficiency and SPARQL-Specific Adjustments. Data generation using query execution is slow; we account for this by applying two data efficiency techniques. First, we include a *time-out* set according to existing optimizers. We effectively truncate our optimization variable while ensuring the optimal query plan will not reach the time-out. Second, we use *experience replay* [4] to store previous (expensive) query executions and reuse them for training.

Relational RL-based optimization approaches use *one-hot encoding* [6] of database attributes to create feature vectors. However, large graphs like Wikidata can contain over 100 million unique entries. One-hot encoding that many attributes would create unwieldy vectors and degrade performance. To improve scalability, we do not use one-hot encoding in our approach, instead, we use feature encoding techniques to capture state information in fixed-size vectors.

Open Challenges. We have not found a way to encode connections between triple patterns. To encode all information in the query graph, these encodings should reflect the possible connections between triple patterns, like object-object, subject-subject, object-subject, and subject-object. Which makes using a simple adjacency matrix infeasible. Furthermore, our approach can only optimize basic graph patterns; in future work, this approach should be extended to more complex SPARQL query operations. Finally, we do not learn feature representations for variables; to enrich our triple pattern representation, we should encode variables based on the other RDF terms in the triple pattern.

3   Initial Experiments

We implement our optimizer in the TypeScript-based Comunica query engine [8] and compare it to the default cardinality-based optimizer. We use the WatDiv benchmark [1] to test our method, and show the performance characteristics of a preliminary version of the model. Table 1 shows that the model can find better plans for 7 templates, which we believe we can improve using the data efficiency and SPARQL-specific adjustments mentioned in Sect. 2. The search time of our method is significantly longer than the standard comunica optimizer. However, we run these benchmarks on a dataset with only about 100,000 triples. For large RDF graphs, like Wikidata, we expect that the execution of the join plan dominates the total query execution time.

Table 1. Comparison of the query optimization and plan execution time, in seconds, of a previous version of our optimizer and the standard Comunica [8] optimizer, with the faster plan execution in bold.

Query Template	C1	C2	C3	F1	F2	F3	F4	F5	L1
Planning (RL)	0.5028	1.000	0.277	0.214	0.347	0.160	0.800	0.278	0.027
Execution (RL)	3.116	2.577	0.583	0.100	0.090	0.062	1.906	**0.059**	**0.006**
Planning (Comunica)	0.007	0.008	0.017	0.002	0.003	0.005	0.005	0.005	0.002
Execution (Comunica)	**0.076**	**0.001**	**0.490**	**0.001**	**0.005**	**0.008**	**0.012**	0.194	0.032
Query Template	L2	L5	S1	S2	S3	S4	S5	S6	S7
Planning (RL)	0.025	0.024	0.689	0.060	0.059	0.066	0.059	0.021	0.028
Execution (RL)	**0.001**	**0.002**	2.242	0.011	**0.005**	**0.000**	**0.002**	0.008	0.002
Planning (Comunica)	0.001	0.001	0.006	0.002	0.002	0.002	0.002	0.002	0.002
Execution (Comunica)	0.006	0.007	**0.139**	**0.009**	0.008	0.005	0.009	**0.001**	**0.000**

4   Conclusion

In this paper, we explore a novel RL-based join plan optimizer for SPARQL endpoint query execution. Initial experiments show that the model can generate better join plans than existing cardinality-based optimizers for 7 query templates of the WatDiv benchmark. We plan to improve the model by enhancing data efficiency during training. We propose to use query *time-outs* based on existing query optimizers to reduce the time spent executing bad query plans. Additionally, we propose to use *experience replay* to reuse query execution information during training. For future work, we should include information on how triple pattern result sets connect to other result sets in the query, encode the RDF terms present in the subject and object locations of a triple pattern, and extend our approach to more complex SPARQL operations.

Acknowledgments. This work is supported by SolidLab Vlaanderen (Flemish Government, EWI and RRF project VV023/10). Ruben Taelman is a postdoctoral fellow of the Research Foundation - Flanders (FWO) (1274521N).

References

1. Aluç, G., Hartig, O., Özsu, M.T., Daudjee, K.: Diversified stress testing of RDF data management systems. In: Mika, P., et al. (eds.) ISWC 2014. LNCS, vol. 8796, pp. 197–212. Springer, Cham (2014). https://doi.org/10.1007/978-3-319-11964-9_13
2. Casals, D., Buil-Aranda, C., Valle, C.: SPARQL query execution time prediction using deep learning
3. Hasan, R., Gandon, F.: A machine learning approach to SPARQL query performance prediction. In: 2014 IEEE/WIC/ACM International Joint Conferences on Web Intelligence (WI) and Intelligent Agent Technologies (IAT) (2014)
4. Lin, L.J.: Self-improving reactive agents based on reinforcement learning, planning and teaching. Mach. Learn. **8**, 293–321 (1992)

5. Marcus, R., et al.: Neo: a learned query optimizer. arXiv preprint arXiv:1904.03711 (2019)
6. Müller, A.C., Guido, S.: Introduction to machine learning with Python: a guide for data scientists (2016)
7. Ristoski, P., Paulheim, H.: RDF2Vec: RDF graph embeddings for data mining. In: Groth, P., et al. (eds.) ISWC 2016. LNCS, vol. 9981, pp. 498–514. Springer, Cham (2016). https://doi.org/10.1007/978-3-319-46523-4_30
8. Taelman, R., Van Herwegen, J., Vander Sande, M., Verborgh, R.: Comunica: a modular SPARQL query engine for the web. In: Vrandečić, D., et al. (eds.) ISWC 2018. LNCS, vol. 11137, pp. 239–255. Springer, Cham (2018). https://doi.org/10.1007/978-3-030-00668-6_15
9. Tai, K.S., Socher, R., Manning, C.D.: Improved semantic representations from tree-structured long short-term memory networks. arXiv preprint arXiv:1503.00075 (2015)
10. Wang, H., et al.: April: an automatic graph data management system based on reinforcement learning. In: Proceedings of the 29th ACM International Conference on Information & Knowledge Management (2020)
11. Yu, X., Li, G., Chai, C., Tang, N.: Reinforcement learning with tree-LSTM for join order selection. In: 2020 IEEE 36th International Conference on Data Engineering (ICDE) (2020)
12. Zhang, W.E., Sheng, Q.Z., Qin, Y., Taylor, K., Yao, L.: Learning-based SPARQL query performance modeling and prediction. World Wide Web **21**, 1015–1035 (2018)

SAP-KG: Synonym Predicate Analyzer Across Multiple Knowledge Graphs

Emetis Niazmand[1,2(✉)] and Maria-Esther Vidal[1,2,3]

[1] TIB Leibniz Information Centre for Science and Technology, Hannover, Germany
{Emetis.Niazmand,Maria.Vidal}@tib.eu
[2] Leibniz University of Hannover, Hannover, Germany
[3] L3S Research Center, Hannover, Germany

Abstract. This demo paper presents SAP-KG, a knowledge graph agnostic tool, to illustrate the benefits of identifying the synonym predicates that provide complementary information; they are used for query rewriting to enhance query answer completeness. SAP-KG proposed a metric to compute the percentage of overlap between pairs of synonym predicate candidates and capture the most similar ones which can complement each other. We present a query processing technique that put in perspective the role of synonym predicates in query answer completeness. The demo code is available online in (https://github.com/SDM-TIB/SAP-KG-ESWC2023Demo) and can be run at (https://mybinder.org/v2/gh/SDM-TIB/SAP-KG-ESWC2023Demo/main?labpath=SAP-KG.ipynb).

Keywords: Knowledge Graphs · Synonym Predicates · Query Answer Completeness

1 Introduction

Community-maintained knowledge graphs, such as Wikidata [5] and DBpedia [3], have the potential to be incomplete due to the decentralized nature of their development and maintenance [1]. These community-maintained knowledge graphs are built collaboratively, enabling everyone to contribute and modify knowledge. Thus, predicates with different names that refer to the same thing can be added by different contributors. These predicates can be discovered as synonym based on different approaches; while they are precise in identifying synonym predicates, they cannot distinguish those with low overlap that represent complementary information. Moreover, the current approaches do not offer a query answering method to evaluate the completeness of answers after query rewriting utilizing identified synonym predicates. Acosta et al. [2] introduce a hybrid SPARQL engine that employs crowdsourcing to improve the completeness of query responses; while incorporating synonym predicates instead of crowd can reduce errors and uncertainty. We demonstrate SAP-KG, a knowledge graph-agnostic tool, to discover synonym predicates that provide complementary

C. Pesquita et al. (Eds.): ESWC 2023, LNCS 13998, pp. 48–53, 2023.
https://doi.org/10.1007/978-3-031-43458-7_9

information, and using them to reformulate the SPARQL queries to enhance query completeness. We illustrate the performance of SAP-KG, and show that rewriting queries based on synonym predicates can enhance answer completeness. Attendees will uncover the predicates with similar meanings but relating complementary entities in community-maintained KGs known as synonym predicates. They will also rewrite queries– which contain incomplete predicates– with their synonym ones to retrieve complete answers.

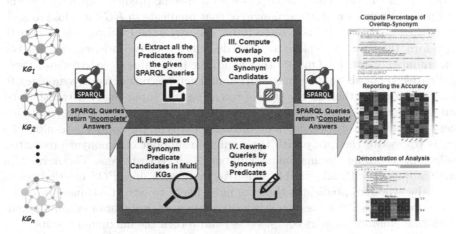

Fig. 1. The SAP-KG Architecture. An SPARQL query over multiple KGs is executed. After extracting predicates, synonym predicate candidates are discovered. The overlap between these candidates is computed. Synonym pairs with a low overlap are selected as synonym predicates to rewrite the query to retrieve the complete answers.

2   The SAP-KG Architecture

The input of SAP-KG is multiple knowledge graphs and SPARQL queries; these queries may retrieve incomplete results. SAP-KG outputs rewritten SPARQL queries based on synonym predicates to ones that retrieve complete answers. As seen in Fig. 1, SAP-KG comprises a step to extract predicates from an input query to find synonym candidates across multiple community-maintained KGs. We assume that the knowledge graphs contain all the links; otherwise, we can use tools such as Falcon 2.0 [4] as an extra step for joint entity and relation linking over the knowledge graphs. Among these candidates, the ones with lower overlap are selected to rewrite the query. For computing the overlap between pairs of synonym predicate candidates, the metric *Percentage of Overlap-Synonym (POS)* is defined. *POS* calculates the overlap between two predicates across multiple knowledge graphs. This metric indicates whether the equivalent predicate can provide additional information to complete the answers retrieved by a query.

Consider a knowledge graph G, a pair of predicates (P', P''), and triple patterns $\mu(.)$. The POS value is computed by the following formulation:

$$POS(P', P'', G) = \frac{min(|\{\mu(P')| \ \mu(?s' \ P' \ ?o') \ in \ G\}|, \ |\{\mu(P'')| \ \mu(?s'' \ P'' \ ?o'') \ in \ G\}|)}{max(|\{\mu(P')| \ \mu(?s' \ P' \ ?o') \ in \ G\}|, \ |\{\mu(P'')| \ \mu(?s'' \ P'' \ ?o'') \ in \ G\}|)} \times 100$$

The percentage of overlapping synonym predicates has a range between 0 and 100%, e.g., if the cardinality of triples with a specific predicate in KG_1 and the cardinality of triples with the synonym of that predicate in KG_2 are close to each other, then the POS value is close to 100%, otherwise the POS value is close to 0. Therefore, the POS value close to 100% describes that two predicates relate the same number of entities. On the other hand, the POS value close to 0 shows these predicates do not share the same entities, and can be considered as synonyms to complement each other. In the step of rewriting, the input query is transformed into an equivalent query that can produce more correct answers. The rewritten query that incorporates synonym predicates returns all the complete results. The aim is to rewrite the query with the minimum number of synonym predicates, while still returning the maximum number of correct answers. The naive tool rewrites queries with all possible synonym predicates, but *POS* metric help to select the synonym predicates that are most likely to return complete answers. Therefore, SAP-KG rewrites a query with a minimum number of synonym predicates that enhance answers completeness and return the maximum results.

3   Demonstration of Use Cases

Consider the following SPARQL queries in Fig. 2. The original query over Wikidata on the left side presents: *Retrieve name of children (wdt:P40), cause of death (wdt:P509), place of birth (wdt:P19), and parent (wdt:P8810) of Marella Agnelli (wd:Q3290404)? - (Retrieval date, Feb 2023)*, and on the right side the rewritten SPARQL query over Wikidata and DBpedia is shown.

Fig. 2. An original SPARQL query comprising four triple patterns executed over Wikidata does not retrieve any answers. The rewritten SPARQL query by detected synonym predicates from Wikidata and DBpedia retrieves eight answers.

By the time this demo was prepared, this query returns no answer. There are four predicates that cause the query to retrieve no result. Simply rewriting query to another query by considering all the synonym predicate candidates retrieve many results which may be incorrect or cannot complete the answers. Therefore, it needs a technique to select the synonym predicates among all discovered synonym predicate candidates with lower overlap for query rewriting. The rewritten SPARQL query returns eight answers.

Effects of *POS* Metric to Provide Complementary Synonym Predicates. A naive tool considers all possible synonym predicate candidates in rewriting queries; while the use of the *POS* metric enables the selection of synonym predicates that are most probable to provide comprehensive answers. As an example, the predicate *manner of death (wdt:P1196)* is a synonym candidate for the predicate *cause of death (wdt:P509)*. The *POS* metric is computed for the predicate candidate pairs. Since, the POS value of these synonym candidates is high (= 87.09%), they cannot be considered as synonym predicates for query rewriting. The high overlap shows these synonym candidates can not complement each other, and they do not lead to retrieve complete results. Thus, predicate *manner of death (wdt:P1196)* is not considered in query reformulation process.

Answer Completeness by Rewriting Queries with Synonym Predicates. For example, by having the predicate *place of birth (wdt:P19)* in the query, only *Florence* is returned as the answer. For predicate *place of birth (wdt:P19)* in Wikidata, there is at least one synonym predicate candidate in DBpedia as *dbp:birthPlace*; where the *POS* value for the above pair is equal to 1.23%. The low overlap value indicates that these synonym predicate candidates are complementary. By rewriting the query with the synonym predicate *dbp:birthPlace* in DBpedia, apart from *Florence*, also *Kingdom of Italy* is returned as the answer. The performance of our tool by running sixty queries over six domains *Person*, *Music*, *History*, *Film*, *Sport*, and *Drug* is shown in Fig. 3. The high value of precision in most of the queries indicates the completeness of answers of rewritten queries compared to the original ones.

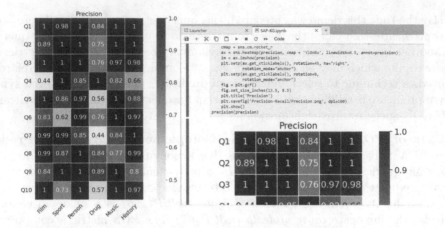

Fig. 3. The performance of SAP-KG where queries rewritten by synonym predicates.

4 Conclusions

We demonstrate SAP-KG and illustrate results that suggest that our proposed technique by considering synonym predicates may return complete answers when faced with queries containing incomplete predicates. Current approaches are not able to differentiate between synonym predicates that provide complementary information. Also, depending on distribution of synonym predicates in multiple community-maintained knowledge graphs, there will be different execution plans to rewrite the queries based on detected synonym predicates. The attendees will evaluate various queries and observe the crucial role of synonym predicates in the completeness of queries executed against Wikidata and DBpedia.

Acknowledgement. This work has been supported by the EU H2020 RIA project CLARIFY (GA No. 875160) and the project TrustKG-Transforming Data in Trustable Insights with grant P99/2020.

References

1. Abiteboul, S.: Querying semi-structured data. In: Afrati, F.N., Kolaitis, P.G. (eds.) Database Theory - ICDT 1997, 6th International Conference, Delphi, Greece, 8–10 January 1997, Proceedings. LNCS, vol. 1186, pp. 1–18. Springer, Cham (1997). https://doi.org/10.1007/3-540-62222-5_33
2. Acosta, M., Simperl, E., Flöck, F., Vidal, M.: Enhancing answer completeness of SPARQL queries via crowdsourcing. J. Web Semant. **45**, 41–62 (2017). https://doi.org/10.1016/j.websem.2017.07.001

3. Auer, S., Bizer, C., Kobilarov, G., Lehmann, J., Cyganiak, R., Ives, Z.G.: DBpedia: a nucleus for a web of open data. In: Aberer, K., et al., (eds.) The Semantic Web, 6th International Semantic Web Conference, 2nd Asian Semantic Web Conference, ISWC 2007 + ASWC 2007, Busan, Korea, 11–15 November 2007. LNCS, vol. 4825, pp. 722–735. Springer, Cham (2007). https://doi.org/10.1007/978-3-540-76298-0_52
4. Sakor, A., Singh, K., Patel, A., Vidal, M.: FALCON 2.0: an entity and relation linking tool over WikiData. In: d'Aquin, M., Dietze, S., Hauff, C., Curry, E., Cudré-Mauroux, P. (eds.) CIKM 2020: The 29th ACM International Conference on Information and Knowledge Management, Virtual Event, Ireland, 19–23 October 2020, pp. 3141–3148. ACM (2020). https://doi.org/10.1145/3340531.3412777
5. Vrandecic, D., Krötzsch, M.: WikiData: a free collaborative knowledgebase. Commun. ACM **57**(10), 78–85 (2014). https://doi.org/10.1145/2629489

Descriptive Comparison of Visual Ontology Change Summarisation Methods

Kornpol Chung[1], Romana Pernisch[1,2](✉) (iD), and Stefan Schlobach[1] (iD)

[1] Department of Computer Science, Vrije Universiteit Amsterdam, Amsterdam,
Netherlands
{k.s.schlobach,r.pernisch}@vu.nl
[2] Discovery Lab, Elsevier, Amsterdam, Netherlands

Abstract. The ontology evolution lifecycle is crucial for usability of
ontologies across applications. Changes that are applied to ontologies
need to be communicated comprehensively to ontology users and engineers. Change visualisation is a simple, yet powerful way of explaining
ontological changes, and different methods come with different short-
comings. This paper introduces and analyses the predominant methods
of ontology change visualisations. As there exists no one-fits-all solution,
we provide simple guidelines for which visualisation to use.

1 Introduction

To help ontology engineers in the engineering process, it is not only important
to have a comprehensive visualisation of the ontology but also of its *changes*.
These changes are often difficult to manage and communicate. Some existing
approaches are widely used by the ontology community [1,4]. While these have
proven their worth in specific application domains, they often fail in other
domains with different application constraints.

This poster presents three predominant methods of visualisations for ontology
change: **graphical notation** represented by OntoDiffGraph (ODG) [2], **list visualisations** represented by Visual Description Delta (VDD) [5] and **abstraction
networks**, specifically the Diff Partial Area Taxonomy (DPAT) [6]. To compare
the methods, we present mock-up visualisations where we applied changes to the
Pizza ontology[1] which were previously used in a user study [7].

2 Ontology Change Visualisation Methods

OntoDiffGraph. ODG [2] is an extension of the Visual Notation for Owl Ontologies (commonly abbreviated as VOWL) [3] for the purposes of highlighting differences between versions of an ontology. The mock-up visualisation shown in

---

[1] https://protege.stanford.edu/ontologies/pizza/pizza.owl.

C. Pesquita et al. (Eds.): ESWC 2023, LNCS 13998, pp. 54–58, 2023.
https://doi.org/10.1007/978-3-031-43458-7_10

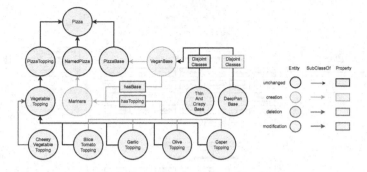

Fig. 1. ODG [2] mock-up visualising changes applied to the Pizza ontology.

Fig. 1 is adapted from its original to only represent entities which are directly affected by the applied changes, instead of visualizing the entire ontology. The ODG uses a graphical notation to present atomic changes and at the same time explicitly represents the ontology's organisation.

Visual Descriptive Delta. The VDD is one (of two) component of the Visual Semantic Delta proposed by Ochs [5] to analyse structural changes to biomedical ontologies. It has the objective to concisely communicate a large number of change concepts into a single notation. The icons use a common colour scheme to connote different editing operations. The affected concepts are listed on the left-hand side ordered in descending order of the number of complex changes. It allows a user to quickly identify where the most relevant and impactful changes occurred. The VDD communicates contextual information concisely by presenting complex changes in a visually aided list.

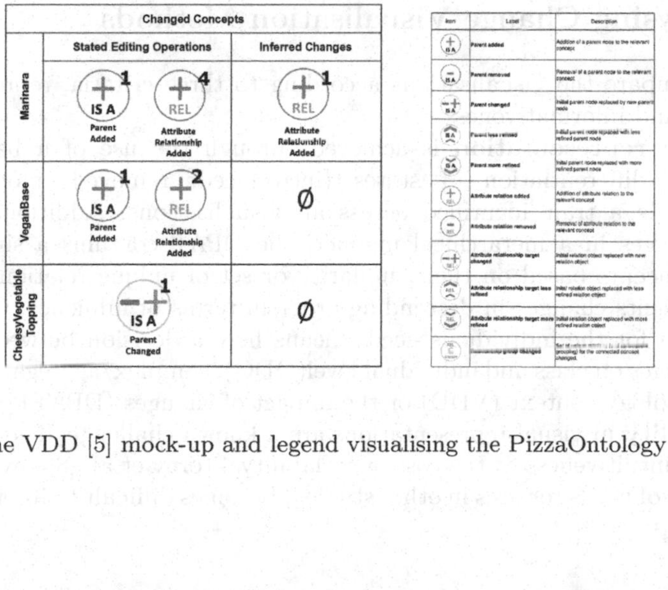

Fig. 2. The VDD [5] mock-up and legend visualising the PizzaOntology changes.

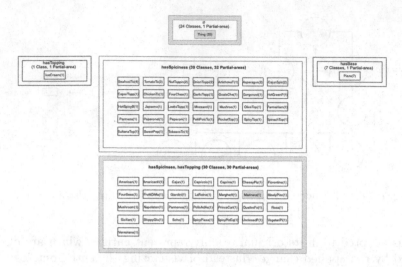

Fig. 3. The DPAT [6] mock-up visualising changes applied to the Pizza ontology.

Diff Partial-Area Taxonomy. The DPAT is based upon the original "abstraction network" [1], and is proposed by Ochs [6] to visualise the *overall impact* of a set of changes. The visualization, shown in Fig. 3 is based upon grouping similar concepts into diff partial-areas. This similarity is defined as the set of relations associated with the concept. These sub-hierarchies come in four states which are: introduced, removed, modified and unchanged, and these are represented by the highlight of their borders. The DPAT's utilisation of sub-hierarchies and diff-partial areas enables it to be particularly proficient at highlighting the global impact of changes to the ontology.

3   Analysing Change Visualisation Methods

We will compare the visualisations according to three criteria, representation, scalability and informativeness.

Change representation is achieved through the use of a basic colour scheme for differentiation of states (introduced, removed, modified and unchanged) is a trait identified across all visualisations. Additionally, ODG reflects changes in a hierarchical manner, the DPAT contains a similar hier-archy of concepts based on their similarity or set of unique relations, and the VDD represents changes in descending order in terms of influence. Choosing a visualisation for the individuals needs means here a decision between showing atomic changes on class and individual level(ODG), complex/aggregated changes without ontology context (VDD) or the impact of changes (DPAT).

Scalability in visual representations are a known challenge. The ODG pro-vide visual intuitiveness at the cost of scalability. Storey et al. [8] have observed that the use of edges (or arcs in other studies) becomes difficult to interpret when the number of relations are too high. Additionally, the scalability of each method is heavily dependent on whether the visualisation provides a representation of the entire ontology, or exclusively the set of applied changes. As such, we identified that the DPAT and the VDD mock-ups have good scalability, because of the characteristic of aggregating atomic changes. Considering scalability when choosing a visualisation method, VDD and DPAT are clearly superior because of their summarizing characteristic, in comparison to ODG who's visualisation only increases with the number of changes applied.

Contextual informativeness is tackled differently in each visualisation. The VDD conveys context primarily through the set of complex change concepts. With the ODG, there is an absence of complex changes, which is supplemented by its representation of the ontology's hierarchical structure. The DPAT takes a different approach in grouping similar entities into sub-hierarchies to convey the overall impact of changes. Conclusively, contextual informativeness remains a challenge as we see each visualisation taking a different approach with its own advantages and disadvantages. Each method provides contextual information in a different way, where intuitively the ODG would be most suitable for novice engineers or users of the subject ontology, as it provides the largest amount of context to the changes.

4   Conclusion

ODG has a hierarchical structure representation but has a major trade-off in scalability, the explored complex changes in the VDD lack general ontological concepts that could be versatile, and the DPAT sub-hierarchy aggregation makes this visualisation hard to interpret when not familiar with the domain. We did not consider the changes to Abox axioms, however, only ODG would be capable of displaying them. To conclude, not any one visualization method alone satisfies all needs. An in-depth study is required to assess the above criteria as well as other ones. We hope to include a visualisation method in the Protégé plugin ChImp [7] in the future.

References

1. Halper, M., Gu, H., Perl, Y., Ochs, C.: Abstraction networks for terminologies: supporting management of "big knowledge". Artif. Intell. Med. **64**(1), 1–16 (2015). https://doi.org/10.1016/j.artmed.2015.03.005
2. Lara, A., Henriques, P.R., Gançarski, A.L.: Visualization of ontology evolution using OntoDiffGraph (2017)
3. Lohmann, S., Negru, S., Bold, D.: The ProtégéVOWL plugin: ontology visualization for everyone. In: Presutti, V., Blomqvist, E., Troncy, R., Sack, H., Papadakis, I., Tordai, A. (eds.) ESWC 2014. LNCS, vol. 8798, pp. 395–400. Springer, Cham (2014). https://doi.org/10.1007/978-3-319-11955-7_55
4. Noy, N.F., Musen, M.A.: PROMPTDIFF: a fixed-point algorithm for comparing ontology versions. AAAI/IAAI **2002**, 744–750 (2002)

5. Ochs, C., Case, J.T., Perl, Y.: Analyzing structural changes in SNOMED CT's bacterial infectious diseases using a visual semantic delta. J. Biomed. Inform. **67**, 101–116 (2017)
6. Ochs, C., et al.: Summarizing and visualizing structural changes during the evolution of biomedical ontologies using a Diff Abstraction Network. J. Biomed. Inform. **56**, 127–144 (2015). https://doi.org/10.1016/j.jbi.2015.05.018
7. Pernisch, R., Dell'Aglio, D., Serbak, M., Gonçalves, R.S., Bernstein, A.: Visualising the effects of ontology changes and studying their understanding with ChImp. J. Web Semant. **74**, 100715 (2022). https://doi.org/10.1016/j.websem.2022.100715
8. Storey, M.A., Lintern, R., Ernst, N., Perrin, D.: Visualization and Protege. In: 7th International Protégé Conference (2004)

AgriNER: An NER Dataset of Agricultural Entities for the Semantic Web

Sayan De[1], Debarshi Kumar Sanyal[2], and Imon Mukherjee[1]

[1] Indian Institute of Information Technology, Kalyani 741235, India
{sayan_jrf22,imon}@iiitkalyani.ac.in
[2] Indian Association for the Cultivation of Science, Jadavpur 700032, India
debarshi.sanyal@iacs.res.in

Abstract. An immense amount of data relevant to agriculture is generated from the vast scholarly literature. To get as much relevant information as possible from the data, we need to extract the context and meaning from them. Semantic web technology can provide context and meaning to the data. Named entity recognition (NER) systems can help to extract the named entities and the relations between the entities. In addition to that, these entities and relations can be used to build a knowledge graph (KG) which can be stored using a resource description framework (RDF) and queried with SPARQL. In this paper, we propose an NER dataset that contains a total of thirty-six types of entities and nine types of relations, which can be used to build a KG.

Keywords: Agricultural Dataset · Named Entity Recognition · Relation Extraction · Knowledge Graph

1 Introduction

Research papers on agriculture contain information about the latest advances in the field, yet it is not always easily accessible to practitioners including scientists and farmers, for a variety of reasons including that the number of papers is huge and that the information is not available in a structured format. Agricultural industries, researchers, food processing companies, and many organizations need to extract entities such as crop names, pesticides, factors that affect plant growth, etc., and their relationships to make useful and strategic decisions. A named entity recognition (NER) system helps to extract knowledge entities from unstructured sources [2]. There are a few works on NER in agriculture, some of which like [1,4] apply deep learning. A few datasets are available to train NER systems. Malarkodi et al. [7] have proposed nineteen entity types in the agriculture domain, but it does not cover many important aspects of agriculture. In addition to that, their corpus is not publicly available. Lun et al. [6] focus on four entity types, namely, Crop, Disease, Pest, and Drug, however, limiting to only Chinese agricultural websites. Gangadharan et al. [3] have worked

C. Pesquita et al. (Eds.): ESWC 2023, LNCS 13998, pp. 59–63, 2023.
https://doi.org/10.1007/978-3-031-43458-7_11

with only three types of entities, namely, Disease, Soil, and Fertiliser, using only Indian agricultural websites. Liu et al. [5] have worked with six types of entities, namely Organism, Trait, Method/Equipment, Chemical, Gene, Environment, and Miscellaneous using article abstracts of ten typical horticultural journals. In contrast to the above works, our corpus is an annotated collection of abstracts from agriculture research papers, and our set of entity types and relations is significantly larger. In this paper, we propose thirty six entity types and nine relations between the entities. Our contributions to this paper are as follows:

1. We introduce a fine-grained tag set comprising 36 useful entities in the agricultural domain.
2. We introduce 9 relations between the entities, including symmetric and asymmetric relations.
3. We introduce a publicly available fully annotated corpus with the above tags.

The corpus is publicly available on GitHub[1]. The rest of our paper is organized as follows. In Sect. 2 we propose a taxonomy for the entities and relations. We provide dataset statistics in Sect. 3. In Sect. 4, we apply a machine learning model for NER on this dataset. We conclude in Sect. 5.

2   Proposed Taxonomy

Our dataset is built from abstracts of research papers in agriculture. After analyzing the abstracts, we have developed a list of entity types and relations to cover most of the important knowledge aspects of the papers. The proposed tag set contains thirty-six named entities that we believe can help in research in the agriculture domain. The named entity types are Agri_Pollution, Agri_Process, Agri_Waste, Agri_Method, Chemical, Citation, Crop, Date_and_Time, Disease, Duration, Event, Field_Area, Food_Item, Fruit, Humidity, Location, ML_Model, Money, Natural_Disaster, Natural_Resource, Nutrient, Organism, Organization, Other, Other_Quantity, Person, Policy, Quantity, Rainfall, Season, Soil, Technology, Temp, Treatment, Vegetable, Weather. The terms are self-explanatory.

We have extracted nine relations to form meaningful connections between the entities. We define three symmetric relation types Coreference_Of, Conjunction, Synonym_Of, and six asymmetric relation types Caused_By, Helps_In, Includes, Originated_From, Used_For, Seasonal. A detailed description of the entity types and relations is available in our GitHub repository.

3   Dataset Statistics

The quality of the dataset influences the knowledge graph constructed and the machine learning models trained on it. We have hand-picked the abstracts of 180 papers from several reputed agricultural journals, such as Asian Journal of

---

[1] https://github.com/Tec4Tric/AgriNER.

Agricultural and Food Sciences (AJAFS)[2], The Indian Journal of Agricultural Sciences[3], and a few journals from IEEE and Springer Nature. We have analyzed the abstracts of these papers and recent trends in agriculture like [8,9], and then we have decided on thirty six entities and nine types of relationships among the entities. Table 1 displays a summary of the number of occurrences of each annotated entity in the proposed dataset in percentage.

Table 1. Entities with their occurrences in AgriNER dataset.

Entity	Frequency	Entity	Frequency	Entity	Frequency
Agri_Method	4%	Other_Quantity	4%	Fruit	3%
Agri_Process	6%	Policy	<1%	Location	15%
Chemical	4%	Rainfall	1%	Money	<1%
Crop	13%	Soil	1%	Natural_Resource	2%
Disease	1%	Temp	1%	Organism	4%
Event	<1%	Vegetable	<1%	Other	<1%
Food_Item	2%	Agri_Ploution	1%	Person	3%
Humidity	<1%	Agri_Waste	2%	Quantity	2%
ML_Model	4	Citation	1%	Season	3%
Natural_Disaster	5	Date_and_Time	2%	Technology	2%
Nutrient	5%	Duration	2%	Treatment	1%
Organization	3%	Field_Area	1%	Weather	<1%

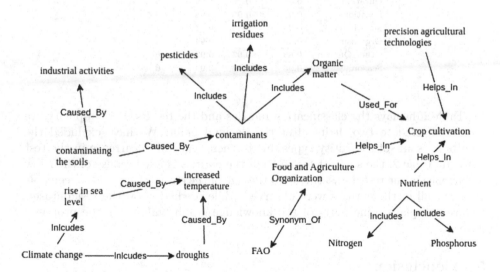

Fig. 1. Some parts of the knowledge graph using the dataset.

[2] https://www.ajouronline.com/index.php/AJAFS/index.
[3] https://epubs.icar.org.in/index.php/IJAgS.

We have used the freely available `brat` tool[4] for annotation. One of the challenges was the entity class imbalance. To solve this problem, we have first counted the occurrences of the mentions of each entity type. Then, we added more data to the corpus to increase the count of the least frequent entity type. In total, we have 14,307 word-tokens and 1348 entity mentions. We have partitioned the dataset in a 70:30 ratio, with 70% data for training, and 30% data for testing.

4   Machine Learning-Based Extraction of Named Entities

To provide a baseline for an automatic NER system for the dataset, we have trained `spaCy`[5] with the entities we have labeled. `spaCy` is a free open-source library for natural language processing in Python. `spaCy v3.0` provides a transformer-based pipeline, where we can train the model with our custom data. We first initialize the `spaCy` pipeline with `tok2vec` and `ner` models and then trained the model for several epochs with our custom entities. This model can recognize entities in unstructured data from the agricultural domain.

Table 2. A sample of the classification report.

	Precision	Recall	F1-Score	Support
Agri_Method	1.00	0.80	0.88	5
Chemical	0.98	0.87	0.91	10
Crop	0.93	0.77	0.84	18
Duration	0.83	0.75	0.80	5
Location	0.93	0.95	0.98	19
ML_Model	0.99	0.85	0.92	7
Organism	0.90	0.97	0.94	9
Other_Quantity	0.85	0.97	0.92	6
Season	0.98	0.97	0.98	6

Table 2 displays the classification metrics and the results. For simplicity, we have restricted to two digits after the decimal point. We have excluded the results for some of the entity types due to their very low occurrence in the test data. In Table 2, the support for some of the entities is low because of their low occurrence in the test dataset. Due to the size of the entity class, it is conceivable that not all of the entities were observed while predicting on the test dataset. Figure 1 displays some parts of the knowledge graph built using the proposed dataset.

5   Conclusion

In this paper, we have introduced a total of thirty six entities, and three symmetric and six asymmetric relations extracted from several agricultural research

---

4 https://brat.nlplab.org.
5 https://spacy.io.

papers. The NER dataset is organized into a knowledge graph. In the future, we intend to use semantic web technologies to make the graph semantically richer by linking it to other relevant knowledge graphs. We hope better ML models will be built to improve the classification performance, and that our dataset will inform and motivate further research on the construction and application of agricultural knowledge graphs.

Acknowledgement. This work is implemented as part of the *"Extraction, Organization and Query of Scholarly Information"*, sponsored by the Science & Engineering Research Board, Govt. of India.

References

1. Devi, M., Dua, M.: ADANS: an agriculture domain question answering system using ontologies. In: Proceedings of the 2017 International Conference on Computing, Communication and Automation (ICCCA), pp. 122–127. IEEE (2017)
2. Drury, B., Fernandes, R., Moura, M.F., de Andrade Lopes, A.: A survey of semantic web technology for agriculture. Inf. Process. Agric. **6**(4), 487–501 (2019)
3. Gangadharan, V., Gupta, D.: Recognizing named entities in agriculture documents using LDA based topic modelling techniques. Procedia Comput. Sci. **171**, 1337–1345 (2020)
4. Li, W., Chen, P., Wang, B., Xie, C.: Automatic localization and count of agricultural crop pests based on an improved deep learning pipeline. Sci. Rep. **9**(1), 7024 (2019)
5. Liu, Z., Luo, M., Yang, H., Liu, X.: Named entity recognition for the horticultural domain. J. Phys. Conf. Ser. **1631**, 012016 (2020). IOP Publishing
6. Lun, Z., Hui, Z., et al.: Research on agricultural named entity recognition based on pre train BERT. Acad. J. Eng. Technol. Sci. **5**(4), 34–42 (2022)
7. Malarkodi, C., Lex, E., Devi, S.L.: Named entity recognition for the agricultural domain. Res. Comput. Sci. **117**(1), 121–132 (2016)
8. Sinha, B.B., Dhanalakshmi, R.: Recent advancements and challenges of internet of things in smart agriculture: a survey. Futur. Gener. Comput. Syst. **126**, 169–184 (2022)
9. Verma, K.K., et al.: Recent trends in nano-fertilizers for sustainable agriculture under climate change for global food security. Nanomaterials **12**(1), 173 (2022)

ClayBot: Increasing Human-Centricity in Conversational Recommender Systems

Fouad Zablith[(✉)]

Olayan School of Business, American University of Beirut,
P.O. Box 11-0236, Riad El Solh, 1107 2020 Beirut, Lebanon
fouad.zablith@aub.edu.lb

Abstract. Conversational recommender systems are increasingly studied to provide more fine-tuned recommendations based on user preferences. However, most existing product recommendation approaches in online stores are designed to interact with people through questions that mainly focus on products or their attributes, and less on buyers' core purchase needs. This work proposes ClayBot, a novel conversational recommendation agent, which aims to capture people's intents and recommend products based on the jobs or actions that their buyers aim to do. Interactions with ClayBot are guided by an openly accessible knowledge graph, which connects a sample of computing products to the actions annotated in product reviews. A demonstration of ClayBot is presented as an Amazon Alexa Skill to showcase the feasibility of handling more human-centered interactions in the product recommendation and explanation process.

Keywords: Conversational Recommender Systems · Knowledge Graphs · Human-centered · Artificial Intelligence · Product reviews

1 Introduction

Conversational recommender systems (CRS) are increasingly gaining research visibility in artificial intelligence (AI). This rising attention can be attributed to several factors, including the challenges in eliciting users' preferences and needs, as well as justifying why does a person prefer an item versus another [4].

In real life, human interaction and questions usually drive the recommendation process and help with discovering people's preferences to reach a recommended product [4]. Asking questions is one of the key components in CRS. In this domain, researchers have been studying "when to ask" and "what to ask" to people, and their approaches mainly focus on formulating questions either around products, or product attributes [3].

While such questions can be effective for experienced buyers, they may be hard to answer by people who are less informed about how products or their attributes can contribute to fulfilling their needs. This work investigates how we can make conversational product recommendation systems more human-centered and aligned with users' needs.

2   Human-Centered Product Recommendations in CRS

Clayton Christensen famously revealed that "when we buy a product, we essentially 'hire' it to get a job done" [2]. This core notion of the Jobs Theory reflects that in most situations, people don't perceive products as a set of attributes, but as a means to perform a certain job. Jobs to be done are often articulated in the form of actions. Designers are usually trained to be sensitive to such potential actions when developing human-centered products. Potential actions that a person is aiming to do may be used as a proxy for further understanding the person's needs and uncovering persona-centered problems in the design thinking process [6]. For example, people may decide to buy a particular laptop to support them while studying, or a certain tablet to be able to stream their favorite TV series in bed. A substantial number of buyers generously share such experiences in product reviews, which often include a description of the actions and jobs to be done [1].

This work aims to shift the focus of questions asked in the majority of existing CRS approaches from a product and product's attributes angle [3], to a human-centered perspective by formulating questions and understanding intents around the jobs or actions that buyers are aiming to fulfill. Drawing on previous efforts to construct a knowledge graph that connects actions detected in product reviews to their products and related entities [8], we propose a framework that leverages the knowledge graph data connections to guide the interaction during the product recommendation process. Figure 1 provides an overview of the CRS framework.

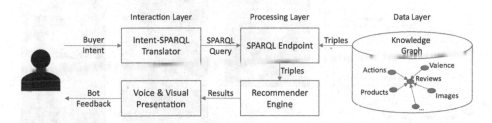

Fig. 1. CRS framework overview for recommending products based on buyers' intents.

The framework includes three layers namely the interaction, processing, and data layers. Following buyers' intents to the CRS, the *Intent-SPARQL Translator* component is responsible for converting the intents into SPARQL queries. The translator is designed to include semantic and pattern-based placeholders to identify the actions and other elements mentioned in the buyer's intents. For example, if a buyer articulates that "she would like a device for drawing," then the translator automatically detects *drawing* as a potential action and integrates it in the SPARQL queries. The queries are then passed to the *SPARQL endpoint* to extract from the knowledge graph the relevant triples needed for the recommendation process. The *Recommender Engine* traverses the triples extracted from the SPARQL endpoint and uses them to rank products and to aggregate relevant action and product-related entities—reviews, images, and others. The *Voice and Visual Presentation* component presents the recommended results to the user through voice and visual features.

3   Demo: Alexa, Ask ClayBot to Recommend a Product

To showcase the feasibility of the proposed approach, this part presents ClayBot, a conversational product recommendation agent. We explore an initial implementation of ClayBot as an Amazon Alexa Skill[1]. The Amazon Alexa Skills platform provides an environment with features that ease the development and deployment of conversational agents. Such features include for example the creation of user intent templates, handling voice and visual interfaces, and customizing slot types that we used in the Intent-SPARQL Translator, among others. Figure 2 shows a sample voice interaction between a person and ClayBot, coupled with visual feedback through the Alexa app[2].

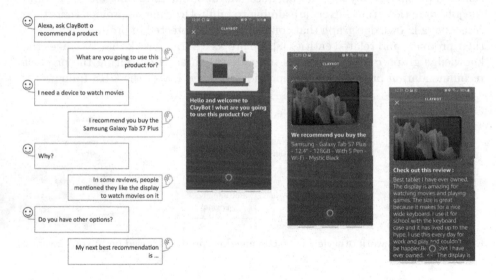

Fig. 2. ClayBot prototype running as an Amazon Alexa Skill.

ClayBot currently relies on a knowledge graph that covers annotated reviews of computing products. Around 3,000 product reviews were annotated as part of another project effort, and the data is accessed through an openly accessible SPARQL endpoint [8]. The knowledge graph includes information pertaining to

---

[1] ClayBot Alexa Skill page: https://www.amazon.com/dp/B0BX6LQQT7.

[2] A video recording of the demo featuring the discussed example in Fig. 2 is available at: https://youtu.be/ZillD_f51MQ.

the actions found in the reviews extracted from a retailer's website that follows the schema.org vocabulary, the valence (i.e., whether the reviewers were positive or negative with the action they were trying to do while using the device), and additional contextual information such as the role of agents and the environment in which the product was used.

A person can invoke the skill by telling Alexa to ask ClayBot to recommend a product. Following this invocation, ClayBot responds with what the person is going to use this product for. This response aims to shift the focus of the interaction on the job or action intended by the buyer, rather than on the traditional products and attributes focus. This design also limits the possibility of the buyer having generic intents, which may drift the conversation to a more generic intent classification task [5,7]. In this example, the person may reply that they would need a device to watch movies. At this level, ClayBot will initiate the Intent-SPARQL Translator component to try to match the action of *watching* with the knowledge graph data. In the current version of ClayBot, the matching is performed by defining in the Alexa app slots of type *Action*. The slot types are then detected through text patterns in the intents. For example, a pattern of *text* + *<to>* or *<for>* followed by an *<action>*. All products that support this action will be fetched from the knowledge graph using SPARQL, along with other data needed by the recommender engine to rank the available products. The ranking of products relies on the relative ratio of positive versus negative review annotations related to the action in focus, as a comparative base among the products.

ClayBot then communicates the recommended product to the user and waits for the person's next instruction. At this stage, the person may ask for explanation why this product was recommended, ask for another recommendation, restart the interaction with another objective, or simply end the conversation. When asked for other options, ClayBot recommends the next best product ranked by the recommender engine. As explanation, ClayBot is currently able to read and visualize a sample of related reviews from the knowledge graph. Figure 3 shows two examples of SPARQL queries. The first query extracts the knowledge graph data needed by the engine for the computation of the products' scores relative to the action detected in the buyer intent. The second query extracts the review data related to the recommended product and action in focus[3].

4   Conclusion

This paper demonstrated a novel attempt to offer more human-centered conversational product recommendation systems. The approach aims to increase human centricity by focusing the agent-people interactions on the jobs and actions that buyers are aiming to fulfill through the products they are seeking.

This work may benefit from several future research paths. First, the recommendation and explanation process can be extended to cover more elements

---

[3] The queries can be tested on the following SPARQL endpoint:
https://linked.aub.edu.lb/actionrec/sparql.

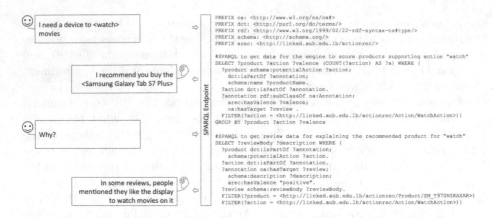

Fig. 3. SPARQL examples to get knowledge graph data relevant to a buyer's intents.

captured in the knowledge graph (e.g., environment of use, product features, and others). Second, it is beneficial to investigate a wider range of questions and their impact on the conversation between a person and the recommender agent. Third, it is valuable to evaluate users' perception of their interaction with the proposed approach compared to existing product recommendation efforts.

This research provides the following contributions: first, it helps CRS with better uncovering buyers' needs that often revolve around performing certain jobs and recommending products accordingly; second, it demonstrates the potential of leveraging knowledge graphs to provide guided and explainable interactions between people and voice-enabled AI recommendation agents.

Acknowledgments. This work was partially supported by the University Research Board of the American University of Beirut. Special thanks to Rayan Al Arab for his support in developing the tools.

References

1. Christensen, C., Hall, T., Dillon, K., Duncan, D.S.: Competing Against Luck: The Story of Innovation and Customer Choice. HarperBusiness, New York (2016)
2. Christensen, C., Hall, T., Dillon, K., Duncan, D.S.: Know your customers' jobs to be done. Harv. Bus. Rev. **94**(9), 54–62 (2016)
3. Gao, C., Lei, W., He, X., de Rijke, M., Chua, T.S.: Advances and challenges in conversational recommender systems: a survey. AI Open **2**, 100–126 (2021)
4. Jannach, D., Pu, P., Ricci, F., Zanker, M.: Recommender systems: trends and frontiers. AI Mag. **43**(2), 145–150 (2022)
5. Moradizeyveh, S.: Intent Recognition in Conversational Recommender Systems (2022). arXiv:2212.03721 [cs]
6. Norman, D.: The Design of Everyday Things. Basic Books, New York (2013)
7. Schuurmans, J., Frasincar, F.: Intent classification for dialogue utterances. IEEE Intell. Syst. **35**(1), 82–88 (2020)
8. Zablith, F.: ActionRec: toward action-aware recommender systems on the web. In: International Semantic Web Conference Demos - CEUR Proceedings, vol. 2980 (2021)

Mining Symbolic Rules to Explain Lung Cancer Treatments

Disha Purohit[1,2](✉)(iD) and Maria-Esther Vidal[1,2,3](iD)

[1] Leibniz University, Hannover, Germany
[2] TIB Leibniz Information Centre for Science and Technology, Hannover, Germany
{disha.purohit,maria.vidal}@tib.eu
[3] L3S Research Center, Hannover, Germany

Abstract. Knowledge Graphs (KGs) represent the convergence of data and knowledge as factual statements; they allow for the enrichment of decision-making semantically. Symbolic inductive learning enables uncovering relevant patterns, expressed, for example, as Horn clauses. Albeit powerful, existing symbolic inductive learning frameworks may mine many rules, being difficult for a user to extract actionable insights. This demo illustrates a pipeline to analyze mined logical rules toward discovering meaningful insights. The demo puts into perspective the role of semantic types in guiding the exploration of mined rules. Participants will observe strategies to traverse the mined logical statements and how the outcomes reveal patterns in the prescription of lung cancer treatments. A video is available online (https://www.youtube.com/watch?v=CN4a3kUjfJ4&ab_channel=TIBSDMGroup), a Jupyter notebook executes a live demos (https://mybinder.org/v2/gh/SDM-TIB/DIGGER-ESWC2023Demo/HEAD?labpath=Mining\%20Symbolic\%20Rules\%20To\%20Explain\%20Lung\%20Cancer\%20Treatments.ipynb), and source-code is available in GitHub (https://github.com/SDM-TIB/Mining_Symbolic_Rules_ESWC2023Demo).

1 Introduction

Knowledge Graphs (KGs) are widely used to represent real-world data in the form of entities and relations. Several open KGs like DBpedia, and Wikidata, are already available to severe the Semantic Web community. KGs are frequently created from heterogeneous sources, which can vary significantly in terms of structure and granularity [3]. The open research challenge of mining Horn rules from facts and analyzing the mined logical rules to uncover meaningful insights has received numerous contributions from the Semantic Web. Exemplary rule mining approaches (e.g., AMIE [1,2,4], AnyBURL [5]) are devised to operate under OWA and mine logical rules. However, these approaches must still be designed to deal with KGs that include semantics and ignore the importance of analyzing the rules. We demonstrate DIGGER, a framework for analyzing mined logical rules. We will illustrate the impact of incorporating semantics and the relevant role of inductive learning in knowledge discovery.

C. Pesquita et al. (Eds.): ESWC 2023, LNCS 13998, pp. 69–74, 2023.
https://doi.org/10.1007/978-3-031-43458-7_13

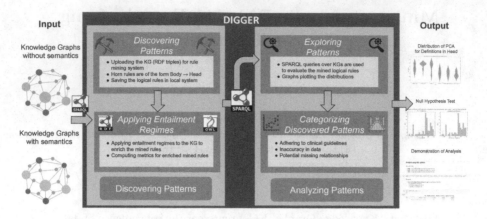

Fig. 1. Architecture. Input includes KGs, ontologies, and entailment regimes. SPARQL queries explore mined rules and perform analysis over KGs. DIGGER demonstrates clinical guidelines' validation, data errors, and missing relationships.

2   The DIGGER Architecture

We aim at providing DIGGER, a framework able to analyze mined logical rules from which true missing facts can be predicted. As a result, KG completion can be achieved with facts inferred from the mined rules and entailment regimes (e.g., RDFS or OWL). DIGGER currently relies on AMIE [4] to efficiently mine logical rules over KGs. Figure 1 depicts the DIGGER architecture; it receives as input KGs and outputs visualizations depicting the results of the analysis of the mined rules on top of the input KGs. DIGGER comprises two steps: a) *Discovering Patterns* and b) *Analyzing Patterns*. The former mines logical rules and then, expands them by applying the entailment regimes. Applying the W3C-recommended Web Ontology Language *(OWL)* and *RDFS* entailment regimes, helps to derive new insights from the KGs. Currently, DIGGER is considering entailment regimes but in the future incorporating *SHACL Integrity Constraints* and *Deductive Systems* to enhance the mined logical rules. Thus, it clearly illustrates that by incorporating the semantics of the KGs the mined logical rules are enriched. The logical rules are loaded in any relational database management system to expedite the process of analysis that can be performed over the mined logical rules. On the other hand, *Analyzing Patterns* explores the mined logical rules towards the discovery of unknown patterns. SPARQL queries are used to explore the mined logical rules. The Partial Completeness Assumption (PCA) assumes that heuristic-based negative edges are possible incomplete edges. Evaluating the logical rules based on the PCA Confidence metrics computed for the rules provides the possibility of identifying the potential prediction of edges over the KGs. Further, using the framework, identifying data errors, missing relationships, and lung cancer patients violating the clinical guidelines is clearly demonstrated which can help oncologists discover insights.

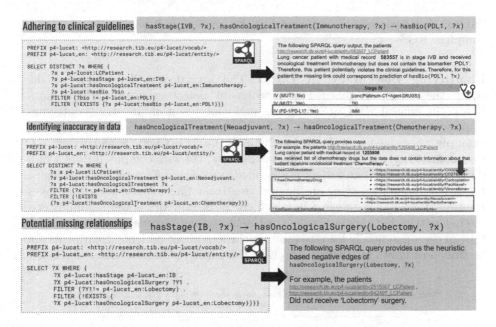

Fig. 2. Use cases: Illustration of use cases with example rules to demonstrate the usage of SPARQL queries over KGs to analyze the mined logical rules. The figure shows all three use cases exhibited in the video demonstration of *DIGGER*.

3   Demonstration of Use Case

The demonstration aims at illustrating the importance of considering the semantics of KGs in mining logical rules from ground facts. Also, use cases in Fig. 2 that help in analyzing the mined logical rules are described in this section.

Adhering to Clinical Guidelines: Attendees will be able to observe the mined logical rules that are used to explain lung cancer treatments. Similarly, attendees will be able to discover the mined logical rules utilized in identifying patients that violate the clinical guidelines. Clinical guidelines are oncologists' treatment protocols for lung cancer. For instance, the logical rule hasStage(IVB, X), hasOncologicalTreatment(Immunotherapy, X) $\Rightarrow$ hasBio(PDL1, X) states if a patient is in cancer stage *IV* and receives an oncological treatment *Immunotherapy* then it is most likely that the patient is positive for biomarker *PDL1*. This rule complies with the clinical guidelines established by oncologists. The PCA Confidence score computed for the above-mentioned rule was 0.966 which states the KG is partially complete and has heuristic-based negative edges. Therefore, there are few patients that do not abide by the clinical guidelines. By running SPARQL queries over the KG, our framework can identify a patient who is not following the guidelines. As a result, we can conclude that the identified patient may be violating clinical guidelines, and the missing link for that patient may correspond to the prediction of hasBio(PDL1, X); to complete KG.

Identifying Inaccuracy in Data: The attendees will be able to discover the usage of mined logical rules in detecting errors in the data. Errors in clinical data are common and can result in incorrect outcomes. Mining logical rules over KGs aids in the detection of data errors. For example, the mined logical rule hasOncologicalTreatment(Neoadjuvant, X) ⇒ hasOncologicalTreatment(Chemotherapy, X) with computed PCA Confidence score of 0.971; one patient is identified as receiving *Neoadjuvant* oncological treatment but not receiving oncological treatment *Chemotherapy*. Further investigation revealed a data error in which chemotherapy drugs were administered to that patient but chemotherapy treatment was not recorded in the data. This type of error potentially leads to false conclusions about patients' treatments and is, thus scrutinized by *DIGGER* to help the oncologists make better decisions.

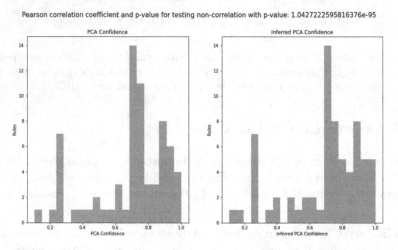

Fig. 3. Distribution of PCA Confidence: Analysis to demonstrate the usage of entailment regimes and inference over KGs. The experimental results of the probability of the correlation between *PCA Confidence* and *Inferred PCA Confidence*. It is represented by the p-value which states that the metrics are statistically significant.

Potential Missing Relationships: Attendees will be able to explore the mined logical rules in identifying the potential incomplete edges of KGs using the *PCA*. The definition of negative edges in a labeled-edge graph $G = (V, E, L)$ is not precise under the OWA. The goal of the PCA is to make accurate predictions that can potentially complete the large incomplete KGs. To illustrate potential missing links in the KG a logical rule hasStage(IB, X) ⇒

hasOncologicalSurgery(Lobectomy, X) states that patients who are in cancer stage *IB* receive oncological surgery as *Lobectomy*. The PCA Confidence score computed for this rule was 0.976. Using a SPARQL query, DIGGER is able to identify two patients who were recorded to be in stage *IB* and did not receive *Lobectomy*. As a result, we can conclude that these two patients in the KG have missing links to oncological surgery and can be regarded as potential predictions. *DIGGER* is domain agnostic but in order to evaluate the accuracy of the use cases used in this work clinical guidelines are considered and humans are in a loop. Another study aims at reporting the impact of injecting entailment regimes on the KGs. In contrast to naive approaches, *DIGGER* takes rdfs:subPropertyOf into account for the experiments in the current example. This yields higher metrics values and demonstrates potential true predictions. For example, higher Inferred PCA Confidence of a rule quantifies the KG's partial completion by identifying more productive rules. The mined logical rules with all the metrics are computed on the KGs first without considering the entailment regimes to obtain *PCA Confidence*. Further, the entailment regimes are injected into the same KG before mining the logical rules. A null hypothesis test (i.e., p-value) shown in Fig. 3 is used to observe the difference in metrics value to compare the results.

4   Conclusion and Future Work

We demonstrate our framework that allows semantically identifying missing information in terms of relationships in the KG or data. Additionally, attendees will be able to observe how we use logical rules to discover potential errors, relationships, and protocol violations in the healthcare domain. To justify the demonstration, the oncologists from the P4-LUCAT project confirmed our experimental findings. By incorporating the analysis discussed in this paper, we aim to design a scalable rule mining system that takes into account all of the semantics of the KGs to discover more meaningful insights. More importantly, evidence of the work presented and the analysis methodology will be provided.

Acknowledgements. This work has been supported by the project TrustKG - Transforming Data in Trustable Insights with grant P99/2020 and the EraMed project P4-LUCAT (GA No. 53000015).

References

1. Galárraga, L., Teflioudi, C., Hose, K., Suchanek, F.: Fast rule mining in ontological knowledge bases with AMIE+. VLDB J. (2015). https://hal-imt.archives-ouvertes.fr/hal 01699866
2. Galárraga, L., Teflioudi, C., Hose, K., Suchanek, F.: Amie: association rule mining under incomplete evidence in ontological knowledge bases. In: WWW 2013 (2013). https://doi.org/10.1145/2488388.2488425
3. Hogan, A., et al.: Knowledge graphs (2021). https://doi.org/10.2200/S01125ED1V01Y202109DSK022

4. Lajus, J., Galárraga, L., Suchanek, F.: Fast and exact rule mining with amie 3. In: Harth, A., et al. (eds.) The Semantic Web (2020)
5. Meilicke, C., Chekol, M.W., Ruffinelli, D., Stuckenschmidt, H.: Anytime bottom-up rule learning for knowledge graph completion. In: IJCAI-2019 (2019). https://doi.org/10.24963/ijcai.2019/435

GLENDA: Querying RDF Archives with Full SPARQL

Olivier Pelgrin[1](✉)(iD), Ruben Taelman[2](iD), Luis Galárraga[3](iD),
and Katja Hose[1,4](iD)

[1] Aalborg University, Aalborg, Denmark
{olivier,khose}@cs.aau.dk
[2] Ghent University, Ghent, Belgium
ruben.taelman@ugent.be
[3] Inria, Rennes, France
luis.galarraga@inria.fr
[4] TU Wien, Vienna, Austria
katja.hose@tuwien.ac.at

Abstract. The dynamicity of semantic data has propelled the research on *RDF Archiving*, i.e., the task of storing and making the full history of large RDF datasets accessible. However, existing archiving techniques fail to scale when confronted with very large RDF datasets and support only simple SPARQL queries. In this demonstration, we therefore showcase GLENDA, a system that can run full SPARQL 1.1 compliant queries over large RDF archives. We achieve this through a multi-snapshot change-based storage architecture that we interface using the Comunica query engine. Thanks to this integration we demonstrate that fast SPARQL query processing over multiple versions of a knowledge graph is possible. Moreover, our demonstration provides different statistics about the history of RDF datasets that can be useful for tasks beyond querying and by providing insights about the evolution dynamics of the data.

Keywords: RDF archives · SPARQL · RDF · temporal queries · versioned queries · time-travel queries · versioning

1 Introduction

Despite most approaches assuming RDF datasets on the Web to be static and providing optimizations for this case, in reality most RDF datasets are consistently evolving [3,5]. Although there has been some work on archiving, where the focus has been more on storing previous versions, research has not yet been paid much attention to efficiently querying past versions of a knowledge graph without depending on specific system setups [1].

A straightforward way to keep track of the history of RDF data is to store each revision of the dataset as an independent copy. Intuitively, this does not scale well and can become prohibitive for large RDF datasets with long histories.

C. Pesquita et al. (Eds.): ESWC 2023, LNCS 13998, pp. 75–80, 2023.
https://doi.org/10.1007/978-3-031-43458-7_14

While few efficient solutions for RDF archiving have been proposed [6,9], they support queries on single triple patterns only. This means that executing full SPARQL queries on RDF archives still requires additional post-processing.

In this demo paper, we therefore present GLENDA, a system for executing full SPARQL queries over RDF archives. GLENDA is built on top of a multi-snapshot change-based storage system for RDF archives [6] that has been integrated with the Comunica [11] SPARQL engine. In the remainder of this paper, we first detail the technical architecture of GLENDA in Sect. 2. Then, we describe and illustrate GLENDA's main functionalities in Sect. 3. Finally, we conclude and discuss future work in Sect. 4.

2   The GLENDA System

Overview. At its core, GLENDA is composed of three distinct and independents components, namely (i) a storage layer composed and an RDF archive store, (ii) a query engine that communicates with the storage layer via an API, and (iii) a user interface in the form of a web application. The query engine is accessible by the client through a SPARQL endpoint.

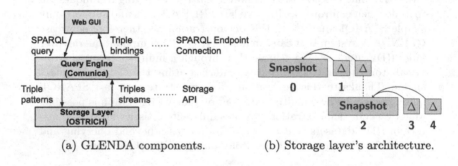

(a) GLENDA components.   (b) Storage layer's architecture.

Fig. 1. GLENDA architecture and components

Figure 1a illustrates the high level architecture of GLENDA. The user interacts with a web-based GUI, where they can write SPARQL 1.1 [8] compliant queries. The query engine is exposed through a SPARQL endpoint with support for versioned queries. The query engine decomposes the full SPARQL query written by the user into versioned triple pattern queries that can be executed natively by the storage layer, which returns answers as triple streams.

Storage Layer. We make use of an extension of the OSTRICH [6] system as storage layer. OSTRICH is a scalable engine for RDF archiving that stores the history of an RDF dataset in a single delta chain. A delta chain is comprised of an initial snapshot followed by a sequence of aggregated changesets (Fig. 1b). OSTRICH supports versioned queries on single triple patterns with optional offsets. It also provides efficient cardinality estimations for triple patterns. We resort to an extension of OSTRICH, presented in [6], that models revision histories using multiple delta chains. As shown in [6], this improves the ingestion time of new revisions drastically – in particular for very long histories.

Query Engine. We chose the *Comunica* [11] query engine to build our SPARQL endpoint. Comunica is a modular, high-performance RDF query engine with full support for the SPARQL 1.1 standard. Building on top of the work from Taelman et al. [10], we opted for a minimal change to the SPARQL language, as a full extension is outside the scope of this demonstration. The semantic of the GRAPH keywork is changed so that it references versions instead of graphs. We implemented support for three standard types of versioned SPARQL queries [2] described in the following.

- **Version Materialization (VM).** These are queries over a specific version of the RDF Archive. These queries use the notation *GRAPH <version:k>* for $k \in \{0, 1, \dots\}$.
- **Delta Materialization (DM).** These are SPARQL queries over the changeset between two versions. This is achieved by using the notation for VM queries in combination with the *FILTER (NOT EXISTS)* construct.
- **Version Queries (VQ).** These are SPARQL queries that yield version-annotated query results. They resort to the notation *GRAPH ?version*.

User Interface. We build our GUI as a regular web-page using HTML, CSS, and Javascript. We resort to the Yasgui[1] library for the SPARQL query interface, and the Plotly[2] library for our graphics and visualizations. More details about the user interface and its functionalities can be found next in Sect. 3.

3   Demonstration of GLENDA

We now demonstrate the capabilities of GLENDA on the BEAR-C dataset [2], which provides 32 snapshots from the Open Data Portal Watch project [4] together with ten full SPARQL queries. To the best of our knowledge, no publicly available system is currently capable of running the queries of this benchmark.

Figure 2a depicts GLENDA's query interface, where the user can write and execute SPARQL 1.1 queries, optionally using our versioning constructs. The queries from the BEAR-C benchmark can be chosen from the dropdown menu on top. The query type can be chosen among VM, DM and VQ queries, and the provided sliders can help the user chose the versions to query.

By selecting the tab "Statistics", the user can have access to various statistics about the underlying dataset (Fig. 2b). These are state-of-the-art metrics that describe the dynamics of an RDF archive [5]. Explanations for the metrics are available as tooltips triggered by hovering the mouse over the metric's name. A video showing all the capabilities of GLENDA can be found on YouTube[3]. The

---

[1] https://triply.cc/docs/yasgui-api.
[2] https://plotly.com/javascript/.
[3] https://youtu.be/DoNjw3V6oSo.

(a) GLENDA main page and query interface.

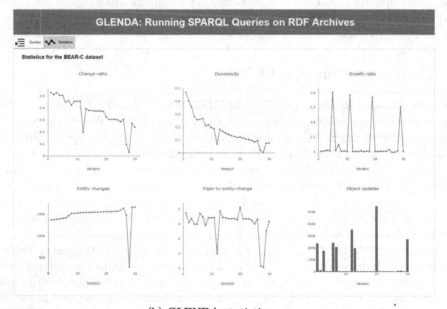

(b) GLENDA statistics page.

Fig. 2. GLENDA's user interface

system is publicly available at https://glenda.cs.aau.dk and more information can be found on our project webpage[4].

4 Conclusion

We have presented GLENDA, a system to execute full SPARQL queries on RDF archives. We detailed the technical makeup of the system and how its different components interact with each other. We explained how queries over archives can be executed with full SPARQL 1.1 via the use of special URIs for named graphs. GLENDA presents itself as a web interface to the user, with user-friendly tools to build and execute queries over RDF archives. We have demonstrated, GLENDA's capabilities on the BEAR-C dataset and queries, which no other system can currently fully support.

In our future work we have planned to consider the development and study of alternative snapshot strategies. Moreover, we envision to reduce the required storage space via more efficient serialization techniques for timestamped deltas. We also expect to improve query processing with advanced RDF representations and novel indexing approaches [7]. Similarly, we envision to study the use of dedicated extensions to the SPARQL language for versioned queries, which would allow for greater flexibility in the querying process, while enabling the simultaneous use of graphs and versions. Finally, we plan to improve the performance of the system further by implementing a more efficient streaming of the results from the storage layer to the query engine.

Acknowledgements. This research was partially funded by the Danish Council for Independent Research (DFF) under grant agreement no. DFF-8048-00051B, the Poul Due Jensen Foundation, and the TAILOR Network (EU Horizon 2020 research and innovation program under GA 952215). Ruben Taelman is a postdoctoral fellow of the Research Foundation - Flanders (FWO) (1274521N).

References

1. Aebeloe, C., Montoya, G., Hose, K.: ColChain: collaborative linked data networks. In: WWW, pp. 1385–1396. ACM/IW3C2 (2021)
2. Fernández, J.D., Umbrich, J., Polleres, A., Knuth, M.: Evaluating query and storage strategies for RDF archives. JWS **10**(2), 247–291 (2019)
3. Hose, K.: Knowledge graph (r)evolution and the web of data. In: MEP-DaW@ISWC, pp. 1–7 (2021)
4. Neumaier, S., Umbrich, J., Polleres, A.: Automated quality assessment of metadata across open data portals. JDIQ **8**(1), 2:1–2:29 (2016)
5. Pelgrin, O., Galárraga, L., Hose, K.: Towards fully-fledged archiving for RDF datasets. SWJ **12**(6), 903–925 (2021)
6. Pelgrin, O., Taelman, R., Galárraga, L., Hose, K.: Scaling large RDF archives to very long histories. In: ICSC (2023)

---

[4] https://relweb.cs.aau.dk/glenda/.

7. Sagi, T., Lissandrini, M., Pedersen, T.B., Hose, K.: A design space for RDF data representations. VLDB J. **31**(2), 347–373 (2022)
8. Seaborne, A., Harris, S.: SPARQL 1.1 query language. W3C Recommendation, W3C (2013). http://www.w3.org/TR/2013/REC-sparql11-query-20130321/
9. Taelman, R., Sande, M.V., Herwegen, J.V., Mannens, E., Verborgh, R.: Triple storage for random-access versioned querying of RDF archives. JWS **54**, 4–28 (2019)
10. Taelman, R., Sande, M.V., Verborgh, R.: Versioned querying with OSTRICH and comunica in MOCHA 2018. In: SemWebEval@ESWC, vol. 927, pp. 17–23 (2018)
11. Taelman, R., Van Herwegen, J., Vander Sande, M., Verborgh, R.: Comunica: a modular sparQL query engine for the web. In: ISWC (2018)

Piloting Topic-Aware Research Impact Assessment Features in BIP! Services

Serafeim Chatzopoulos[(✉)][ID], Kleanthis Vichos[ID], Ilias Kanellos[ID], and Thanasis Vergoulis[ID]

IMSI, Athena RC, Athens, Greece
{schatz,kvichos,ilias.kanellos,vergoulis}@athenarc.gr

Abstract. Various research activities rely on citation-based impact indicators. However these indicators are usually globally computed, hindering their proper interpretation in applications like research assessment and knowledge discovery. In this work, we advocate for the use of topic-aware categorical impact indicators, to alleviate the aforementioned problem. In addition, we extend BIP! Services to support those indicators and showcase their benefits in real-world research activities.

1 Introduction

Citation-based impact indicators, like citation counts, have found a variety of uses during the previous years as a way to facilitate various research-related activities. First of all, they are used by scientific literature search engines (e.g., Semantic Scholar[1], BIP Finder[2]) to rank keyword search results assisting researchers in prioritising their reading. Moreover, they have been exploited as facilitators in research assessment activities [4], while they have also become the basis for monitoring scientific output (e.g., [2]). The majority of these indicators are based on network analysis algorithms that rely on citation data and publication metadata (e.g., publication year, author lists etc.).

However, impact indicators have been related to various problems that plague research community at large. For instance, scientific literature search engines incorporate a limited number of indicators that capture a narrow perspective of scientific impact [5]. Specifically, most of them only support citation count, which has specific known issues (e.g., bias against recent articles, vulnerable to excessive self citation attacks). Moreover, in research assessment, evaluators often tend to over-rely on impact indicators without delving into the researchers' CVs and publications. Using indicators as "evaluation shortcuts" has been identified as a problematic approach [4] that often results in unfair research assessment.

But an even more important problem is that, in the aforementioned applications, users are allowed to compare articles from different fields, something that can lead to misconceptions. Academic search engines often return results

---

[1] Semantic Scholar: https://www.semanticscholar.org/.
[2] BIP! Finder: https://bip.imsi.athenarc.gr/.

© The Author(s), under exclusive license to Springer Nature Switzerland AG 2023
C. Pesquita et al. (Eds.): ESWC 2023, LNCS 13998, pp. 81–85, 2023.
https://doi.org/10.1007/978-3-031-43458-7_15

from different topics, since the same keywords can be related to various fields. Similarly, academic CVs usually contain publications from multiple fields, hence directly comparing impact indicators likely results in misjudgements.

Since it is not realistically possible to alleviate all impact-indicator-related problems, they should always be used with caution and only supplementary to other (qualitative) evidence. However, impact indicators can still have an assisting role in various applications, therefore alleviating some of their problems remains valuable. Motivated by this, we adapt the multi-perspective impact indicators provided by BIP! DB [7] into a set of topic-aware, categorical indicators. To transform the numerical values of the original indicators into categorical, we translate them into percentile rank classes (similarly to the approaches described in [1]). We believe that this is useful since the categorical indicators are easier to interpret. Finally, we showcase the benefits of these topic-aware indicators in real-world applications by extending the BIP! Services[3] to incorporate them.

2   Implementation

2.1   Topic-Aware, Categorical Impact Indicators

As mentioned, to alleviate the problems mentioned in Sect. 1, we advocate on the use of a variation of the impact indicators offered by BIP! DB [7]. This database already follows a multi-perspective approach providing a variety of indicators that capture different aspects of publication scientific impact. For this work we focus on the following indicators:[4]

- *Popularity.* It reflects the "current" impact/attention (the "hype") of an article based on the underlying citation network.
- *Influence.* It reflects the overall/diachronic impact of an article in the research community at large, based on the underlying citation network.
- *Citation Count.* The number of citations an article has received (it also reflects overall/diachronic impact).
- *Impulse.* It reflects the initial momentum of an article directly after its publication, based on the underlying citation network.

BIP! DB calculates scores on the whole citation network. Based on the indicator value, it is possible to assign a global categorical value to each paper according to the percentile[5] into which it belongs. Hence, in this way, it is possible to define five categorical impact indicators, one for each of the initial indicators. We refer to these categorical indicators as "Popularity class", "Influence class", "Citation count class", and "Impulse class", respectively.

---

[3] BIP! Services: https://bip.imsi.athenarc.gr/.

[4] More details (e.g., the calculation algorithms) for these indicators can be found here: https://bip.imsi.athenarc.gr/site/indicators.

[5] Percentiles are not strongly affected by outlier values, and can be easily calculated even if the underlying data are heavily skewed.

We proceed a step further by annotating each article with its relevant topics (details in Sect. 2.2) and, then, calculating topic-specific versions of the afore-mentioned categorical indicators. In this way, for each article, apart from its global impact classes we also calculate topic-specific ones for all its related topics. In particular, for each topic, we compute the percentiles for all indicators as follows: first, we rank the topic-related articles by the given impact indicator in descending order; then, each publication is assigned a percentile based on the distribution of scores and we assign the respective class to the article. For all categorical indicators, the following impact classes are used: Top 0.01%, Top 0.1%, Top 1%, Top 10%, Average (rest 90%).

2.2 Data Collection, Processing, and Publishing

To calculate the topic-aware, categorical impact indicators, we get the respective impact indicator scores from BIP! DB. The version used for the needs of the current paper was version 8 containing indicators for almost 134M articles.[6] We then associated these articles with (L2) topics from OpenAlex [3] (284 in total). We chose to keep only the three most dominant topics for each publication, based on their confidence score, and only if this score was greater than 0.3. After this process, we ended up with more than 75% of the articles in BIP! DB being associated to at least one topic. Subsequently, we calculated the topic-specific impact classes for each publication. Given a specific topic, each publication was assigned with an impact class from the set {C1, C2, C3, C4, C5}, with C1 corresponding to the Top 0.01% class and C5 to that of Average impact. We integrated those indicators in BIP! DB dataset that is openly available on Zenodo.

2.3 BIP! Services Extensions

To demonstrate how the previous indicators can be useful in practice, we focused on two use-cases: scientific knowledge discovery and research impact monitoring. For the former case, we have extended the BIP! Finder [5] academic search engine accordingly by modifying the UI to (a) display the topics of each result and its impact class according to each topic and (b) support topic-based filtering. To visualise the impact classes, we have used a compact visualisation based on icons that get particular color-codes for each class. Figure 1a illustrates the results list and the filter for the query "semantic web". For the latter case, we have extended the BIP! Scholar [6] service that offers researcher profile pages summarising research careers. Specifically, we have added a topic facet allowing the researchers to reveal their impact on selected topics (Fig. 1b).

3 Demonstration Scenarios

At the conference, the audience will have the opportunity to interact with the BIP! Services and examine the benefits that the topic-specific impact indicators bring in various use-cases. We will also demonstrate the following scenarios.

---

[6] https://doi.org/10.5281/zenodo.4386934.

(a) Scientific knowledge discovery.   (b) Monitoring a researcher's impact.

Fig. 1. Topic-aware publication impact indicators in BIP! Services.

Scientific Knowledge Discovery. An audience member searches for the key-words "semantic web" in BIP! Finder and determines (using the topic filter) that only articles related to the "Artificial Intelligence" topic are of interest (Fig. 1a). Each result contains the associated topics and for each of them the impact icons inform the user about the topic-specific impact class of the result.

Monitoring a Researcher's Impact. The same audience member, uses BIP! Scholar, to display the profile of Tim Berners-Lee, a well-known researcher in field of web technologies (Fig. 1b). By selecting each of the topic facets on top of the profile ("Data science"), the user can reveal the impact of Berners-Lee in the respective topic (e.g., how many popular works he has).

Acknowledgements. This work was co-funded by the EU Horizon Europe projects SciLake (GA: 101058573) and GraspOS (GA: 101095129) and the EU H2020 project OpenAIRE-Nexus (GA: 101017452).

References

1. Bornmann, L., Leydesdorff, L., Mutz, R.: The use of percentiles and percentile rank classes in the analysis of bibliometric data: opportunities and limits. J. Informet. **7**(1), 158–165 (2013)
2. Papastefanatos, G., et al.: Open science observatory: monitoring open science in Europe. In: ADBIS/TPDL/EDA Workshops, vol. 1260, pp. 341–346 (2020)
3. Priem, J., Piwowar, H., Orr, R.: OpenAlex: a fully-open index of scholarly works, authors, enues, institutions, and concepts (2022). https://arxiv.org/abs/2205.01833
4. Strinzel, M., Brown, J., Kaltenbrunner, W., de Rijcke, S., Hill, M.: Ten ways to improve academic CVS for fairer research assessment. Human. Soc. Sci. Commun. **8**(1), 1–4 (2021)
5. Vergoulis, T., Chatzopoulos, S., Kanellos, I., Deligiannis, P., Tryfonopoulos, C., Dalamagas, T.: Bip! Finder: facilitating scientific literature search by exploiting impact-based ranking. In: CIKM, pp. 2937–2940 (2019)

6. Vergoulis, T., et al.: Bip! Scholar: a service to facilitate fair researcher assessment. In: JCDL, pp. 1–5 (2022)
7. Vergoulis, T., et al.: Bip! DB: a dataset of impact measures for scientific publications. In: Companion Proceedings of the Web Conference 2021, pp. 456–460 (2021)

Explanation-Based Tool for Helping Data Producers to Reduce Privacy Risks

Hira Asghar[(✉)], Christophe Bobineau, and Marie-Christine Rousset

Université Grenoble Alpes, CNRS, Grenoble INP, LIG, Grenoble, France
{hira.asghar,christophe.bobineau,
marie-christine.rousset}@univ-grenoble-alpes.fr

Abstract. This paper demonstrates the interactive user interface *PrivEx* that helps data producers to reduce privacy risks raised by data collection from service providers in the Semantic Web of Things. *PrivEx* provides several types of support to data producers in their management of the tension between the privacy risks and the utility of the data they accept to publish. *PrivEx* is grounded on the formal framework presented in [1] for detecting automatically privacy risks raised by utility queries. In the demonstration, we will illustrate the functionalities of *PrivEx*, on a smart meter scenario inspired by a real-world use case providing time series of electrical consumptions of different customers associated with some metadata on their demographics, home sizes and equipment.

Keywords: Privacy risks · Data exchange · Semantic Web of Things

1 Introduction

Personal data are increasingly disseminated over the Web through mobile devices and smart environments. They are exploited for developing more and more sophisticated services and applications. All these advances come with serious risks for privacy breaches that may reveal private information wanted to remain undisclosed by data producers. It is therefore of utmost importance to help them to identify privacy risks raised by requests of service providers for utility purposes. In [1], we have presented a formal framework supporting utility-aware privacy preservation in the setting of applications where service providers request collecting data from data producers to perform useful aggregate data analytics. The approach that we promote to face the privacy versus utility dilemma in this setting can be summarized as follows:

– Data producers specify by a set of *privacy queries* (kept secret) the (possibly aggregated) data they *do not want* to be disclosed.

Partially supported by MIAI@Grenoble Alpes (ANR-19-P3IA-0003), PERSYVAL-Lab (ANR-11-LABX-0025-01) and TAILOR, a project funded by EU Horizon 2020 research and innovation programme under GA No 952215.

C. Pesquita et al. (Eds.): ESWC 2023, LNCS 13998, pp. 86–90, 2023.
https://doi.org/10.1007/978-3-031-43458-7_16

- Data consumers make explicit by a set *utility queries* the data they request to each data producer for offering them services in return.
- The compatibility between privacy and utility queries is automatically verified, and in case of incompatibility data producers get an explanation that can be exploited later to help them find an acceptable privacy-utility trade-off.

In this paper, we demonstrate *PrivEx* an interactive user interface that we have built[1] on top of the implementation of the formal results presented in [1] for detecting automatically privacy risks raised by utility queries. The user interface *PrivEx* provides several types of support to data producers in their management of the tension between the privacy risks and the utility of the data they accept to publish. First, it presents in an interpretable form the requests of a service provider for utility purpose. Second, it provides a form-based interface for guiding data producers in construction of privacy queries. Third, it detects the privacy risks and provides a factual explanation for each detected privacy risk. Last, it provides several options for modifying the utility queries to reduce the detected privacy risks.

2   Smart Meter Use Case

We consider a smart meter scenario inspired by a real-world use case provided by the *Irish Social Science Data Archive (ISSDA) Commission for Energy Regulation (CER)*[2]. This dataset includes time series of electrical consumptions of different house owners. In addition, pseudonymized metadata are available on customers' demographics, home sizes and equipment associated to the electric consumption time series. For capturing the properties describing the smart meter data and the associated customers' metadata in a uniform way, we have designed a simple RDFS ontology[3].

This ontology provides a shared vocabulary used by service providers to express their utility queries (as illustrated in Fig. 1) and by data producers to express their privacy queries (as shown in Fig. 2).

In their most general form, the (privacy and utility) queries have 4 parts: *(i)* a *core pattern* that specifies the combinations between properties to be satisfied by the requested data; *(ii)* a *constraints* part on the values of some of the properties for filtering more precisely the requested data; *(iii)* a *result* defining the target properties the values of which must be returned by the query evaluation, and possibly an aggregate function to be computed on groups; and *(iv)* a *time window* part, if the aggregate function is computed on a dynamic property (such as *issda:consumption*), to specify the time intervals over which the aggregation must be computed.

Time windows are specified with two parameters: a *size* to express the duration of each time window, and a *step* to express the time interval separating

---

[1] Code is available at https://github.com/repository-code/PrivEx.
[2] https://www.ucd.ie/issda/data/commissionforenergyregulationcer/.
[3] Available at https://raw.githubusercontent.com/fr-anonymous/puck/main/issda_schema.ttl.

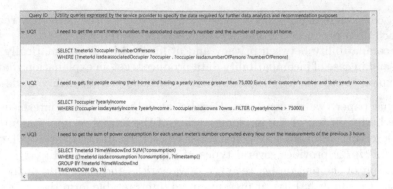

Fig. 1. Example of 3 utility queries expressed in their textual and SPARQL-like syntax

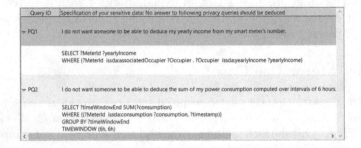

Fig. 2. Example of 2 privacy queries expressed in their textual and SPARQL-like syntax

consecutive time windows, which can thus be sliding (like in the UQ3 query in Fig. 1 or tumbling (like in the PQ2 query in Fig. 2).

3 Demonstration Scenario

In the demo, the following functionalities of *PrivEx* will be demonstrated.

1. *Guided construction of privacy queries:* The form-based interface facilitates the step by step construction of each privacy query as illustrated in Fig. 3. In first step, the user enters the textual description of the query to be constructed. The second step (construction of the core pattern of each query) is guided by the display of the ontology to help the user choose properties. For the other parts, the user is guided by the interface to enter their choices easily. During the demo, the attendees can see the interactive construction of privacy query PQ2.
2. *Detection and explanation of privacy risks:* Each detected privacy risk comes with an explanation based on the proof produced by the incompatibility checking algorithm described in [1]. Each privacy risk is explained using two

different levels as illustrated in Fig. 4. The first level simply points out the privacy queries likely to be violated by some utility queries that are also shown to the user. The second level exhibits the corresponding privacy risk by providing a counter example in the form of synthetic data built from the ontology and the (utility and privacy) queries involved. In the demo, attendees can see the explanation for each detected privacy risk.

3. *Guided negotiation to reduce privacy risks:* As illustrated in Fig. 5, the interface lists several options for negotiating the utility queries involved in privacy risks, either by refusing to answer them, or by modifying their result, or by generalizing their conditions, or by changing the aggregate function, or by changing the time window size or step. In the demo, attendees can observe how the interface guides users for interactively removing or reducing the privacy risks.

Fig. 3. Screenshot of the steps followed for the construction of privacy query PQ2

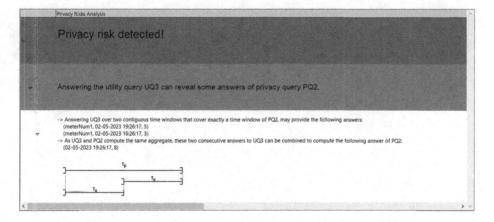

Fig. 4. Screenshot illustrating the explanation of detected privacy risk

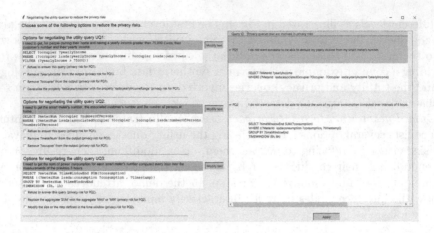

Fig. 5. Screenshot of the interface for guiding the negotiation of privacy risks

The functionalities of *PrivEx* are demonstrated in a demo video that is accessible via the following link: https://www.veed.io/view/3f1f8db3-0ca8-4ebc-b143-52bdc26f73de?panel=share.

References

1. Asghar, H., Bobineau, C., Rousset, M.C.: Identifying privacy risks raised by utility queries. In: Chbeir, R., Huang, H., Silvestri, F., Manolopoulos, Y., Zhang, Y. (eds.) WISE 2022. LNCS, vol. 13724, pp. 309–324. Springer, Cham (2022). https://doi.org/10.1007/978-3-031-20891-1_22

PathWays: Entity-Focused Exploration of Heterogeneous Data Graphs

Nelly Barret[1] , Antoine Gauquier[2], Jia-Jean Law[3],
and Ioana Manolescu[1(✉)]

[1] Inria and Institut Polytechnique de Paris, Paris, France
{nelly.barret,ioana.manolescu}@inria.fr
[2] Institut Mines Télécom, Paris, France
antoine.gauquier@etu.imt-nord-europe.fr
[3] Ecole Polytechnique, Palaiseau, France
jia-jean.law@polytechnique.edu

Abstract. Graphs, and notably RDF graphs, are a prominent way of sharing data. As data usage democratizes, users need help figuring out the useful content of a graph dataset. In particular, journalists with whom we collaborate [3] are interested in identifying, in a graph, the *connections between entities*, e.g., people, organizations, emails, etc.

We propose PathWays, an interactive tool for exploring data graphs through *their data paths connecting Named Entities (NEs, in short)*; each data path leads to a tabular-looking set of results. NEs are extracted from the data through dedicated Information Extraction modules. Path-Ways leverages the ConnectionLens platform [4,6] and follow-up work on dataset abstraction [5]. Its novelty lies in its interactive and efficient approach to enumerate, compute, and analyze NE paths.

Keywords: Data graphs · Graph exploration · Information Extraction

1 Motivation and Problem Statement

Data graphs, including RDF knowledge graphs, as well as Property Graphs (PGs), are often used to represent and share data. More generally, *any structured or semistructured dataset can be viewed as a graph*, having: (*i*) an internal node for each structure element of the original dataset, e.g., relational tuple, XML element or attribute, JSON map or array, URI in an RDF graph; (*ii*) a leaf node for each value in the dataset, e.g., attribute value in a relational tuple, text node or attribute value in XML, atomic (leaf) value in a JSON document, or literal in RDF. The connections between the data items in the original dataset lead to edges in the graph, e.g. parent-child relationship between XML or JSON nodes, edges connecting each relational tuple node with their attributes, etc. In a relational database, when primary key-foreign key pairs are present, they lead to further edges allowing one tuple, e.g., an Employee, to "point to" the Company tuple representing their employer. This graph view of a dataset has been introduced to support unstructured (keyword-based) search on (semi)structured data, since [2,8] and through many follow-up works [12].

C. Pesquita et al. (Eds.): ESWC 2023, LNCS 13998, pp. 91–95, 2023.
https://doi.org/10.1007/978-3-031-43458-7_17

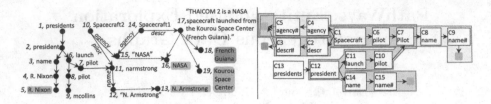

Fig. 1. Sample data graph (left), and corresponding collection graph (right) on which paths linking entities are explored (highlighted areas). (Color figure online)

1.1 Entity-Rich Graphs

Building on this idea of integrating heterogeneous data into graphs, the ConnectionLens system [4,6] has been developed to facilitate, for users lacking IT skills, such as data journalists, the exploration of datasets of various models, including relational/CSV, XML, JSON, RDF, and PGs. ConnectionLens turns *any (set of) datasets into a single graph as outlined above.* For instance, the data graph at left in Fig. 1 features RDF triples about NASA spacecrafts (labeled edges), and an XML document describing presidents who attended spacecraft launches (tree with labeled node and unlabeled edges). ConnectionLens also includes Information Extraction modules, which extract, from any leaf node in the data graph, Named Entities (People, Locations and Organizations) [4], as well as other types of entities that journalists find interesting: temporal moments (date, time); Web site URIs; email addresses; and hashtags. We designate any of these pieces of information as *entities*, and we model them as extra nodes, e.g., in the data graph in Fig. 1, organizations appear on a pink background, people on yellow and locations on green, respectively. Each entity is extracted from a leaf text node, to which it is connected by a dashed edge. When an entity is extracted from more than one text node, the edges connecting it to those nodes increase the connectivity of the graph, e.g., "NASA" extracted from the nodes with IDs 15 and 17.

1.2 Entity Paths

Journalists are interested in *the paths connecting entities* in a given dataset. For instance, in Fig. 1, they may want to know "how people are connected to places". Similarly, an article describes French real estate bought by family members of dictators abroad; here, journalists ask "what are the paths between people and cities (where real estate is)?". Importantly, we should consider paths *irrespective of the direction of the edges in the data graph.* This is because, depending on how the data is modeled, we may encounter $x \xrightarrow{\text{boughtProperty}} y \xrightarrow{\text{locatedIn}} c$, or $x \xleftarrow{\text{hasOwner}} y \xrightarrow{\text{locatedIn}} c$; both paths are interesting.

Goal: Efficient Exploration of Entity Connections. Journalist questions such as those above ask for *data paths ending in entity pairs of certain kinds.* When shown the set of corresponding labeled paths, users may pick one to *further* *explore*: how many pairs of entities are connected by each path? which entities are most frequent, e.g., in which cities are most properties located? how do the cities spread across countries, etc. Such analysis requires *materializing the entity pairs connected by the paths*, which may be very costly, if (*i*) the graph is large, and/or (*ii*) there are many paths (the latter is almost always true, especially since our paths may traverse edges in both directions. To mitigate this problem, PathWays includes a *materialized view recommender and view-based rewriting module* (Sect. 3), which significantly improve performance. Thus, PathWays enumerates paths between entities of user-selected types, (*i*) independently of the edge direction, (*ii*) asking for user input to focus on the paths most useful to them, and (*iii*) efficiently. To our knowledge, PathWays is the first system built for this flavor of graph exploration (see also Sect. 4).

2 Demonstration Scenarios

PathWays is developed in Java 11, on top of [4,5] which build the data and, respectively, the collection graph (see below), and store them in PostgreSQL.

User interaction with PathWays starts by making some choices: *"Which types of entities to connect?"* (in Fig. 1, organizations and people); *"How many paths to enumerate?"* (say, 20) and *"What is the maximum allowed length for a path?"* (say, 10). In Fig. 1, four paths connect organizations and people; two are shown in yellow and red highlight. Computing the paths on large data graph may be costly. Instead, PathWays leverages a *collection graph* [5], a (much smaller) summary of the data graph, grouping similar data nodes in a single collection node, e.g., the spacecraft nodes 10 and 14 in the data graph are grouped in collection C1. For each collection of nodes having text children, e.g., C8 labeled name, the collection of these text children is denoted, e.g., name#; entities (people, locations, etc.) are extracted from such texts. *Any path in the data graph also exists in the collection graph*, thus PathWays enumerates paths on the smaller collection graph. Each path is then translated in a query over the data graph, to obtain data paths between actual entities. PathWays displays sample entity pairs connected by each path, e.g., Nixon is connected to NASA because he attended a launch involving N. Armstrong. Users can then apply more aggregation/analysis on the entity pairs, look for frequent entities, etc. We will also show how PathWays optimizes path evaluation (see below). We will use real-life datasets, such as PubMed, the NASA dataset, RDF benchmarks, and GeoNames, to investigate connections between people and organizations, e.g., companies funding PubMed article authors, geographic repartition of papers (PubMed) and launches (NASA), etc. A preview of our demonstration can be found at https://team.inria.fr/cedar/projects/abstra/pathways/.

3 View Materialization and View-Based Rewriting

When the data graph is large, paths are long, and/or many, evaluating path queries on the graph may be inefficient, despite the graph being extensively indexed. However, as illustrated at right in Fig. 1, paths may *overlap*, e.g., the edges connecting C1, C6 and C7 are common between the two highlighted paths. Leveraging this observation, PathWays identifies the subpaths common to at least two path queries. Then, with the help of a cost model, based on PostgreSQL's estimations, it *materializes the most profitable shared subpath* s_1 where profit is: the decrease in the total path evaluation cost *if the subpath is materialized and its results used to evaluate the paths enclosing it*, minus the cost to materialize the subpath. PathWays then *rewrites* every path query $p_1^1, \ldots, p_1^{n_1}$ containing s_1, using it as a materialized view. Then, we remove $p_1^1, \ldots, p_1^{n_1}$ from the path set, and, in a greedy fashion, again look for the most profitable common subpath s_2 for the remaining paths, etc. We stop when no subpath is profitable (materializing it costs more than its cost savings). The complexity of the above view selection algorithm is $O(N^2 L + N^3)$, for N paths of length at most L.

Sample Performance Saving. On the NASA RDF dataset (100.000 triples), we enumerated 100 paths, of length 2 to 8, between locations and people. Evaluating them all took 419 s, including 12 that timed-out at 30 s. PathWays found 89 common subpaths; 16 were selected by our algorithm, which rewrote 98 path queries using them as materialized views. Materializing the 16 paths took 0.1 s, and the total path query evaluation shrank to 6.93 s, a speedup of 60×.

4   Related Work and Conclusion

Many graph exploration methods exist, see, e.g., [11]. Modern graph query languages such as GPML [7] (no implementation so far) or the JEDI [1] SPARQL extension allow asking for paths between nodes matching some query variables. Other systems interact with users to incrementally build SPARQL queries interesting for them, e.g., [10] for queries with aggregation. In keyword-based search (KBS, in short) [2,4,6,8,12], one asks, e.g., for connections between "Sivel Aliev" (related to the Azeirbadjan president) and "Nice" (where she owns villas). KBS is handy when users *know keywords (entities) to search for*. Complementing the above, PathWays is focused on *identifying and computing all paths between certain extracted entities*, to give a first global look at the dataset content, for graphs obtained from multiple data models. For performance, PathWays leverages a compact graph summary and efficiently materializes views; our view materialization problem, focusing only on paths, is a restriction of that considered, e.g., in [9], enabling a low complexity while being very effective. We are currently adapting our algorithm to other graph data management systems.

Acknowledgments. This work has been funded by the DIM RFSI PHD 2020-01 project and the AI Chair SourcesSay (ANR-20-CHIA-0015-01) chair.

References

1. Aebeloe, C., Setty, V., Montoya, G., Hose, K.: Top-K diversification for path queries in knowledge graphs. In: ISWC Workshops (2018)

2. Agrawal, S., Chaudhuri, S., Das, G.: DBXplorer: a system for keyword-based search over relational databases. In: ICDE (2002)
3. Anadiotis, A., Balalau, O., Bouganim, T., et al.: Empowering investigative journalism with graph-based heterogeneous data management. IEEE DEBull. (2021)
4. Anadiotis, A., Balalau, O., Conceicao, C., et al.: Graph integration of structured, semistructured and unstructured data for data journalism. Inf. Syst. **104** (2022)
5. Barret, N., Manolescu, I., Upadhyay, P.: Abstra: toward generic abstractions for data of any model (demonstration). In: CIKM (2022)
6. Chanial, C., Dziri, R., Galhardas, H., et al.: ConnectionLens: finding connections across heterogeneous data sources (demonstration). PVLDB **11**(12) (2018)
7. Deutsch, A., Francis, N., Green, A., Hare, K., Li, B., Libkin, L., et al.: Graph pattern matching in GQL and SQL/PGQ. In: SIGMOD (2022)
8. Hristidis, V., Papakonstantinou, Y., Balmin, A.: Keyword proximity search on XML graphs. In: ICDE (2003)
9. Le, W., Kementsietsidis, A., Duan, S., et al.: Scalable multi-query optimization for SPARQL. In: ICDE (2012)
10. Lissandrini, M., Hose, K., Pedersen, T.B.: Example-driven exploratory analytics over knowledge graphs. In: EDBT (2023)
11. Lissandrini, M., Mottin, D., Hose, K., Pedersen, T.B.: Knowledge graph exploration systems: are we lost? In: CIDR (2022). www.cidrdb.org
12. Yang, J., Yao, W., Zhang, W.: Keyword search on large graphs: a survey. Data Sci. Eng. **6**(2) (2021)

A Geological Case Study on Semantically Triggered Processes

Yuanwei Qu[✉], Eduard Kamburjan, and Martin Giese

SIRIUS Center, University of Oslo, Oslo, Norway
{quy,eduard,martingi}@ifi.uio.no

Abstract. We present an approach to connect semantic descriptions of situations to program-based descriptions of processes. The main mechanism is a semantically formalised *trigger* that initiates a process. We demonstrate the viability of the approach by modelling scenarios and processes in petroleum geoscience.

1 Introduction

Semantic technologies are designed to build graph-based models to represent and reason about static relationships between entities and their properties, but not to represent dynamic behavior and changes. Although there is research focusing on formalisation of the concept of change [6] and top-level ontology frameworks to describe processes [1], there is still limited support for exploiting these models, e.g. in simulations, to build conditionals and loops to model the scenario that is described by the knowledge representations.

The distinction between utilizing semantic technologies to represent knowledge of dynamic processes and programming languages to implement the dynamics remains pronounced. The current work of [3] introduces a core programming language called 'Semantic Micro Object Language' (SMOL) to map the dynamic expression of an object-oriented programming language to the static description of semantic knowledge models, which demonstrates a structural approach for closing the gap between descriptive and computational modeling languages. Combined with the notion of programs as behavioural specifications, this enables hybrid semantic and behavioural models.

In this work, we propose an architecture to connect the modeling of processes in ontologies and the implementation of these processes in a simulator program. To illustrate our approach, we explore petroleum geological process modeling, which often involves complex reasoning, and for which various ontologies and knowledge graphs have been constructed to represent knowledge [4].

Traditional quantitative geological process simulation produces results that sometimes do not follow the geological knowledge and require experts to interpret the results. Such challenges can be avoided in knowledge-based qualitative simulation. Previous efforts [5] have shown that it is possible but still challenging to simulate geological processes based on formal domain knowledge. Geological

C. Pesquita et al. (Eds.): ESWC 2023, LNCS 13998, pp. 96–100, 2023.
https://doi.org/10.1007/978-3-031-43458-7_18

processes usually take place when a set of conditions are met and lead to certain consequences. For each geological process, the corresponding conditions can be summarized as a trigger. Therefore, in addition to modeling the domain knowledge of the process, it is also important to model the condition that triggers the process and the entities related to the process. The program can thus utilize the trigger to query entities when a process starts.

Through our case study, we show how the notion of triggers is used to close the gap between semantic technologies and programming languages. This approach is not only easy to apply to other domains but also provides a clear structure for describing processes and implementing their simulation.

2   Architecture and Case Study

Our architecture is based on a split between so-called *event triggers* in the domain knowledge, and *event handlers* in the program. A process on some entity e is described two-fold. The ontology contains (a) the domain knowledge about e, (b) the domain knowledge when a process is triggered on e and (c) the domain knowledge of how this process relates to other processes. The program contains (1) the computational knowledge about e and (2) the computational knowledge of how the processes affect e.

The trigger bridges the gap between computation and description: while described in the domain, it can be used to query *inside the program* all entities where a process is about to start.

Domain Knowledge. We first introduce some basic geological terms. The geothermal maturation and migration of organic matter is a pivotal geological process for the energy industry, which makes it a fitting use case for our study. This process involves the transformation of subsurface kerogen into oil and/or gas, as a result of geothermal maturation, followed by its migration through stratigraphic layers. The kerogen is dehydrated organic matter and compacted by overlying rocks. The oil transformation window of kerogen is roughly around 90 to 150 °C, while the gas transformation window is mainly above 150 °C [2]. We molded these processes triggers, namely cooking and burning. The oil and gas may eventually be trapped and stopped by an impermeable layer or escape to reach the surface. Temperature and permeability are the two key factors in the process, as oil and gas need the sufficient temperature to be generated, and rock needs to be permeable to allow the petroleum to flow through.

In this use case, we are modeling the process of organic matter in the rock transferring into oil or gas and migrating upward toward the surface. As a proof of concept, we consider that the migration path is vertically upwards through the stratigraphic layers. Each stratigraphic layer is homogeneous as it is constituted by only one type of rock. The only barrier to stop the migration is the impermeable stratigraphic layer that petroleum can not flow through.

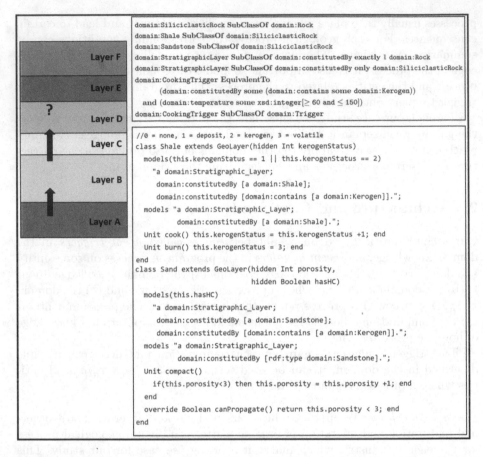

Fig. 1. Illustration of migration in rock layers (left); part of the domain ontology of the scenario (upper); and the simulation code of shale layers in SMOL (lower)

Domain Model. The concepts of the stratigraphic layers and their rock types as well as domain knowledge about their properties and process trigger conditions are modeled in an ontology which is partly illustrated in the upper part of Fig. 1 upper part. Note that the ontology formalises only process *triggers* but not models of the process themselves.

A *trigger* is equivalent to a physical entity that meets the required conditions to trigger some processes. In this use case, the physical entity is the *stratigraphic layer*. A *stratigraphic layer* is a layer that consists of one type of rock. We considered two petroleum-relevant rock types, namely *sandstone* and *shale*.

In the perspective of Petroleum Geoscience, instead of fresh organic matter, *oil* and *gas* is transferred from *kerogen*. This thermal transformation process is modeled as *cookingTrigger*.

Programming with Domain Knowledge. So far, entities are described in the knowledge graph. To program with them, we use *semantically lifted programming (SLP)*. SLP is based on the idea of lifting a program state *during* program execution into a knowledge graph, in our case, the geological knowledge, and query it from within the very same program to use the domain knowledge for computations. Our implementation is based the SMOL [3] implementation of SLP. Our simulator has a general setup with classes for different kinds of layers and rocks, and can simulate different actions, such as the deposition of material, or its erosion. Here we show only the relevant part of the class for shale layers.

The class declares a field `status` that models the state of the hydrocarbons within. In this field, two methods operate: `cook`, for cooking and `burn` for burning. Note that this modeling is optimized towards computations: it requires no knowledge about the exact nature of these processes, or even a concept of hydrocarbons. Instead, it can be manipulated with simple arithmetic operations.

Let us turn our attention to the **models** clause. It extends the semantic lifting by adding additional knowledge about the *program object*. If the status is between 0 and 3, then additional axioms are added, namely that the object is constituted by shale and contains kerogen, i.e., deposited and non-volatile hydrocarbons. In case the status is different, only the axiom to describe is constitution is added.

This allows us now to interpret a *program object* in terms of the domain. To facilitate an effective connection, the simulator is round-based, where each round models the progressing of time by a certain step. During this time, some action (erosion or deposition) is performed and the simulator state updated accordingly. After each time round, the simulator queries *itself*, i.e., its own lifted objects, for triggers. If the query for all entities that are triggering a cooking process, returns a non-empty set, then on all these objects the `cook` method is called. This is shown in Fig. 1, in the lower box. We stress again that this query is not performed on external data, but on internal objects with external knowledge.

Our model implements a separation of concerns between domain modeling of static structures, done in OWL, and modeling of dynamic behavior, done in a standard object-oriented programming language. This reduces the redundancy between code and ontology and provides a very clear interface between these two worlds: the modeling bridge that interprets an object in the domain. Note, however, that a SMOL object is *not* a geological layer, instead it is explicitly linked to one. Similarly, a trigger remains purely in the domain, it is not a concept of the programming language, but a technique to implement guards in our setting.

The case study is available at smolang.org. We performed two experiments, based on different sequences of deposition and erosion and can comprehend the resulting hydrocarbon migration in great detail and with more domain knowledge than the prior approach [5]. We note however that for now but we consider a simpler setup with only a single column of uniform layers.

3   Conclusion and Future Work

We presented an architecture to model processes by connecting knowledge and computation: the same concept is modeled once in a knowledge graph and once in a program, where the program entities can be connected with the knowledge graph using semantical lifting. A process is modeled as (a) a *trigger*, which is a domain description of entities where a process can start (e.g., cooking starts), and (b) a method, a program description of the effects of the process (cooking itself). An event handler is used to repeatedly query the program for triggered entities, on which the method is subsequently executed.

This is the first work on modeling and simulating a geological process by using semantic technologies and a programming language. We plan to extend this work to model more complex geological processes and apply this to other domains as a general method.

References

1. Arp, R., Smith, B., Spear, A.D.: Building Ontologies with Basic Formal Ontology. MIT Press, Cambridge (2015)
2. Bjørlykke, K.: Source rocks and petroleum geochemistry. In: Bjørlykke, K. (ed.) Petroleum Geoscience, pp. 361–372. Springer, Heidelberg (2015). https://doi.org/10.1007/978-3-642-34132-8_14
3. Kamburjan, E., Klungre, V.N., Schlatte, R., Johnsen, E.B., Giese, M.: Programming and debugging with semantically lifted states. In: ESWC, vol. 12731 (2021)
4. Ma, X.: Knowledge graph construction and application in geosciences: a review. Comput. Geosci. **161**, 105082 (2022)
5. Yu, I.C., et al.: Subsurface evaluation through multi-scenario reasoning. In: Patel, D. (ed.) Interactive Data Processing and 3D Visualization of the Solid Earth, pp. 325–355. Springer, Cham (2022). https://doi.org/10.1007/978-3-030-90716-7_10
6. Zamborlini, V.C., Guizzardi, G.: An ontologically-founded reification approach for representing temporally changing information in OWL. In: COMMONSENSE (2013)

A System for Repairing $\mathcal{EL}$ Ontologies Using Weakening and Completing

Ying Li[1,2] and Patrick Lambrix[1,2,3]

[1] Linköping University, Linköping, Sweden
patrick.lambrix@liu.se
[2] The Swedish e-Science Research Centre, Linköping, Sweden
[3] University of Gävle, Gävle, Sweden

Abstract. The quality of ontologies in terms of their correctness and completeness is crucial for developing high-quality ontology-based applications. Traditional debugging techniques repair ontologies by removing unwanted axioms, but may thereby remove consequences that are correct in the domain of the ontology. We propose an interactive approach to mitigate the negative effects of removing unwanted axioms for $\mathcal{EL}$ ontologies by axiom weakening and completing. This is the first approach that allows for different ways to combine removing, weakening and completing. The choice of combination strategy influences the amount of work for a domain expert as well as the completeness of the repaired ontology. In this paper we describe a system based on a repairing approach that allows for different such combinations (This is a companion paper to [3], a paper accepted at the main track of ESWC 2023, and presents one of the two systems proposed in [3].).

1 Introduction

Debugging ontologies aims to remove unwanted knowledge in the ontology. This can be knowledge that leads to logical problems such as inconsistency or incoherence (semantic defects) or statements that are not correct in the domain of the ontology (modeling defects) (e.g., [1]). The workflow consists of several steps including the detection and localization of the defects and the repairing [2]. In the classical approaches for debugging the end result is a set of axioms to remove from the ontology that is obtained after detection and localization, and the repairing consists solely of removing the suggested axioms. However, first, these approaches are usually purely logic-based and therefore may remove correct axioms (e.g., [4]). Therefore, it is argued that a domain expert should validate the results of such systems. Furthermore, removing an axiom may remove more knowledge than necessary. Correct knowledge that is derivable with the help of the wrong axioms may not be derivable in the new ontology.

In this paper, we discuss one of two implemented systems based on the approach in [3]. The system supports an interactive repairing approach using weakening and completing to mitigate the negative effects of removing unwanted

C. Pesquita et al. (Eds.): ESWC 2023, LNCS 13998, pp. 101–105, 2023.
https://doi.org/10.1007/978-3-031-43458-7_19

axioms in $\mathcal{EL}$ ontologies. For formal definitions, the underlying algorithms and experimental results, we refer to [3].

2 Repairing system

We implemented a Protégé plugin for repairing based on the Algorithm C9 in [3]. Using this algorithm the user can repair all unwanted axioms at once, or one at a time by iteratively invoking this plugin, thereby allowing for two of the possible choices presented in [3][1]. We use the Mini-GALEN ontology, visualized in Fig. 1a as a running example for the use of the system. After loading the target ontology into Protégé, starting the built-in reasoner and entering the wrong axiom(s) by selecting left/right-hand concepts from the list of concepts in the ontology (Fig. 1b), the user starts a repairing by weakening the wrong axioms first.

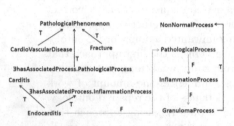

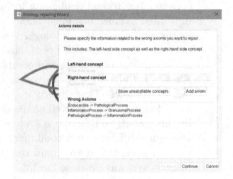

(a) The domain expert's knowledge about the subsumption axioms in the Mini-GALEN ontology is marked with T (true) or F (false) at the arrows.

(b) Input the whole wrong axioms set.

Fig. 1. Ontology and ontology repairing wizard.

Weakening aims to mitigate the effect of removing wrong axioms by replacing them with correct weaker axioms. This means that a wrong axiom $\alpha \sqsubseteq \beta$ would be replaced by a correct weaker axiom $sb \sqsubseteq sp$ such that sb is a sub-concept of α and sp is a super-concept of β. In the weakening step, the set of sub-concepts of α (sub) and the set of super-concepts of β (sup) are generated, thereby representing the possible choices for weaker axioms. The weaker axioms are visualized in two ways: (i) as a list of axioms and (ii) by the sub and sup sets. In the former case weakened axioms are chosen by clicking the *Validate relations*

---

[1] We also implemented a stand-alone system based on the $\mathcal{EL}$ version of the RepOSE system [5] where the user can choose different ways to combine removing, weakening, completing and updating strategies, thereby providing a choice in the trade-off between validation work and completeness of the repaired ontology. The systems are available at https://www.ida.liu.se/~patla00/publications/ESWC2023/ and a demo for the Protégé plugin is available at https://www.ida.liu.se/~patla00/publications/ESWC2023/Demo-video.mp4.

button, selecting the axioms in the list and clicking the *Validate* button. In the latter case the user can choose weakened axioms by clicking on a concept in the sub set and a concept in the sup set and validate the axiom by clicking the *Validate* button. The weakening step is finished by clicking the *Weakening done* button. The completion step is started using the *Continue* button.

Example. Figure 2a shows the sub and sup of the wrong axiom PathologicalProcess $\sqsubseteq$ InflammationProcess. The weaker axiom PathologicalProcess $\sqsubseteq$ NonNormalProcess is correct and can thus be selected by choosing the PathologicalProcess from sub and NonNormalProcess from sup (visualization) or by choosing from the axiom list as in Fig. 2b.

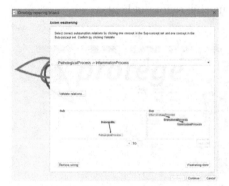 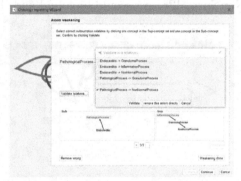

(a) Sub and sup of PathologicalProcess⊑InflammationProcess. (b) The candidate weaker axioms list of PathologicalProcess⊑InflammationProcess.

Fig. 2. Axiom weakening.

Completing aims to find correct axioms that are not derivable from the ontology yet and that would make a given axiom derivable. For the repairing, after a weakened axiom $\alpha \sqsubseteq \beta$ is validated, the completion step finds correct axioms $sp \sqsubseteq sb$ such that sp is a super-concept of α and sb is a sub-concept of β. If $sp \sqsubseteq sb$ is added to the ontology, then $\alpha \sqsubseteq \beta$ would be derivable. We compute two sets, source and target. These are similar to sup and sub, respectively, but exclude concepts that would introduce equivalence relations in the ontology. These sets represent the possible choices for completing axioms. These axioms are visualized in two ways: (i) as a list of axioms and (ii) by the source and target sets. In the former case completing axioms are chosen by clicking the *Validate relations* button, selecting the axioms in the list and clicking the *Validate* button. In the latter case the user can choose completing axioms by clicking on a concept in the source and a concept in the target and validate the axiom by clicking the *Validate* button. As adding completed axioms adds new knowledge to the ontology that was not earlier derivable, the system allows to find additional correct axioms by invoking the completion process again[2]. Clicking the < and > buttons allows to work on the completing for other axioms.

Example. After the weakening step, we obtained the weakened axioms set {PathologicalProcess ⊑ NonNormalProcess, InflammationProcess ⊑ NonNormalProcess}. Fig. 3a shows the source and target sets of InflammationProcess ⊑ NonNormalProcess. The axiom InflammationProcess ⊑ PathologicalProcess is a correct axiom and was not derivable from the ontology yet. Adding this axiom (by using the visualization or by using the axiom list) makes the ontology more complete. Similar operations can be performed for the other axiom in the weakened axiom set. In this case no stronger axiom than PathologicalProcess ⊑ NonNormalProcess would be found and thus this axiom is kept as is.

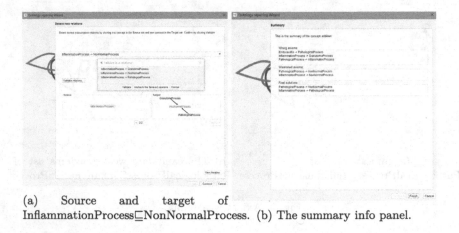

(a) Source and target of InflammationProcess⊑NonNormalProcess. (b) The summary info panel.

Fig. 3. Completing axioms and repairing process summary.

When all the desired axioms are added, clicking the *Finish* button closes this wizard and the new ontology is updated automatically. A summary panel is shown (Fig. 3b), displaying the original wrong axioms, the computed weakened axioms and the completing axioms. The final ontology is created by removing the wrong axioms and adding the completing axioms. The weakened axioms will be derivable from the final ontology.

3 Conclusion

In this paper, we introduced a tool for repairing wrong axioms in an ontology, which uses an interactive way that contains the removing, weakening and completing operations to preserve as much correct knowledge as possible to mitigate

---

[2] The possibility of multiple iterations of the completing phase is an extension of the method in [3]. This can be done by clicking the *Next iteration* button.

the influence of removing wrong axioms. To our knowledge it is the first system that combines all these operations. In the demonstration we show a repairing session for parts of the experiments in [3].

References

1. Kalyanpur, A., et al.: Debugging unsatisfiable classes in OWL ontologies. J. Web Semant. **3**(4), 268–293 (2005)
2. Lambrix, P.: Completing and debugging ontologies: state of the art and challenges in repairing ontologies. J. Data Inf. Q. (2023)
3. Li, Y., Lambrix, P.: Repairing $\mathcal{EL}$ ontologies using weakening and completing. In: Pesquita, C., et al. (eds.) ESWC 2023. LNCS, vol. 13870, pp. 298–315. Springer, Cham (2023). https://doi.org/10.1007/978-3-031-33455-9_18
4. Pesquita, C., et al.: To repair or not to repair: reconciling correctness and coherence in ontology reference alignments. In: 8th Ontology Matching, pp. 13–24 (2013)
5. Wei-Kleiner, F., Dragisic, Z., Lambrix, P.: Abduction framework for repairing incomplete $\mathcal{EL}$ ontologies: complexity results and algorithms. In: AAAI, pp. 1120–1127 (2014)

A User Interface Model for Digital Humanities Research: Case BookSampo – Finnish Fiction Literature on the Semantic Web

Annastiina Ahola[1]([⊠]) [iD], Eero Hyvönen[1,2]([⊠]) [iD], and Heikki Rantala[1]([⊠]) [iD]

[1] Semantic Computing Research Group (SeCo), Aalto University, Espoo, Finland
[2] Helsinki Centre for Digital Humanities (HELDIG), University of Helsinki, Helsinki, Finland
{annastiina.ahola,eero.hyvonen,heikki.rantala}@aalto.fi
https://seco.cs.aalto.fi

Abstract. This paper presents the implementation of a new user interface (UI) for the Finnish fiction literature BOOKSAMPO knowledge graph. The UI utilizes possibilities of semantic web technologies to provide the end-user an enhanced search and browsing experience through faceted search and data-analytical tools for Digital Humanities research.

Keywords: Digital Libraries · Linked Data · User Interfaces · Portals

1 Introduction

BOOKSAMPO[1] is a semantic portal containing information on virtually all Finnish fiction literature. The portal makes use of the BOOKSAMPO knowledge graph (KG) consisting of Linked Data (LD) descriptions of literary works and other objects related to those works, e.g., authors and covers, that have been systemically recorded for works in Finnish libraries since 1997 [6]. While the usage of LD for library collections is not new [1], the BOOKSAMPO KG is a uniquely rich fiction literature dataset on an international scale that offers countless possibilities for data analysis and literary research.

The currently available BOOKSAMPO PORTAL was published in 2011. It is part of the series of *Sampo portals*[2] based on the "Sampo Model" for LD publishing [3]. The six principles of the Sampo Model are listed in Table 1. The currently available portal's user interface (UI) was built with Drupal, and the portal offers a text-based search engine for searching and exploring the underlying KG. While the search engine makes use of links between records, the full potential of what LD could offer for digital libraries is not realized in the portal. The reliance on a single text-based search field limits the user's ability to place

---

[1] See project research homepage at: https://seco.cs.aalto.fi/applications/kirjasampo/.
[2] See the homepage of Sampo portals at: https://seco.cs.aalto.fi/applications/sampo/.

C. Pesquita et al. (Eds.): ESWC 2023, LNCS 13998, pp. 106–111, 2023.
https://doi.org/10.1007/978-3-031-43458-7_20

Table 1. Sampo Model Principles P1–P6

P1	Support collaborative data creation and publishing
P2	Use a shared open ontology infrastructure
P3	Make clear distinction between the LOD service and the user interface (UI)
P4	Provide multiple perspectives to the same data
P5	Standardize portal usage by a simple filter-analyze two-step cycle
P6	Support data analysis and knowledge discovery in addition to data exploration

exact filters on the results. A single filter (e.g., setting) can be made more exact by clicking on the property value links in the information pages of the works, but placing multiple different filters (e.g., setting *and* genre of a work) requires relying on just the text-based search for the additional filters. The user interface also lacks meaningful ways of analyzing the returned results, limiting the use of the portal for research purposes, even though the BOOKSAMPO KG data behind it has immense potential for literary digital humanities (DH) research.

As a part of a project revisiting the BOOKSAMPO KG in 2022, a new semantic UI based on integrated data analytic tools and faceted search was developed for the BOOKSAMPO KG. The new portal makes it possible for users to browse and filter the results in a more effective way that was not possible with the previous user interface, and provides easy ways of visualizing and studying the data in different ways, using, e.g., charts, timelines, and maps. This paper presents this new UI developed using the Sampo-UI Framework[3] [5] based on the Sampo Model.

2   BookSampo Knowledge Graph

The original BOOKSAMPO PORTAL[4] deployed in 2011 was developed as a part of the national FinnONTO research initiative (2003–2012) [2]. The portal has then been maintained by the Finnish Public Libraries[5] and had more than 1.1 million distinct visitors in 2021[6]. The original data came from legacy library databases that were harmonized and transformed into RDF format. After this, the librarians have maintained and enriched the data [7] by themselves. The original transformed dataset contained more than 3 million triples with around 90 000 new triples being added monthly. Today the KG consists of nearly 9 million triples with over 210 000 abstract literary works and nearly 220 000 publications.

---

[3] See code and documentation at: https://github.com/SemanticComputing/sampo-ui.
[4] Available at: http://kirjasampo.fi.
[5] https://kirjastot.fi.
[6] Statistics (in Finnish) available at: https://www.kirjasampo.fi/fi/kirjasammon-tilastot-2021.

3   Using the New User Interface for the BookSampo KG

Based on the Sampo-UI framework, the landing page of the portal contains *application perspectives* through which instances of the major classes of the underlying KG can be searched. In this case, there are five perspectives: Three of them deal directly with literary works—*novels, nonfiction books*, and *publications*—and the other two deal with *people* (e.g., authors and translators) and *covers*. The novels and nonfiction books perspectives contain information about those books on the *abstract work level* while the publications perspective has information on all works on the *physical work level* following the conceptual distinction made in the original data [7].

Clicking on an application perspective card on the landing page opens up a faceted search view of the perspective. The user can then use the available facets to filter the results to match specific criteria or explore the result set as a whole. The perspectives offer various tabs for visualizing the result set in different forms, e.g., as a traditional table, on maps, on a time line, and using pie and other charts. Detailed information on individual result entities can be seen on their *instance pages*.

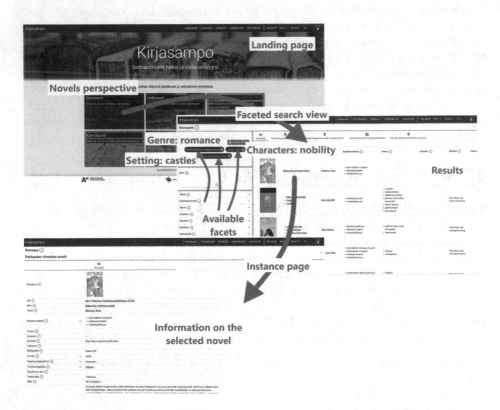

Fig. 1. An example use case of the portal: Finding a novel fulfilling criteria.

Figure 1 illustrates an example use case of the portal where the user wants to find novels that match specific criteria. The user first chooses the novels perspective and then makes selections on three facets: genre=*romance novels*, setting=*castles* and characters=*nobility*. The end results and facet hit counts are automatically updated after the user makes a choice. The user can finally choose a novel that looks appealing and open its instance page to see aggregated information regarding the novel.

Figure 2 illustrates another use case. Here the user has chosen the publications perspective willing to analyze the evolution of novel themes in time. The user has made facet selections publications=*original*, i.e., not translations, type=*novels*, and language=*Finnish*. The visualization tab of *Annual themes and keywords* consists of two parts: The upper part shows the number of publications per the top 10 themes throughout the years. The lower visualization has the same idea but for keywords, which are used in the BOOKSAMPO KG to supplement themes when no appropriate theme entity is found for a novel.

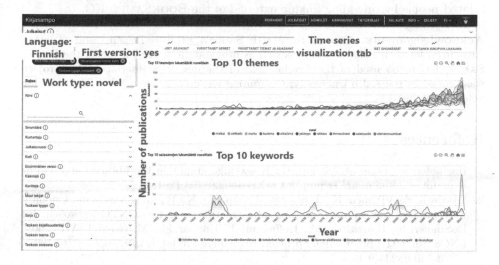

Fig. 2. A time series visualization of the top 10 themes and keywords.

Using BOOKSAMPO is demonstrated in more detail in this online video[7].

4   Discussion and Future Work

The presented UI utilizes the possibilities of semantic web technologies to enhance the search, browsing, and data analysis experience for the end-user. The faceted search make it possible to perform intricate searches without the users having to familiarize themselves with the underlying data model in the

---

[7] Demo video available at: https://vimeo.com/805561697.

BOOKSAMPO KG nor having to learn to write queries in SPARQL. The integrated visualizations then offer ways of easily visualizing and analyzing those results. This opens up the possibility of humanities researchers with less technical skills using the BOOKSAMPO KG data for research through the portal or as a stepping stone towards more in-depth research carried out by querying the KG directly.

Our end-goal is to publish this new UI alongside the original portal. This requires some cleaning of the underlying KG, which is already underway. Making the portal available for public use opens up the possibility of gathering feedback from end-users on how the portal and its functionalities can be improved or changed to better accommodate the end-users' needs. We also plan to publish the KG openly for data analytic research.

The underlying KG could also be enriched with data from other KGs in the Cultural Heritage (CH) domain, such as the BIOGRAPHYSAMPO KG [4], which already contains over 700 links to people (e.g., authors) in the BOOKSAMPO KG. This would allow the users to better explore the world of Finnish literature and related people by providing linking external of the BOOKSAMPO KG.

Acknowledgements. Thanks to Matti Sarmela, Kaisa Hypén, and Tuomas Aitonurmi for their collaborations as well as providing a newer version of the BOOK-SAMPO KG to be used in the development of the new user interface. This project was funded by the Aalto University; Computing resources of the CSC – IT Center for Science were used.

References

1. Haslhofer, B., Isaac, A., Simon, R.: Knowledge graphs in the libraries and digital humanities domain. arXiv preprint arXiv:1803.03198 (2018)
2. Hyvönen, E., Viljanen, K., Tuominen, J., Seppälä, K.: Building a national semantic web ontology and ontology service infrastructure –the FinnONTO approach. In: Bechhofer, S., Hauswirth, M., Hoffmann, J., Koubarakis, M. (eds.) ESWC 2008. LNCS, vol. 5021, pp. 95–109. Springer, Heidelberg (2008). https://doi.org/10.1007/978-3-540-68234-9_10
3. Hyvönen, E.: Digital humanities on the semantic web: sampo model and portal series. semantic web - interoperability, usability, applicability (2022). http://semantic-web-journal.org/content/digital-humanities-semantic-web-sampo-model-and-portal-series accepted
4. Hyvönen, E., et al.: BiographySampo – publishing and enriching biographies on the semantic web for digital humanities research. In: Hitzler, P., et al. (eds.) ESWC 2019. LNCS, vol. 11503, pp. 574–589. Springer, Cham (2019). https://doi.org/10.1007/978-3-030-21348-0_37
5. Ikkala, E., Hyvönen, E., Rantala, H., Koho, M.: Sampo-UI: A Full Stack JavaScript Framework for Developing Semantic Portal User Interfaces. Semantic web - interoperability, usability, applicability **13**(1), 69–84 (2022). https://doi.org/10.3233/SW-210428

6. Mäkelä, E., Hypén, K., Hyvönen, E.: BookSampo—lessons learned in creating a semantic portal for fiction literature. In: Aroyo, L., et al. (eds.) ISWC 2011. LNCS, vol. 7032, pp. 173–188. Springer, Heidelberg (2011). https://doi.org/10.1007/978-3-642-25093-4_12
7. Mäkelä, E., Hypén, K., Hyvönen, E.: Fiction literature as linked open data - the BookSampo dataset (2013). https://doi.org/10.3233/SW-120093

Modeling Grammars with Knowledge Representation Methods: Subcategorization as a Test Case

Raúl Aranovich$^{(\boxtimes)}$ ⓘD

University of California Davis, One Shields Avenue, Davis, CA 95616, USA
raranovich@ucdavis.edu

Abstract. An OWL ontology is used to model a grammar that accounts for subcategorization, showing that ontologies are able to generate (mildly) context-sensitive languages. Semantic Web knowledge representation methods offer a useful way to model the implicit knowledge that defines human linguistic abilities. When a grammar is modeled as a set of ontological constraints (i.e. classes with restrictions on their properties), ungrammatical sentences are defined as facts that lead to inconsistencies which can be discovered by a reasoner. Property chains are used to "pass on" the category of a syntactic complement as the value of a head's subcategorization feature, modeling the concept of structure sharing that is central to constraint-based theories of syntax like HPSG. By treating utterances as instances and syntactic constraints as axioms, this approach offers points of contact with efforts to model grammars as Linguistic Linked Open Data in the Semantic Web.

Keywords: Syntax · Subcategorization · Property Chain

1 Introduction

In this paper I will argue that knowledge graphs built with RDF/OWL offer sufficient resources to model a grammar whose strong generative power goes beyond that of context-free grammars. I will focus on the problem of subcategorization in natural languages [1]. This approach points to the usefulness of formal knowledge representation methods for modeling the implicit human knowledge about natural language grammars, and as a testbed for theories of syntax.

Ontologies represent knowledge as a hierarchy of concepts and instances interconnected by relations. Declarative languages like RDF and OWL [2] allow for consistency checks on ontologies by modeling complex logical aspects of knowledge representation, and for the extraction of inferred knowledge. Applications of OWL ontologies to linguistics exists mostly for practical purposes (e.g. domain-specific terminologies, automatic population of ontologies from text), but they can also serve as a tool for theoretical research [3, 4]. More specifically, I am interested in showing that the declarative approach to knowledge representation behind RDF graphs and OWL ontologies provides a fruitful framework to formalize constraint-based approaches to syntax, and to

© The Author(s), under exclusive license to Springer Nature Switzerland AG 2023
C. Pesquita et al. (Eds.): ESWC 2023, LNCS 13998, pp. 112–116, 2023.
https://doi.org/10.1007/978-3-031-43458-7_21

discuss the formal complexity of such grammars. The main insight of this paper is that, when a grammar is modeled as a set of ontological restrictions on admissible structures, ungrammatical sentences can be formalized as sets of syntactic assertions that are in contradiction with the rest of the ontology. By modeling sentence structures as instances, then, syntactic theories can be tested by reasoning over them, since only grammatical sentences will be consistent with the rest of the ontology.

2   Knowledge Representation and Constraint-Based Syntax

Following work in constraint-based theories of syntax [5–7], I model syntactic categories as classes, and the immediate constituency relations that build phrase structure as relations. A :headDtr relation with domain :Phrase and range :Word, for instance, describes the relation between a phrase and its head, as follows:

```
:Phrase a owl:Class .
:Word a owl:Class ;
    owl:disjointWith :Phrase .
:headDtr a owl:ObjectProperty ;
    rdfs:domain :Phrase ;
    rdfs:range :Word .
```

Likewise, complements are modeled with the object property :compDtr. The grammar includes subclasses of words (e.g. :Noun, :Verb) as well as the corresponding subclasses of phrases (:NounPhrase, :VerbPhrase, etc.). Local constraints on constituency, like the fact that a (transitive) verb phrase is headed by a verb, and has a noun phrase for a complement, are modeled as restrictions.

```
:Verb a owl:Class ;
  rdfs:subClassOf :Word .
:VerbPhrase a owl:Class ;
  rdfs:subClassOf :Phrase ;
  owl:equivalentClass [
    owl:intersectionOf ( [
      a owl:Restriction ;
      owl:onProperty :headDtr ;
      owl:someValuesFrom :Verb ] [
        a owl:Restriction ;
        owl:onProperty :compDtr ;
        owl:someValuesFrom :NounPhrase ] ) ] .
```

A grammar, then, is made of classes representing categories (phrasal or lexical). Well-formedness condition on syntactic structure are represented as restrictions. The actual syntactic structures generated by the grammar are instances of its classes and object properties. Take a sentence like (1), for example:

(1) Pan mocked Hook.

The verb *mocked* and its object form a constituent, which is an instance of the class :VerbPhrase. *Mocked* is also an instance, in a :headDtr relation with the mother node, while :Hook is its :compDtr.[1]

```
:Mocked a owl:NamedIndividual , :Verb .
:Hook a owl:NamedIndividual , :NounPhrase .
:Mocked_Hook a owl:NamedIndividual , :VerbPhrase ;
   :headDtr :Mocked ;
   :compDtr :Hook .
```

3 Subcategorization and Structure Sharing in OWL

Adding these assertions to the ontology will not lead to contradiction, since they follow from the class axioms. But the ontology is not yet powerful enough to rule out an ungrammatical sentence like (2) where a verb like *listen* is followed by an NP, not a PP:

(2) Pan listened *(to) Wendy.

A first step is to subcategorize verbs according to the class of their complements, with a property :complement with domain :Word and range :Phrase. The :Verb subclass :TransitiveVerb would be restricted so that the value of its :complement relation had to be an NP.[2] Likewise, :PrepositionalVerb subcategorizes for a PP. The second step is to come up with an implementation that will define the value of :compDtr to match the restriction on the verb. One way to achieve that is to define the relation :complement as a **property chain**, so that the instance that occurs as the syntactic complement in the VP is passed on to the verb's :complement value. The chain links the inverse of the :headDtr relation (getting to the mother VP from the V) and the :compDtr relation (getting from the VP to the complement NP).

```
:complement owl:propertyChainAxiom (
      [ owl:inverseOf :headDtr ]  :compDtr )
```

---

[1] As instances, constituents need to be given unique identifiers, like "Mocked_Hook", and not generic class names like VP.

[2] This is similar to the use of syntactic frames in LexInfo [8].

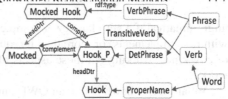

This is how the notion of **structure-sharing**, central to constraint-based theories like HPSG, can be implemented in OWL. If a sentence has a syntactic VP complement that does not match the restriction on the verb's subclass, as in (2), then the ontology becomes inconsistent. This result has been confirmed in an ontology designed with the help of the Protégé editor (Fig. 1).[3]

Fig. 1. Ontology schematic for "mocked Hook"

4 Consequences and Conclusions

Syntactic theory has an important role to play in the development of the Semantic Web. Automatic sentence parsing, for instance, is a component of systems that allow users to access semantic content through natural language queries, which must be converted into formal SPARQL queries [9]. But these approaches use syntactic tools that are external to the ontology itself, and are usually procedural. My proposal, by contrast, develops a declarative approach to sentence structure which is built using native OWL constructs, and is formalized as an ontology.

Moreover, there are ontologies of linguistics (e.g. GOLD [10], LexInfo [8]), but the purpose of these is mainly to define the concepts that linguists use in their discipline, with the associated terminology, rather than as a generative model (i.e. a system that defines the set of grammatical sentences of a language with their associated structures). Here is where an important ontological difference with the current proposal stems from. While models like GOLD or LexInfo treat parts of speech and other linguistic categories as instances, I treat them as classes. In my system, the only instances are concrete utterances, with their latent structure.[4] That is because my goal is to formalize the *implicit* knowledge that a speaker has of their language (the Chomskyan notion of *competence*, if you may), while other ontologies formalize the *explicit* knowledge that a linguist has about their discipline. To the extent that I use that explicit knowledge to model the implicit knowledge, there should be a point of contact between the approaches.

The approach sketched here is not intended to compete with statistical models of language in terms of scale and empirical coverage. Rather, it offers a method to model the constructs that syntactic theory has proposed to account for sentence structure. There are two directions in which this method can be extended. First, there are other verb classes besides transitive verbs that should be modeled with similar tools: intransitives (*glitter*, *work*), ditransitives (*give*, *tell*), prepositional (*rely on*), verbs with sentential complements (*hope*, *think*), etc. Each of these classes is defined by a different restriction. Second, there are different contexts in which a verb may or may not appear (including verbs with variable behavior). In this paper I have dealt with the problem of a verb with a complement of the wrong class (a PP instead of an NP). But a sentence may also be

---

[3] https://github.com/RaulAranovich/OnSyDE/blob/main/OnSyDE.owl.

[4] My treatment of individual utterances as instances is similar to efforts to serialize syntactically-annotated corpora as RDF documents, sharable as Linguistic Linked Data [11, 12].

ungrammatical if a verb has fewer complements than it requires (e.g. a transitive verb with no complements) or more than it requires (an intransitive verb with a complement of any kind). Working out those aspects of the problem should be the matter of future work.

What I have shown is that an OWL ontology can be used to model a grammar that goes beyond simple context free generation to account for strict subcategorization. This result is important, in that it shows that ontologies can be used to generate context-sensitive languages. The knowledge representation methods that have been developed for the Semantic Web may prove to be a useful tool to model syntactic competence, understood as the implicit knowledge that defines the human linguistic abilities.

References

1. Joshi, A.K., Shanker, K.V., Weir, D.: The Convergence of Mildly Context-Sensitive Grammar Formalisms. University of Pennsylvania Department of Computer and Information Science Technical Report No. MS-CIS-90-01 (1990)
2. Hitzler, P.: A review of the semantic web field. Commun. ACM **64**(2), 76–83 (2021)
3. Cimiano, P., Unger, C., McCrae, J.: Ontology-Based Interpretation of Natural Language. Morgan & Claypool, San Rafael (2014)
4. Schalley, A.C.: Ontologies and ontological methods in linguistics. Lang. Linguist. Compass **13**(11) (2019). https://doi.org/10.1111/lnc3.12356
5. Pollard, C., Sag, I.: Head-Driven Phrase Structure Grammar. University of Chicago Press, Chicago (1994)
6. Copestake, A.: Implementing Typed Feature Structure Grammars. CSLI Publications, Stanford (2002)
7. Francez, N., Wintner, S.: Unification Grammars. Cambridge University Press, Cambridge (2012)
8. Cimiano, P., Buitelaar, P., McCrae, J., Sintek, M.: LexInfo: a declarative model for the lexicon-ontology interface. J. Web Semant. Sci. Serv. Agents World Wide Web **9**(1), 29–51 (2011)
9. Unger, C., Cimiano, P.: Pythia: compositional meaning construction for ontology-based question answering on the semantic web. In: Muñoz, R., Montoyo, A., Métais, E. (eds.) NLDB 2011. LNCS, vol. 6716, pp. 153–160. Springer, Heidelberg (2011). https://doi.org/10.1007/978-3-642-22327-3_15
10. Farrar, S., Lewis, W.D.: The GOLD community of practice: an infrastructure for linguistic data on the web. Lang. Resour. Eval. **41**(1), 45–60 (2007)
11. Chiarcos, C., Glaser, L.: A tree extension for CoNLL-RDF. In: Proceedings of the 12th Conference on Language Resources and Evaluation, pp. 7161–7169. ELRA (2020)
12. Chiarcos, C.: POWLA: modeling linguistic corpora in OWL/DL. In: 9th Extended Semantic Web Conference, Heraklion, pp. 225–239 (2012)

TRIC: A Triples Corrupter for Knowledge Graphs

Asara Senaratne[✉], Pouya Ghiasnezhad Omran, Peter Christen,
and Graham Williams

School of Computing, The Australian National University, Canberra, Australia
{asara.senaratne,p.g.omran,peter.christen,graham.williams}@anu.edu.au

Abstract. We study the problem of corrupting triples in Knowledge
Graphs (KG) for the purpose of assisting anomaly detection and error
detection techniques developed for KG quality enhancement. Our goal is
to provide users with the highest possible level of control over the triples
corruption process, and simultaneously develop a solution that scales to
large KGs. Hence, we introduce TRIC, an approach for corrupting triples
considering both semantic and type information to generate errors in a
KG. In this paper, we discuss how the problem of triples corruption
is challenging, and different from existing negative sampling techniques
used in link prediction. To the best of our knowledge, there is no approach
in the literature dedicated for generating abnormal triples in KGs to
support anomaly detection and error detection tasks.

Keywords: Anomalous triples · Erroneous triples · Knowledge Graph
quality enhancement · Negative sampling

1 Introduction

Large scale Knowledge Graphs (KG) such as YAGO, DBpedia, and Wikidata are
published and widely used at present. However, these KGs are far from perfect
and have many quality issues. For example, these KGs may contain inaccurate,
or abnormal triples which limit the credibility and further utility of the KGs [8].
The domain of data quality assessment in the field of traditional relational data
roots in the literature, and has recently attracted experts from the domain of
knowledge representation. Inspired by our recent work in anomaly detection [4,
5], we consider the problem of empirically evaluating anomaly detection and
error detection algorithms developed for quality enhancement of KGs, in the
absence of labelled data.

The essence of this study is the absence of a standardized technique to
systematically corrupt triples in a KG considering both semantics and entity
types of triples. As none of the real-world KGs contain labelled data (ground
truth data), developers of existing KG quality enhancement techniques adopt
impromptu means of corrupting triples for their evaluation purposes [1]. This
further demotivates the development of unsupervised and human-independent

C. Pesquita et al. (Eds.): ESWC 2023, LNCS 13998, pp. 117–122, 2023.
https://doi.org/10.1007/978-3-031-43458-7_22

approaches for anomaly and error detection in KGs. As a result, many of the existing KG error detection techniques depend on external sources to validate their proposed approaches during experimental evaluation [6]. However, this is a costly process, and not every KG has a gold standard [2].

To overcome the stated problem, we introduce a triples corrupter for knowledge graphs (TRIC). It is unsupervised, and can introduce a wide range of errors (inaccurate, unusual, contradicting, invalid, redundant triples, and data quality errors) in a KG by corrupting either of subject, predicate, or object, whilst considering type and semantic information. This is in contrast to negative sampling, where negative triples are generated by corrupting a known positive triple by replacing either subject, predicate, or object. TRIC introduces different types of errors by corrupting a set of randomly chosen triples in a KG, where it can corrupt both entity-based and literal-based triples. Furthermore, TRIC allows the user to have complete control over the triples corruption process. While TRIC operates on a default setting, if required, a user can determine the types of errors to be introduced, the percentage of errors from each error type to be introduced, and the overall percentage of triples to be corrupted such that the KG has 10%, 20%, and so on of its triples corrupted.

Our Contribution: We introduce TRIC, a pioneer in generating errors in a KG to support anomaly and error detection techniques. The novelty of TRIC is its ability to corrupt both entity-based and literal-based triples by considering the semantics, data types, and entity types of the associated relations, literals, and entities, respectively. TRIC is automated, and requires no user assistance. Furthermore, the corruptions of TRIC will introduce inaccurate, unusual, contradicting, invalid, redundant triples, and data quality errors in a KG.

2   Related Work

There are many techniques proposed in the literature for KG evaluation. One common evaluation strategy is to use a partial gold standard. In this methodology, a subset of graph entities or relations are selected and labeled manually. Another evaluation strategy is to use the given KG itself as a test dataset, which is known as silver standard evaluation. For retrospective evaluations, the output of a given approach is given to human judges for annotation, who then label identified errors as correct or incorrect [2]. While it is costly and time consuming to perform manual evaluation involving human experts, obtaining a gold standard KG for every KG is infeasible. Hence, most existing KG evaluation approaches depend on silver standard evaluation, where the developers of these these techniques synthetically generate errors. Negative sampling is one such technique used to introduce corrupted triples [2].

Negative sampling techniques [7] generate negative triples by corrupting a known positive triple $(s, p, o) \in G$ by replacing either s, p, or o. Usually, the corruption of relations (predicate) is omitted as the evaluation of KG embedding models on the link prediction task only considers the suitability of head (subject) prediction and tail (object) prediction, but not relation (predicate) prediction. Due to the simplicity in thus generated corrupted triples (as this approach has no specific interest in corrupting the semantics nor the data types of literals), and given that real-world errors and anomalies in KGs are much complex [5], there exists the requirement of a triples corruption approach dedicated for the evaluation of anomaly detection and error detection techniques developed for KGs.

3 Methodology

Even though large scale KGs such as YAGO-4 contains semantic constraints in the form of SHACL to keep data clean [3], such a validation layer is not often available in custom built KGs. Hence, during the designing process of TRIC, we considered all possible quality issues that can exist in such real-world KGs, where there is no adoption of constraints such as SHACL or ShEx.

We consider a directed edge-labelled KG, $G = (V, E)$ containing a set of nodes (or vertices) V, and a set of labelled edges E connecting these vertices. Each edge $e \in E$, together with the connecting nodes are considered as a triple t. A triple (also named as a triplet) contains the three elements subject (head) $s \in S$, predicate (relation) $p \in P$, and object (tail) $o \in O$. A triple t is denoted as (s, p, o), where $(s, o) \in V$. While a subject $s \in t$ is considered as a real-world entity, an object $o \in t$ can either be an entity n, or a literal l (an entity's attribute value) [5]. We refer triples of the form (s, p, n) as entity-based triples, and (s, p, l) as literal-based triples.

Table 1 provides the fifteen types of errors TRIC can generate considering both (s, p, n) and (s, p, l) triples. Furthermore, algorithm 1 provides the pseudocode of TRIC under the default setting (assuming there are no user inputs). To replace an element of t, TRIC extracts the new content within the KG itself. While TRIC randomly selects the triples for corruption based on the percentage of errors required, the entities and predicates to use as replacements are also selected randomly after analyzing the type information associated with the entities. We obtain entity type information via inferencing. Implementation of TRIC is available on our GitHub repository[1].

---

[1] https://github.com/AsaraSenaratne/SEKA.

Table 1. Types of errors TRIC can generate in a KG.

Error Types	Original Triple/Status	Corrupted/New Triple
(1) Change *s* while preserving entity type.	\<personA, isMarriedTo, personB\>	\<personC, isMarriedTo, personB\>
(2) Change *o* while preserving the entity type	\<personA, isMarriedTo, personB\>	\<personA, isMarriedTo, personD\>
(3) Change *p* while preserving the predicate type	\<personA, isMarriedTo, personB\>	\<personA, hasChild, personB\>
(4) Change both (*s, o*) while preserving the entity types.	\<personA, isMarriedTo, personB\>	\<personE, isMarriedTo, personF\>
(5) Change *s* while also changing the entity type.	\<personA, isMarriedTo, personB\>	\<moon, isMarriedTo, personB\>
(6) Change *o* while also changing the entity type.	\<personA, isMarriedTo, personB\>	\<personA, isMarriedTo, london\>
(7) Change both (*s, o*) while also changing their entity types.	\<personA, isMarriedTo, personB\>	\<moon, isMarriedTo, london\>
(8) Change *p* while also changing its semantic meaning. That is replace predicates used for a person with a predicate that is not used for a person.	\<personA, isMarriedTo, personB\>	\<personA, livesIn, personB\>
(9) Add an edge between two entities, such that there is a type inconsistency in the predicate introduced.	The entities *personP* and *personQ* have no relationship	\<personP, produced, personQ\>
(10) Add an edge between two entities, such that there is no type inconsistency in the predicate introduced.	The entities *personP* and *personQ* have no relationship	\<personP, hasChild, personQ\>
(11) Introduce semantically incorrect literals to entities.	Add *DateOfBirth* to a *location* entity	\<london, hasDateOfBirth, "10/10/1990" \>
(12) Introduce semantically correct literals to entities (avoiding duplicates).	Add *hasWebsite* to a *person*	\<personA, hasWebsite, "www.a.com"
(13) Corrupt *t* such that the literal value changes to a value of a different data type.	A date gets changed to a name.	\<personA, hasDateOfBirth, "Sarah"\>
(14) Corrupt *t* by removing the literal value, thus generating a triple with a missing literal.	\<personA, hasDateOfBirth, "12/02/1989"\>	\<personA, hasDateOfBirth, ""\>
(15) Corrupt *t* such that the new literal value is a duplicate of an existing literal value of the same entity under consideration.	\<personA, hasDateOfBirth, "12/02/1989"\>	\<personA, hasDateOfBirth, "12/02/1989"\>

ALGORITHM 1: Error generation steps of TRIC.

Input: G: The KG to be subjected for triples corruption.
Output: $\mathbf{G}_c$: The KG with corrupted triples.

//If no user input, default percentage of errors is 1%
1: $p \leftarrow defineAnomalyPercentage()$
   //Get total number of triples in G.
2: $sizeG \leftarrow getSize(G)$
   //Find count of errors required from the percentage
3: $errorscount \leftarrow sizeG * p$
   //Number of errors required from each error type (from 15 error types)
4: $errorseach \leftarrow round(errorscount/15)$
   //Select the triples to corrupt
5: $triplestocorrupt \leftarrow getTriplesRandomly(G)$
   //Remove triples to corrupt from G
6: $reducedG = \mathbf{G}_c \leftarrow removeTriples(G, triplestocorrupt)$
   //Iterate over the types of errors TRIC can generate
7: **for** $error$ in $errortypes$:
8:     $count = 0$
       //Iterate to generate specified number of errors from each error type.
9:     **while** $count <=$ errorseach:
          //Add corrupted triples to graph
10:        $\mathbf{G}_c+ = generateErrors(error, reducedG, triplestocorrupt)$
          //Increment count
11:        $count + +$
12: **return** $\mathbf{G}_c$

---

4   Conclusion and Future Work

In this paper, we introduced TRIC, a triples corrupter for Knowledge Graphs
(KG) that is aimed at supporting the KG quality enhancement tasks; anomaly
detection and error detection. Even though there exists negative sampling techniques dedicated for link prediction, the triples corrupted via negative sampling
cannot fully exercise the capabilities of anomaly and error detection approaches,
as negative sampling does not consider semantic and type information of the
predicates, literals, and entities. As future work, we aim to publish TRIC as a
Python library for the use of the wider research community.

References

1. Jia, S., Xiang, Y., Chen, X., Wang, K.: Triple trustworthiness measurement for
   knowledge graph. In: The World Wide Web Conference, pp. 2865–2871 (2019)
2. Paulheim, H.: Knowledge graph refinement: a survey of approaches and evaluation
   methods. Semant. Web **8**(3), 489–508 (2017)

122   A. Senaratne et al.

3. Pellissier Tanon, T., Weikum, G., Suchanek, F.: YAGO 4: a reason-able knowl-edge base. In: Harth, A., et al. (eds.) ESWC 2020. LNCS, vol. 12123, pp. 583–596. Springer, Cham (2020). https://doi.org/10.1007/978-3-030-49461-2_34
4. Senaratne, A., Christen, P., Williams, G., Omran, P.G.: Unsupervised identification of abnormal nodes and edges in graphs. JDIQ **15**(1), 1–37 (2022)
5. Senaratne, A., Omran, P.G., Williams, G., Christen, P.: Unsupervised anomaly detection in knowledge graphs. In: IJCKG, pp. 161–165 (2021)
6. Wang, Y., Ma, F., Gao, J.: Efficient knowledge graph validation via cross-graph representation learning, pp. 1595–1604. ACM, New York (2020)
7. Xie, R., Liu, Z., Lin, F., Lin, L.: Does william shakespeare really write hamlet? knowledge representation learning with confidence. In: AAAI, vol. 32 (2018)
8. Xue, B., Zou, L.: Knowledge graph quality management: a comprehensive survey. In: TKDE (2022)

ExeKGLib: Knowledge Graphs-Empowered Machine Learning Analytics

Antonis Klironomos[1,2]([✉]), Baifan Zhou[3], Zhipeng Tan[1,4], Zhuoxun Zheng[1,5], Gad-Elrab Mohamed[1], Heiko Paulheim[2], and Evgeny Kharlamov[1,3]

[1] Bosch Center for Artificial Intelligence, Renningen, Germany
`antonis.klironomos@de.bosch.com`
[2] University of Mannheim, Mannheim, Germany
[3] University of Oslo, Oslo, Norway
[4] RWTH Aachen, Aachen, Germany
[5] Oslo Metropolitan University, Oslo, Norway

Abstract. Many machine learning (ML) libraries are accessible online for ML practitioners. Typical ML pipelines are complex and consist of a series of steps, each of them invoking several ML libraries. In this demo paper, we present `ExeKGLib`, a Python library that allows users with coding skills and minimal ML knowledge to build ML pipelines. `ExeKGLib` relies on knowledge graphs to improve the transparency and reusability of the built ML workflows, and to ensure that they are executable. We demonstrate the usage of `ExeKGLib` and compare it with conventional ML code to show `ExeKGLib`'s benefits.

Keywords: Machine learning · Knowledge graphs · Python library

1 Introduction

Due to the significant advancements in the realm of computer science, particularly in the field of machine learning (ML), there is a plethora of ML algorithms and corresponding libraries publicly accessible [2,3,9,10]. The use of ML is steadily rising in both academic and industrial settings [11]. Experts in various domains are also learning ML for the sake of applying it to solve domain-specific challenges, e.g. biologists [5,7], oncologists [1,6], and engineers in the industry [4,8,12]. The development of functional and useful ML workflows can be complex and time-consuming, which can pose a barrier for non-ML experts. Thus, there is a need for a user-friendly approach that neither requires excessive knowledge nor training in ML. While, existing tools such as Amazon Sage Maker[1] or Google AutoML[2] provide convenient graphical user interfaces (GUI) and application programming interfaces (API), yet do not provide open-source code libraries.

---

[1] https://aws.amazon.com/sagemaker
[2] https://cloud.google.com/automl

© The Author(s), under exclusive license to Springer Nature Switzerland AG 2023
C. Pesquita et al. (Eds.): ESWC 2023, LNCS 13998, pp. 123–127, 2023.
https://doi.org/10.1007/978-3-031-43458-7_23

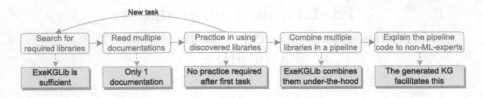

Fig. 1. Improvements on conventional data science workflow

In this paper, we introduce ExeKGLib, an easily-extendable Python library that supports a variety of methods for data visualization, data preprocessing and feature engineering, and ML modeling. ExeKGLib works in two steps: (1) Generate executable ML pipelines using knowledge graphs (KGs), (2) Convert generated pipelines into functional Python scripts, and execute these scripts. We rely on KGs for expressing the created pipelines to make them more understandable and reusable, and to verify that they are executable [13]. ExeKGLib can be used by a wide range of users and in a variety of scenarios: from domain experts that want to do ML to teachers and students for teaching and learning ML.

In the following sections, we start with demonstrating ExeKGLib's usage. Then, we describe the used KG schemata and discuss the underlying details of KG construction and pipeline generation in Sect. 3.

2   Usage Demonstration

Our target user can generate an ML pipeline either by importing ExeKGLib's ExeKG Python module or by interacting with the provided Typer CLI without writing code [3]. We demonstrate the former usage with three sample Python files [4]. The pipelines represented by the generated sample KGs are briefly explained below:

1. **ML pipeline**: Loads features and labels from an input CSV dataset, splits the data, trains and tests a k-NN model, and visualizes the prediction errors.
2. **Statistics pipeline**: Loads a feature from an input CSV dataset, normalizes it, and plots its values (before and after normalization) using a scatter plot.
3. **Visualization pipeline**: Loads a feature from an input CSV dataset and plots its values using a line plot.

The above pipelines (in form of executable KGs) can be executed using the provided Typer CLI [5]. To exhibit the pipelines' transparency, we have visualized the sample pipelines using Neo4j [6]. The script to perform this visualization for any executable KG is also provided.

---

[3] https://github.com/boschresearch/ExeKGLib#usage
[4] https://github.com/boschresearch/ExeKGLib/tree/main/examples
[5] https://github.com/boschresearch/ExeKGLib#executing-an-ml-pipeline
[6] https://bit.ly/exe-kg-lib-visualizations

Table 1. Comparison between conventional code and `ExeKGLib` for a classification task

Pipeline steps	Conventional code	Code using ExeKGLib
1. Load data	`pd.read_csv()` + convert to numpy	`ExeKG.create_data_entity()` `ExeKG.create_pipeline_task()`
2. Split data	`sklearn...train_test_split()`	`ExeKG.add_task()`
3. Train	`sklearn...Classifier().fit()`	`ExeKG.add_task()`
4. Evaluate	`sklearn...Classifier().predict()`	`ExeKG.add_task()`
5. Visualize	`matplotlib.pyplot...()`	`ExeKG.add_task()`

Experimentation with the offered resources can verify the benefits of `ExeKGLib` on the traditional data science process (Fig. 1). In particular, using our tool to solve a task reduces the overhead prior to the implementation, reduces the effort during the code development, and increases the explainability of the resulting ML pipeline. A brief display of the tool's practical advantages for a generic classification task is illustrated in Table 1. In a conventional setting (table's middle column), the user needs to separately import three different libraries (*i.e.* `pandas`, `scikit-learn`, `matplotlib`) and use five of their modules. On the other hand, when using `ExeKGLib` (table's right column), the user needs a limited number of libraries and modules, and thus learning is easier and faster by skipping reading extensive documentation of various libraries.

3   System Design

`ExeKGLib` relies on KG schemata to construct executable KGs (representing an ML pipeline) and execute them. Both of these processes use the `rdflib` Python library combined with SPARQL queries to find and create KG components.

3.1   Underlying KG Schemata

`ExeKGLib` utilizes an upper-level KG schema (Data Science – namespace: `ds`) that describes data science concepts such as data entity, task, and method. The supported tasks and methods are separated into bottom-level KG schemata [7]:

- **Visualization** tasks schema, which includes two types of methods: (1) The plot canvas methods that define the plot size and layout. (2) The various kinds of plot methods (e.g. line plot, scatter plot, or bar plot).
- **Statistics and Feature Engineering** tasks schema including methods such as Interquartile Range calculation, mean and standard deviation calculation, etc., which can also form more complex methods like outlier detection and normalization.
- **ML** tasks schema representing ML algorithms like Linear Regression, MLP, and k NN and helper functions that perform e.g. data splitting and ML model performance calculation.

`ExeKGLib`'s Python implementations of the above methods utilize common libraries such as `matplotlib` and `scikit-learn`.

---

[7] https://github.com/boschresearch/ExeKGLib#kg-schemata

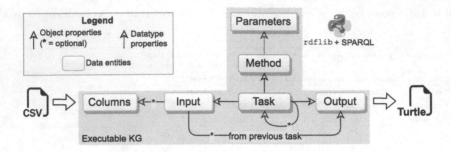

Fig. 2. Executable KG construction phase

3.2 Executable KG Construction

As shown in Fig. 2, the internal process of creating an executable KG starts with extracting the columns from the input dataset (CSV file). `ExeKGLib` populates the KG with data entities representing the target columns. Data entities are then used as input to the ML pipeline tasks.

Afterward, `ExeKGLib` adds to the KG the entities representing the user-specified task type (e.g. classification) and method type (e.g. k-NN), which are taken from the provided bottom-level KG schemata; and links the current task with the chosen method, input data entities, datatype properties, and the next task. Throughout the process, the compatibility of the aforementioned KG components is ensured by `ExeKGLib` based on the KG schemata. Finally, the created KG is serialized and saved on the disk in Turtle.

3.3 ML Pipeline Execution

To execute a given KG, `ExeKGLib` parses the KG with the help of the above KG schemata (Sect. 3.1). After that, the pipeline's *Tasks* (`owl:Individuals`) are sequentially traversed using the object property `ds:hasNextTask`. Based on the IRI of the next *Task* (`owl:Individual`), the *Task*'s type and properties are retrieved and mapped dynamically to a Python object. Such mapping allows for extending the library without modifying the KG execution code. Finally, for each *Task*, the Python implementation of the selected method type is invoked.

4 Future Work

We plan to add additional algorithms to `ExeKGLib` to support a wider variety of ML-related tasks, which can be conveniently done due to its good extendability. In the future, we will build a system by integrating `ExeKGLib` with a graph-based database. This will allow for easier management of the produced executable KGs, quick visualization, and more convenient reuse.

Acknowledgements. The work was partially supported by EU projects Dome 4.0 (GA 953163), OntoCommons (GA 958371), DataCloud (GA 101016835), Graph Massiviser (GA 101093202), and EnRichMyData (GA 101093202).

References

1. Abreu, P.H., Santos, M.S., Abreu, M.H., Andrade, B., Silva, D.C.: Predicting breast cancer recurrence using machine learning techniques: a systematic review. ACM Comput. Surv. **49**(3), 52:1–52:40 (2016). https://doi.org/10.1145/2988544
2. Bartschat, A., Reischl, M., Mikut, R.: Data mining tools. Wiley Interdisc. Rev. Data Min. Knowl. Disc. **9**(4), e1309 (2019). https://doi.org/10.1002/widm.1309
3. Heidrich, B., et al.: pyWATTS: python workflow automation tool for time series. arXiv preprint arXiv:2106.10157 (2021). https://doi.org/10.48550/arXiv. 2106.10157
4. Huang, Z., Fey, M., Liu, C., Beysel, E., Xu, X., Brecher, C.: Hybrid learning-based digital twin for manufacturing process: modeling framework and implementation. Robot. Comput.-Integr. Manuf. **82**, 102545 (2023). https://doi.org/10.1016/j.rcim. 2023.102545
5. Kim, J., Ahn, I.: Infectious disease outbreak prediction using media articles with machine learning models. Sci. Rep. **11**(1), 4413 (2021). https://doi.org/10.1038/ s41598-021-83926-2
6. Kourou, K., Exarchos, T.P., Exarchos, K.P., Karamouzis, M.V., Fotiadis, D.I.: Machine learning applications in cancer prognosis and prediction. Comput. Struct. Biotech. J. **13**, 8–17 (2015). https://doi.org/10.1016/j.csbj.2014.11.005
7. Libbrecht, M.W., Noble, W.S.: Machine learning applications in genetics and genomics. Nat. Rev. Genet. **16**(6), 321–332 (2015). https://doi.org/10.1038/ nrg3920
8. Meng, L., et al.: Machine learning in additive manufacturing: a review. JOM **72**(6), 2363–2377 (2020). https://doi.org/10.1007/s11837-020-04155-y
9. Mikut, R., et al.: The MATLAB toolbox SciXMiner: user's manual and programmer's guide. arXiv preprint arXiv:1704.03298 (2017). https://doi.org/10.48550/ arXiv.1704.03298
10. Obulesu, O., Mahendra, M., ThrilokReddy, M.: Machine learning techniques and tools: a survey. In: 2018 International Conference on Inventive Research in Computing Applications (ICIRCA), pp. 605–611. IEEE (2018). https://doi.org/10.1109/ ICIRCA.2018.8597302
11. Sarker, I.H.: Machine learning: algorithms, real-world applications and research directions. SN Comput. Sci. **2**(3), 1–21 (2021). https://doi.org/10.1007/s42979- 021-00592-x
12. Zeng, L., Al-Rifai, M., Chelaru, S., Nolting, M., Nejdl, W.: On the importance of contextual information for building reliable automated driver identification systems. In: 2020 IEEE 23rd International Conference on Intelligent Transportation Systems (ITSC), pp. 1–8. IEEE (2020). https://doi.org/10.1109/ITSC45102.2020. 9294439
13. Zheng, Z., et al.: Executable knowledge graphs for machine learning: a Bosch case of welding monitoring. In: Sattler, U., et al. The Semantic Web - ISWC 2022. ISWC 2022, LNCS, vol. 13489, pp. 791–809. Springer, Cham (2022). https://doi. org/10.1007/978-3-031-19433-7_45

Hannotate: Flexible Annotation for Text Analytics from Anywhere

Tan-Tai To[1], Hoang Dao[2], Huyen Nguyen[1], Thanh-Ha Do[1], and Tuan-Anh Hoang[3(✉)]

[1] Hanoi University of Science, Hanoi, Vietnam
{totantai_ch2020,huyennt,dothanhha}@hus.edu.vn
[2] Worcester, USA
[3] RMIT University Vietnam, Ho Chi Minh City, Vietnam
anh.hoang62@rmit.edu.vn

Abstract. Data annotation is a critical but the most expensive step in any text analytics project. There have been several frameworks built for enabling and easing this step. Most of these frameworks are however either not easy to be configured to specific users' needs, have no functionalities for annotating text pairs, or lack of efficient mechanism for data management and progress monitoring. Moreover, they have mostly no graphical user interfaces that are specifically designed for mobile devices. In this paper, we introduce Hannotate, a highly flexible, lightweight web-based framework that provides functionalities for a wide range of text annotation from both desktop and mobile devices. Our framework inherits the advantages of the typical existing ones while allowing users to easily customize the annotation work according to their demand and budget. The framework also supports users in managing data, monitoring the progress, and giving feedback to annotators.

1 Introduction

Labeled datasets are essential for any text analytics project. These datasets are however not always available at the beginning of the projects. Moreover, the available datasets, if there is any, are not always suitable for the projects, for various reasons, including mismatch in the domains, modalities, languages, and size of the datasets and the projects' requirements. Hence, annotating new datasets is a critical step for enabling the projects. This step is however time consuming and expensive, which requires efficient frameworks for distributing and crowd-sourcing the annotation work [9].

There have been a number of frameworks constructed for text annotation in different contexts and for different purposes [7]. Most of these frameworks however suffer from some of the following shortcomings:

– Limited options and not intuitive interfaces for customization. For example, several existing frameworks require complicated interactions for setting the possible labels to be assigned, and the number of annotations required for each text.

H. Dao—Independent Researcher. Email: hoangdhph04904@gmail.com.

C. Pesquita et al. (Eds.): ESWC 2023, LNCS 13998, pp. 128–132, 2023.
https://doi.org/10.1007/978-3-031-43458-7_24

- No functionalities for annotating pairs of texts. This type of annotation is used for entailment inference [1], and semantic similarity measurement [2], which are crucial in natural language understanding applications.
- Limited functionalities for giving feedback to annotators. This is critical for training the annotator in order to improve the quality of the annotation jobs.
- No interfaces tailored for mobile devices. This would drastically reduces the productivity of a large number of annotators who work on their handheld smart devices.

In this work, we would like to address the aforementioned shortcomings in existing frameworks by developing a lightweight, flexible one for a wide range of text annotation jobs. We aim to provide users with friendly interfaces for designing and customizing their jobs, monitoring the annotation progress, giving feedback to annotators, and managing the datasets. We also want to provide annotators with convenient interfaces for performing the annotation tasks efficiently from both desktop or mobile devices. In summary, the notable features of our framework are as follows.

- **Highly flexible**: it allows users to customize their jobs easily and intuitively
- **Highly accessible**: it is accessible from a wide range of devices with consistent user experience across the devices
- **Convenient**: it is a lightweight framework that integrates user-friendly interfaces for managing data and monitoring the progress.

In the rest of this paper, we briefly discuss the existing frameworks in Sect. 2. We then describe our framework in detail in Sect. 3. Lastly, we conclude the paper and sketch some directions for further improvement for the framework in Sect. 4.

2   Related Work

Among the frameworks that have been widely used in text mining communities, **brat**[1], is considerably the most popular one. This framework was originally designed for linguistic annotation (e.g., part-of-speech tagging and named entity recognition). One can configure **brat** for non-linguistic annotation, e.g., aspect-specific sentiment analysis [8]. However, the configuration is performed through a text file, which is not intuitive. Moreover, the configuration, once set, is shared among all the projects, which do not allow different types of annotation to be performed concurrently. This shortcoming has been partially addressed in **WebAnno**[2] [3] and **INCEpTION**[3] [5] – the successors to **brat** with most recent releases. These two frameworks have major extensions for project-specific configuration and interfaces for data curation. The configuration is however still quite complicated with required sequences of interactions. Also, these two frameworks provide no mechanism for giving feedback to the annotators.

There are also existing frameworks that are more specifically designed for non-linguistic annotation, e.g., **doccano**[4], **WARP-Text** [6], **prodigy**[5], and **Label Studio**[6].

---

[1] https://brat.nlplab.org.
[2] https://webanno.github.io/webanno.
[3] https://inception-project.github.io.
[4] https://github.com/doccano/doccano.
[5] https://prodi.gy.
[6] https://github.com/heartexlabs/label-studio.

These frameworks are however limited to annotating of single texts, and therefore not suitable for tasks that require annotating of pairs of texts. Moreover, to the best of our knowledge, there is no existing open-source frameworks that provide convenient interfaces for performing the annotation from mobile devices.

Certainly, there are commercial frameworks and platforms that provide customizable services for annotating texts, e.g., **Labelbox**[7], **CloudFactory**[8], and **Amazon Mechanical Turk**[9]. These services are however expensive while may suffer from low quality annotation and data confidentiality risks [4].

3 Hannotate

We now highlight the notable features of our framework. We start by describing the types of annotation that our framework is designed for. We then specify the users of the frameworks and the functionalities we would like to provide them. Finally, we describe the components for deploying the framework. Please refer to the extended version of this paper[10] for more detailed information on the framework's design, its enable technologies, and its implementation.

3.1 Annotation Types

Currently, our framework is facilitated for the following types of annotation.

- **Single text annotation**, which includes topic labeling, and sentiment recognition.
- **Text pair annotation**, e.g., entailment inference and semantic similarity measurement.
- **Span annotation** such as key-phrase detection named entity recognition.
- **Span pair annotation** such as relational extraction and co-reference recognition.
- **Sentence rewriting**, e.g., translation and paraphasing.

3.2 User Role and Functionalities

Our framework is designed to server the **job managers** – who manage dataset(s) to be annotated and the annotation process, the **annotators** – who would like to perform the annotation jobs, and the **admin** – who manages an operate the whole system. We provide the user-friendly graphical interfaces for the following functionalities for each user role.

The **job managers** are supported to

- Create and customize annotation job. Here, a job will be created for each dataset to be annotated. Current options for customization includes specifying the label sets, the number of labels, and the number of annotation for each data instance.

---

[7] https://labelbox.com.
[8] https://www.cloudfactory.com.
[9] https://www.mturk.com.
[10] Hannotate's full version.

- Approve or reject bids from annotators who register to perform the job, and assign tasks to the approved annotators. Here, a task is the annotating of a data instance, and tasks are assigned to annotators in batches. This help to better distribute the job among the annotators while managing their progress and annotation quality better.
- Monitor the work progress of the whole project, and that of each individual annotator.
- Examine the annotated data instance, then approve or reject the annotation, and give feedback to the corresponding annotator.
- Export the annotated text and related information (including the annotators and their labels for each data instance, timestamp, etc.) to local for later use.

The **annotators** are supported to

- Search and bid for open jobs. Each annotator can bid for and perform multiple jobs concurrently.
- Perform the assigned annotation tasks and submit the result
- View feedback from the job's manager, revise and re-submit the tasks.

Lastly, the **admin** is supported to manage user accounts and to perform basic customization regarding the operating of the whole system.

3.3 Components

Our whole framework is packed into front-end and back-end components separately. Each component is indeed a stand-alone package that can be run as it. This allows each part of the framework to be deployed independently from different environments. We also provide a walk-through video presentation about our framework and an online demo. Please refer to our project's repository[11] for those components and their usage.

4   Conclusion

We have introduced Hannotate, a lightweight yet highly flexible and accessible framework for a wide range of text annotation. Our framework inherits the advantages of the existing ones while addressing their main issues by providing users with user-friendly interfaces for customizing, managing, and monitoring their annotation jobs. We also provide annotators with interfaces for annotating smoothly and consistently across devices.

Possible extensions to our framework include adding functionalities for more types of annotations and analyzing the annotation results. We would also like to add smart suggestion mechanisms for aiding annotators in performing the tasks, which have been shown to significantly improve the annotators' productivity [10].

Acknowledgement. This work is supported by Vingroup Innovation Foundation (VINIF) in project code VINIF.2020.DA14

---

[11] https://github.com/smutahoang/hannotate.

References

1. Bowman, S.R., Angeli, G., Potts, C., Manning, C.D.: A large annotated corpus for learning natural language inference. In: EMNLP 2015 (2015)
2. Cer, D., Diab, M., Agirre, E., Lopez-Gazpio, I., Specia, L.: Semeval-2017 task 1: semantic textual similarity multilingual and crosslingual focused evaluation. In: SemEval-2017 (2017)
3. De Castilho, R.E., et al.: A web-based tool for the integrated annotation of semantic and syntactic structures. In: COLING 2016 Workshop (2016)
4. Fort, K., Adda, G., Cohen, K.B.: Amazon mechanical turk: Gold mine or coal mine? Comput. Linguist. **37**(2), 413–420 (2011)
5. Klie, J.C., Bugert, M., Boullosa, B., de Castilho, R.E., Gurevych, I.: The inception platform: machine-assisted and knowledge-oriented interactive annotation. In: COLING 2018 (2018)
6. Kovatchev, V., Martí, M.A., Salamó, M.: Warp-text: a web-based tool for annotating relationships between pairs of texts. In: COLING 2018 (2018)
7. Neves, M., Ševa, J.: An extensive review of tools for manual annotation of documents. Briefings Bioinf. **22**(1), 146–163 (2021)
8. Pontiki, M., Papageorgiou, H., Galanis, D., Androutsopoulos, I., Pavlopoulos, J., Manandhar, S.: Semeval-2014 task 4: aspect based sentiment analysis. In: SemEval 2014 (2014)
9. Sabou, M., Bontcheva, K., Derczynski, L., Scharl, A.: Corpus annotation through crowdsourcing: Towards best practice guidelines. In: LREC'14 (2014)
10. Yang, J., Zhang, Y., Li, L., Li, X.: Yedda: a lightweight collaborative text span annotation tool. In: ACL 2018 (2018)

Study-Buddy: A Knowledge Graph-Powered Learning Companion for School Students

Fernanda Martinez[2], Diego Collarana[1,2]([envelope]), Davide Calvaresi[3], Martin Arispe[2], Carla Florida[2], and Jean-Paul Calbimonte[3,4]

[1] Fraunhofer IAIS, Dresden, Germany
diegocollarana@upb.edu
[2] Universidad Privada Boliviana, Cochabamba, Bolivia
fernandamartinez@upb.edu, martinarispe@upb.edu, carlaflorida@upb.edu
[3] University of Applied Sciences and Arts Western Switzerland HES-SO, Sierre, Switzerland
davide.calvaresi@hevs.ch, jean-paul.calbimonte@hevs.ch
[4] The Sense Innovation and Research Center, Lausanne, Switzerland

Abstract. Large Language Models (LLMs) have the potential to substantially improve educational tools for students. However, they face limitations, including factual accuracy, personalization, and the lack of control over the sources of information. This paper presents Study-Buddy, a prototype of a conversational AI assistant for school students to address the above-mentioned limitations. Study-Buddy embodies an AI assistant based on a knowledge graph, LLMs models, and computational persuasion. It is designed to support educational campaigns as a hybrid AI solution. The demonstrator showcases interactions with Study-Buddy and the crucial role of the Knowledge Graph for the bot to present the appropriate activities to the students. A video demonstrating the main features of Study-Buddy is available at: https://youtu.be/DHPTsN1RI9o.

Keywords: Knowledge Graphs · NLP · Personalized Education

1 Introduction

The emergence of Large Language Models (LLMs) such as ChatGPT has revolutionized the field of AI, enabling machines to process natural language and handle human-like conversations [1,5]. LLMs have gained significant attention in education, potentially enhancing students' learning experiences worldwide [3]. However, several challenges hinder their widespread adoption, including factual correctness, lack of personalization, and control over information sources [4]. These challenges are even more prominent in developing regions, where access to digital educational content is limited. In this paper, we present a demonstrator of a conversational AI assistant for school students, leveraging the latest advances in LLMs, Knowledge Graphs (KGs), and Computational Persuasion

C. Pesquita et al. (Eds.): ESWC 2023, LNCS 13998, pp. 133–137, 2023.
https://doi.org/10.1007/978-3-031-43458-7_25

methods (Hybrid-AI). Our assistant is designed to run educational campaigns meeting each student's unique needs through multi-modal interactions. Powered by a KG, our assistant can connect teachers, students, topics, learning material, and learning sessions to enhance school students' study experience, improve their ability to retain information and increase their motivation and engagement with their studies. Through this prototype, we aim to showcase the potential of Hybrid-AI in developing educational tools that bridge the digital divide and empower students with equal access to high-quality educational content. The demonstrator is actively being developed/piloted in collaboration with two schools in Bolivia.

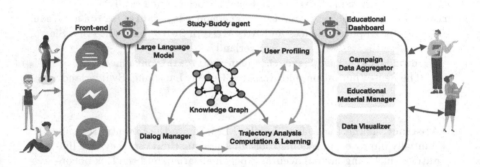

Fig. 1. Architecture of Study-Buddy: connecting students with content/teachers.

2   The Study-Buddy Architecture

Students interact with Study-Buddy via a chatbot agent deployed in Telegram, which uses computational persuasion principles to motivate students to review the learning material uploaded by teachers. Teachers can run learning session campaigns and visualize user engagement and interaction, adjusting to students' needs through the tracking of user behaviour in the Study-Buddy KG.

Knowledge Graph: A KG powers the Study-Buddy assistant, linking students with learning sessions on topics defined by teachers for different subjects. Figure 2 depicts the KG. These links help to identify specific topics and concepts that are not clear to students and need to be reinforced through the dynamic learning material of their preference. For dialog The KG links also support dialog management. Specifically, the KG is used to identify and retrieve information relevant to the current dialog context, i.e., the student's subject, grade, an learning path, which can help the LLM generate appropriate responses. The KG indicates not only the subjects of the dialog but also provide additional semantics that the LLM used to enhance the quality and relevance of its responses. The KG flexible model allows the integration of different activities in learning sessions, which teachers can supervise to follow up on the student's progress and strengthen weak areas. In this version of Study-Buddy, the learning path is based on paragraphs from a guiding textbook uploaded by the teacher for a specific subject with defined topics in the grade curricula. The application allows students to play in practice sessions to increase their scores. It is also possible to show a ranking per course and topic according to practice time and earned scores.

Conversational Agent and Learning Activities Platform: The Study Buddy chatbot is targeted for students aged between 13 and 18 to make studying more engaging and interactive. It is developed on RASA and connected to Telegram. It relies on a KG that models elements including grades, subjects, selected topics and related learning materials. The bot proposes study sessions with multiple-choice questions and possible rewards for correct answers. Users can switch between topics, choose to study a topic again, or enter into competition mode where they have to provide written answers without hints. The bot uses LLM models from HuggingFace to provide learning activities, such as Question Answering over Paragraphs and Tables, evaluating the user's answer, and providing feedback. Users earn points for each correct answer, and their scores can increase with rewards earned by studying.

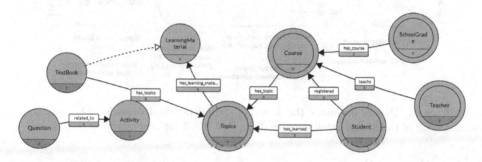

Fig. 2. Study-Buddy KG links students, teachers, courses, topics, textbooks, and learning sessions, making the discovery of unforeseen learning trajectory paths possible.

Study-Buddy also provides a web platform with different learning activities to reinforce and clarify questions about topics. The web platform presents key concepts from the material so students can quickly assimilate the main ideas. The platform uses gamification techniques, i.e., earning points for each question about the topic in the paragraph or table, to motivate the user to continue learning a subject. We use LLMs to implement these activities for text analysis and question answering over tables (e.g., the TAPAS model [2]).

Educational Dashboard for Teachers: The educator can see reports of the student's progress, such as the average number of questions per day, percentage of time per topic, percentage of questions per topic, and the result of the tests of correct and failed answers of a student in a range of determined dates. This role has the functionality available to load the information on the topics such as texts and books.

3   Prototype Demonstrator

The demonstrator is focused on the learning experience for students, i.e., it will showcase students' interactions with the chatbot using Telegram and the learning activities platform. A registered student picks a topic to start studying. Then the bot will send a motivational message for correct answers; for wrong answers, it will send the correct one along with engagement elements. This loop only ends when the student explicitly asks for it. Then, the student moves on to the platform and makes questions related to the text proposed by the teacher. Next, the student explores a table containing the knowledge about a topic, e.g., history, and asks questions to learn the subject. Finally, after earning points with three different dynamics, the user returns to the chatbot and asks for the course topic ranking, which can be seen as a message or in a leaderboard on the web page. These activities motivate the user to continue learning (Fig. 3).

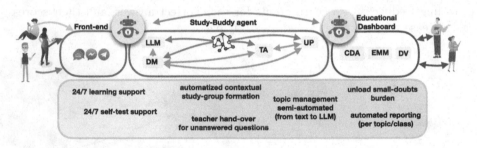

Fig. 3. Study-Buddy improves the learning experience and provides 24/7 support, automation of tasks, and intelligent analysis (see Fig. 1 for acronyms).

Helping Students to Reach Learning Goals. Using competition through the gamification of a topic is a critical factor for engaging the student in practicing. Studying becomes a game, reducing the reluctance to complete the proposed activities. The main difference is personalizing the content proposed during the session, going beyond a pure memorization activity. Besides, the chatbot integration on Telegram allows the bot to reach the user whenever an event of interest happens. For example, if a student's ranking drops in a gamified learning environment, Study-Buddy can send a message encouraging them to continue practicing. Additionally, if the teacher adds new questions or content to a topic, Study-Buddy can notify the student, encouraging them to revisit and review the material. Those reminders keep the student taking at least a session per day. By leveraging the convenience and accessibility of chatbots, students can stay engaged and motivated to reach their learning goals.

Helping Teachers to Evaluate Learning Trajectories. Thanks to Study-Buddy, teachers can use technology to assess students' learning trajectories more accurately and comprehensively. With the help of Study-Buddy, teachers can gather data on students' learning behaviors and track their progress over time. For example, by analyzing the frequency and accuracy of students' answers to specific questions, teachers can identify areas where students may be struggling or making common mistakes. This data can then be used to adapt instruction better to meet the needs of individual students or the class. Additionally, once Study-Buddy collects enough data, machine learning algorithms can be used to predict students' future performance based on their past performance, providing teachers with valuable insights that can be used to design personalized learning experiences for each student. Study-Buddy helps teachers evaluate learning trajectories more accurately, provide targeted support, and ultimately, help students achieve their full potential.

4   Conclusions

This demonstrator presents Study-Buddy, a personalized conversational AI assistant for school students, which uses Large Language Models, Knowledge Graphs, and Computational Persuasion methods to motivate students to review learning material uploaded by teachers. Study-Buddy provides a gamified learning experience for the students, and teachers can track learning trajectories. Study-Buddy is a promising tool for addressing issues such as factual accuracy, personalization, and control over the sources of information used in educational settings. The prototype is being developed in collaboration with two high schools in Bolivia, showcasing the importance of introducing digital education technologies in environments where access to pedagogical resources is limited and expensive.

We plan to expand Study-Buddy to other subjects, grades, and countries in future work. We also aim to implement additional features, such as sentiment analysis, to detect the students' emotions during the learning process to enable more accurate and personalized responses. Additionally, we plan to investigate using additional data sources, such as educational videos, to enhance the learning experience. Finally, they intend to conduct more extensive system evaluations, including user studies with students and teachers, to gather feedback and improve Study-Buddy's usability and effectiveness.

Acknowledgments. This work is supported by the Research Partnership Grant RPG2106 funded by the Swiss Leading House for Latin America.

References

1. Bommasani, R., et al.: On the opportunities and risks of foundation models (2021). arXiv2108.07258
2. Herzig, J., Nowak, P.K., Müller, T., Piccinno, F., Eisenschlos, J.M.: TaPas: weakly supervised table parsing via pre-training. In: ACL, Online, pp. 4320–4333 (2020)
3. Hosseini, M., et al.: An exploratory survey about using ChatGPT in education, healthcare, and research. medRxiv, pp. 2023–03 (2023)
4. Kasneci, E., et al.: ChatGPT for good? On opportunities and challenges of large language models for education. Learn. Individ. Differ. **103**, 102274 (2023)
5. Schulman, J., et al.: ChatGPT: optimizing language models for dialogue (2022)

On the Problem of Automatically Aligning Indicators to SDGs

Mario Soriano, Rafael Berlanga$^{(\boxtimes)}$, and Indira Lanza-Cruz

Department de Llenguatges i Sistemes Informàtics,
Universitat Jaume I, Castelló de la Plana, Spain
{berlanga,magregor,lanza}@uji.es

Abstract. In this paper we present a first approach to the application of transformer-based language models to the automatic alignment to sustainable development goals (SDGs). This task is quite relevant for the development of new tools that aim at measuring the engagement degree of the organization's indicators to the SGDs. Our first experiments show that this task is hard, and that even powerful large language models do not achieve a high accuracy as in other NLP tasks.

Keywords: Transformers · Indicators · Knowledge Graphs

1 Introduction

In 2015, the UN defined the Agenda 2030 to establish a series of goals for the sustainable development of the World [6]. The sustainable development goals (SDGs) consist of 17 main objectives covering different perspectives related to sustainability. These goals are described in detail by defining their context and the main indicators that must be tracked to measure their achievement. As a consequence, all kind of organizations must align their indicators and goals towards the SDGs. Indeed, most public funding is currently conditioned to define appropriate indicators related to SGDs.

Aligning specific indicators to the global SDGs is a challenging task. Firstly, this is a very open scenario which involves many perspectives and knowledge areas. Secondly, we have to find a causal chain between indicators and SDGs, which requires a deep understanding of both the organization and the SDGs.

In this paper, we present a first approach to this problem by applying deep learning language models. The main idea is to measure the quality of automatic alignments produced by these models. We evaluate language models trained for English and Spanish over the indicators proposed in the Agenda 2030. We show in this paper that the connection between indicators and goals are not so evident and, in some cases, it requires a reasoning process to find out them.

2   Related Work

2.1   Goals, Actions and Indicators

Strategic maps usually represent the knowledge in terms of goals, actions and indicators. The goals express the future state we aim at in terms of some measurable quantities [5]. For example, the SDG-2 "Zero hunger" implies that some global measure for "hunger" must be reduced to 0. This global measure relies on many indicators, which express the different perspectives involved in such an abstract goal. For example, the indicator "Prevalence of anaemia in women aged 15 to 49 years, by pregnancy status" is used in the SDG-2 to account for the nutrition status of woman in reproductive age. Reducing this indicator directly implies approaching to the goal according to the following causal chain: if anemia has been reduced is because the nutrition status was improved, so hunger was indeed reduced.

2.2   Dynamic SLOD-BI

The activities and indicators of any organization must also be aligned to the SGDs, so that they can impact positively towards the sustainability goals. For this purpose, the context of this paper is the semantic infrastructure for business intelligence named Dynamic SLOD-BI [4]. This infrastructure deals with streams of open and corporate data which feed a live knowledge graph (KG) for analytical purposes. Goals and indicators are also represented in this graph, along with their connections to the streamed data. A first prototype of this infrastructure is being developed in the scenario of sustainable tourism, where the UNWTO defined its own indicators before the SDGs were established.

2.3   SDGs-Based Classification

There are some work about using text classifiers to assign SDGs to arbitrary documents. For example, in [3], authors apply NLP techniques to articles from peer-reviewed journals in order to classify them according to the 17 SDGs. They compare the performance of different multi-label text classification models with datasets of different characteristics. On the other hand, authors in [1] tried to map the Environmental Higher Education Ranking Systems Indicators (ESH-ERS) to the SGD indicators using NLP and document similarity techniques. Finally, the work in [2] fine-tune a BERT multi-class model to classify documents into the SDGs. All these approaches uses a labelled set of documents (e.g., scientific articles) to predict labels for arbitrary documents. Instead, in our work, we focus on classifying indicators and sub-goals, which are very short descriptions with clear semantics.

It is worth mentioning that there are some online tools like Escaner2030[1] provided by the Political Watch and the Spanish Ministry of Foreign Affairs, which classifies any paragraph into their most likely SDGs.

---

[1] https://escaner2030.es/.

3   Methods and Results

For the experiments, we directly use the inventory of sub-goals and indicators proposed in 2015 by the UN to define the 17 SDGs. Thus, the dataset contains 400 sentences describing different sub-goals and indicators labelled with their SDG code.

The experiments in this paper make use of the pre-trained BERT-like models from HuggingFace. We conducted two experiments. The first one consists of directly encoding the sentences of the whole dataset to find out if the database is consistently distributed in a metric semantic space. That is, sentences should be somehow clustered around their goals. The second experiment consists of fine-tuning pre-trained models as multi-class models for SDGs. The first experiment is intended to link sentences to goals in an unsupervised way, whereas the latter needs a train/test partitions of the dataset (we used a 90/10 partition).

Table 1 shows the precision when linking sentences by using a similarity text (ST) encoder. Precision is calculated with the K-nearest sentences to each sentence, considering success if they belong to the same goal. Notice that the best score always occur at K=1, which indicates that the semantic space is quite heterogeneous. Notice that ST performs similarly in the two languages.

Table 2 shows the results of the trained multi-class models. For these experiments we use 9:1 train/test partitions and 6 epochs. We show best models and best scores. Surprisingly, these results are not much better than those in Table 1. Moreover, quality results of the trained models are affected by the language.

Table 1. Precision for text similarity in both languages.

Text Similarity Models			
hiiamsid/sentence_similarity_spanish_es		distiluse-base-multilingual-cased-v1	
K	Score	K	Score
1	**0.66268**	1	**0.66427**
2	0.62081	2	0.60312
3	0.58214	3	0.57234

We performed further experiments over the zero-shot pipelines of Huggingface resulting in very poor results. Also, the tool Escaner2030 showed very poor results when classifying indicators from this dataset (below 0.4). Finally, we report the results of the large language model chatGPT. We prepared 5-folds for each language, containing 30 random samples each. We used the new API with the following prompt:

Prompt: "Please, assign sustainability goals (SDGs) to a series of texts. When I write a text you must assign it to one SDG code followed by the words from the text that are relevant to your decision (relevant words). You have to answer simply with this format: <SDG Code> | <relevant words>"

With this prompt we also extract the explanations for the chosen SDGs. Usually, chatGPT returned the right keywords involved in the connection. In Table 2, we report the accuracy with confidence intervals for the 5-folders. Each fold takes approximately one minute, making this method no scalable. Like supervised methods, chatGPT performs much better in English than Spanish.

Table 2. Accuracy of supervised and chatGPT.

Language Model	Language	Accuracy
Multi-class Fine-tuned Models		
XLM-Roberta	Spanish	0.6415
Roberta	English	0.6981
Large Language Model		
chatGPT	Spanish	0.76 ± 0.07
chatGPT	English	**0.84 ± 0.04**

4   Conclusions

This paper presents a first approach to the SGD alignment problem for indicators. Results show that scores are still far from the ideal ones. Even the powerful chatGPT does not achieve high enough scores, being them also dependent on the target language. Future work will focus on enhancing text similarity methods and few-shot classifiers by means of explainable methods that rely on knowledge graphs. These techniques will allow us to align texts and indicators at a larger scale than chatGPT can currently do.

Acknowledgement. This research has been partially funded by the Spanish Ministry of Science under grants PID2021-123152OB-C22 and PDC2021-121097-I00 both funded by the MCIN/AEI/10.13039/501100011033 and by the European Union and FEDER/ERDF (European Regional Development Funds). Mario Soriano is granted by the Generalitat Valenciana through the project INVESTIGO (INVEST/2022/308).

References

1. Buzaboon, A., Alboflasa, H., Alnaser, W., Shatnawi, S., Albinali, K.: Automated mapping of environmental higher education ranking systems indicators to SDGs indicators using natural language processing and document similarity (2021)
2. Guisiano, J., Chiky, R.: Automatic classification of multilabel texts related to sustainable development goals (SDGs). In: TECHENV EGC2021, France (2021)
3. Morales-Hernández, R.C., Jaguey, J.G., Becerra-Alonso, D.: A Comparison of multi-label text classification models in research articles labeled with sustainable development goals (2022)
4. Lanza-Cruz, I., Berlanga, R., Aramburu, M.J.: Modeling analytical streams for social business intelligence. Informatics 5(3), 33 (2018)

5. Parmenter, D.: Key Performance Indicators: Developing, Implementing, and Using Winning KPIs. Wiley, Hoboken (2015)
6. UN general assembly, transforming our world : the 2030 agenda for sustainable development, 21 October 2015, A/RES/70/1. https://www.refworld.org/docid/57b6e3e44.html

Automating Benchmark Generation for Named Entity Recognition and Entity Linking

Katerina Papantoniou$^{(\boxtimes)}$, Vasilis Efthymiou, and Dimitris Plexousakis

FORTH-ICS, Heraklion, Greece
{papanton,vefthym,dp}@ics.forth.gr

Abstract. Named Entity Recognition (NER) and Linking (NEL) have seen great advances lately, especially with the development of language models pre-trained on large document corpora, typically written in the most popular languages (e.g., English). This makes NER and NEL tools for other languages, with fewer resources available, fall behind the latest advances in AI. In this work, we propose an automated benchmark data generation process for the tasks of NER and NEL, based on Wikipedia events. Although our process is applied and evaluated on Greek texts, the only requirement for its applicability to other languages is the availability of Wikipedia events pages in that language. The generated Greek datasets, comprising around 19k events and 41k entity mentions, as well as the code to generate such datasets, are publicly available.

1 Introduction

We are witnessing a proliferation of news articles available on the Web, making it difficult for readers to identify good-quality journalism with well-formulated and factually supported arguments. Despite the abundance of news articles available, it is still challenging to retrieve information related to a specific entity of interest (e.g., person, event, organization), in order to compare the arguments in favor of, or against a specific claim about them and shape an informed opinion. This often leads to easy spread of misinformation and conspiracy theories, sometimes with huge political, socio-economical or health impact. The DebateLab project[1] is conducting research towards representing, mining and reasoning with online arguments. The goal of this project is to offer a suite of tools and services that will assist both professional journalists in accomplishing everyday tasks, and readers who wish to be well-informed about topics or entities of interest.

A main component of DebateLab is EL-NEL [14], a tool responsible for *named entity linking (NEL)* in Greek news articles. NEL is the task of mapping parts of a text (called *entity mentions* or *surface mentions*) to uniquely identified entity descriptions provided in a target knowledge graph (KG). Consequently, it

---

[1] https://debatelab.ics.forth.gr/.

C. Pesquita et al. (Eds.): ESWC 2023, LNCS 13998, pp. 143–148, 2023.
https://doi.org/10.1007/978-3-031-43458-7_27

requires a step of detecting such entity mentions, along with their possible entity type, in the given texts, a task known as *named entity recognition* (NER).

Although NEL tools have recently seen great advances with language models pre-trained on large document corpora in English, few models exist for less popular languages. Worse yet, those few models are trained and evaluated on document corpora of much smaller scale, and tested by far fewer people than their popular-language counterparts. Due to those challenges, NEL tools in those low-resource languages fall far behind the latest advances in AI. To deter this gap, in this work, we propose an automated, language-agnostic benchmark data generation process for NER and NEL tasks using Wikipedia events pages[2]. We use the manually curated links in those event pages as the ground truth for NER and NEL tools and show how existing tools can be evaluated using such data. Although we use Wikipedia events in the Greek language as a use case, and release our data in Greek, our publicly available source code is language-agnostic and can be easily used for other languages.

It is not until recently that benchmark dataset for Greek NER have become publicly available (e.g., a NER dataset for spaCy [10], and a manually annotated corpus of Greek newswire articles, elNER [4]). Among the works that adopt multilingual approaches for the creation of benchmark datasets for NER based on Wikipedia articles, only two (Polyglot [2] and WikiAnn [13]) include Greek and only one (WikiAnn) also covers the NEL task. Unlike those benchmarks, the datasets generated by our method are news-/events-oriented. MEANTIME [11] and [8] are also targeting news/events. The MEANTIME [11] corpus consists of 120 manually annotated English Wikinews articles. [8] extracted 170k events from Wikipedia event pages from 9 languages (not including Greek). The main differences of our work compared to [8], are that we attribute entity types to the recognized entities, enabling its applicability to state-of-the-art NER tools, and that we perform a data enrichment step to fix red links.

In summary, the contributions of this work are the following:

- We offer publicly available benchmark datasets[3] for NER and NEL in Greek, with a permissive license (CC BY-SA 3.0), generated from Wikipedia events.
- We open-source the code[4] that generated those datasets, which can be adapted to generate similar datasets in more languages and, potentially, from more data sources.
- We show that these benchmarks can be used to evaluate existing NER and NEL tools, posing new challenges for such tools.

2   Methodology

In this section, we describe the methodology for the construction of the NER and NEL benchmark data.

---

[2] Greek wikinews page is not currently active. We expect that this may also be the case for many other languages.

[3] https://zenodo.org/record/7429037.

[4] https://gitlab.isl.ics.forth.gr/debatelab/elwiki_events_benchmark.

Data Extraction. We extracted Greek Wikipedia events, redirects, mappings between Wikidata and Wikipedia articles, the Wikidata type(s) for each article, and the Greek Wiktionary, between 2009 (when the first Greek Wikipedia Events appeared in the template used today) and 2022.

Cleaning and Filtering. Our cleaning and filtering process includes the attribution of surface mentions to specific entity types, the removal of surface mentions not related to those types, and the concatenation of consecutive sentences referring to the same event. For the latter, we rely on heuristics. The entity types selected in this work are: event, facility, geopolitical entity, location, organization, person, product and work of art. For the attribution for each annotation to the entity types above, we use the instanceOf property of Wikidata. **Data Enrichment.** In addition to cleaning and filtering, we also enrich the extracted data, by filling in some of the so-called "red links", i.e., links to non-existing Wikipedia pages. Instead of disregarding red links, we tried to match such links with the corresponding (language-agnostic) Wikidata identifier, in order to increase the linkage of this dataset. For the collected dataset, approximately 14K out of 64K (~21%) links were originally red links. We managed to recover ~10K of those red links, by following the processing steps described below: (*i*) lexical transformations, e.g., convert first letter of placeholder suffix to uppercase, re-order words within the same entity mention, (*ii*) using the surface mention text as a wikidata search query, and (*iii*) translating the surface mention to English, using M2M100 [6], and repeating the same process in English.

3   Experiments

In this section, we evaluate the following NER methods: *EL-NEL* [14], *Neural-ILSP* [16], *NLP-AUEB* [17], *spaCy* [9], and *Polyglot* [2]; then, we evaluate the following NEL methods: *EL-NEL* [14], *WAT* [15], *spaCy fishing* [1], and *ReFinED* [3]. For all NEL tools, except *EL-NEL* which supports Greek, we translate the texts and the surface mentions in English to get the results.

NER Evaluation Methodology. For NER, we follow the so-called partial evaluation schema [5], that defines the following cases: A correct case (COR), when the surface mention and entity type in the ground truth match exactly with the NER tool. A partially correct case (PAR), when the surface mention in the ground truth overlaps with the surface mention returned by the NER tool (ignoring entity type). A missing case (MIS), when a ground truth annotation is not returned at all by a NER tool. A spurious case (SPU), when a NER tool suggest an annotation that does not exist in the ground truth. Then, precision and recall are defined as $Precision = \frac{COR+0.5\,PAR}{COR+PAR+SPU}$, and $Recall = \frac{COR+0.5\,PAR}{COR+PAR+MIS}$.

NEL Evaluation Methodology. For NEL, we follow the spaCy scorer[5] app-roach that considers only the links provided for entity mentions that overlap with the NER ground truth. We consider the following cases: A true positive (TP) occurs when a NEL tool suggests the same link as the ground truth. A false positive (FP) occurs when a NEL tool suggests a different link than the correct link. This includes the case of a NEL tool suggesting any link for a known red link in the ground truth. A false negative (FN) occurs when a NEL tool returns no link (or an incorrect link) for an entity mention that appears in the NEL ground truth (not a red link). True negatives (TN) are ignored. As a consequence, precision and recall are almost identical, so we report only the micro- and macro-averaged F1-scores. Due to the imbalance of the entity types, F1-micro that takes into account proportion of every type is more meaningful.

NER Evaluation Results. The results of NER, presented in Table 1, show that the NER benchmark is challenging for all evaluated methods, with the highest F1 being 0.56 for the EL-NEL system. Polyglot, which detects a small portion of the entity types (which are, nonetheless, the most representative in the dataset), shows the highest precision, but also the lowest recall. The low recall for all the tools is explainable due to spurious cases, since there is a gap between what the Wikipedians choose to annotate and the tools' predictions, which are usually more exhaustive.

Table 1. NER results.

Tool	Types	Precision	Recall	F1
EL-NEL	8	0.76	0.46	0.56
Neural-ILSP	8	0.51	0.46	0.46
NLP-AUEB	8	0.84	0.34	0.47
spaCy	6	0.75	0.43	0.53
Polyglot	3	0.86	0.33	0.47

Table 2. NEL results.

Tool	F1-micro	F1-macro
EL-NEL	0.91	0.82
WAT	0.96	0.96
SpaCy fishing	0.77	0.78
ReFinED	0.95	0.90

NEL Evaluation Results. The results of NEL are shown in Table 2. Overall, WAT shows the best performance among all NEL tools, followed by the neural-based ReFinED. A more detailed analysis, as presented in Table 3, reveals that all NEL tools struggle with events, while they show impressive results for persons. WAT does not categorize surface mentions into entity types, so it is skipped from this table.

In terms of computational time, SpaCy fishing and ReFinED that do not require calls to web APIs are significantly faster (few minutes vs a few hours). An efficiency evaluation of the tools falls beyond the scope of this work.

---

[5] https://github.com/explosion/spaCy/blob/master/spacy/scorer.py.

Table 3. NEL results (F1-macro) per entity type.

	EL-NEL	SpaCy fishing	ReFinED
EVENT	0.61	0.47	0.78
FAC	0.78	1	0.88
GPE	0.92	0.72	0.96
LOC	0.92	0	0.94
ORG	0.9	0.81	0.94
PERSON	0.92	0.92	0.94
PRODUCT	0.58	1	1
WORK_OF_ART	1	0.6	0.71

4 Conclusion and Future Work

In this work, we have presented an open-source benchmark dataset for NER and NEL, built from Greek Wikipedia Events. The dataset consists of 24k sentences and includes 41k entity mentions. We plan to follow the same methodology and release similar benchmark datasets in more languages. We also plan an experimental comparison with other benchmark datasets and models, as well as the enrichment of the collection with annotations that Wikipedians have not considered in their annotations. For the latter the structure of Wikipedia (e.g., anchor links, disambiguation pages) as well as co-reference information can be exploited as in [12] and [7].

Acknowledgement. This project has received funding from the Hellenic Foundation for Research and Innovation (HFRI) and the General Secretariat for Research and Technology (GSRT), under grant agreement No 4195.

References

1. entity-fishing. https://github.com/kermitt2/entity-fishing
2. Al-Rfou, R., Kulkarni, V., Perozzi, B., Skiena, S.: POLYGLOT-NER: massive multilingual named entity recognition. In: SIAM, pp. 586–594 (2015)
3. Ayoola, T., Tyagi, S., Fisher, J., et al.: ReFinED: an efficient zero-shot-capable approach to end-to-end entity linking. In: NAACL, pp. 209–220 (2022)
4. Bartziokas, N., Mavropoulos, T., Kotropoulos, C.: Datasets and performance metrics for Greek named entity recognition. In: SETN, pp. 160–167 (2020)
5. Chinchor, N., Sundheim, B.: MUC-5 evaluation metrics. In: MUC, pp. 69–78 (1993)
6. Fan, A., Bhosale, S., Schwenk, H., et al.: Beyond English-centric multilingual machine translation. J. Mach. Learn. Res. **22**, 107:1–107:48 (2021)
7. Ghaddar, A., Langlais, P.: Winer: a Wikipedia annotated corpus for named entity recognition. In: IJCNLP, pp. 413–422 (2017)
8. Hienert, D., Wegener, D., Paulheim, H.: Automatic classification and relationship extraction for multi-lingual and multi-granular events from Wikipedia. In: DeRiVE, pp. 1–10 (2012)

9. Honnibal, M., Montani, I.: spaCy 2: natural language understanding with Bloom embeddings, convolutional neural networks and incremental parsing (2017)
10. Daras, I., Markos Gogoulos, P.L.: gsoc2018-spacy. GitHub (2018). https://github.com/eellak/gsoc2018-spacy
11. Minard, A., Speranza, M., Urizar, R., et al.: MEANTIME, the newsreader multilingual event and time corpus. In: LREC (2016)
12. Nothman, J., Ringland, N., Radford, W., Murphy, T., Curran, J.R.: Learning multilingual named entity recognition from Wikipedia. Artif. Intell. **194**, 151–175 (2013)
13. Pan, X., Zhang, B., May, J., Nothman, J., Knight, K., Ji, H.: Cross-lingual name tagging and linking for 282 languages. In: ACL, pp. 1946–1958 (2017)
14. Papantoniou, K., Efthymiou, V., Flouris, G.: EL-NEL: entity linking for Greek news articles. In: ISWC Posters, Demos and Industry Tracks (2021)
15. Piccinno, F., Ferragina, P.: From TagMe to WAT: a new entity annotator. In: ERD@SIGIR, pp. 55–62 (2014)
16. Prokopidis, P., Piperidis, S.: A neural NLP toolkit for Greek. In: SETN, pp. 125–128 (2020)
17. Smyrnioudis, N.: A transformer-based natural language processing toolkit for Greek-Named entity recognition and multi-task learning. BSc thesis, AUEB (2021)

VRKG-CollaborativeExploration - Data-Driven Discussions in the Metaverse

Alberto Accardo, Daniele Monaco, Maria Angela Pellegrino[✉],
Vittorio Scarano, and Carmine Spagnuolo

Dipartimento di Informatica, Università degli Studi di Salerno, Fisciano, Italy
{damonaco, mapellegrino, vitsca, cspagnuolo}@unisa.it

Abstract. The metaverse is an immersive, multi-user, virtual world where humans, represented by avatars, can entertain, socialize, and collaborate. This demo proposes VRKG-CollaborativeExploration, a Virtual Reality application that enables users to join thematic and collaborative data-driven discussions in the social metaverse where data are retrieved from Knowledge Graphs via SPARQL queries.

Keywords: Knowledge Graph · Collaboration · Exploration · Virtual reality · SPARQL queries

1 Introduction and Background

The term metaverse was first coined by the novelist Neal Stephenson in 1992 in his science fiction novel "Snow Crash" [4] to denote a virtual universe created beyond the real one where humans could freely access a 3D space that reflects the real world through digital agents (avatars) and interact with each other. As a new term, researchers discussed the metaverse with broad insights without reaching a consensus [7]. Mark Zuckerberg defined the metaverse as an embodied online world where people can work collaboratively and socialize with avatars, often in the form of headsets or glasses [10]. Common metaverse features are persistent, multi-user, immersive environments [4,7], where immersion is achieved by digital technologies such as augmented reality, virtual reality (VR), and mixed reality [3], avatar-based platforms [6], where humans spend time performing their day-to-day activities, such as entertaining and socializing [5], where any user can create virtual rooms freely accessible to others.

This demo proposes VRKG-CollaborativeExploration, a VR application where users can join thematic virtual rooms and perform collaborative data-driven discussions supported by structured data. We achieved this by exploiting Knowledge Graphs (KGs) as the data source and SPARQL query results to model topics of interest. The proposed application, tested on Meta Quest Pro, relies on VR technologies by using a lightweight head-mounted display to give the user a sense of visual and audio immersion. Users will be immersed in a meta world of knowledge represented by 3D *sphere of knowledge* (SK) (a.k.a. the nodes of the KG induced by SPARQL query results) and may navigate

C. Pesquita et al. (Eds.): ESWC 2023, LNCS 13998, pp. 149–153, 2023.
https://doi.org/10.1007/978-3-031-43458-7_28

this world using relations between SK (a.k.a. the links of the KG induced by SPARQL query results). During an exploration session, users may have real-time interaction with other users (represented by avatars) using gestures and voice communication.

Our proposal grounds on the literature of 3D visualization of ontologies and KGs, such as Ontodia3D [2], that leads to the possibility of representing data interactively and entertainingly. Thanks to the collaborative dimension, the opportunity to freely author publicly available and persistent virtual rooms via SPARQL queries, and an avatar-based representation of users able to mimic hands and head movements, our proposal moves a step forward in the direction of enabling thematic collaborative discussions in the social metaverse. While research combining metaverse and KGs mainly focuses on the interoperability issues and data modeling aspects [1,5,8,9], we focus on the collaborative exploration and data-driven discussion enabled by a 3D representation of the Semantic Web data in the metaverse. A video of our proposal is freely available[1].

2   VRKG-CollaborativeExploration

VRKG-CollaborativeExploration is a VR application where users can join data-driven discussions enabled by a 3D representation of a KG induced by SPARQL query results that determine the topic of the thematic virtual rooms. Instead of proposing a VR application bounded to a specific data source, VRKG-CollaborativeExploration lets users choose the topic of interest from a publicly available and persistent repository of virtual thematic rooms determined by SPARQL query results.

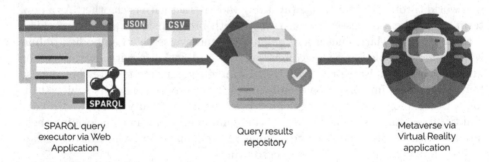

| SPARQL query executor via Web Application | Query results repository | Metaverse via Virtual Reality application |

Fig. 1. Approach to enable data-driven discussions in the metaverse by querying KG.

The proposed workflow at the basis of VRKG-CollaborativeExploration is graphically represented in Fig. 1. A publicly available web application[2] lets users author a virtual room by performing a SPARQL query on a user-defined working

---

[1] Video presenting the demo: http://www.isislab.it:12280/submission/VRKG.mp4.
[2] Web application http://www.isislab.it:12280/applications.html.

SPARQL endpoint. The SPARQL query results is constrained as it serves as an input for the visualization step, and it must retrieve subject, property, object, with their respective labels and subject description. While labels will be used on nodes and edges in the metaverse to improve readability, textual descriptions will provide further details on demand based on users' interactions.

Any executed query stores a persistent virtual room modelled by a CSV containing query results and a JSON file to configure the VR application in a public repository. Each room in the metaverse has a topic strictly connected to the retrieved SPARQL query results. For example, Fig. 2 shows users who joined the thematic virtual room dedicated to stars and constellations available in DBpedia. In each virtual room, users can collaboratively discuss with others using a 3D representation of the KG as evidence.

Fig. 2. Example of the demo in action while exploring the *stars* room in the metaverse. The screen projects what each participant joining the metaverse can explore via the Meta Quest Pro. The two avatars reflecting the real users and the KG on the background modeling starts and constellations retrieved by querying DBpedia are observed by a third user out of the scene. Users can see each other in the metaverse even if they join the same room from geographically distant physical places.

Hence, users can manipulate the KG induced by SPARQL query results where nodes and edges are referred to by English labels, focus on nodes and visualize node details on dedicated panels, and perform a data-driven discussion enabled by the possibility to manipulate the graph in the same virtual place and discuss each other about the explored content using real-time voice streaming, overcoming any geographical distance.

Users can also customise the graphic room profile. At the moment, authors can choose between *Universe* and *Blue sky*. The source code is publicly available on GitHub with an Open License[3].

Technical Details. Our implementation of `VRKG-CollaborativeExploration` is developed using the Unity game engine 2021.3.2f1 version. The main packages used are Mixed Reality Toolkit 2.8 to handle the input from the headset touch controllers, Photon Unity Networking 2.39 to implement the multi-user capability. The application has been tested on Meta Quest Pro headsets. The resulting graph is limited to a maximum of 50 nodes total and 16 edges per node. This limit has been handpicked to both avoid performance issues (due to the complexity of the graphics and physics simulation in VR) and to not create complex and overcrowded graphs which are difficult to navigate for the users.

3 Demonstration and Conclusions

The metaverse is in an early developmental stage but is promising to occupy prominent space in the next phase of the Internet [5]. This demo focuses on enabling data-driven discussions in the metaverse implemented by the VR technology exploiting KGs as a data source. It represents an opportunity to entertain and engage users in data-driven thematic discussions and KG exploration without requiring any technical skills in SPARQL query language. SPARQL knowledge is only required when users want to author virtual rooms in the metaverse. In future directions, we will support Prezi-like presentations by predefined navigation of nodes and edges configured by a presenter.

Demonstration. During the demo, we will show how to configure the VR application[4] to join a virtual room, such as *the stars room*, by accessing to a publicly available SPARQL query results repository, and how to author a data-driven discussion room in the metaverse. The demo will take place by exploiting the Meta Quest Pro and by collaboratively exploring KGs with remote users.

References

1. Awan, A., Prokop, S., Vele, J., Dounas, T., Lombardi, D., Agkathidis, A.: Qualitative knowledge graph for the evaluation of metaverse (s). ASCAAD **28** (2022)
2. Daniil, R., Wohlgenannt, G., Pavlov, D., Emelyanov, Y., Mouromtsev, D.: A new tool for linked data visualization and exploration in 3D/VR space. In: Hitzler, P., et al. (eds.) ESWC 2019. LNCS, vol. 11762, pp. 167–171. Springer, Cham (2019). https://doi.org/10.1007/978-3-030-32327-1_33

---

[3] Source code: https://github.com/DanieleBubb/VRKG-CollaborativeExploration.
[4] APK link: http://www.isislab.it:12280/submission/VRKG.apk.

3. Di Natale, A.F., Repetto, C., Riva, G., Villani, D.: Immersive virtual reality in K-12 and higher education: a 10-year systematic review of empirical research. Br. J. Educ. Technol. **51**(6), 2006–2033 (2020)
4. Díaz, J., Saldaña, C., Ávila, C.: Virtual world as a resource for hybrid education. Int. J. Emerg. Technol. Learn. (iJET) **15**(15), 94–109 (2020)
5. Jaimini, U., Zhang, T., Brikis, G.O., Sheth, A.: iMetaverseKG: industrial metaverse knowledge graph to promote interoperability in design and engineering applications. IEEE Internet Comput. **26**(6), 59–67 (2022)
6. Jin, S.A.A.: Leveraging avatars in 3D virtual environments (second life) for interactive learning: the moderating role of the behavioral activation system vs. behavioral inhibition system and the mediating role of enjoyment. Interact. Learn. Environ. **19**(5), 467–486 (2011)
7. Mystakidis, S.: Metaverse. Encyclopedia **2**(1), 486–497 (2022). https://doi.org/10.3390/encyclopedia2010031
8. Shu, X., Gu, X.: An empirical study of a smart education model enabled by the edu-metaverse to enhance better learning outcomes for students. Systems **11**(2), 75 (2023)
9. Wang, X., Wang, J., Wu, C., Xu, S., Ma, W.: Engineering brain: metaverse for future engineering. AI Civil Eng. **1**(1), 2 (2022)
10. Zuckerberg, M.: Connect 2021 keynote: our vision for the metaverse. https://tech.fb.com/ar-vr/2021/10/connect-2021-our-vision-for-the-metaverse (2021). Accessed Mar 2023

FOO: An Upper-Level Ontology for the Forest Observatory

Naeima Hamed[1](✉)(iD), Omer Rana[1](iD), Benoît Goossens[2](iD),
Pablo Orozco-terWengel[2](iD), and Charith Perera[1](iD)

[1] School of Computer Science and Informatics, Cardiff University, Cardiff, UK
{hamednh,ranaof,pererac,goossensbr,orozco-terwengelpa}@cardiff.ac.uk
[2] School of Biosciences, Cardiff University, Cardiff, UK

Abstract. Wildlife and preservation research activities in the tropical forest of Sabah, Malaysia, can generate a wide variety of data. However, each research activity manages its data independently. Since these data are disparate, gaining unified access to them remains a challenge. We propose the Forest Observatory Ontology (FOO) as a basis for integrating different datasets. FOO comprises a novel upper-level ontology that integrates wildlife data generated by sensors. We used existing ontological resources from various domains (i.e., wildlife) to model FOO's concepts and establish their relationships. FOO was then populated with multiple semantically modelled datasets. FOO structure and utility are subsequently evaluated using specialised software and task-based methods. The evaluation results demonstrate that FOO can be used to answer complex use-case questions promptly and correctly.

Keywords: Wildlife data · Internet of Things · Ontology · Knowledge Graph · Question-answering

1 Introduction

Over the past 15 years, the Danau Griang Field Centre (DGFC)[1], a scientific research facility in Sabah, Malaysia, has collected various data. Collars with GPS chips have been put on elephants, and images from camera traps are also available. However, each research activity maintains its collected data independently, resulting in disparate data. Hence, decision-makers face challenges when accessing these data collectively to search for and discover meaningful information. To address this challenge, we suggest using semantic web technologies, which make it possible to search multiple data sources in a detailed way and to

Resource type: Ontology and Knowledge Graph.
License: Creative Commons 4.0 International SA (CC BY-SA 4.0).
Ontology's URL https://naeima.github.io/foo_html/.
Knowledge Graph's URL https://naeima.github.io/fooKG/.
Main website URL: https://www.ontology.forest-observatory.org.
[1] https://www.dgfc.life/home/.

reason about data. Our poster paper contributes an upper-level ontology named the Forest Observatory Ontology (FOO). Following past research methodologies, FOO reuses classes from existing ontologies to connect the Internet of Things (IoT) and wildlife concepts. Then we populated FOO with four semantically modelled datasets to form knowledge graphs. These knowledge graphs enable users to access and query disparate data types in a unified manner, facilitating semantically-enriched information exchange between humans and computer systems.

2   Approach

We searched several previous research archives (e.g., the ACM digital library and Google Scholar) for a suitable methodology. We acknowledge the significance of NeOn Methodology [7]. However, we selected the Linked Open Terms (LOT) methodology by Poveda et al. [6], which builds on Neon Methodology and has features that best match our ontology requirement. For example, competency questions, natural statements and tabular data can all be used at the requirements stage. Figure 1 depicts the development process.

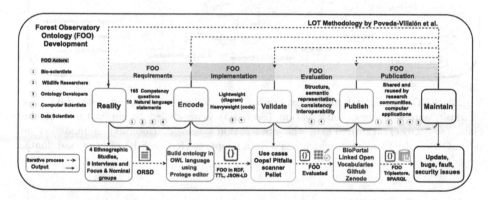

Fig. 1. FOO Ontology Development phases, inspired by Linked Open Terms (LOT) methodology

The Ontology Requirements Specification Document (ORSD)[2] was made to collect information about FOO's scope, its intended purpose, and how it can be used in real life. We compiled 106 competency questions, ten natural language statements (NLS), different use cases from ethnographic studies at DGFC, semi-structured interviews with eight wildlife researchers, and focus and nominal groups at DGFC. For implementation, we searched the existing literature for relevant ontologies. We found many of them, such as SAREF[3], IoT-lite[4],

---

[2] https://naeima.github.io/FOO-Book/lifecycle/requirements.html.

[3] https://ontology.tno.nl/saref/.

[4] https://www.w3.org/Submission/iot-lite/.

SWEET[5] and African wildlife ontology [3]. We chose to reuse the self-contained ontology Sensor, Observation, Sample and Actuator (SOSA) [2] from the second version of the Semantic Sensor Network (SSN) Ontology [1] as it closely matches our requirements. Furthermore, we adopted the BBC Wildlife Ontology[6], which contained sufficient classes to model our wildlife data entities. We discussed the conceptual model (Fig. 2) with FOO's actors. Following that, we encoded FOO in the Web Ontology Language (OWL2) (https://www.w3.org/TR/owl2-overview/), edited it with Protégé[7], and wrote pipeline codes in Python to map and serialise the datasets that populated FOO. Figure 2 shows FOO's lightweight conceptual model.

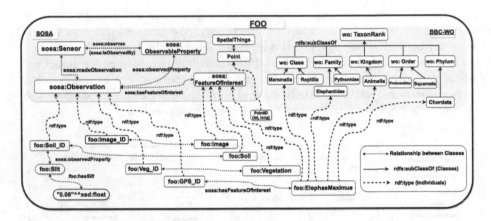

Fig. 2. FOO conceptual model explaining the classes instantiated with data. For example, our soil sensor observation (Soil_ID) is modelled as an instance of the class (sosa:Observation). Then, the observation's metric, (foo:Silt) is modelled as (sosa:ObservableProperty), which has a data property (foo:hasSilt) of type (xsd:float).

We evaluated FOO's structure, semantic representation, and interoperability using open-source online scanners, Oops![8], and Pellet[9] and SPARQL queries that answered competency questions. We instantiated FOO with four distinct wildlife datasets about the forest of Sabah, Malaysia. The datasets compromise sensor observations about (i) soil properties, (ii) GPS elephant tracking collars, (iii) vegetation scanners, and (iv) camera trap images. We programmatically transformed these heterogeneous datasets into RDF graphs. We wrote modular Python codes using the RDFlib[10] library. The approach used is similar to

---

[5] https://bioportal.bioontology.org/ontologies/SWEET.

[6] https://github.com/rdmpage/bbc-wildlife.

[7] https://protege.stanford.edu/.

[8] oops.linkeddata.es.

[9] github.com/stardog-union/pellet.

[10] https://github.com/RDFLib/rdflib.

the RDF Mapping Language (RML) mapping technique[11]. The pipeline codes declare the namespaces specific to FOO, iterate through the data, and map the observation id columns to the subjects, the observable property columns to the objects, and their relationship to the predicates. The data source entities were modelled as instances (rdf:type) of FOO's classes, as shown in Fig. 2. Nevertheless, the mapping codes generate RDF triples that could be serialised into various output formats, such as Turtle, RDF, N3, and JSON-LD. The serialised RDF graphs are loaded into Stardog triple-stores containing FOO to form the knowledge graphs. Each knowledge graph resides in a separate triple-store, representing a data source. Our criteria for creating the federation of knowledge graphs focused on applying a common vocabulary (i.e., a shared ontology) and achieving interoperability (i.e., the disparate knowledge graphs can exchange information using common standards and protocols). To link these knowledge graphs, we used federated SPARQL queries to retrieve data from multiple knowledge graphs simultaneously. The competency question shown in Listing 1.1 retrieved accurate and prompt information about an Asian elephant's GPS tracking information and the soil condition in a particular area from different knowledge graphs. In order to publish FOO, we used the WIZARD for DOCumenting Ontology (WIDOCO) [5] to generate W3C-compliant documentation. Then, FOO was shared on Github, Bioportal and its dedicated website. FOO's maintenance plan entails routine inspection, scanning, and documenting updates. There will always be issues to resolve, such as bugs or new data to add or remove. Hence, we rely on Github[12] for maintenance, collaboration, and version control. A noteworthy research project by Mussa et al. [4] implemented an AI application, specifically a chatbot, to enhance access to FOO by non-domain experts. As such, we encourage contributions from the research community to support us in extending FOO and identifying additional use cases.

Listing 1.1. What is elephant Aqeela's GPS collar information on 13 November 2011 and the soil sensor information installed at Danum Valley Conservation Area?

```
Prefix  foo :  <http://www.ontology/ns/foo/1.1#>
Prefix  sosa :  <http://www.w3.org/ns/sosa/>
Prefix  xsd :  <http://www.w3.org/2001/XMLSchema#>
Prefix  dgfc :  <http://www.w3.org/schema.org/dgfc/elephant#>
Prefix  wgs84_pos :  <http://www.w3.org/2003/01/geo/wgs84_pos#>

SELECT DISTINCT * {
  ?UniqueID a   sosa:Observation ;
  sosa:madeObservation  dgfc:Aqeela ;
  foo:hasSpeed  ?Speed ;
  wgs84_pos:lat  ?Lat ;
  wgs84_pos:long  ?Long ;
  sosa:resultTime  "2011-11-13"^^xsd:date .
  foo:ElephasMaximus a   ?info ;
  {SERVICE <username:password@https://[host].stardog.cloud:
```

---

[11] https://rml.io/specs/rml/.

[12] https://github.com/Naeima/Forest-Observatory-Ontology.

```
port/Soil/query>
{?Soil_ID a sosa:Observation ;
?Site "Danum_Valley_Conservation_Area" ;
foo:hasSilt ?Silt;
foo:hasSoil_pH ?pH.}}
Limit 1
```

3 Conclusion and Future Work

We propose the Forest Observatory Ontology (FOO), an upper-level ontology that semantically integrates heterogeneous wildlife data. It provided answers to complex questions to aid bio-scientists and wildlife researchers in making informed decisions. We instantiated FOO using diverse datasets modelled as RDF graphs. The resultant knowledge graphs contain six million triples capable of performing various operations. First, end-users can remotely query them, as demonstrated in our usage documentation and SPARQL query examples. Secondly, wildlife researchers can incorporate reasoning rules to assert conditions that constitute a threat to wildlife. In the future, we plan to use FOO's knowledge graphs for predictive analytics.

References

1. Haller, A., et al.: The modular SSN ontology: a joint W3C and OGC standard specifying the semantics of sensors, observations, sampling, and actuation. Semantic Web 10(1), 9–32 (2019)
2. Janowicz, K., Haller, A., Cox, S.J., Le Phuoc, D., Lefrançois, M.: SOSA: a lightweight ontology for sensors, observations, samples, and actuators. J. Web Semant. 56, 1–10 (2019)
3. Keet, C.M.: The African wildlife ontology tutorial ontologies. J. Biomed. Semant. 11(1), 1–11 (2020)
4. Mussa, O., Rana, O., Goossens, B., Orozco-terWengel, P., Perera, C.: ForestQB: an adaptive query builder to support wildlife research. arXiv preprint arXiv:2210.02640 (2022)
5. Garijo, D.: WIDOCO: a wizard for documenting ontologies. In: d'Amato, C., Fernandez, M., Tamma, V., Lecue, F., Cudré-Mauroux, P., Sequeda, J., Lange, C., Heflin, J. (eds.) ISWC 2017. LNCS, vol. 10588, pp. 94–102. Springer, Cham (2017). https://doi.org/10.1007/978-3-319-68204-4_9
6. Poveda-Villalón, M., Fernández-Izquierdo, A., Fernández-López, M., García-Castro, R.: LoT: an industrial oriented ontology engineering framework. Eng. Appl. Artif. Intell. 111, 104755 (2022)
7. Suárez-Figueroa, M.C., Gómez-Pérez, A., Fernández-López, M.: The NeOn methodology framework: a scenario-based methodology for ontology development. Appl. Ontol. 10, 107–145 (2015). https://doi.org/10.3233/AO-150145

RoXi: A Framework for Reactive Reasoning

Pieter Bonte$^{(\boxtimes)}$ⓘ and Femke Ongenaeⓘ

Ghent University - imec, Belgium, Technologiepark-Zwijnaarde 126, 9052 Ghent, Belgium
pieter.bonte@ugent.be

Abstract. The Stream Reasoning research paradigm aims to target application domains that need to solve both data variety and velocity at the same time. Many of these domains benefit from processing the data as close to the source as possible, e.g. in Internet of Things applications we see a paradigm shift towards Edge processing, and in the Web, we see more and more effort towards decentralization of the Web where applications run directly inside the browser. However, current Stream Reasoning engines are not able to reuse the same code-base to run applications in the cloud, edge, or browser.

In this paper, we present RoXi, a Reactive Reasoning framework that provides the needed building blocks to realize Stream Reasoning applications that can target cloud, edge, and browser environments.

Keywords: RDF Stream Processing · Edge Processing · Reasoning · Decentralized Web

1 Introduction

In recent years, the interest in streaming data has increased for application domains that combine data variety, i.e. data that require some form of data integration, with the requirement to process data in a reactive fashion, i.e., as soon as possible and before the data are no longer useful [1]. Examples of such application domains include Smart Cities, Industry 4.0, Web Analytics, etc. Stream Reasoning (SR) is a research initiative that combines Semantic Web with Stream Processing technologies to target both the data variety and velocity at the same time [8]. Semantic Reasoning allows to target the data variety, by providing means to integrate and abstract data from various sources. Furthermore, it provides a way to interpret any defined domain knowledge.

Many of the application domains that target both data variety and velocity can offload parts of the processing closer to where data is being produced in order to speed up computation. In Internet of Things (IoT) applications, this means to the Edge of the network, while in Web applications, this means to the browser of the user. Running computation in the browser has become more popular with the rise of the decentralized Web, as supported by the Solid project [6].

C. Pesquita et al. (Eds.): ESWC 2023, LNCS 13998, pp. 159–163, 2023.
https://doi.org/10.1007/978-3-031-43458-7_30

Both the Edge environment and browsers provide limited resources compared to processing all data in the cloud. However, many of the same building blocks should be able to run both in the cloud and at the edge/browser. This calls for a Reasoning framework where the same code-base can be used for running applications both in the cloud or at the edge/browser.

We introduce RoXi, a framework for Reactive Reasoning that is fully written in Rust. RoXi allows to use the same code-base to develop applications that require Reactive Reasoning, disregardless of performing computation at the cloud, edge or browser. RoXi can run in the browser through the support of WebAssembly, at the edge through Rust's ability to optimize code for low-level devices and at the cloud.

2   Related Work

Various reasoners and Stream Reasoners have been proposed over the years [9], however, typically focusing on running high-performance hardware as found in the cloud. RDFox [4] is a highly-scalable reasoning-enabled RDF store and has shown to be able to run at the Edge, however, it does not support any browser run-time, nor stream processing capabilities. Fed4Edge [5] is an RDF Stream Processing engine optimized to run in an edge environment, it focuses on query answering on RDF data streams. However, it does not provide any reasoning capabilities or functionality to run inside the browser. DIVIDE [2] allows to optimize reasoning rules for the evaluation at the edge, however, it does not support any browser run-time or optimized code for running on low-level devices. Hylar [7] is a reasoner written in Javascript and designed to run in the browser. However, the Javascript run-time makes it an unsuited candidate to efficiently run at the Edge, in the cloud or efficiently handle high-velocity data streams.

3   Architecture

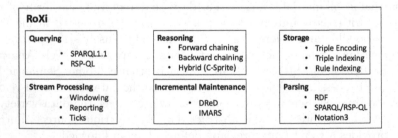

Fig. 1. Overview of the supported components in RoXi's architecture

RoXi is a framework for Reactive Reasoning, providing Querying, Reasoning and Stream Reasoning functionality. Figure 1 visualizes RoXi's architecture, consisting of the following components:

1. **Querying**: RoXi provides support for both SPARQL1.1 queries on static data and RSP-QL queries on streaming data.
2. **Reasoning**: RoXi has at this point support for rule-based reasoning, with Datalog expressivity. We support a subset of *Notation3* rules[1] that relate to the expressivity of *Datalog*. RoXi supports both forward- and backward-chaining reasoning algorithms. For efficient reasoning over RDF data streams, RoXi implements the C-Sprite algorithm [1], i.e. a hybrid approach that optimizes the reasoning based on the registered queries.
3. **RDF Stream Processing**: RoXi aims to provide the same RDF Stream Processing interfaces and functionality as RSP4J [8], which aims to unify RDF Stream Processing. RoXi provides *Time-based Windows* that allow to cut the unbounded streams in processable chunks. *Different Reporting* dimensions are supported that allow to configure when the window triggers: *(a) Content Change*: reports when the content of the current window changes, *(b) Window Close*: reports when the current window closes, *(c) Non-empty Content*: reports when the current window is not empty, and *(d) Periodic* reports periodically. Various *Ticks* are supported that can configure how the evaluation of the reporting should be triggered: time-driven, tuple-driven, or batch-driven. Once the window triggers, different components can be called, such as *Querying* and *Reasoning*.
4. **Incremental Maintenance**: incremental maintenance programs allow to keep an updated view on all inferred triples through forward-chaining. These programs update the view when triples are added or removed. At this point, DReD [3] and IMARS incremental maintenance programs are supported in RoXi. The latter focus specifically on Window-based maintenance. In the future, the more optimized Forward-Backward-Forward [3] and the naive counting-based [3] approaches will be provided as well.
5. **Storage**: To reduce memory usage, RoXi employs dictionary encoding on the consumed triples. To speed up query evaluation, RoXi supports Indexed Datastores for all triples and rules.
6. **Parsing**: RoXi supports parsing of RDF, SPARQL, RSP-QL and Notation3.

RoXi is implemented in Rust and can be compiled to run at the edge, cloud or browser. The code is available on our Github-page[2]. RoXi's functionality can be tested directly in the browser using the Web UI[3].

4   Conclusion and Future Work

This paper presents RoXi, a framework for Reactive Reasoning. RoXi provides components for querying, reasoning, incremental maintenance and RDF Stream Processing. RoXi can be compiled to run in the cloud, edge and inside the browser, allowing the same code-base to be used while targeting IoT, Edge and decentralized Web applications.

---

[1] https://w3c.github.io/N3/spec/.

[2] https://github.com/pbonte/roxi.

[3] https://pbonte.github.io/roxi/index.html.

In our future work, we aim to support more implementations of different technologies for each component in RoXi's hierarchy. For *Querying*, we wish to support SHACL and research its applicability in combination with the *RDF Stream Processing* component. In terms of *Reasoning*, we wish to investigate the integration of more expressive reasoning algorithms both for reasoning over static data, e.g. to support OWL2 DL, and streaming data e.g. using temporal reasoning such as datalogMTL. For *RDF Stream Processing*, we aim to support more advanced types of windowing, such as session windows. We also aim to formalize the connection between reasoning and RDF Stream processing while using RoXi as a prototype. For *Incremental Maintenance*, we aim to integrate the more optimized Forward-Backward-Forward [3] and the naive counting-based [3]. In terms of *Storage*, we wish to experiment with different indexing techniques and their relation with streaming data, i.e. researching data structures that optimize trade-offs between the added value of the indexes and the cost of performing the indexing on data that changes frequently.

RoXi brings us one step closer to realize the Stream Reasoning vision by providing a Reactive Reasoning framework that allows the same code-base to be run in the cloud, edge or even in the browser.

Acknowledgement. This work is funded by Pieter Bonte's postdoctoral fellowship of Research Foundation Flanders (FWO) (1266521N) and by SolidLab Vlaanderen (Flemish Government, EWI, and RRF project VV023/10).

References

1. Bonte, P., Tommasini, R., De Turck, F., Ongenae, F., Valle, E.D.: C-sprite: efficient hierarchical reasoning for rapid RDF stream processing. In: Proceedings of the 13th ACM International Conference on Distributed and Event-Based Systems, pp. 103–114 (2019)
2. De Brouwer, M., et al.: Context-aware and privacy-preserving homecare monitoring through adaptive query derivation for IOT data streams with divide. Semantic Web J.
3. Motik, B., Nenov, Y., Piro, R., Horrocks, I.: Maintenance of datalog materialisations revisited. Artif. Intell. **269**, 76–136 (2019)
4. Nenov, Y., Piro, R., Motik, B., Horrocks, I., Wu, Z., Banerjee, J.: RDFox: a highly-scalable RDF store. In: Arenas, M., et al. (eds.) ISWC 2015. LNCS, vol. 9367, pp. 3–20. Springer, Cham (2015). https://doi.org/10.1007/978-3-319-25010-6_1
5. Nguyen-Duc, M., Le-Tuan, A., Calbimonte, J.-P., Hauswirth, M., Le-Phuoc, D.: Autonomous RDF stream processing for IoT edge devices. In: Wang, X., Lisi, F.A., Xiao, G., Botoeva, E. (eds.) JIST 2019. LNCS, vol. 12032, pp. 304–319. Springer, Cham (2020). https://doi.org/10.1007/978-3-030-41407-8_20
6. Sambra, A.V., et al.: Solid: a platform for decentralized social applications based on linked data. MIT CSAIL & Qatar Computing Research Institute, Tech. Rep. (2016)
7. Terdjimi, M., Médini, L., Mrissa, M.: Hylar+ improving hybrid location-agnostic reasoning with incremental rule-based update. In: Proceedings of the 25th International Conference Companion on World Wide Web, pp. 259–262 (2016)

8. Tommasini, R., Bonte, P., Ongenae, F., Della Valle, E.: RSP4J: an API for RDF stream processing. In: Verborgh, R., et al. (eds.) ESWC 2021. LNCS, vol. 12731, pp. 565–581. Springer, Cham (2021). https://doi.org/10.1007/978-3-030-77385-4_34
9. Tommasini, R., Bonte, P., Spiga, F., Della Valle, E.: Web Stream Processing Systems and Benchmarks, pp. 109–138. Springer, Cham (2023). https://doi.org/10.1007/978-3-031-15371-6_5

SummaryGPT: Leveraging ChatGPT for Summarizing Knowledge Graphs

Giannis Vassiliou[1], Nikolaos Papadakis[1], and Haridimos Kondylakis[1,2(✉)]

[1] ECE, Hellenic Mediterranean University, Heraklion, Greece
giannisvas@ics.forth.gr, npapadak@cs.hmu.gr
[2] FORTH-ICS, Heraklion, Greece
kondylak@ics.forth.gr

Abstract. Semantic summaries try to extract compact information from the original knowledge graph (KG) while reducing its size for various purposes such as query answering, indexing, or visualization. Although so far several techniques have been exploited for summarizing individual KGs, to the best of our knowledge, there is no approach summarizing the interests of the users in exploring those KGs, capturing also how these evolve. SummaryGPT fills this gap by enabling the exploration of users' interests as captured from their queries over time. For generating these summaries we first extract the nodes appearing in query logs, captured from a specific time period, and then we classify them into different categories in order to generate quotient summaries on top. For the classification, we explore both the KG type hierarchy (if existing) and also a large language model, i.e. ChatGPT. Exploring different time periods enables us to identify shifts in user interests and capture their evolution through time. In this demonstration we use WikiData KG in order to enable active exploration of the corresponding user interests, allowing end-users to visualize how these evolve over time.

1 Introduction

The explosion of the information now available in big KGs requires effective and efficient methods for quickly understanding their content, enabling the exploitation of the information they contain.

Semantic summaries have been proposed as methods for condensing information available in such KGs [4,5]. According to our survey [1] a semantic summary is a piece of compact information, extracted from the original KG that can be used instead of the original graph for performing certain tasks more efficiently such as query answering, indexing or visualization.

Recent approaches (e.g., [6,7]) have generated efficient summaries over large KGs such as DBpedia, WikiData, and Bio2RDF by capturing users' interests as they appear in their queries. The idea in those approaches is to identify the most frequently queried nodes in large query logs as the most important ones, and extract and link them exploiting paths from the original graph. Those summaries have nice properties regarding query answering, however, they fail to provide an overview of the overall graph as they only focus on the few most queried nodes, pretty much ignoring the information contained in the remaining graph.

SummaryGPT, demonstrated in this paper, focuses on presenting an overview of the *entire KG for visualization* purposes by constructing *quotient* summaries. Quotient summaries establish a notion of "equivalence" for identifying node's representatives, and presenting those representatives instead of the original graph, enabling users to quickly understand the main groups of the underlying graph.

For the classification of the extracted nodes into the various groups we exploit and compare two methods: a) one based on the existing type hierarchy and b) one identifying (and labeling) generic categories generated by ChatGPT. ChatGPT is a large language model (LLM) that is trained on a substantial corpus of text data to perform natural language processing tasks such as text summarization and question answering. The ability of LLMs to pack large amounts of knowledge into their large parameter set has raised the possibility of using their implicit knowledge without domain training.

In this demonstration, we move beyond single quotient summaries, considering the fact that ontologies and KGs evolve over time [2,3] along with user interests. As such instead of a single summary, we present a *series* of summaries, summarizing how users' interests evolve over time, allowing KG curators to appropriately visualize and explore shifts in users' interests. To the best of our knowledge, this is the first time that the notion of a *series of summaries* appears in the bibliography for enabling the exploration of KGs.

The system is available online[1] however we have disabled the configuration screen.

2   Architecture

Figure 1 (left) depicts the high-level architecture of SummaryGPT. It consists of three layers, the GUI layer, the Service layer and the Data layer.

Using the GUI layer the user is able to upload query logs to be processed for a specific KG (SPARQL endpoint) and visualize the result summaries. The user is able to explore how those summaries evolve through time identifying the main categories targeting those queries. The more nodes in a specific category the bigger the node that appears in the result summary. The category nodes are linked based on the links in the processed query logs using the same philosophy (bigger lines as more queries include this link). Further, additional statistics are presented on the distribution of the queried nodes in the various groups. The main graph is interactive allowing users to click on the nodes and get further information on the nodes that appear in a specific group.

The service layer includes initially the query parser, extracting and storing the various nodes and edges in user queries, and also it implements the algorithm

---

[1] https://giannisergo.pythonanywhere.com/.

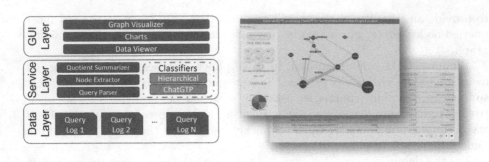

Fig. 1. SummaryGPT high-level architecture (left) and example screenshots of the system (right).

for constructing the quotient summaries. The algorithm summarizes a graph by assigning a representative to each class of equivalence of the nodes in the original graph.

Definition 1. (Quotient graph) Let $G = (V, E)$ be a KG graph and $\equiv\ \subseteq V \times V$ be an *equivalence relation* over the nodes of V. The *quotient graph of G using* $\equiv$, denoted $G_{/\equiv}$, is a graph having:

– a node u_S for each set S of $\equiv$-equivalent V nodes;
– an edge (v_{S_1}, l, v_{S_2}) iff there exists an E edge (v_1, l, v_2) such that v_{S_1} (resp. v_{S_2}) represents the set of V nodes $\equiv$-equivalent to v_1 (resp. v_2).

A particular feature of the quotient methods is that each graph node is represented by exactly one summary node, given that one node can only belong to one equivalence class. For determining the equivalence classes the service layer implements two classifiers.

The first classifier is based on ChatGPT, grouping query nodes into common-sense categories returned by the large language model. For each node (i.e., its label) appearing in user queries, we requested a one-word generic category that this node belongs to (i.e. "for each item in the list return a word that defines under which broad category it belongs"), and then we grouped the ones with the same description, building as such a classifier for the nodes appearing in each query log.

The second classifier queries the KG directly in order to retrieve the types of the queries' nodes, ignoring the ones that have no type, and then grouping the queried nodes based on their types.

Finally, the data layer includes the various query logs initially uploaded by the end user. SummaryGPT was implemented in Python Dash, whereas Cytoscape was used for the interactive graphs. ChatGPT API was used for querying Chat-GPT and standard SPARQL was for querying the KGs.

3   Demonstration

To demonstrate the functionalities of SummaryGPT (an instance is shown in Fig. 1 (right)), we will use the Wikidata KG along with the query logs available online[2]. The query logs are already split into seven batches, each one covering user queries for around a month, starting from June 2017. We used organic queries ranging between 200K and 800K queries per batch.

The demonstration will proceed in six phases:

1. **Configuration.** The summarization process starts by selecting the KG to be summarized along with the corresponding query logs. In the configuration menu, the user should provide a SPARQL endpoint for each KG and also a set of files, each one containing a distinct query log.
2. **Summary over a single query batch using existing hierarchy.** In this phase we will select a single query batch and we will demonstrate the quotient summary returned by the system. We will explain that the size of each group depends on the frequency of the nodes of the corresponding type that appears in the query batch and we will demonstrate the various statistics available.
3. **Summary over a single query batch using ChatGPT.** Then we will demonstrate the summary over the same query batch using the ChatGPT constructed classifier. The classifier automatically suggests groups and labels for these groups.
4. **Mini-Game.** In this phase we will discuss the quality of the summaries as perceived by conference participants. We will play a mini-game with the conference participants by examining a few nodes of the query logs and trying to assign those nodes in groups.
5. **Assessment.** Then we will discuss also that the results using the ChatGPT classifier seem to be more natural and very close to what a human classifier would do if s/he was asked to do the same process.
6. **Evolution of Summaries in Time.** Finally, we will demonstrate how those summaries evolve over time based on users' interests as they are captured by the query logs. We will identify that the 1st interval has a significant portion of nodes related to politics, mostly related to US elections, retaining traction for the following months, whereas after elections this portion is practically eliminated.

4   Conclusions

In this demonstration, we generate quotient summaries for KG based on user queries. We exploit query batches to explore how those summaries evolve through time making several interesting observations and comparing two classification methods for assigning queried entities into summary groups. To our knowledge, no other system today is available, enabling the rapid summarization of big KGs and no other system is able to explore how those summaries evolve over time.

---

[2] https://iccl.inf.tu-dresden.de/web/Wikidata_SPARQL_Logs/en.

Acknowledgments. Work reported in this paper has been partially supported by the Hellenic Foundation for Research and Innovation (H.F.R.I.) under the "2nd Call for H.F.R.I. Research Projects to support Post-Doctoral Researchers" (iQARuS Project No. 1147). Further is has been partially supported by the Hoirizon SafePolyMed EU project under grant agreement No. 101057639.

References

1. Cebiric, S., et al.: Summarizing semantic graphs: a survey. VLDB J. **28**(3), 295–327 (2019)
2. Kondylakis, H., Flouris, G., Plexousakis, D.: Ontology and schema evolution in data integration: review and assessment. In: Meersman, R., Dillon, T., Herrero, P. (eds.) OTM 2009. LNCS, vol. 5871, pp. 932–947. Springer, Heidelberg (2009). https://doi.org/10.1007/978-3-642-05151-7_14
3. Kondylakis, H., Plexousakis, D.: Ontology evolution in data integration: query rewriting to the rescue. In: Jeusfeld, M., Delcambre, L., Ling, T.-W. (eds.) ER 2011. LNCS, vol. 6998, pp. 393–401. Springer, Heidelberg (2011). https://doi.org/10.1007/978-3-642-24606-7_29
4. Trouli, G.E., Pappas, A., Troullinou, G., Koumakis, L., Papadakis, N., Kondylakis, H.: Summer: structural summarization for RDF/S kgs. Algorithms **16**(1), 18 (2023)
5. Troullinou, G., Kondylakis, H., Stefanidis, K., Plexousakis, D.: Exploring RDFS KBs using summaries. In: Vrandečić, D., et al. (eds.) ISWC 2018. LNCS, vol. 11136, pp. 268–284. Springer, Cham (2018). https://doi.org/10.1007/978-3-030-00671-6_16
6. Vassiliou, G., Alevizakis, F., Papadakis, N., Kondylakis, H.: iSummary: workload-based, personalized summaries for knowledge graphs. In: ESWC (2023)
7. Vassiliou, G., Troullinou, G., Papadakis, N., Kondylakis, H.: WBSum: workload-based summaries for RDF/S kbs. In: SSDBM, pp. 248–252. ACM (2021)

Entity Typing with Triples Using Language Models

Aniqa Riaz[1], Sara Abdollahi[2]([✉])[ID], and Simon Gottschalk[2][ID]

[1] Universität Bonn, Bonn, Germany
`s6anriaz@uni-bonn.de`
[2] L3S Research Center, Leibniz Universität Hannover, Hanover, Germany
{abdollahi,gottschalk}@L3S.de

Abstract. Entity Typing is the task of assigning a type to an entity in a knowledge graph. In this paper, we propose ETwT (Entity Typing with Triples), which leverages the triples of an entity, namely its label, description and the property labels used on it. We analyse which language models and classifiers are best suited to this input and compare ETwT's performance on coarse-grained and fine-grained entity typing. Our evaluation demonstrates that ETwT is able to predict coarse-grained entity types with an F_1 score of 0.994, outperforming three baselines.

1 Introduction

The availability of entity types in a knowledge graph (e.g., *Microsoft* is a *Company*)[1] is important for a series of tasks including question answering and named entity linking. However, type information is often not complete. For example, in the well-established cross-domain knowledge graph DBpedia [1], $2,447,977$ out of $6,266,949$ entities do not have a type in the DBpedia ontology, including persons like Leonard E. Barrett and buildings like Deel Castle[2]. Therefore, entity typing is an essential sub-task of knowledge graph completion, aiming at full coverage of entity types in a knowledge graph.

Triples in a knowledge graph provide rich information describing an entity which can be used to detect the entity's type. This information includes both textual information, namely the label and description of an entity, as well as relationships to other entities (e.g., `dbr:Berlin dbo:country dbo:Germany`). Following the intuition behind [7], we expect that the properties used in an entity's triples can hint at the entity type, as well as its textual information [2,4]. In this paper, we propose ETwT (Entity Typing with Triples) which exploits both types of information simultaneously to perform highly precise entity typing.

To train a model that best deals with the given entity information, we perform an analysis of how different language models (BERT [6], XLNet [10] and GPT [8])

---

[1] This entity type assignment can be expressed as a triple in the DBpedia knowledge graph: `dbr:Microsoft rdf:type dbo:Company`.
[2] In the DBpedia dumps of December 2022, considering all entities that have a Wikipedia page ID but do not redirect or disambiguate.

C. Pesquita et al. (Eds.): ESWC 2023, LNCS 13998, pp. 169–173, 2023.
https://doi.org/10.1007/978-3-031-43458-7_32

and classifiers (Fully Connected, Convolutional and Recurrent Neural Networks) perform on entity typing.

We compare ETwT's best configuration on the DBpedia630k [9] dataset. The results demonstrate that ETwT outperforms three state-of-the-art baselines for coarse-grained entity typing, reaching an F_1 score of 0.994 on average. Thus, we highlight the effectiveness of leveraging entity properties along with entity labels and descriptions as input to a language model.

2 Related Work

Biswas et al. [2] combine a language model with a character embedding model to encode the entity label and detect its type. Cat2Type [3] instead utilises a Wikipedia category graph as an input to a language model. GRAND [4] employs BERT and RDF2Vec-based graph walking strategies. KLMo [5] uses translational embeddings of whole triples as an input to an attention layer. In contrast, ETwT focuses on an entity's properties including its label and description.

3 Approach

Figure 1 gives an overview of ETwT where, given an entity e (here, a node representing *Berlin*), a ranking of entity types is generated of which the top-ranked entity type is chosen (here, *Place*). To do so, we (i) first extract triples describing the entity, (ii) embed them using a language model, and (iii) train a classifier.

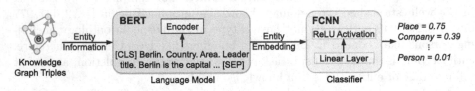

Fig. 1. The ETwT approach at the example of using BERT as language model and a fully connected neural network (FCNN) as classifier.

- **Knowledge Graph Triples**: We extract the property labels in the triples used on entity e plus its label and description as its entity information.
- **Language Model**: We fine-tune a pre-trained language model on the entity information. Figure 1 exemplifies ETwT using BERT as the language model, where we use BERT's [CLS] token as input to the subsequent classifier.
- **Classification**: A multi-class classifier is trained to predict the type of an entity. Figure 1 exemplifies ETwT using a fully connected neural network (FCNN) as classifier, where we use a ReLU activation for the final prediction.

4   Evaluation

4.1   Data

We use three splits (DB1, DB2 and DB3) of DBPedia630k [9][3] for evaluating our model. Each split is divided into a train, test, and validation set with a ratio of 50:30:20 [3]. We consider coarse-grained (14 entity types) and fine-grained (37 entity types[4]) entity typing.

4.2   Comparison with Baselines

We compare ETwT (using BERT and FCNN) against **JBN** (Judge an Entity by its Name) [2], **C2T** (Cat2Type) [3] and **GRAND** [4], as described in Sect. 2.

Table 1 shows that ETwT outperforms all baselines for coarse-grained entity typing based on Micro F_1 (MiF$_1$) and Macro F_1 (MaF$_1$) scores.[5] With F_1 scores of 0.994 on average, ETwT types entities nearly without a miss. For 37 fine-grained types, ETwT is outperformed by **GRAND** on DB1 but still performs best on DB3 with a Micro F_1 score of 0.947.

Table 1. Evaluation of coarse-grained (14 types) and fine-grained (37 types) entity typing. For ETwT, we use FCNN as classifier and BERT as language model.

| | Coarse-grained | | | | | | Fine-grained | | | |
| | DB1 | | DB2 | | DB3 | | DB1 | | DB3 | |
	MaF$_1$	MiF$_1$	MaF$_1$	MiF$_1$	MaF$_1$	MiF$_1$	MaF$_1$	MiF$_1$	MaF$_1$	MiF$_1$
JBN	0.714	0.720	0.606	0.657	0.446	0.511	0.231	0.521	0.318	0.531
C2T	0.983	0.984	0.983	0.983	0.985	0.985	0.402	0.732	0.847	0.915
GRAND	0.911	0.911	0.990	0.990	0.989	0.989	**0.745**	**0.870**	0.880	0.931
ETwT	**0.996**	**0.996**	**0.994**	**0.994**	**0.993**	**0.993**	0.404	0.765	**0.885**	**0.947**

4.3   Analysis of Language Models and Classifiers and Ablation Study

To identify which language models and classifiers are best to be used with ETwT, we evaluated all combinations of three language models (BERT [6], XLNet [10] and GPT [8]) and three classifiers: Fully Connected Neural Network (FCNN), Convolutional Neural Network (CNN) and Recurrent Neural Network (RNN). Table 2 shows the results of selected configurations and reveals that BERT with an FCNN performs best in most cases. Only for fine-grained entity types on DB3, XLNet performs best regarding Macro F_1.

---

[3] https://github.com/russabiswas/GRAND-Entity-Typing-in-KGs.

[4] We omit DB2 for fine-grained entity typing as its selection of classes deviates from the other splits.

[5] Before train/test/validation split, the coarse-grained types are distributed evenly over the datasets. Therefore, MaF$_1$ and MiF$_1$ are similar.

Table 2. Analysis of classifiers (Class.) and language models (LM).

Class.	LM	Coarse-grained						Fine-grained			
		DB1		DB2		DB3		DB1		DB3	
		MaF_1	MiF_1	MaF_1	MiF_1	MaF_1	MiF_1	MaF_1	MiF_1	MaF_1	MiF_1
FCNN	XLNet	0.995	0.995	0.993	0.993	0.992	0.992	0.365	0.760	**0.896**	0.944
FCNN	GPT	0.989	0.989	0.988	0.988	0.987	0.987	0.368	0.753	0.868	0.937
FCNN	BERT	**0.996**	**0.996**	**0.994**	**0.994**	**0.993**	**0.993**	**0.404**	**0.765**	0.885	**0.947**
RNN	BERT	0.988	0.988	0.990	0.990	0.989	0.989	0.349	0.757	0.700	0.902
CNN	BERT	0.991	0.991	0.988	0.988	0.972	0.972	0.295	0.705	0.567	0.859

We further analyse the contribution of the inputs into the language model in an ablation study shown in Table 3. In the case of coarse-grained entity typing, the F_1 score drops from 0.994 to 0.959 (averaged over all splits) when removing the entity label and description and to 0.989 when removing the property labels. This indicates that both inputs are best used in combination.

Table 3. Ablation study for coarse-grained and fine-grained types.

Model	Coarse-grained			Fine-grained			
	DB1	DB2	DB3	DB1		DB3	
	MaF_1	MaF_1	MaF_1	MaF_1	MiF_1	MaF_1	MiF_1
ETwT	**0.996**	**0.994**	**0.993**	**0.404**	**0.765**	**0.885**	**0.947**
without description	0.972	0.953	0.951	0.358	0.758	0.817	0.898
without property	0.990	0.989	0.988	0.341	0.737	0.839	0.930

5   Conclusion

We introduced ETwT, an approach for predicting entity types in a knowledge graph using the entity label, description and property labels as input to a language model. ETwT outperforms state-of-the-art baselines and reaches average $F1$ scores of 0.994 for predicting coarse-grained entity types in DBpedia.

Acknowledgments. This work was partially funded the Federal Ministry for Economic Affairs and Climate Action (BMWK), Germany ("ATTENTION!", 01MJ22012D).

References

1. Auer, S., Bizer, C., Kobilarov, G., Lehmann, J., Cyganiak, R., Ives, Z.: DBpedia: a nucleus for a web of open data. In: Aberer, K., et al. (eds.) ASWC/ISWC -2007. LNCS, vol. 4825, pp. 722–735. Springer, Heidelberg (2007). https://doi.org/10.1007/978-3-540-76298-0_52

2. Biswas, R., et al.: Do judge an entity by its name! Entity typing using language models. In: Proceedings of the Extended Semantic Web Conference (2021)
3. Biswas, R., et al.: Wikipedia category embeddings for entity typing in knowledge graphs. In: Proceedings of the Knowledge Capture Conference (2021)
4. Biswas, R., et al.: Entity type prediction leveraging graph walks and entity descriptions. In: Proceedings of the International Semantic Web Conference (2022)
5. He, L., et al.: KLMo: knowledge graph enhanced pretrained language model with fine-grained relationships. In: Findings of EMNLP (2021)
6. Jacob, D., et al.: BERT: pre-training of deep bidirectional transformers for language understanding. In: Proceedings of NAACL-HLT (2019)
7. Paulheim, H., Bizer, C.: Type inference on noisy RDF data. In: Proceedings of the International Semantic Web Conference (2013)
8. Radford, A., Wu, J., Child, R., Luan, D., Amodei, D., Sutskever, I.: Language Models are Unsupervised Multitask Learners. OpenAI blog (2019)
9. Zhang, X., et al.: Character-level convolutional networks for text classification. In: Advances in Neural Information Processing Systems, vol. 28 (2015)
10. Zhilin, Y., et al.: XLNet: generalized autoregressive pretraining for language understanding. In: Advances in Neural Information Processing Systems, vol. 32 (2019)

Industry

Addressing the Scalability Bottleneck of Semantic Technologies at Bosch

Diego Rincon-Yanez[1,2(✉)], Mohamed H. Gad-Elrab[1], Daria Stepanova[1],
Kien Trung Tran[1], Cuong Chu Xuan[1], Baifan Zhou[3,4],
and Evgeny Karlamov[1,3]

[1] Bosch Center for AI, Renningen, Germany
drinconyanez@unisa.it
[2] University of Salerno, Fisciano, Italy
[3] SIRIUS Centre, University of Oslo, Oslo, Norway
[4] Oslo Metropolitan University, Oslo, Norway

1 Introduction

At the heart of smart manufacturing is real-time semi-automatic decision-making. Such decisions are vital for optimizing production lines, e.g., reducing resource consumption, improving the quality of discrete manufacturing operations, and optimizing the actual products, e.g., optimizing the sampling rate for measuring product dimensions during production. Such decision-making relies on massive industrial data thus posing a real-time processing bottleneck.

Indeed, consider an example of automated welding that is present in multiple Bosch production sites where real-time decisions include welding machine adjustment when welding quality (welding spots) degrades [11]. Such processes are data-intensive, including sensor measurements, e.g., temperature, pressure, and electrical conductivity, settings of welding parameters, and replacement of accessories (welding caps), etc. When the welding is performed during car body manufacturing, each such body has up to 6.000 welding spots, generating a large amount of data instances. The data is distributed across several analytical pipelines in charge of feed statistics, training traditional ML models, quality control measures, and many more [8].

This decision-making for welding requires both integration of heterogeneous data and real-time computation on top of it, thus leading to scalability bottleneck. Delivering a consistent and accurate industry-grade solution as long as the data grows in time, increases the complexity in scalability and performance terms. These challenges combined with the need of maintaining daily operations, increase further scalability requirements, creating the need to implement additional machine learning, knowledge engineering, and data management solutions transversely into a unified framework.

Bosch is a multinational company with a strong emphasis on manufacturing and engineering in automotive, energy, consumer goods, and other industries. Smart and AI-powered manufacturing is one of the central pillars of the Bosch strategy, thus real-time effective and efficient processing of extreme data chains

C. Pesquita et al. (Eds.): ESWC 2023, LNCS 13998, pp. 177–181, 2023.
https://doi.org/10.1007/978-3-031-43458-7_33

of heterogeneous, distributed [3], fast-growing, and often disconnected or hardly compatible information is critical for the company's success.

2   Semantic Approach to Industrial-Scale Data

In Bosch, we follow a semantic approach [10] to deal with large-scale industrial data, as depicted in Fig. 1. The idea is to unlock the value of data by exploiting industrial knowledge graphs to support decision-making. In particular, the data is first converted into KGs via ETL processes [4], then analyzed using Neuro-Symbolic AI methods that combine both semantic technology and Machine Learning, and finally, the results of analyses are transferred to industrial applications. This allows to bridge the data challenge and the value generation part of manufacturing.

In order to ensure that the proposed approach offers the expected value, Bosch does a strong focus on both research and system development in scalability. In particular, Bosch does it via in-house research efforts and libraries and as a part of several EU projects such as enRichMyData on at-scale data annotation pipelines (https://enrichmydata.eu/), GraphMassivizer on massive processing of graph data (https://graph-massivizer.eu/), DataCloud on scalable automated deployment of data pipelines to the Cloud (https://datacloudproject.eu/), and SmartEdge on edge-driven computations (https://www.smart-edge.eu/).

Our scalable Neuro-Symbolic AI-powered ecosystem as can be seen in Fig. 2, comprehend a set of tools, libraries, and frameworks destined to integrate, process, and deploy traditional data pipelines, and Industrial KG; these orchestrated components have the objective to empower the experienced and non-experienced internal users to leverage value from incoming from the data generated by the production lines in the different Bosch manufacturing scenarios.

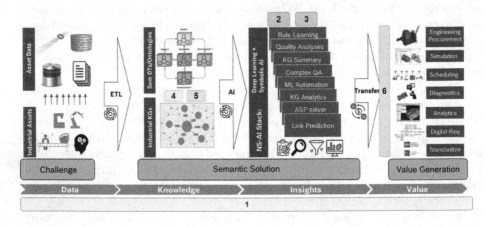

Fig. 1. Semantic approach at Bosch to deal with large industrial data

The solution to address the scalability bottleneck covers the transversely company semantic approach, a high-level view is given in Fig. 1, following characteristics:

1. *Semantic Powered Scalable Computing platform:* Consists of a scalable execution environment specially designed for simulating and executing data pipelines, this environment implements underlying semantic capabilities to assist in the pipeline description as well as exploiting the hardware configurations to find the best deployment scenario based on an initial requirement set.
2. *Embedding Training Pipeline:* Provides a standardized pipeline for embeddings computation, merging symbolic reasoning with traditional low-dimension vector representations, delivering a fast prototyping experimentation tool seamlessly integrated with the internal data silos in the company environment.
3. *Embedding Explainability Tool:* Library with the capability of analyzing semantic enhanced KG with previously trained embedding models comparing different models providing understandability methods for knowledge representation tasks [1, 7].
4. *Knowledge Graph Consistency Check:* Tool to discover inconsistency patterns in KGs with respect to ontological rules, this allows to processing of the data as well as the recognition of inconsistency patterns in the evaluated KG [5].
5. *Knowledge Driven Optimization:* Package for encoding generic KG-based optimization problems in Answer Set Programming (ASP) language, which is currently used in suppliers optimization, factory planning, and scheduling.
6. *Semantically Enhanced Automatized pipelines:* In order to deliver efficiency to the internal teams template-typed pipelines were prepared to leverage the use of mappings techniques to create KB's to exploit traditional ML knowledge [2, 9].

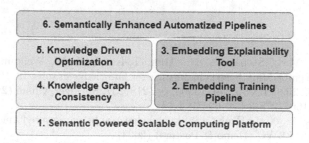

Fig. 2. Stacked view of semantic solutions for Neuro-Symbolic use-cases at Bosch

3   Conclusion

Given the specific nature of the use case and the particular needs of a company like Bosch, there is no off-the-shelf software solutions able to adapt the constantly grow and demands in terms of data streaming speed, security and volume. As lessons learned, we deeply understand that semantic technology not offers shared data schema that unifies different data syntax and semantics but also offers unambiguous "lingua franca" for cross-domain communication, that unifies the language and understanding of stakeholders [6]. This greatly helps the stakeholders to perform tasks of a remote domain (e.g., semantic technology) that otherwise would be error-prone, time-consuming and cognitively demanding. Meanwhile, it is important to be flexible in adopting combined technology of relational database and KG, such as a mixture of both or virtual KG, to exploit the flexibility of KG as well as the computational performance of relational databases.

Modern automatic manufacturing requires real-time decision-making for quality optimization tasks. ML methods face new challenges and opportunities to holistically analyze the massive and unprecedented data integrated across these chains, In this tailored ecosystem the goal is to speed up the experimentation capabilities of the onsite teams by providing a set of state-of-the-art semantically enhanced evaluation approaches, to support decisions that change the manufacturing processes towards a sustainable, circular, and climate-neutral industry.

Finally, we are excited to present our Bosch challenges and solutions to address the scalability bottleneck for semantic data to the ESWC community. We believe our case of large industrial data is rather typical for large manufacturing and service industries and thus will be of interest to a wide audience.

Acknowledgements. The work was partially supported by EU projects: Dome 4.0 (GA 953163), OntoCommons (GA 958371), DataCloud (GA 101016835), Graph Massiviser (GA 101093202) and enRichMyData (GA 101093202), SMARTEDGE (GA 101092908) and the SIRIUS Centre, (NRC, No. 237898).

References

1. Gad-Elrab, M.H., Stepanova, D., Tran, T.-K., Adel, H., Weikum, G.: ExCut: explainable embedding-based clustering over knowledge graphs. In: Pan, J.Z., et al. (eds.) ISWC 2020. LNCS, vol. 12506, pp. 218–237. Springer, Cham (2020). https://doi.org/10.1007/978-3-030-62419-4_13
2. Klironomos, A., et al.: ExeKGLib: knowledge graphs-empowered machine learning analytics. In: ESWC (Demo & Posters) (2023)
3. Rincon-Yanez, D., Crispoldi, F., Onorati, D., Ulpiani, P., Fenza, G., Senatore, S.: Enabling a semantic sensor knowledge approach for quality control support in cleanrooms. In: ISWC, vol. 2980 (2021)
4. Rincon-Yanez, D., Lauro, E.D., Falanga, M., Senatore, S., Petrosino, S.: Towards a semantic model for IoT-based seismic event detection and classification. In: 2020 IEEE SSCI, pp. 189–196. IEEE, December 2020

5. Tran, T.K., Gad-Elrab, M.H., Stepanova, D., Kharlamov, E., Strötgen, J.: Fast computation of explanations for inconsistency in large-scale knowledge graphs. In: Proceedings of the Web Conference 2020, pp. 2613–2619. WWW (2020)
6. Yahya, M., Zhou, B., Breslin, J.G., Ali, M.I., Kharlamov, E.: Semantic modeling, development and evaluation for the resistance spot welding industry. IEEE Access **11**, 37360–37377 (2023)
7. Zheng, Z., Zhou, B., Zhou, D., Khan, A.Q., Soylu, A., Kharlamov, E.: Towards a statistic ontology for data analysis in smart manufacturing. In: ISWC (Demo & Posters) (2022)
8. Zheng, Z., Zhou, B., Zhou, D., Soylu, A., Kharlamov, E.: Executable knowledge graph for transparent machine learning in welding monitoring at Bosch. In: CIKM, pp. 5102–5103 (2022)
9. Zheng, Z., Zhou, B., Zhou, D., Soylu, A., Kharlamov, E.: Executable knowledge graph for transparent machine learning in welding monitoring at Bosch. In: Proceedings of the 31st ACM International Conference on Information & Knowledge Management, pp. 5102–5103 (2022)
10. Zheng, Z., et al.: Executable knowledge graphs for machine learning: a Bosch case of welding monitoring. In: Sattler, U., et al. (eds.) ISWC 2022. LNCS, vol. 13489, pp. 791–809. Springer, Cham (2022). https://doi.org/10.1007/978-3-031-19433-7_45
11. Zhou, B., et al.: SemML: facilitating development of ML models for condition monitoring with semantics. J. Web Semant. **71**, 100664 (2021)

Knowledge Injection to Counter Large Language Model (LLM) Hallucination

Ariana Martino$^{(\boxtimes)}$ (iD), Michael Iannelli (iD), and Coleen Truong (iD)

Yext, New York, NY 10011, USA
{amartino,miannelli,ctruong}@yext.com
https://www.yext.com/

Abstract. A shortfall of Large Language Model (LLM) content generation is hallucination, i.e., including false information in the output. This is especially risky for enterprise use cases that require reliable, fact-based, controllable text generation at scale. To mitigate this, we utilize a technique called Knowledge Injection (KI), where contextual data about the entities relevant to a text-generation task is mapped from a knowledge graph to text space for inclusion in an LLM prompt. Using the task of responding to online customer reviews of retail locations as an example, we have found that KI increases the count of correct assertions included in generated text. In a qualitative review, fine-tuned bloom-560m with KI outperformed a non-fine-tuned text-davinci-003 model from OpenAI, though text-davinci-003 has 300 times more parameters. Thus, the KI method can increase enterprise users' confidence leveraging LLMs to replace tedious manual text generation and enable better performance from smaller, cheaper models.

Keywords: large language model · knowledge graph · prompt engineering · hallucination · bloom · gpt-3

1 Introduction

One limitation of Large Language Model (LLM) content generation is hallucination, or false assertions in the generated text [2]. Enterprise use cases require reliable, fact-based text generation at scale, making investment into LLM-generated text risky. To mitigate hallucination, we utilize a technique called Knowledge Injection (KI) where contextual data about entities relevant to a task is mapped from a knowledge graph to text space for inclusion in an LLM prompt. In our use case of responding to online customer reviews of retail locations, KI increases the rate at which assertions are correct while improving overall text quality.

While LLM parameters encode knowledge [7], they are still susceptible to hallucination because: (1) not all current data can be present during training of the model (e.g., updates to business information made post-training) and (2) it is difficult to encode all knowledge into the models parameters [6].

All work in this paper was supported by and conducted at Yext.

KI begins with a knowledge graph that includes the entity relevant to the task and connections to other entities from which context can be derived. KI aims to generate controllable text with business information from a knowledge graph that is not general knowledge (e.g., the business' phone number will not likely be common knowledge that the LLM knows from base training). Controllable Text Generation (CTG) is subject to controlled constraints such as sentiment or, in our use case, alignment with source-of-truth business information [8].

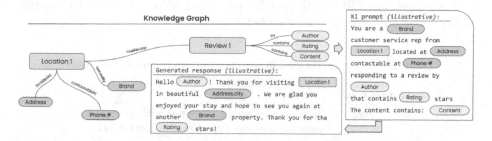

Fig. 1. A templated text prompt with KI is compiled by navigating the entity's neighborhood and inserting relevant contextual fields. In this example, the KI prompt requests the model generate a text response to an online customer review based on the relevant review, location, and brand entities. In contrast, a review-only prompt would contain only the yellow fields (author, rating, and content). (Color figure online)

Text fields from the knowledge graph are inserted into a templated prompt to map the graph-based context to text space, forming the input to the LLM. This is demonstrated in Fig. 1, where an LLM generated response to an online customer review is requested. The relevant entity, Review 1, and its neighbors, e.g., Location 1, in the knowledge graph are mapped to a templated prompt.

2   Problem Setup and Experiments

2.1   Hallucination

We set out to determine if KI reduces hallucination in LLM-generated responses to online customer reviews. LLMs using bloom-560m [4] were fine-tuned using reviews and responses written by human customer service agents. Generated responses from a review-only model fine-tuned with only information from the review (i.e., author, rating, and content) vs. a KI-prompted model fine-tuned with added context about the linked entities were evaluated. The models were fine-tuned on a dataset of ∼35K review-response pairs.

Domain experts counted correct and incorrect assertions in each generated response. Assertions included specification of a location name, contactable at phone number or web address, owned by brand name, and located at location address. Incorrect (i.e., hallucinated) assertions contained untrue information contradicted by the knowledge graph, like directing customers to call a fictitious phone number. Factual assertions were those not otherwise marked as incorrect.

2.2 Generated Response Quality

In addition to testing KIs impact on hallucination, we also tested its impact on overall quality of generated review responses. Subject matter experts graded generated responses from non-KI prompted OpenAIs text-davinci-003 text generation model, aka GPT-3 [1], and KI prompted bloom-560m on the overall quality based on a 3-point scale (Table 1).

Table 1. Scoring rubric used in qualitative response quality analysis

Score	Quality	Criteria
1	Bad	Unusable generated response with potential negative business brand reputation impact
2	Good	Usable generated response with potential for human-intervention to refine using business brand standards
3	Great	Usable generated response with minimal to no requirement for human- intervention and aligns with business brand standards

3 Results and Discussion

3.1 Hallucination

The KI increased the count of correct assertions while decreasing the count of incorrect assertions (Table 2), suggesting it is useful for enterprise tasks like review response, which are manual and costly when done by humans, but require factual context about the business to produce trustworthy generated text.

Table 2. Assertions in generated text from review-only vs. KI LLMs (bloom-560m)

Avg. # of assertions per inference	Review-only prompt $n = 64$	KI prompt $n = 78$	Δ
Correct	0.61	1.86	+205%
Incorrect	0.23	0.19	−18%
Total	0.84	2.05	+143%

3.2   Generated Response Quality

The KI model received higher quality scores for generated responses, suggesting KI is useful for helping models to align with business brand standards (Table 3). Though text-davinci-003 has ~300 times as many parameters as bloom-560m, the smaller model fine-tuned with KI outperformed the larger OpenAI model. Thus, fine-tuning with KI could help businesses save on cost by training and hosting a smaller model while producing higher quality generated responses [5]. Furthermore, using smaller models could improve inference speed [3].

Table 3. Quality of Generated Responses

Model	Params.	Avg. Score
OpenAI text-davinci-003 *(n = 94)*	175b	1.80
bloom-560m fine-tuned with KI *(n = 94)*	**0.56b**	**2.14**

4   Conclusions and Future Work

Experiments on both hallucination and generated response quality highlighted how KI can help businesses generate more reliable, fact-based, and higher quality text from LLMs. In order to take advantage of this, businesses would require a factual and robust knowledge graph of entities relevant to their business, like locations, reviews, products, documents, etc.

   To help mitigate this limitation, in future experimentation, we intend to continue researching methods to build out robust knowledge graphs for businesses through entity and edge extraction leveraging LLMs.

References

1. Brown, T.B., et al.: Language models are few-shot learners. CoRR abs/2005.14165 (2020). https://arxiv.org/abs/2005.14165
2. Ji, Z., et al.: Survey of hallucination in natural language generation. ACM Comput. Surv. **55**(12), 1–38 (2023). https://doi.org/10.1145/3571730
3. Menghani, G.: Efficient deep learning: a survey on making deep learning models smaller, faster, and better. ACM Comput. Surv. **55**(12), 1–37 (2023)
4. Scao, T.L., et al.: BLOOM: a 176B-parameter open-access multilingual language model (2022). https://doi.org/10.48550/ARXIV.2211.05100
5. Sharir, O., Peleg, B., Shoham, Y.: The cost of training NLP models: a concise overview. arXiv preprint arXiv:2004.08900 (2020)
6. Singhal, K., et al.: Large language models encode clinical knowledge (2022)
7. Wang, C., Liu, X., Song, D.: Language models are open knowledge graphs (2020). https://arxiv.org/abs/2010.11967
8. Zhang, H., et al.: A survey of controllable text generation using transformer-based pre-trained language models. ArXiv abs/2201.05337 (2022)

Towards the Deployment of Knowledge Based Systems in Safety-Critical Systems

Florence De-Grancey[✉] and Amandine Audouy

Thales AVS France, SAS, Vélizy-Villacoublay, France
{florence.de-grancey,amandine.audouy}@fr.thalesgroup.com

Abstract. At Thales, we studied the use of Knowledge-Based System (KBS) to create a crew-assistant, inserted inside the safety-critical cockpit systems. Developing a KBS as a safety-critical system induced new needs such as a high amount of verification activities or a bounded reasoning time. This paper aims at presenting our needs and related new challenges to the scientific community.

Keywords: safety-critical system · ontology · knowledge-based system

1 Introduction

When you get on a plane or charge your smartphone with electricity produced by nuclear plants, you rely on safety-critical systems (SCS). Development of such high reliable systems must provide evidences that the system performs well its intended function and does not have any undesirable behavior that could lead to human injury or environmental damages. Since a few years the introduction of AI's technics in SCS is extensively studied, in particular Machine Learning. Knowledge-Based Systems (KBS) are also considered for information retrieval or reasoning-based decision-making tasks. Their ability to add value to existing domain knowledge or to provide a causal explanation makes them attractive.

At Thales, we considered the application of KBS to create a cockpit-assistant supporting crew decision-making during normal and abnormal situation. As example, it should detect automatically if aircraft's landing airport becomes unreachable, explain the causes to the crew, and suggest diversion airports. This assistant relies on an OWL DL ontology where the TBox represent domain knowledge and the ABox represents current situation. Contextualized assistance or suggestions are built in soft real time using a combination of standard reasoning tasks: a *"query task"* extracting implicit information, a *"consistency task"* which uses consistency checks to assess if current situation status is correct, an *"explanation task"* which provides a comprehensible explanations to the crew if errors exists inside ABox, followed by *"root-cause task"* which identifies a way to correct errors. These tasks are based on the Hermit reasonner[1].

Application in a safety-critical system context unveils new requirements concerning knowledge-based technologies that, to our best knowledge, are open scientific challenges. In this paper, illustrating by our results, we want to highlight three of them.

---

[1] HermiT Reasoner: Home (https://www.hermit-reasoner.com.).

© The Author(s), under exclusive license to Springer Nature Switzerland AG 2023
C. Pesquita et al. (Eds.): ESWC 2023, LNCS 13998, pp. 186–190, 2023.
https://doi.org/10.1007/978-3-031-43458-7_35

2 Facilitating the Design of a Task-Fit Knowledge Base

Context: Safety-critical systems traditionally follow a certification process that ensure that enough evidences are collected to demonstrate the trustworthiness of the system. KBS introduce a novelty: demonstrating that the knowledge base design is *task-fitted*, meaning that it contains necessary and sufficient elements to perform the intended function inside the desired operational domain, and no more.

Our Work: To guide the knowledge base design, we used seminal work of [6] as a guidance: starting from aeronautics domain ontology SESAR BEST[2] AIRM, we refined them to select only the necessary elements for the expected tasks. During design, as proposed in [3], we performed error checking using OntoDebug[3] and monitored metric using OntoMetrics[4]. Metrics of the original and obtained ontology are given in Table 1.

Remaining Challenge: During ontology design, we noted that selecting pertinent concepts and relations required a high expertise in KB design, making difficult KB assessment. To accelerate the conception of KB, some **methods to help** traditional software engineers would be appreciable. One valuable track could be to **facilitating the assessment of ontology high-level properties** described in [6] using **ontology metrics**. For example, if minimizing the *depth*, can easily be understood as a contributor to ontology *intelligibility* (explanations less complex) or *deployability* (paths explored quickly), impact of *tangledness* or *attribute richness* is hardly understandable.

Table 1. Ontologies Metrics

Ontology	Classes	Axioms	Richness	Depth	Breadth	Tangledness	Path Nb
BEST	1177	34576	0.167	8	135	0.403	2256
our	97	5989	0.1857	5	14	0.103	127

3 Enhancing Black Box Verification and Validation

Context: To allow deployment of KBS in SCS, in addition to classical verification and validation (VV) practices, one must verify that the whole KBS (eg. Knowledge base, reasoner and additional algorithm) performs well its intended function and does not present any unintended behaviour. A property of determinism (e.g. same output is obtained for same input), is also required. These verifications can be performed either by testing (called *"black box testing"* in [4]) either by formal demonstration.

---

[2] https://www.project-best.eu/.
[3] http://isbi.aau.at/ontodebug/.
[4] https://ontometrics.informatik.uni-rostock.de/ontologymetrics/.

Our Work: We explored black box testing methods, designing several test-based campaigns where a test is defined by a manually created ABox or a set of variations around theses ABox. Especially for *"consistency-tasks"*, *"root-cause-tasks"*, and *"explanation task"* tests, we introduced erroneous axioms leading to ABox inconsistency. In ours campaigns, we defined an *accuracy* criteria as for *"query task"*, the percentage of right answers provided for any possible query on an A-box element; for *"consistency tasks"*, the percentage of detected inconsistency in test cases; for *"root-cause tasks"* and *"explanation task"*, the quantity of tests where algorithm provides the right and same root cause or explanation. As expected, we effectively verified that the KBS provided always the expected output and has deterministic outputs.

Remaining Challenges: Even if black-box test-based campaigns provide confidence elements, they do not ensure that the system would perform its intended function **whatever** the ABox e.g. operational conditions. Indeed, as test sets are manually created, we are not able to prove that **every possible ABox** was tested. For low criticality task, we can consider automatic test generation as proposed in [1] but – to our best knowledge – there is no tools to generate automatically inconsistencies in ontology. Developing new tools managing inconsistency would be valuable.

For high criticality tasks, a formal demonstration approach, based on the decidability criteria would be preferable. Developing a tool to demonstrate decidability would be valuable. Furthermore, as to our best knowledge, not all description logics currently satisfy these criteria, proving decidability of new logics would be pertinent.

4   An Acceptable and Bounded Execution Time

Context: In typical SCS, outputs must be provided with a guaranteed accuracy and within an acceptable and bounded execution time. For KBS, this requirement translates into the ability to *finish the reasoning task* whatever the A-Box filling, within an acceptable time and without saturating the selected hardware.

Our Work: During the test-based campaigns detailed above, we launched each test at least 100 times to measure execution time statistics. We notice a high variability of the execution time for all tasks except query, sometimes leading to execution timeout with respect to specifications. Results are illustrated Fig. 1.

Remaining Challenges: The variability and the excess of execution time is currently not acceptable. It's well known that OWL DL reasoners have difficulties to scale on large ontology, over than 1000 axioms ([3, 11]) and our ontology clearly overtakes this limit. **Scaling, accelerating and bounding the execution time of reasoning task** is then a crucial point to enable the deployment of our crew assistant. We note that several interesting tracks are currently studied by scientific community such creating an optimized reasoner ([5, 8, 9]), incremental reasoning [2], parallel reasoning [7] or reasonner composition [10]. They will be explored in additional work.

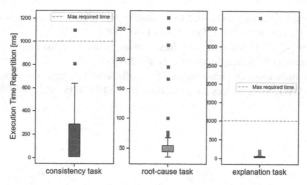

Fig. 1. Repartition of measured execution time and required execution time (1000 ms)

5 Conclusion

In Thales, we develop a knowledge-based system (KBS) to address the needs of crew assistance in complex and critical situations. Even if the technology presents promising capacities, we are confronted to important challenges before a concrete deployment. Increasing the amount of confidence elements collectable during VV is the first one and concerns both evaluation of the knowledge base itself and the whole KBS. The second challenge is the reasoning acceleration to reach an acceptable and bounded execution time for large ontologies. We encourage the semantic web community to seize these challenges in the next years to enable the deployment of such systems.

Acknowledgements. We thanks V. Charpenay, C. Rey and F. Toumani for their valuable comments and inspiring discussions.

References

1. Banerjee, S., Debnath, N.C., Sarkar, A.: An ontology-based approach to automated test case generation. SN Comput. Sci. **2**, 35 (2021)
2. Bento, A., Médini, L., Singh, K., Laforest, F.: Do Arduinos dream of efficient reasoners? In: The Semantic Web, ESWC 2022 (2022)
3. Bobed, C., Yus, R., Bobillo, F., Mena, E.: Semantic reasoning on mobile devices: do androids dream of efficient reasoners? J. Web Semant. **35**, 167–183 (2015)
4. McDaniel, M., Storey, V.: Evaluating domain ontologies: clarification, classification, and challenges. ACM Comput. Surv. **52**, 1–44 (2019)
5. Motik, B., Horrocks, I., Kim, S.M.: Delta-reasoner: a Semantic Web reasoner for an intelligent mobile platform. In: 21st World Wide Web Conference (WWW 2012) (2012)
6. Vizedom, A., Neuhaus, F., et al.: Toward Ontology Evaluation across the lifecycle. Applied Ontology (2013)
7. Steigmiller, A., Glimm, B.: Parallelized ABox reasoning and query answering with expressive description logics. In: The Semantic Web, ESWC 2021 (2021)
8. Sinner, A., Kleemann, T.: KRHyper – in your pocket. In: Nieuwenhuis, R. (ed.) CADE 2005. LNCS (LNAI), vol. 3632, pp. 452–457. Springer, Heidelberg (2005). https://doi.org/10.1007/11532231_33

9. Steller, L., Krishnaswamy, S., Gaber, M.M.: Enabling scalable semantic reasoning for mobile services. Int. J. Semant. Web Inf. Syst. **5**, 91–116 (2009)
10. Tai, W., Keeney, J., O'Sullivan, D.: Resource-constrained reasoning using a reasoner composition approach. Semantic Web **6**, 35–59 (2015)
11. Pan, Z.: Benchmarking DL reasoners using realistic ontologies. In: Proceedings of the Workshop on OWL: Experiences and Directions (OWLED 2005), vol. 188. CEURWS (2005)

A Source-Agnostic Platform for Finding and Exploring Ontologies at Bosch

Lavdim Halilaj[1]([✉]), Stefan Schmid[1], Khushboo Goutham Chand[2], Santhosh Kumar Arumugam[2], and Sahu Sajita Kumari[2]

[1] Bosch Center for Artificial Intelligence, Renningen, Germany
{lavdim.halilaj,stefan.schmid5}@de.bosch.com
[2] Bosch Global Software Technologies Private Limited, Bangalore, India
{khushboo.gouthamchand,santhoshkumar.arumugam,
sajitakumari.sahu}@in.bosch.com

Keywords: Ontology Finding and Exploration · Reusability and Visualization

1 Introduction

The usage of semantic technologies for purposes like data integration, information retrieval, search, and decision-making is steadily on the rise [2,10]. Bosch is leveraging these technologies to enhance the ability to represent, integrate, and query various data sources [7]. The main objectives are enabling data understanding, interlinking, and analysis [15]. To achieve this, a number of ontologies for various domains are developed over time, i.e. autonomous driving [5–7,9,14], manufacturing [3,8,13], smart home and IoT[1] [1,11,12]. These ontologies result from research and development activities carried out across several projects, groups, and departments. Subsequently, various stakeholders with diverse backgrounds and expertise are utilizing and repurposing the ontologies for their specific use cases and scenarios. Therefore, it is crucial that these ontologies, which may be hosted on different platforms, are easily discoverable and explorable by both humans and intelligent agents. This paper discusses how we at Bosch tackle the obstacles and barriers of finding and exploring ontologies by providing a source-agnostic solution. We underscore the ability to access and explore ontologies using user-friendly interfaces enhances comprehension, particularly for domain experts, thus facilitates the adoption of semantic technologies.

2 Approach

The objective of our platform is to serve as a centralized point for ontology finding and exploration and facilitate easy discovery, exploration, and reuse. For this

---

[1] https://www.boschbuildingsolutions.com/xc/en/news-and-stories/building-ontologies.

C. Pesquita et al. (Eds.): ESWC 2023, LNCS 13998, pp. 191–194, 2023.
https://doi.org/10.1007/978-3-031-43458-7_36

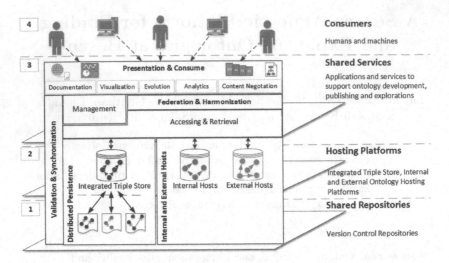

Fig. 1. Our solution comprises various layers: 1) *Shared Repositories* - git-based repositories for ontologies; 2) *Hosting Platforms* - triple-based repositories for ontologies; and 3) *Shared Services* - providing different services for management and exploration.

purpose we designed the architecture illustrated in Fig. 1 which is inspired by the approach presented in [4]. We extended it with the mechanisms to incorporate any SPARQL-based ontology repository, either hosted internally within Bosch or externally. Our approach enables users to search for relevant ontologies through various criteria, including domain, format, and language. Additionally, via dedicated views it is possible to check further how ontologies are interconnected to each other, thus supporting tasks for ontology mapping and alignment.

The architecture comprises three layers with a clear separation of concerns: 1) *Shared Repositories* - at the bottom layer various version control systems such as *git* can be plugged in. These systems are used to manage ontology development activities; 2) *Hosting Platforms* - contains internal and external hosted triple-stores where the ontologies are maintained or developed. Access to these stores is achieved through the standard SPARQL interface; and 3) *Shared Services* - offers a number of different functionalities related to the ontology finding, exploration, and analysis. Further, a separate module enables the administration of the system, including adding, configuring, or deleting hosting repositories. A simultaneous access to all sources of ontologies is realized via the distributed query processing mechanism. It sends queries, including user-provided values, to the selected sources and clusters the retrieved results into joint sets. These sets are then shown to the user as unified views, where additional filtering criteria can be applied. The functionalities are decoupled into two main components: back-end and front-end, allowing for an independent development and easier maintenance. To ensure the scalability and resilience of the platform, the following characteristics are implemented:

- Templated queries - enabling standardization and reusability of queries, thus saving integration time and reducing the risk of errors. They offer various placeholders for variables that are dynamically filled in at run-time according to the storage and representation characteristics of ontologies in the respective hosting repositories. Therefore, regardless of the underlying repository, each component can consume ontologies via a common interface.
- Configurable hosts - provide flexibility in deployment, and customization of features to be provided by each individual repository. This enables the platform to scale up by adding new repositories, thus facilitating the reusability and interoperability of ontologies for different domains.
- Extensible architecture - internally or of-the-shelf developed components can be easily integrated. This allows for extending its base functionalities with new features, such as ontology evaluation or evolution. As a result, users are able to have a more comprehensive view while deciding on the reuse of the ontologies for their applications.

3   Conclusion

At Bosch, we are utilizing semantic technologies to enhance the representation, integration, and querying of heterogeneous data sources. To facilitate ontology exploration, a source-agnostic platform is implemented serving as a centralized point for finding and exploring ontologies. At the moment, our platform serves more than 500 ontologies that are built inside Bosch. It also provides access to public external SPARQL endpoints, which serve more than 700 ontologies. At any time, new SPARQL endpoints can be added by simply specifying the connection details and defining a few SPARQL-based templates that resemble the way how ontologies can be accessed in the given source. On a daily basis, more than 100 users are accessing our platform to explore ontologies and the defined concepts.

Our ultimate objective is to simplify the process of ontology development and adoption by making it more efficient, cooperative, and accessible. A crucial aspect of this objective is to enable domain experts to have a better comprehension of ontologies. We support this through our platform by providing various views, such as visualization, documentation, hierarchical navigation, and connectivity.

References

1. Bercher, P., et al.: Do it yourself, but not alone: companion-technology for home improvement - bringing a planning-based interactive DIY assistant to life. Künstliche Intell. **35**(3), 367–375 (2021)
2. Dibowski, H., Schmid, S., Svetashova, Y., Henson, C., Tran, T.: Using semantic technologies to manage a data lake: Data catalog, provenance and access control. In: Proceedings of the 13th International Workshop on Scalable Semantic Web Knowledge Base Systems (SSWS 2020) co-located with 19th International Semantic Web Conference (ISWC) (2020)

3. Grangel-González, I., Lösch, F., ul Mehdi, A.: Knowledge graph-based support for automated manufacturability analysis. In: 27th IEEE International Conference on Emerging Technologies and Factory Automation, ETFA, pp. 1–8. IEEE (2022)
4. Halilaj, L.: An approach for collaborative ontology development in distributed and heterogeneous environments. Ph.D. thesis, University of Bonn, Germany (2019). http://hss.ulb.uni-bonn.de/2019/5315/5315.htm
5. Halilaj, L., Dindorkar, I., Lüttin, J., Rothermel, S.: A knowledge graph-based approach for situation comprehension in driving scenarios. In: Verborgh, R., et al. (eds.) ESWC 2021. LNCS, vol. 12731, pp. 699–716. Springer, Cham (2021). https://doi.org/10.1007/978-3-030-77385-4_42
6. Halilaj, L., Luettin, J., Henson, C., Monka, S.: Knowledge graphs for automated driving. In: 5th IEEE International Conference on Artificial Intelligence and Knowledge Engineering, AIKE, pp. 98–105. IEEE (2022)
7. Henson, C., Schmid, S., Tran, A.T., Karatzoglou, A.: Using a knowledge graph of scenes to enable search of autonomous driving data. In: Proceedings of the ISWC Satellite Tracks (Posters & Demonstrations, Industry, and Outrageous Ideas) co-located with 18th International Semantic Web Conference (ISWC). CEUR Workshop Proceedings, vol. 2456, pp. 313–314. CEUR-WS.org (2019)
8. Kalaycı, E.G., et al.: Semantic integration of Bosch manufacturing data using virtual knowledge graphs. In: Pan, J.Z., et al. (eds.) ISWC 2020, Part II. LNCS, vol. 12507, pp. 464–481. Springer, Cham (2020). https://doi.org/10.1007/978-3-030-62466-8_29
9. Kaleeswaran, A.P., Nordmann, A., ul Mehdi, A.: Towards integrating ontologies into verification for autonomous driving. In: Proceedings of the ISWC Satellite Tracks (Posters & Demonstrations, Industry, and Outrageous Ideas) co-located with 18th International Semantic Web Conference (ISWC), CEUR Workshop Proceedings, vol. 2456, pp. 319–320. CEUR-WS.org (2019)
10. Khiat, A., Halilaj, L., Hemid, A., Lohmann, S.: VoColReg: a registry for supporting distributed ontology development using version control systems. In: IEEE 14th International Conference on Semantic Computing, ICSC, pp. 393–399. IEEE (2020)
11. Kim, J.E., Boulos, G., Yackovich, J., Barth, T., Beckel, C., Mossé, D.: Seamless integration of heterogeneous devices and access control in smart homes. In: Eighth International Conference on Intelligent Environments, pp. 206–213. IEEE (2012)
12. Svetashova, Y., Schmid, S., Harth, A.: Towards semantic model extensibility in interoperable IoT data exchange platforms. In: Global Internet of Things Summit, GIoTS, pp. 1–6. IEEE (2018)
13. Svetashova, Y., et al.: Ontology-enhanced machine learning: a Bosch use case of welding quality monitoring. In: Pan, J.Z., et al. (eds.) ISWC 2020, Part II. LNCS, vol. 12507, pp. 531–550. Springer, Cham (2020). https://doi.org/10.1007/978-3-030-62466-8_33
14. Westhofen, L., Neurohr, C., Butz, M., Scholtes, M., Schuldes, M.: Using ontologies for the formalization and recognition of criticality for automated driving. CoRR abs/2205.01532 (2022). https://doi.org/10.48550/arXiv.2205.01532
15. Zhou, B., et al.: The data value quest: a holistic semantic approach at Bosch. In: Groth, P., et al. (eds.) ESWC 2022. LNCS, vol. 13384, pp. 287–290. Springer, Cham (2022). https://doi.org/10.1007/978-3-031-11609-4_42

Wisdom of the Sellers: Mining Seller Data for eCommerce Knowledge Graph Generation

Petar Ristoski[✉], Sathish Kandasamy, Aleksandr Matiushkin, Sneha Kamath, and Qunzhi Zhou

eBay Inc., San Jose, USA
{pristoski,satkandasamy,amatiushkin,snkamath,qunzhou}@ebay.com

Abstract. Query understanding is a fundamental part of an e-commerce search engine, and it is crucial for correctly identifying the buyer intent. To perform a semantic query understanding, in this work we introduce a relationship-rich product Knowledge Graph (KG), mined from seller provided data, which captures entities and relationships to model the whole product inventory, allowing us to identify the buyer intent more accurately.

Keywords: Knowledge Graphs · e-Commerce · Query Understanding

1 Introduction

The main task of an e-commerce search engine is to semantically match the user query to the product inventory and retrieve the most relevant items that match the user's intent. This task is not trivial as often there can be a mismatch between the user's intent and the product inventory, which is the main cause for customer churn and loss of revenue. To bridge this gap, plethora of query understanding approaches have been introduced [1]. However, generating a precise knowledge base with high coverage for semantic query understanding remains a main challenge. In this work we mine seller provided information, to generate a high-quality KG covering the whole product inventory. To assure data quality, all the knowledge in the KG must be confirmed by a number of sellers, i.e., "wisdom of the sellers". The KG contains entities and relations describing millions of products, e.g., brands, colors, materials, sizes etc. To perform semantic query understanding, we perform entity linking using the KG [5]. Through the identified entities we can explore the graph to draw additional information about each entity and analyze the relations to other entities in the graph. For example, given the query "Oyster Bracelet Submariner", we first identify the query category in our inventory, and we pull the corresponding KG for that category, i.e., "Wristwatches". As shown in Fig. 1, we are able to link each text mention to the corresponding KG entity, e.g., "Submariner" is linked to an entity of type "model". Along with the entities, we can retrieve the number of listings

C. Pesquita et al. (Eds.): ESWC 2023, LNCS 13998, pp. 195–199, 2023.
https://doi.org/10.1007/978-3-031-43458-7_37

associated with the given entity. This allows us to capture the buyer intent, i.e., the buyer is interested in "luxury" and "classic" watches, and we can identify similar models that they might be interested in.

In this work, we use the product KG in several query understanding applications, which significantly improve the buyer experience.

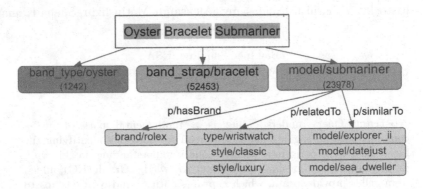

Fig. 1. KG-based semantic query understanding

2 Approach

We build a directed weighted graph based on co-occurring aspect-value pairs in listings provided by sellers partitioned by category. Formally, we represent the product inventory as a set of product listings $L = \{l_1, l_2, \ldots, l_n\}$, where each listing l_n is represented as a set of aspect-value pairs $AV_n = \{av_1, av_2, \ldots, av_n\}$, where a is the aspect name, and v is the aspect value. Each aspect name a is converted to an *rdf:Class*, *class/A*, and the corresponding value v is converted to an instance of the class *class/A*. For example the aspect value pair *Brand:Apple* is converted to the following triple: `kg:brand/Apple rdf:type kg:class/Brand`. Each pair of co-occurring aspect-value pairs within at least one product listing, av_i and av_j is converted into 2 triples as follows: $kg : a_i/v_i\ kg : p/a_j\ kg : a_j/v_j$ and $kg : a_j/v_j\ kg : p/a_i\ kg : a_i/v_i$, where the predicates are derived from the class of the object entity. For each pair av_i and av_j, we calculate the co-occurrence frequency c_{ij}, as well as the total frequency of each aspect-value pair, c_i and c_j respectively. Then the predicate e_{ij} between these two pairs is assigned a weight $w_{ij} = c_{ij}/c_i$. Similarly, we set a weight $w_{ji} = c_{ji}/c_j$ on the symmetric edge e_{ji}. Such weights give higher relevance to aspect-value pairs that co-occur more often together, normalized by their global popularity. This results in a directed weighted graph, which is generated separately for each category.

For example, for the co-occurring aspect-values *Brand:Apple* and *Color:Sierra Blue*, we will generate the following quadruples:

```
kg:brand/apple kg:p/color kg:color/sierra_blue 0.01
kg:color/sierra_blue kg:p/brand kg:brand/apple 0.99
```

The fourth element is the weight of the triple, and in this case indicates that the color *Sierra Blue* is almost fully conditioned on the brand *Apple*, while the other direction is not significant.

To assure high-quality data, we filter out noisy entities based on their frequency, consolidate entities appearing under different surface forms, and prune edges with low weight. The KG generation pipeline, shown in Fig. 2 runs weekly, using Spark jobs, automated through Apache Airflow. The resulting KG contains tens of millions of entities, and hundreds of millions of relations.

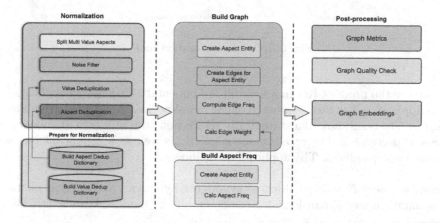

Fig. 2. KG Generation Pipeline

To ease the use of such KG in downstream tasks, we use the graph embedding approach using biased walks [4]. We perform biased walks on the weighted graph to flatten the graph in sequences that can later be embedded by any of the existing language models. This imparts a locality as well as some global contextual information to the nodes across the graph. This approach is able to capture the neighborhood of each entity in a single vector, which then can be used for similarity calculation or context inference. Such embeddings can then be ingested in various machine learning models to solve a variety of downstream tasks, in this case query rewriting.

3 Applications

The knowledge graph is available for exploration and querying within the enterprise, as shown in Fig. 3. Internal users regularly use this tool to perform exploratory data analysis, and scope new opportunities.

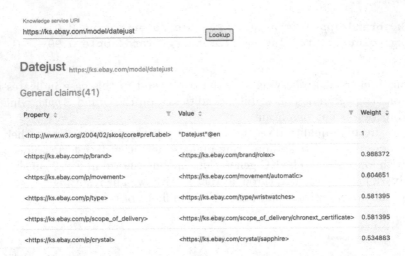

Fig. 3. KG data exploration tool

We use the product KG in a handful fundamental e-Commerce applications. Each application has been evaluated offline or online, i.e., A/B tests with millions of users. The tests showed a statistically significant drop in search abandonment rate and decrease in low recall search sessions, as well as a significant increase in purchased products. The applications include:

Semantic Query Expansion: Identify synonyms, hyponyms and subtype relations for semantic query expansions, for colors, materials, models, brands, etc. [3].

KG-Enhanced Query Reformulation: Neural generative query rewriting model using KG embeddings, trained on user search logs. We build a KG-enhanced token dropping model, which is able to identify and remove least significant tokens in a query in order to increase relevant recall. Furthermore, we train a generative model for end-to-end query rewriting, which is able to identify entity substitutes or increase the query abstraction in order to increase the recall [2].

Multi-faceted Item Recommendation: Recommend diverse items related to the initial buyer intent, by expanding on different entities. We identify entity substitutes and allow the user to pivot on different aspects of the query in order to easier identify the products they are interested in.

Listing Autocomplete and Validation: Infer missing aspect values and remove inconsistent aspect values to assist sellers when listing new items on the platform.

References

1. Chang, Y., Deng, H.: Query Understanding for Search Engines. Springer, Heidelberg (2020). https://doi.org/10.1007/978-3-030-58334-7

2. Farzana, S., Zhou, Q., Ristoski, P.: Knowledge graph-enhanced neural query rewriting. In: Companion Proceedings of the Web Conference, The 2nd Workshop on Interactive and Scalable Information Retrieval Methods for eCommerce (2023)

3. Liang, L., Kamath, S., Ristoski, P., Zhou, Q., Wu, Z.: Fifty shades of pink: understanding color in e-commerce using knowledge graphs. In: Proceedings of the 31st ACM International Conference on Information & Knowledge Management, pp. 5090–5091 (2022)

4. Ristoski, P., Paulheim, H.: RDF2Vec: RDF graph embeddings for data mining. In: Groth, P., et al. (eds.) ISWC 2016. LNCS, vol. 9981, pp. 498–514. Springer, Cham (2016). https://doi.org/10.1007/978-3-319-46523-4_30

5. Zhou, Q., et al.: Leveraging knowledge graph and deepner to improve uom handling in search. In: ISWC (Posters/Demos/Industry) (2021)

Supplier Optimization at Bosch with Knowledge Graphs and Answer Set Programming

Cuong Xuan Chu[✉], Mohamed H. Gad-Elrab, Trung-Kien Tran,
Marvin Schiller, Evgeny Kharlamov, and Daria Stepanova

Bosch Center for Artificial Intelligence, Renningen, Germany
{cuongxuan.chu,mohamed.gad-elrab,trung-kien.tran,marvin.schiller,
evgeny.kharlamov,daria.stepanova}@de.bosch.com

Abstract. The automotive industry is constantly facing the challenge of optimizing their suppliers to meet customer demands while keeping costs low. Knowledge graphs have proven to be effective tools for modeling complex supply chains, but their use for optimization is limited. In this paper, we report on our experience at Bosch to use Answer Set Programming (ASP) to optimize component suppliers in the automotive industry based on knowledge graphs. Evaluation on industrial products shows both efficiency and effectiveness of our modeling framework in generating optimal solutions for supply chain management problems.

1 Introduction

Supplier Optimization. The challenge of *supplier optimization* in the automotive industry concerns identifying the best suppliers for automotive parts and components based on various criteria, *e.g.* quality, reliability, cost, and delivery time. Usually the production of a single system relies on a large number of suppliers providing various parts and components. Managing relationships with a large network of suppliers is time-consuming and resource-intensive. Therefore, supplier optimization is essential to ensure the timely delivery of high-quality components at a competitive cost.

Supply Chain Knowledge Graph. Following our semantic driven strategy [7], we rely on semantic technologies for solving the supplier optimization problem. More specifically, we represent the suppliers and their products (i.e., characteristics, such as the price, quality, lead time, delivery options, certifications, etc.) in knowledge graphs (KGs) [5]. The supplier graph is integrated with the KG representing the bill of materials (BOM), i.e., the components and materials needed for product manufacturing.

Answer Set Programming for Optimization. To compute the optimal set of suppliers, we utilize *answer set programming (ASP)* [3,4,6], i.e., a declarative programming paradigm which provides a simple modeling language allowing

C. Pesquita et al. (Eds.): ESWC 2023, LNCS 13998, pp. 200–204, 2023.
https://doi.org/10.1007/978-3-031-43458-7_38

for a succinct representation of search and optimization problems. Problems are encoded in programs, i.e., finite sets of rules, whose answer sets (which are special models) computed by dedicated ASP solvers, yield the solutions of a problem.

Supplier Optimization. In our solution, we utilize the flexibility of KGs and the power of ASP to optimize the suppliers for materials and components of a given product. This problem is particularly challenging due to the large size of the input KG, and directly invoking ASP solvers on the full data is not feasible. Thus, we develop strategies for extracting only relevant facts required for the optimization. Moreover, to ensure wide usage of our service, we make it accessible also for users without ASP background.

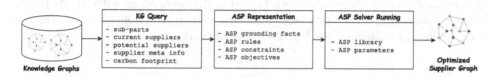

Fig. 1. Architecture overview of the supply chain optimization service.

2   Supplier Optimization

Figure 1 describes the overview of the process for using ASP in optimizing suppliers for different parts of a product in the KG. We proceed with describing the required data, the details of each component of our pipeline, as well as discuss the user experience.

Required Input. To model the supplier optimization problem, the following components are required: (1) *input facts*, related to the target product. In our use-case, we are working on multiple knowledge graphs, including **supplier KGs**, containing over 4.2M *part–plant–supplier* relationships, along with information about suppliers, such as supplier types (`producer or reseller`), location and carbon footprint; **BOM KGs**, containing a hierarchical structure of the parts of a target product and their current suppliers. Usually a product contains thousands of parts and sub-parts; (2) the *objectives* of the optimization problem, *e.g.*, minimizing the number of suppliers for the product and the total carbon footprint; (3) *constraints*, depending on customers' requirements, e.g., "avoiding reseller", "restrictions on the number of suppliers per part", etc.

Optimization Process. The process starts with querying the KGs to extract the relevant facts including the product, its parts, as well as current and potential suppliers and defining the optimization objectives, rules and constraints. Then, the retrieved facts, rules, and objectives are represented in the Answer Set Programming modeling language [6].

We pass the constructed ASP encoding to the state-of-the-art ASP solver `clingo` [4] to compute possible solutions to the problem, i.e., sets of optimal suppliers for each product, along with the relevant meta information (*e.g.,* number of optimal suppliers, their total carbon footprint, etc.).

User Experience. We have implemented our ASP-based optimization approach as a webservice (i.e. API) that supports asynchronous interaction, allowing the users to define new optimization problems, specify KGs used in the input, set optimization objectives as well as product-specific constraints. The customers are able to interact with the system by adding further simple constraints (e.g., exclusion or inclusion of certain potential suppliers) in an iterative fashion if the computed solution does not meet their expectations. In the output, a KG with the optimal selection of suppliers is returned to the user. Along with the API, we also provide a simple web interface to facilitate the interaction with our system for supplier optimization (see Fig. 2 for illustration).

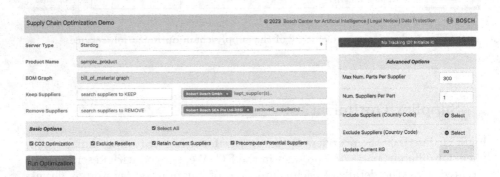

Fig. 2. Web interface for the supply chain optimization service.

Table 1. Sample statistics for the suppliers of a **single** product and the optimization results obtained by the service. ([1] two current suppliers & one new supplier)

Number of **product parts**	362
Number of **current** suppliers	171
Number of **potential** suppliers	3302
Number of **optimal** suppliers	3[1]
Total carbon footprint of **current** suppliers	44245
Total carbon footprint of **optimal** suppliers	50

Optimization Results. We have evaluated our service for supplier optimization on real industrial data. As an example, in Table 1 we present the statistics of the input dataset and the supplier optimization results for an electronic device. One can observe that with the help of our supplier optimization service, we have managed to reduce the number of suppliers from 171 to only 3 suppliers. In Fig. 3 we additionally report the detailed results of the optimization process, *i.e.,* intermediate solutions with the number of suppliers, their total carbon footprint as well as the time required for their computation. The optimal number of suppliers with the best carbon footprint has been computed in only 15 s, demonstrating the usability of our service in real industrial settings.

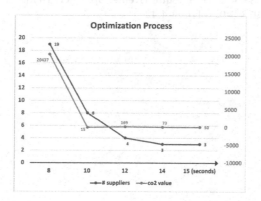

Fig. 3. Optimization results on the sample product.

3   Discussion and Future Work

Our solution for supplier optimization paves the way towards wide adoption of KGs and ASP-based technology for industrial use cases. As future work, we are going to improve the scalability of the presented service by exploiting recent extensions of answer set programming solvers with large neighborhood optimization strategies [1,2]. We also plan to automatically learn complex ASP constraints from the user feedback in order to iteratively improve the quality of the resulting solutions.

Acknowledgement. The work was partially supported by EU projects Dome 4.0 (GA 953163), OntoCommons (GA 958371), DataCloud (GA 101016835), Graph Massiviser (GA 101093202), enRichMyData (GA 101070284), and SMARTEDGE (GA 101092908).

References

1. Eiter, T., Geibinger, T., Ruiz, N.H., Musliu, N., Oetsch, J., Stepanova, D.: Large-neighbourhood search for optimisation in answer-set solving. In: AAAI (2022)

2. Eiter, T., Geibinger, T., Ruiz, N.H., Musliu, N., Oetsch, J., Stepanova, D.: ALASPO: an adaptive large-neighbourhood ASP optimiser. In: KR 2022 (2022)
3. Eiter, T., Ianni, G., Krennwallner, T.: Answer set programming: a primer. In: Tessaris, S., Franconi, E., Eiter, T., Gutierrez, C., Handschuh, S., Rousset, M.-C., Schmidt, R.A. (eds.) Reasoning Web 2009. LNCS, vol. 5689, pp. 40–110. Springer, Heidelberg (2009). https://doi.org/10.1007/978-3-642-03754-2_2
4. Gebser, M., Kaminski, R., Kaufmann, B., Schaub, T.: Multi-shot ASP solving with clingo. Theory Pract. Log. Program. **19**(1), 27–82 (2019)
5. Hogan, A., et al.: Knowledge graphs. ACM Comput. Surv. **54**, 1–37 (2021)
6. Lifschitz, V.: Answer Set Programming. Springer, Heidelberg (2019)
7. Zhou, B., et al. The data value quest: a holistic semantic approach at Bosch. In: The Semantic Web: ESWC 2022 Satellite Events. Springer, Heidelberg (2022). https://doi.org/10.1007/978-3-031-11609-4_42

Ontologies for Formalizing the Process of Configuring and Deploying Building Management Systems

Hervé Pruvost[✉] and Andreas Wilde

Division Engineering of Adaptive Systems (EAS), Fraunhofer Institute for Integrated Circuits
(IIS), Münchner Straße 16, 01187 Dresden, Germany
{herve.pruvost,andreas.wilde}@eas.iis.fraunhofer.de

1 Introduction

For tackling the current energy crisis and increasing energy demand worldwide, it has become urgent to rationalize energy use and decrease energy waste. Buildings are responsible for about one third of the global energy consumption in the world [1], and 30% of this energy is even wasted due to e.g. malfunctions of heating, ventilation and air conditioning systems (HVAC), wrong operation strategies or unaware user behavior. Building management systems (BMS) can bring support through optimal control and continuous monitoring of building energy systems, but their design and configuration is a complex process that requires much expert knowledge and labor cost.

This paper presents a method relying on knowledge graphs to automate this process. Starting from a semantic description of a building, it characterizes its energy system to identify applicable monitoring and control tasks. Following a risk paradigm, it then configures and deploys these tasks as BMS functions selecting for each their required sensor data. The industrial adoption of the method is foreseen as an expert system add-on to BMS that would accelerate and scale up their deployments for energy saving.

2 System and Process Ontologies

The expert system is composed of ontologies which conceptualize the domains of building energy systems and automation. In the field, several metadata schemas have emerged and are for a part reused in the ontology system. These include ifcOWL that was released by buildingSMART as an OWL (Web Ontology Language) representation of IFC (Industry Foundation Classes) [2]. The automation domain was formally described into SSN/SOSA [3] and CTRLont [4]. The Brick ontology [5] has emerged a few years ago for representing HVAC systems. The Building Topology Ontology (BOT) is a lightweight ontology for describing the spatial structure of buildings [6], and the QUDT ontologies were initiated by the Constellation Program at NASA [7].

© The Author(s), under exclusive license to Springer Nature Switzerland AG 2023
C. Pesquita et al. (Eds.): ESWC 2023, LNCS 13998, pp. 205–209, 2023.
https://doi.org/10.1007/978-3-031-43458-7_39

As each ontology covers a specific domain with its limitations, we developed further ontologies [8] that enable a full description of a building in its operation phase (see Fig. 1). Additional ontologies consist of the Energy System Information Model (ESIM) that extends Brick with concepts about energy systems at building and urban levels. The Metric model consists of a set of quantities that complement QUDT and SSN/SOSA with specific metrics for HVAC engineering. The Risk model provides a catalog of possible faults that can lead to energy wastes, together with corrective energy conservation measures. The BAF (Building Automation Functions) model is a catalogue of generic control functions usually implemented by automation engineers.

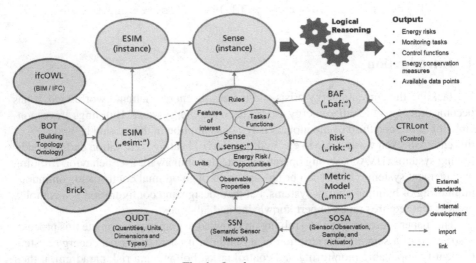

Fig. 1. Ontology system

Finally, the Sense ontology represents the central knowledge model that aggregates all the concepts, and in which logical axioms and rules are encoded for formalizing expert knowledge. This contrasts with the other ontologies that rather focus on system description while the Sense ontology aims at emulating the process of BMS setup by characterizing the system and prescribing BMS functions. These functions consist of algorithms that can process real-time data of buildings gained from sensors and meters in order to detect faults or energy waste. If energy is being wasted, different actions can be taken by a facility manager or a building user. Accordingly, a set of corrective actions are formalized as energy conservation measures inside the ontology. Figure 2 represents some fundamental concepts composing the Sense ontology that share causal relationships to support the setup of BMS functions for e.g. fault detection. More specifically, Table 1 shows some examples of rules written in SWRL (Semantic Web Rule Language). They are used by a reasoner for identifying potential energy risks in air handling units and deploy related monitoring functions to check if they occur.

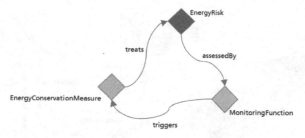

Fig. 2. Some fundamental concepts and their relationships for configuring fault detection

Table 1. Examples of SWRL rules for energy risk identification.

id	Rule definition in human-readable syntax
R1	brick:AHU(?ahu) ∧ brick:Heating_Coil(?hc) ∧ brick:Cooling_Coil(?cc) ∧ brick:hasPart(?ahu, ?hc) ∧ brick:hasPart(?ahu, ?cc) → risk:hasRisk(?ahu, risk:SimultaneousAirHeatingAndAirCooling)
R2	brick:AHU(?ahu) ∧ brick:Heating_Coil(?hc) ∧ brick:Supply_Fan(?sf) ∧ brick:hasPart(?ahu, ?hc) ∧ brick:hasPart(?ahu, ?sf) → risk:hasRisk(?ahu, risk:AirHeatedButNotVentilated)
R3	risk:hasRisk(?e, ?ri) ∧ risk:assessedBy(?ri, ?mf) ∧ sense:MonitoringFunction(?mf) → sense:hasFunction(?e, ?mf)

3   Knowledge Extraction for Task Configuration

A prerequisite for an automated configuration process is on the one hand the availability of building information i.e. metadata to create assertions in the ontology. On the other hand, real-time sensor data are necessary for BMS functions. While sensor data can be nowadays extensively supplied in modern or retrofitted buildings, metadata are rather difficult to gather for easy ontology instantiation which remains a work in progress. Basically, there exist three possible use cases which consist of getting metadata from either 1) a sensor database, 2) a graph database, or 3) a building information model (BIM) gained from CAD design. Then a two-step workflow consisting of metadata processing followed by data processing can be realized (see Fig. 3).

A first prototype workflow was developed as part of an energy assistant system [9]. In that context, some metadata from a sensor database could be reused in the ontology. They describe topological objects and locations in the building that relate to specific sensor data points. During metadata processing which is performed using a reasoner, the Sense model enables to classify thermal zones and associate them with relevant monitoring functions. As an example, if a room hosts one or more radiators, it will be classified as a heating zone and associated with a function that checks potential overheating using indoor temperature data. During data processing, it can then generate as output notifications to reduce heating in this zone if overheating really occurs.

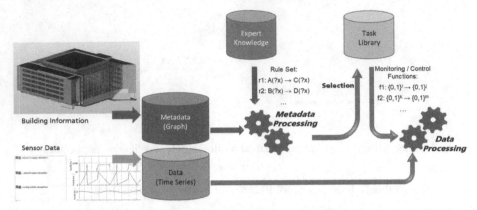

Fig. 3. Workflow for automated building energy system monitoring and control

The second use case was tested using the Brick schema that aims at generalizing the use of graphs for modeling building energy systems [5]. While a classical sensor database may only provide few metadata, Brick can describe HVAC systems in sufficient detail. On that basis, the rules from Table 1 were used to automatically select all entities that should be analyzed for some fault detection if they are threatened by some energy risk. Potential risks can be identified in an air handling unit (AHU) according to its built-in components (e.g. heating coil, cooling coil, fans, humidifier, air filters...). Accordingly, if an AHU carries a certain energy risk, the metadata processing will select relevant monitoring functions in order to identify related faults from real operation data.

4   Industrial Application - Barriers and Opportunities

First tests proved that BMS functions can be derived from an ontological description of an energy system. A necessary pre-condition for the proposed method is the availability of building information to populate the instance ontologies. Digitalization in building sector, supported by the Brick paradigm and the BIM method, shall ensure availability of computer-readable data models to generate graphs in an automated manner. Since BIM models consist of comprehensive descriptions of buildings at high level of detail, they can provide larger amount of metadata that can serve an extensive configuration of BMS systems. This BIM use case is currently under development.

References

1. IEA: Tracking report. https://www.iea.org/reports/buildings. Accessed 22 May 2023
2. ISO 16739-1: Industry foundation classes (IFC) for data sharing in the construction and facility management industries—part 1: Data schema. International Organisation for Standardisation, Geneva, Switzerland (2018)
3. W3C: Semantic Sensor Network Ontology. https://www.w3.org/TR/vocab-ssn/. Accessed 22 May 2023
4. Schneider, G.F., Pauwels, P., Steiger, S.: Ontology-based modeling of control logic in building automation systems. IEEE Trans. Industr. Inf. **13**(6), 3350–3360 (2017)

5. Fierro, G., et al.: Shepherding metadata through the building lifecycle. In: 7th ACM International Conference on Systems for Energy-Efficient Buildings, Cities, and Transportation, pp. 70–79 (2020)
6. Rasmussen, M.H., Lefrançois, M., Schneider, G.F., Pauwels, P.: BOT: the building topology ontology of the W3C linked building data group. Semantic Web J., 1–19 (2021)
7. FAIRsharing.org: QUDT; Quantities, Units, Dimensions and Types. https://doi.org/10.25504/FAIRsharing.d3pqw7. Accessed 22 May 2023
8. Pruvost, H.: SENSE ontology system. https://w3id.org/sense. Accessed 25 May 2023
9. Pruvost, H., Calleja-Rodríguez, G., Enge-Rosenblatt, O., Jiménez-Redondo, N., Peralta-Escalante, J.J.: A recommendation system for energy saving and user engagement in existing buildings. Proc. Inst. Civ. Eng. Smart Infrastruct. Constr. 176(1), 1–11 (2023)

PhD Symposium

Metaphor Processing in the Medical Domain via Linked Data and Language Models

Lucía Pitarch[(✉)] [ID]

University of Zaragoza, Zaragoza, Spain
lpitarch@unizar.es

Abstract. This thesis proposes a hybrid approach that benefits from Natural Language Processing and Semantic Web technologies for computational metaphor processing. Metaphors are linguistic devices that enable us to perceive and express a concept in terms of another similar one. Designing systems that allow their explicit identification and interpretation can highly facilitate communication in sensitive and obscure contexts such as the medical one. This proposal seeks the identification, understanding, generation, and manipulation of metaphors while providing novel datasets and baselines to exploit Languages Models and Linked Data in the context of figurative knowledge. The developed methodologies will be validated by their application into a specific communication tool between cancer patients and healthcare professionals.

Keywords: Metaphors · LLOD · Ontologies · PTLMs · Medical Domain

1 Introduction

Metaphors are not only poetic resources to embellish communication, but very common linguistic devices that enable us to talk about one thing in terms of another in every kind of communication [19]. Metaphors establish correspondences between a target domain[1], which is the one implicitly trying to be expressed, and one or more source domains, which are explicitly represented on the text. By doing so, some characteristics of the target domain are highlighted while others are shadowed. In short, metaphors focus and shape how we perceive the world [19]. By establishing associations between source and target domains, metaphors make communications more economical and efficient. They

---

Supported by the Spanish project PID2020-113903RB-I00 (AEI/FEDER, UE), by DGA/FEDER, and by the EU research and innovation program HORIZON Europe 2021 through the "4D PICTURE" project under grant agreement 101057332.

[1] Domains in this linguistic field are understood differently than in the Semantic Web community, in this work we consider domains as the background knowledge needed to understand a concept, it is to some extent similar to a semantic field.

C. Pesquita et al. (Eds.): ESWC 2023, LNCS 13998, pp. 213–223, 2023.
https://doi.org/10.1007/978-3-031-43458-7_40

can be used to fill in lexical gaps, motivate semantic change, describe personal experience and ground it into some common knowledge shared between speakers, or influence decision making by priming the speaker with a different idea [35].

Having such big impact in communication, it is no surprise how common they are in the medical environment. As studied by Semino et al. [32], patients used journey and violence metaphors around 1.5 times per 1000 words in their discourse. Complementary, Casarett [3] pointed our that oncologists use at least one metaphor in every conversation with advanced cancer patients. Benefits of metaphor usage in the medical domain are twofold. For patients, they have been proven as useful communicative devices by aiding them make sense of difficult and abstract experiences [17] and when used as coping mechanisms [16]. For clinicians, they can help them explain complex medical terms [28], reinforce or reorient potentially unhealthy misconceptions [10], help patients gain foresight on their condition [27], aid the initiation of difficult topics [9] or make patients aware about risks [20]. Yet, as shown by Landau et al., using the wrong metaphor can backfire [20]; thus, studying what metaphors are beneficial for individual patients under particular conditions (e.g., illness, treatment phase) becomes crucial.

While previous research on metaphors in the medical domain has been mainly conducted using manual effort, it is very time and resource-consuming, and hardly adaptable to new patients or to changes in the patient's condition. Thus, complementing manual effort with Computational Metaphor Processing (CMP) seems like the logical way to go. The aim of this thesis is to generate a CMP tool that facilitates the understanding and generation of metaphors in the medical domain. The tool must be transparent, highly interpretable, adaptable to individual needs, scalable, and dynamic.

The underlying hypothesis behind this thesis is that a mixed approach that uses both Language Models and Linked Data will provide the needed flexibility, adaptability, interpretability, transparency, and dynamic processing of metaphors. The development of such hybrid technology will lead to a powerful communication tool between clinicians and patients. Moreover, by pursuing this goal, the thesis will contribute to the technological field by gaining insights into the abilities of Natural Language Processing (NLP) and current Ontological models to encode and represent figurative knowledge, and in the humanistic domain by providing large structured data which can further be used to understand the cognitive processes that guide metaphoric expression or the socio-cultural and medical preferences for different metaphors in the medical domain.

2   State of the Art

2.1   Computational Metaphor Processing

Tasks: In previous systematic reviews [14,30] CMP has been split into 4 different tasks: a) metaphor identification, which consists in finding the words in a text being used metaphorically; b) metaphor interpretation, which groups metaphor

paraphrasing, metaphor best fitting definition selection, and metaphoric impli-
cation selection; c) metaphor mapping, consisting in explicitly showing the correspondences between source and target domains, and d) metaphor generation.

Methods: CMP has gained attention in recent years [14], since the seminal work
of Shutova [33]. Shutova described how in 2015 approaches towards metaphor
processing were shifting from hand-coded knowledge to statistical modeling.

Then, after the arousal of transformer architectures [8], a renewed attention
towards metaphors can be seen in the literature, and the usage of Pre-Trained
Language Models (PTLMs) has become the state of the art for metaphor identification [1] and interpretation [34]. Distributional methodologies (e.g., with the
usage of Language Models) rely on a discourse analysis approach, and while
being promising to identify the metaphorical expressions used in a text or being
able to superficially interpret them by paraphrasing them, they lack the ability
to run a finer graded analysis and conceptualization of metaphors.

A more symbolic approach (e.g., through Linked Data and Knowledge
Graphs) would contribute in structuring the different elements involved in
metaphors and the relations between them. Structured representation of knowledge would provide models which enable inference discovery to uncover individual preferences for particular metaphors, the patterns used to create metaphors,
and an understanding of how the different lexical entries in the text metaphorically relate to each other. Overall, using Semantic Web technologies would facilitate the prediction of the effect, usage, and preference for a particular metaphor.
Efforts towards symbolic representations of metaphor have already been initiated [12,13,15], yet, they are too generic and should be adapted to cover the
medical and individual-centered approach of this thesis.

Hybrid approaches mixing symbolic and distributional models, while promising, are very scarce and new. Song et al., [34] represent similes (a similar device
to metaphor) as triples and extract them using LMs, but they only encode three
entity types (source domain, target domain, and attribute) which is not enough
to represent a metaphor.

Datasets: Two different kinds of data should be used in this thesis to meet
the hybrid approach necessities. On the one hand, Structured data covering
metaphoric knowledge [12,13,15], and, on the other hand, available datasets to
train and test Language Models with metaphors, a summary of which can be
found in Ge's et al., survey [14]. Among these, most focus on computational
metaphor identification [2,18,25,31] and leave mostly uncovered other tasks
such as metaphor interpretation, mapping, and generation. Available datasets
for computational metaphor processing are too general, they do not differentiate between different figurative (e.g., between analogies, metaphors, idioms,
or metonymy), they usually cover a small number of examples, and they do
not control socio-cultural or individual differences though being key aspects in
metaphor comprehension, and, finally, and as a core limitation that motivates
one of the goals of this thesis, they do not cover the medical domain.

Baselines: Among the different tasks in CMP, metaphor identification has obtained the most attention, thus, most baselines available are for this task [14], and results are already very promising with baselines around 80% of accuracy. Yet, this is only for English and little has been done for other languages. Moreover, among the different things which could be controlled for bias in the prediction of metaphoric expressions in the texts (e.g., different underlying metaphors, domains, or metaphor types), just part of speech is controlled. Regarding the rest of the tasks, research is not only scarce but also there is a lot of heterogeneity in the approaches taken. Baselines and evaluation criteria are defined particularly per paper, making comparability among them very hard.

2.2   Metaphors in the Medical Domain

Studies regarding metaphors in the medical domain have mostly been conducted by manually harvesting physicians' and patients' discourse to identify, classify and study the implications of using a limited group of metaphors in the medical domain [10,28,32]. Most studies have focused either on studying the usage of figurative expressions by non-neurotypical patients to gain insights into cognition or, on analyzing the discourse surrounding oncological processes. In this latter setting violence and journey metaphors have been the most discussed, leaving the rest unattended. It is relevant to extend this kind of research to other metaphors and gain a bigger adaptation ability to each patient [10,32], their sociocultural background [11], treatment phase, and illness [26]. At the moment, large databases and computational tools to automate this process, to the best of our knowledge are not available, thus, conveying a key goal of this thesis. The only communication tool through metaphors currently available is the Metaphor Menu [32], an inventory of narratives exploring different metaphors that can be used to talk about cancer. A limitation of such a tool is that it covers only a small and closed number of metaphors, it is only openly available in English and it has not been thoroughly researched on how to be adapted to individual patients' necessities. An additional limitation of the Metaphor Menu is that it only covers the underlying metaphor in a text but it does not provide an structured inventory of the metaphoric mappings that can be selected to express a particular metaphor or to reframe an existing one through particular lexical expressions (e.g., if a nurse wants to express treatment in terms of the journey metaphor, a tool containing such correspondences, would relate the patient to the traveler, and the treatment to the path). Extension of tools such as the Metaphor Menu in this direction becomes relevant as researchers such as Landau et al., [20] have pointed out extending the same metaphor (through different lexical entries) throughout the text to talk about both the risks and prevention possibilities is more effective than changing metaphor across discourse.

3   Problem Statement and Contributions

Metaphoric expressions identification in texts, or what it has usually been called metaphor identification, has been the most research task in CMP. However, unless some further effort is conducted afterwords, the identified words, relations between them, and what they are implicitly trying to express, cannot be interpreted. Thus, metaphoric expressions identification needs to be complemented by the joint development of resources and research in related tasks such as metaphor interpretation, generation and mapping. The first contribution from this thesis is then, shifting towards a more holistic exploration of metaphors. The proposed pipeline towards fulfilling this kind of approach is represented in Fig. 1 and described bellow.

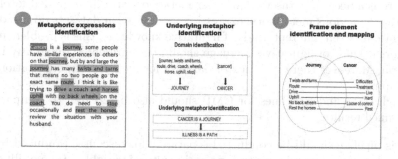

Fig. 1. Metaphor processing road map

1. **Metaphoric expressions identification**, traditionally coined *metaphor identification*. This task consists of identifying the words used metaphorically in a text.
2. **Underlying metaphor identification**, this next task derives from a rather cognitive approach to metaphor processing in comparison to the main discourse analysis approach[2]. It consists of, given a list of the lexical entries used metaphorically in the text, identifying the source and target domains of the metaphor.
3. **Frame elements' identification and mapping** consists of given the lexical entries used metaphorically in the discourse, the underlying metaphors that relate them, and their source and target domains, go a step further and uncover the semantic roles they play inside that the expressed domain in the text and the correspondent entities in the target domain.

The described pipeline makes use, on the one hand, of Knowledge Graphs to represent the metaphors and elements in them (e.g., domains, frame elements, lexical entries or mappings), and, on the other hand, of LMs for the identification of new metaphoric expressions in the text, prediction of relations between them, and further population of the ontology.

---

[2] Cognitive approach to metaphor complements discourse approach and provides cues to following the patterns of creation and understanding of metaphors as well as structured and abstracted examples which facilitate ontological representation of metaphors.

Right now, the main challenges that need to be addressed to make the execution of the pipeline possible are:

1. Finding the best way to encode not only metaphors in the ontology, but also the context and corpus characteristics they appear in. We hypothesize this could be done by adapting current available ontologies and linking them to resources as Ontolex-Frac [4] for corpus annotation.
2. Understanding how figurative knowledge is encoded in LMs and how to exploit them to further populate the metaphor Knowledge Graph.
3. There is a need of datasets that cover metaphors at a finer-graded level. For instance previous metaphoric expression identification datasets do not differenciate between different kinds of figurative knowledge, this is problematic as different kinds of figurative language should be represented differently in the graph. Moreover there is a lack of datasets for metaphor interpretation and mapping.
4. Benchmarks and Baselines for CMP should also be created to compare the obtained results.

This pipeline should be conducted separately for discourse produced by different subgroups of people, controlling socio-cultural variables, type of illness or affliction, and treatment phase factors. Once discourse has been processed, the outcome should consist of different subgraphs per population type. These graphs should be compared to try and grasp if any different patterns arise from them.

By pursuing these outcomes, this thesis will contribute to the technological field by providing further understanding and development of NLP and Ontological models to encode metaphorical knowledge, algorithms, and architectures mostly based on Language Models that enhance them, databases that can be further exploited, and, baselines for the newly created tasks. Moreover, the outcoming structured datasets will provide data that can be used to explore cognitive and sociocultural patterns behind metaphor processing.

4   Research Methodology and Approach

The first step of this thesis should cover the available **ontological model's adaptation**. A great ontology to start could be Framester [12] and derived resources from it such as ImageSchemaNet [15]. After its adaptation to our necessities, it should be linked to cognitive resources such as Small World of Words [7], factual knowledge bases such as Wikidata [37] and lexicographic resources such as Ontolex-Frac [4] and Ontolex-Core [24] modules.

The next step should cover the **dataset creation**. This dataset should consist on texts produced on the medical environment, annotated with metadatate controlling for the patient and clinician particular circumstances. A starting point, which could also serve to validate the ontological models creating in the first step, is the transformation of the Metaphor Menu [32] in structured data. Further data should be collected and parsed from questionnaires and internet forums, similarly to [32].

The third step consists of the **exploitation of Language Models** to perform the tasks described in Sect. 3 while further populating the ontology. At this point technical questions such as the following ones will be addressed, pushing the SotA in CMP forward: What figurative knowledge is encoded in Language Models? How? What kind of knowledge injection boosts Language Models performance in each of the CMP tasks described in Sect. 3.

Our first approach covers only Pre-Trained Language Models, as they provide higher control and interpretability of the outputs. Working with Large Language Models and comparing them to our contributions, is currently out of the scope of this thesis and would remain as future work, that could be pursued after the delivery of the thesis.

Finally, the applicability of our outcomes and their effect in the medical domain will be validated in a real-world scenario by interviews in collaboration with the Horizon Europe 4DPicture project.

5 Evaluation Plan

The proposed **ontological model** for representing metaphors should follow the best practices described in the Linguistic Linked Data community [5].

Metaphoric expressions identification will be tested on general domain metaphor identification datasets and benchmarks as the ones described in [14].

Identification of the underlying metaphors behind texts and **metaphor mapping** can be evaluated by using as gold dataset the data extracted from ontological resources such as Framester [12], or datasets with metaphoric analogies encoding their domains such as the one from Czinczoll et al., [6]. Superficially it can be compared to similar works such as the one conducted by Song et al., [34]; yet, the work with analogies rather than metaphors. Given the lack of resources to compare the latter-named tasks with other works, we would consider at this point the creation of a benchmark for CMP.

The resulting communication tool will be validated in a **real-world scenario** by interviews with healthcare professionals, linguists, and patients. This will be possible through collaboration with the Horizon Europe 4DPicture project.

6 Preliminary Results

Our first experiments dealt with the metaphor identification task. In a first attempt to uncover how much linguistic knowledge is encoded in the available pre-trained language models to classify words between figurative and literal expressions. Even when following a very simple approach we obtained promising and competitive results when compared with the SotA approaches which support the model with external linguistic features and theories [1,21,38,39].

Our approach is in line with research such as [29,36] that goes towards the idea that PTLMs already encode a large amount of linguistic knowledge, and thus can be directly exploited, or with minimal fine-tuning to perform a wide range of language-related tasks.

For this first approach, we use minimal prompting to fine-tune and exploit RoBERTa [23] model. This prompting procedure derives from the idea that PTLMs have been trained with a masked language model objective where given a correctly verbalize sentence they need to predict a masked word in it. Thus, providing the model with the instructions in a well-verbalized way, more similar to how the model was trained, is supposed to boost the model's performance, this has been coined as prompting [22]. In our first experiments, we fine-tune a PTLM with a sequence classification layer on the top. We train the model with the input prompt "[SEP] sentence with target word [SEP] target word" and the regarding label, 1, if the target word is a metaphor in the sentence, otherwise 0. The following Table 1 summarizes the obtained results, which even with such a simple methodology are results are not far behind the current SotA. In the future and by taking advantage of the metaphor modeling as structured data, we aim to inject the PTLMs with additional lexical features from BabelNet or Ontolex following the minimal prompting technique.

Table 1. F1 Score report for metaphor identification datasets

	Babieno, 22	Lin, 21	Yang, 21	Wan, 21	Ours
VUA-20	**72.5**	–	–	–	68.9
VUA-V	68.8	75.6	**80.7**	75.0	71.1
MOH-X	80.8	**84.7**	–	–	76.9
TroFi	61.7	74.5	–	**89.3**	73.1

Further analysis should make use of visualization techniques to check how the model is learning through different layers and epochs.

7   Conclusions

Explicit metaphor representation should aid communication in sensitive contexts such as the medical one. While previous tools such as the Metaphor Menu required huge manual efforts to produce them, they are still very case oriented, small, not flexible and with limitations. This thesis proposes a mixed exploitation of Natural Language Processing and Semantic Web technologies to further enrich them, while providing new extense databases and guidelines that will boost figurative knowledge computational processing.

Acknowledgements. I would like to thank my supervisors Dr.Jorge Gracia del Río and Dr.Jorge Bernad Lusilla for their support and feedback, and Javier Fernández for his valuable insight and questions.

References

1. Babieno, M., Takeshita, M., Radisavljevic, D., Rzepka, R., Araki, K.: Miss RoBERTa wilde: metaphor identification using masked language model with wiktionary lexical definitions. Applied Sciences **12**(4), 2081 (2022)
2. Birke, J., Sarkar, A.: A clustering approach for nearly unsupervised recognition of nonliteral language. In: Conference of the European Chapter of the Association for Computational Linguistics (2006)
3. Casarett, D., et al.: Can metaphors and analogies improve communication with seriously ill patients? J. Palliat. Med. **13**(3), 255–260 (2010)
4. Chiarcos, C., et al.: Modelling frequency and attestations for ontolex-lemon. In: Proceedings of the 2020 Globalex Workshop on Linked Lexicography, pp. 1–9 (2020)
5. Cimiano, P., Chiarcos, C., McCrae, J.P., Gracia, J.: Linguistic linked open data cloud. In: Cimiano, P., Chiarcos, C., McCrae, J.P., Gracia, J. (eds.) Linguistic Linked Data, pp. 29–41. Springer, Cham (2020). https://doi.org/10.1007/978-3-030-30225-2_3
6. Czinczoll, T., Yannakoudakis, H., Mishra, P., Shutova, E.: Scientific and creative analogies in pretrained language models. arXiv preprint arXiv:2211.15268 (2022)
7. De Deyne, S., Navarro, D.J., Perfors, A., Brysbaert, M., Storms, G.: The "small world of words" English word association norms for over 12,000 cue words. Behav. Res. Methods **51**, 987–1006 (2019)
8. Devlin, J., Chang, M.W., Lee, K., Toutanova, K.: BERT: pre-training of deep bidirectional transformers for language understanding. In: Proceedings of the 2019 NACL. ACL, Minneapolis (2019)
9. Fadul, N., et al.: Supportive versus palliative care: what's in a name? Cancer **115**, 2013–2021 (2009)
10. Fatehi, A., Table, B., Peck, S., Mackert, M., Ring, D.: Medical metaphors: increasing clarity but at what cost? Arch. Bone Joint Surg. **10**(8), 721–728 (2022)
11. Fernandez, J.R., Richmond, J., Nápoles, A.M., Kruglanski, A.W., Forde, A.T.: Everyday discrimination and cancer metaphor preferences: the mediating effects of needs for personal significance and cognitive closure. SSM - Popul. Health **17**, 100991 (2021)
12. Gangemi, A., Alam, M., Asprino, L., Presutti, V., Recupero, D.R.: Framester: a wide coverage linguistic linked data hub. In: Blomqvist, E., Ciancarini, P., Poggi, F., Vitali, F. (eds.) EKAW 2016. LNCS (LNAI), vol. 10024, pp. 239–254. Springer, Cham (2016). https://doi.org/10.1007/978-3-319-49004-5_16
13. Gangemi, A., Alam, M., Presutti, V.: Linked metaphors. In: International Workshop on the Semantic Web (2018)
14. Ge, M., Mao, R., Cambria, E.: A survey on computational metaphor processing techniques: from identification, interpretation, generation to application (2022)
15. Giorgis, S.D., Gangemi, A., Gromann, D.: ImageSchemaNet: a framester graph for embodied commonsense knowledge. Semant. Web (2022)
16. Gustafsson, A.W., Hommerberg, C., Sandgren, A.: Coping by metaphors: the versatile function of metaphors in blogs about living with advanced cancer. Med. Humanit. **46**, 267–277 (2019)
17. Harrington, K.J.: The use of metaphor in discourse about cancer: a review of the literature. Clin. J. Oncol. Nurs. **16**(4), 408–12 (2012)

18. Krennmayr, T., Steen, G.: VU Amsterdam metaphor corpus. In: Ide, N., Puste-jovsky, J. (eds.) Handbook of Linguistic Annotation, pp. 1053–1071. Springer, Dordrecht (2017). https://doi.org/10.1007/978-94-024-0881-2_39
19. Lakoff, G., Johnson, M.: Metaphors We Live By. The University of Chicago Press (1980)
20. Landau, M.J., Cameron, L.D., Arndt, J., Hamilton, W., Swanson, T.J., Bultmann, M.N.: Beneath the surface: abstract construal mindset increases receptivity to metaphors in health communications. Soc. Cogn. 37(3), 314–340 (2019)
21. Lin, Z., Ma, Q., Yan, J., Chen, J.: Cate: A contrastive pre-trained model for metaphor detection with semi-supervised learning. In: Proceedings of the 2021 EMNLP, pp. 3888–3898 (2021)
22. Liu, P., Yuan, W., Fu, J., Jiang, Z., Hayashi, H., Neubig, G.: Pre-train, prompt, and predict: a systematic survey of prompting methods in natural language processing. ACM Comput. Surv. 55, 1–35 (2023)
23. Liu, Y., et al.: RoBERTa: a robustly optimized bert pretraining approach. arXiv preprint arXiv:1907.11692 (2019)
24. McCrae, J.P., Bosque-Gil, J., Gracia, J., Buitelaar, P., Cimiano, P.: The Ontolex-Lemon model: development and applications. In: Proceedings of eLex 2017 Conference, pp. 19–21 (2017)
25. Mohammad, S.M., Shutova, E., Turney, P.D.: Metaphor as a medium for emotion: an empirical study. In: International Workshop on Semantic Evaluation (2016)
26. Munday, I., Newton-John, T.R.O., Kneebone, I.I.: Clinician experience of metaphor in chronic pain communication. Scand. J. Pain 23, 88–96 (2022)
27. Penson, R.T., Schapira, L., Daniels, K.J., Chabner, B.A., Lynch, T.J.: Cancer as metaphor. Oncologist 9(6), 708–16 (2004)
28. Pinheiro, A.P.M., Pocock, R.H., Dixon, M.D., Shaib, W.L., Ramalingam, S.S., Pentz, R.D.: Using metaphors to explain molecular testing to cancer patients. Oncologist 22(4), 445–449 (2017)
29. Pitarch, L., Dranca, L., Bernad, J., Gracia, J.: Lexico-semantic relation classification with multilingual finetuning. In: LLOD Approaches for Language Data Research and Management, pp. 86–88 (2022)
30. Rai, S., Chakraverty, S.: A survey on computational metaphor processing. ACM Comput. Surv. (CSUR) 53(2), 1–37 (2020)
31. Sanchez-Bayona, E., Agerri, R.: Leveraging a new Spanish corpus for multilingual and crosslingual metaphor detection. arXiv preprint arXiv:2210.10358 (2022)
32. Semino, E., Demjén, Z., Hardie, A., Payne, S., Rayson, P.: Metaphor, Cancer and the End of Life: A Corpus-Based Study. Routledge (2017)
33. Shutova, E.: Design and evaluation of metaphor processing systems. Comput. Linguist. 41(4), 579–623 (2015)
34. Song, W., Guo, J., Fu, R., Liu, T., Liu, L.: A knowledge graph embedding approach for metaphor processing. IEEE/ACM Trans. Audio Speech Lang. Process. 29, 406–420 (2021)
35. Thibodeau, P.H., Matlock, T., Flusberg, S.J.: The role of metaphor in communication and thought. Lang. Linguist. Compass 13(5), e12327 (2019)
36. Ushio, A., Camacho-Collados, J., Schockaert, S.: Distilling relation embeddings from pretrained language models, pp. 9044–9062. Association for Computational Linguistics (2021)
37. Vrandečić, D., Krötzsch, M.: WikiData: a free collaborative knowledgebase. Commun. ACM 57, 78–85 (2014)

38. Wan, H., Lin, J., Du, J., Shen, D., Zhang, M.: Enhancing metaphor detection by gloss-based interpretations. In: Findings of the Association for Computational Linguistics: ACL-IJCNLP 2021, pp. 1971–1981 (2021)
39. Yang, L., Zeng, J., Li, S., Shen, Z., Sun, Y., Lin, H.: Metaphor recognition and analysis via data augmentation. In: Wang, L., Feng, Y., Hong, Yu., He, R. (eds.) NLPCC 2021, Part I. LNCS (LNAI), vol. 13028, pp. 746–757. Springer, Cham (2021). https://doi.org/10.1007/978-3-030-88480-2_60

Knowledge-Based Multimodal Music Similarity

Andrea Poltronieri[(✉)] [iD]

Department of Computer Science and Engineering, University of Bologna,
Bologna, Italy
andrea.poltronieri2@unibo.it

Abstract. Music similarity is an essential aspect of music retrieval, recommendation systems, and music analysis. Moreover, similarity is of vital interest for music experts, as it allows studying analogies and influences among composers and historical periods.

Current approaches to musical similarity rely mainly on symbolic content, which can be expensive to produce and is not always readily available. Conversely, approaches using audio signals typically fail to provide any insight about the reasons behind the observed similarity.

This research addresses the limitations of current approaches by focusing on the study of musical similarity using both symbolic and audio content. The aim of this research is to develop a fully explainable and interpretable system that can provide end-users with more control and understanding of music similarity and classification systems.

Keywords: Music Similarity · Computational Musicology ·
Knowledge Graphs

1 Introduction

Music similarity is a central area of research in the field of Music Information Retrieval (MIR) [11] as it enables various applications, such as music recommendation, playlist generation, music search, and classification. The ability to measure the similarity between music tracks is essential for providing personalised and relevant recommendations to users based on their listening history and preferences [26]. Music similarity also facilitates the discovery of new music that matches the user's taste [28]. Additionally, music similarity can be used for content-based music classification, such as genre classification [10]. It is also useful in musicological research, as it allows for the exploration of musical patterns and structures across different styles and genres [36].

1.1 Problem Statement

The study of musical similarity is approached from various perspectives, which can be summarised in *content-based systems* and *context-based systems* [20]. The

C. Pesquita et al. (Eds.): ESWC 2023, LNCS 13998, pp. 224–233, 2023.
https://doi.org/10.1007/978-3-031-43458-7_41

former approach extracts information directly from the musical content (whether symbolic or audio), while the latter obtains information from non-musical data, such as metadata or information related to the song's popularity or listener characteristics. Content-based approaches allow a quantitative measurement of similarity based on factual music data, and make it possible to investigate similarities independently of the availability and accuracy of metadata [19].

However, studying content-based similarity poses several challenges, given the multidisciplinary nature of the research, which encompasses music theory, ethnomusicology, cognitive science, and computer science [36].

In content-based music similarity, a further distinction must be made concerning the representation of music. Two types of representations have been identified: *signal representations* that are recordings of sound sources, and *symbolic representations* that represent discrete musical events [37]. Symbolic representations are context-aware and offer a structured representation from which is easy to extract information from. On the other hand, signal representations are content-unaware and not structured, which makes extracting information from them a challenging task [38]. Signal representations are by far more studied than symbolic representations, since they are more interesting from a commercial point of view (e.g. for streaming services) and the data availability is higher.

Depending on the type of musical representation, several features can be used for similarity analysis: *descriptive metadata*, *low-level features*, and *high-level features* [39]. Descriptive metadata is text-based information about the song, while low-level features are extracted from the audio signal (e.g., beat, tempo) and are efficient but difficult to interpret. High-level features, on the other hand, are content descriptors that reflect the knowledge of experienced or professional listeners, making them the most intuitive approach for music classification tasks.

Most of the available music similarity systems, especially those based on audio signals [30], rely on low-level features. Annotating high-level content descriptors is also expensive and requires the expertise of musicians and musicologists [35]. As a result, most available systems cannot explicitly recognise similarity motives, and their lack of interpretability and transparency can lead to biased recommendations.

This results in a measure of similarity that is neither interpretable nor transparent, which may result in biased results [21].

1.2   Expected Contribution

This research proposes a fully explainable and interpretable system that provides information on musical similarity based on both symbolic and audio content, with a focus on factual musical data such as melodic and harmonic patterns.

RQ1 *What is an effective method to create high-quality datasets that incorporate multimodal data that links symbolic annotations (both melodic and harmonic) and audio?*

To achieve this, the symbolic content needs to be studied first to assess similarity in a transparent and explainable way.

RQ2 *How can similarity measures be derived from this knowledge graph in order for it to be objectively measured and quantified?*

Next, an alignment of the symbolic content with the audio signal using multimodal datasets must be performed. Finally, a deep learning system is trained to analyse the audio signal informed by the symbolic content. By doing so, it is possible to provide end-users with more control and understanding of the music similarity and classification systems they use, regardless of the representation under analysis.

RQ3 *How can score-informed audio analysis be used to identify similarities and patterns in audio data, and what are the benefits of this approach for the study of music similarity?*

The current study focuses on the application of Semantic Web technologies, particularly in the representation and alignment of multimodal data. One of the key challenges is how to effectively encode knowledge graphs (KGs) to enable their use as input and mapping onto various mathematical models, such as time-series and embedding.

2   Related Works

2.1   Symbolic Music Similarity

The study of similarity on symbolic content has been studied in depth in recent years. Various approaches have been proposed, ranging from harmonic similarity to melodic and rhythmic similarity.

Melodic similarity is the most extensively researched category. Algorithms that handle melodic similarity in symbolic form are typically rule-based and aim to define various types of context-dependent similarity functions, which rely on music theory [30]. However, these algorithms lack a shared definition of similarity and primarily focus on studying similarity in monophonic sequences [36].

On the other hand, algorithms for harmonic similarity has not received much attention in recent years. To the best of my knowledge, current state-of-the-art methods for this task are the *Tonal Pitch Step Distance* (TPSD) [15] and the *Chord Sequence Alignment System* (CSAS) [16]. These studies consider tracks similar only if their harmonic profiles are globally aligned, providing no information on local similarity.

Studies using a combination of harmonic and melodic content to calculate similarity are limited to a few contributions [14].

2.2   Audio Music Similarity

Music similarity in the audio signal domain has been studied for a wide range of applications, ranging from cover song identification [32] to recommendation systems [12]. These algorithms are based on the extraction of low-level features directly from the signal, such as spectrograms, MFCCs and Chorma Features [13].

One of the main limitations of these approaches is their reliance on deep learning approaches. These methods are based on end-to-end algorithms that do not provide valuable information regarding fundamental aspects of similarity, such as the explanation for why two or more tracks are similar, and the highlight of parts in common between different tracks.

2.3   Multimodal Music Similarity

Multimodality refers to the integration of multiple representation modes, such as visual, auditory, and textual.

In the realm of music, multimodality has become an increasingly popular field of research in recent years and has proven to provide better results in different tasks, if compared to approaches that consider a single modality [3,33].

One of the primary areas of research in multimodal MIR is the integration of audio and textual data. Moreover, multimodality has been explored also for other tasks, such as audio-to-score alignment [29] and classification [22].

However, less emphasis has been placed on algorithms that combine audio and symbolic annotations, particularly in the field of classification and similarity. Some methods, like [2] and [34], aim to identify audio tracks through symbolic queries, but they rely on converting either audio into symbolic or symbolic into audio, respectively. In contrast, [24] proposes a score-informed analysis of audio. Although this approach represents a promising development, it has to be considered a preliminary study, with a small sample size of only 20 violin-only tracks.

3   Research Metodology

The primary objective of this research is to develop algorithms that can accurately measure musical similarity based on both audio and symbolic content. The proposed approach will consider factual musical data and provide an interpretable model for computing music similarity between music pieces.

Dataset Creation. To achieve this goal, the first step is to create a multimodal dataset, which includes various types of data for each song in the dataset (c.f. *RQ1*). Specifically, the dataset must consist of four key elements for each track: (i) an audio track, (ii) melodic annotations, (iii) harmonic annotations, and (iv) track metadata.

The dataset will be encoded as a RDF/OWL Knowledge Graph (KG) [7], which will define semantic relationships between the various multimodal elements. The KG will also contain alignment data between different types of annotations, such as audio, melodic and harmonic data.

Similarity Computation. Similarity measures based on symbolic data will then be defined (c.f. *RQ2*), focusing on both melodic and harmonic elements. To achieve this, it is first necessary to define the concept of music similarity both musicologically and perceptually. First, repositories and datasets of known patterns will serve as a basis for the definition of similarity functions. Then, various types of matches, such as exact and fuzzy matches, will be considered between symbolic annotations at different levels, such as phrases, form, cadences, and melodies. This approach enables the investigation of musical similarity from a purely musical perspective, which would allow to the resulting similarity functions to be both explainable and transparent.

The research will also enable the definition of local similarities, allowing for the analysis of influences between different songs, as well as the detection of plagiarism in specific song sections. Moreover, the similarity analysis will be conducted by jointly analysing the harmonic and melodic data to provide more realistic and musicologically grounded similarity information.

Multimodal Analysis. In the final step, the similarities extracted from the symbolic data will be used to study similarity on the audio signal. This will involve training deep learning architectures on the aligned audio and symbolic data through the application of data fusion techniques (c.f. *RQ3*). Great care will be given in selecting an architecture that is both explainable and allows for analogies to be drawn between the various components of the multimodal analysis, such as deep learning architectures and neuro-symbolic reasoning.

An architecture that will be explored is transformers [9], which in this context can be employed for the unsupervised matching between symbolic annotations and audio features. Hence, the produced unsupervised model will be fine-tuned using the similarity measures extracted from the symbolic annotations.

3.1 Evaluation

The validation of the results obtained will focus on two main elements: (i) similarity measures based on symbolic content; and (ii) similarity based on audio signals.

Firstly, the similarity measures calculated on symbolic content will be evaluated to determine if the output of the defined similarity functions produces a musicologically or perceptually relevant output. Moreover, known pattern datasets [1,27] will be used to evaluate the output of the similarity measures. Secondly, crowdsourced surveys will be conducted to gather more data on the perceptual relevance of the extracted similarities.

Regarding the similarities calculated on audio signals, global results will be evaluated on typical music information retrieval tasks, such as cover song detection. For local similarities, the audio extracted similarities will be evaluated using the symbolic-aligned data.

Similarly, we will assess the transparency and explainability of the model. While the explainability of the symbolic similarity models is inherent in their design, the explainability of the model on audio signal will be evaluated by comparing the results to the aligned symbolic annotations.

4 Current Results

As initial contributions to the development of this research project, work was conducted on several fronts, including the creation of a dataset, the study of harmonic similarity, the embedding of harmonic annotations, and the construction of ontologies for modeling musical content.

4.1 Dataset Creation

As the first contribution of my research, I focused on the creation of a dataset of harmonic annotations (c.f. RQ1): ChoCo, the largest available *Chord Corpus* [4]. Choco is a large-scale dataset that semantically integrates harmonic data from 18 different sources in various representations and formats (Harte, Leadsheet, Roman numerals, ABC). The corpus leverage JAMS (JSON Annotated Music Specification) [18], a popular data structure for annotations in Music Information Retrieval, to effectively represent a variety of chord-related information (chord, key, mode, etc.) in a uniform way. ChoCo also consists of a converter module that takes care of standardising chord annotations into a single format, the Harte Notation [17]. On top of it, a novel ontology modelling music annotations and involved entities (artists, scores, etc.) has been proposed, and a 30M triple knowledge graph[1] has been built.

The proposed workflow is highly scalable and enables the seamless integration of additional data types, including melodic and structural annotations. Moreover, the Knowledge Graph utilised in ChoCo facilitates the alignment of its annotations with various metadata available on the web, such as MusicBrainz[2] and Discogs[3].

As a result, these resources provide an accurate and distinct reference point for each track, which will allow the identification of the audio recording which refers to the annotations contained in the dataset.

4.2 Studies on Harmonic Similarity

In accordance with the second research question (RQ2), a preliminary investigation into the similarity measures has been conducted.

Based on the limitations found in the state-of-the-art study of harmonic similarity, I worked on LHARP, a *Local Harmonic Agreement of Recurrent Patterns*. LHARP is a measure of harmonic similarity formulated for emphasising shared repeated patterns among two arbitrary symbolic sequences, thereby providing

---

[1] ChoCo SPARQL Endpoint: https://polifonia.disi.unibo.it/choco/sparql.

[2] MusicBrainz: https://musicbrainz.org/.

[3] Discogs: https://www.discogs.com/.

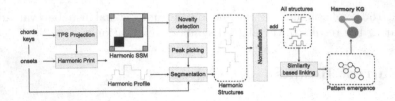

Fig. 1. Workflow used for the production of the Harmonic Memory (Harmory).

a general framework for the analysis of symbolic streams based on their local structures.

To evaluate the efficacy of LHARP as a method for harmonic similarity, two separate experiments were carried out – each pertaining to a case study that the function can potentially accommodate. First, a graph analysis was performed to encode harmonic dependencies (edges) between music pieces (nodes) based on their similarity values. Second, to conform with the literature, a cover song detection experiment was conducted.

As an evolution of LHARP, I worked on the *Harmonic Memory* (Harmory) [5]. Harmory is a Knowledge Graph (KG) of harmonic patterns extracted from a large and heterogeneous musical corpus. By leveraging a cognitive model of tonal harmony, chord progressions are segmented into meaningful structures, and patterns emerge from their comparison via harmonic similarity. Akin to a music memory, the KG holds temporal connections between consecutive patterns, as well as salient similarity relationships (c.f. Fig. 1).

During the creation of Harmory, I focused on the developement of both harmonic segmentation and harmonic similarity state-of-the-art algorithm.

Digital Signal Processing (DSP) algorithms were used to perform harmonic segmentation on symbolic content. Tonal Pitch Space (TPS) [23] was used to encode the harmonic sequences and generate a Self-Similarity Matrix (SSM) [6], from which a novelty curve was extracted to identify the harmonic segment boundaries [29].

Additionally, a new algorithm for computing harmonic similarity using Dynamic Time Warping (DTW) [31] on TPS-encoded sequences was proposed, which is more efficient than the previous state-of-the-art approach [15].

4.3   Music Chord Embeddings

Another aspect of my work involved the definition of embeddings to enable the expressive encoding of harmonic annotations. To achieve this goal, I developed *pitchclass2vec*, a novel type of embedding that effectively preserves the harmonic characteristics of a chord.

The efficacy of this embedding was evaluated in a Music Structure Analysis task, where it outperformed other approaches, including those based on chord encoding [25] or textual encoding [8].

4.4   Semantic Integration of Musical Data

For the development of the aforementioned works, ontologies were created to model various types of data related to the music domain. These works respond to RQ1, and aim to provide new methods for the representation of musical knowledge. These ontologies include the *JAMS Ontology*, which models musical notations (such as chords, patterns, and musical structures), the *Roman Chord Ontology*, which models chords expressed in Roman numeral notation, and the *Music Note Ontology*, which models musical notes and their realisation (i.e., the note played in a performance). These ontologies are part of an ontological framework named *Polifonia Ontology Network* (PON).

5   Conclusion and Next Steps

This paper presents a research project that employs a symbolic-informed architecture to study music similarities on audio signals. This allows an explainable and interpretable musically-grounded analysis of similarities in music which can be performed both on symbolic annotations and audio signal.

The use of Knowledge Graphs (KG) and Semantic Web tools is crucial to this research as they provide a foundation for data alignment and interoperability across various data types.

Moving forward, the research will focus on expanding the dataset (as described in Sect. 4.1) by incorporating new data types, such as melodic data and audio signals, into the knowledge graph. This will facilitate exploration of novel similarity functions that enable the study of symbolic data, integrating diverse musical elements such as melody, harmony, and structure.

Subsequently, the research will aim to align the produced data with audio signals, with the objective of training a model informed by symbolic data that is capable of analysing similarity on audio signals.

Finally, a crucial objective of this study is to extend the ontological models developed to enable multimodal analysis of other data types and in other domains.

References

1. Adegbija, T.: JazzNet: a dataset of fundamental piano patterns for music audio machine learning research. In: IEEE International Conference on Acoustics, Speech and Signal Processing (ICASSP). IEEE (2023)
2. Balke, S., Arifi-Müller, V., Lamprecht, L., Müller, M.: Retrieving audio recordings using musical themes. In: 2016 IEEE International Conference on Acoustics, Speech and Signal Processing (ICASSP), pp. 281–285 (2016)
3. Baltrušaitis, T., Ahuja, C., Morency, L.P.: Multimodal machine learning: a survey and taxonomy (2017)
4. de Berardinis, J., Meroño-Peñuela, A., Poltronieri, A., Presutti, V.: Choco: a chord corpus and a data transformation workflow for musical harmony knowledge graphs. In: Manuscript Under Review (2022)

5. de Berardinis, J., Meroño-Peñuela, A., Poltronieri, A., Presutti, V.: The harmonic memory: a knowledge graph of harmonic patterns as a trustworthy framework for computational creativity. In: The Web Conference (2023)
6. de Berardinis, J., Vamvakaris, M., Cangelosi, A., Coutinho, E.: Unveiling the hierarchical structure of music by multi-resolution community detection. Trans. Int. Soc. Music Inf. Retrieval **3**(1), 82–97 (2020)
7. Bizer, C., Heath, T., Berners-Lee, T.: Linked data - the story so far. Int. J. Semant. Web Inf. Syst. **5**(3), 1–22 (2009)
8. Bojanowski, P., Grave, E., Joulin, A., Mikolov, T.: Enriching word vectors with subword information. Trans. Assoc. Comput. Linguist. **5**, 135–146 (2017)
9. Chefer, H., Gur, S., Wolf, L.: Transformer interpretability beyond attention visualization (2020)
10. Corrêa, D.C., Rodrigues, F.A.: A survey on symbolic data-based music genre classification. Expert Syst. Appl. **60**, 190–210 (2016)
11. Downie, J.S.: The scientific evaluation of music information retrieval systems: foundations and future. Comput. Music. J. **28**(2), 12–23 (2004)
12. Du, X., Chen, K., Wang, Z., Zhu, B., Ma, Z.: Bytecover2: towards dimensionality reduction of latent embedding for efficient cover song identification. In: ICASSP 2022–2022 IEEE International Conference on Acoustics, Speech and Signal Processing (ICASSP), pp. 616–620 (2022)
13. Dörfler, M., Bammer, R., Grill, T.: Inside the spectrogram: convolutional neural networks in audio processing. In: 2017 International Conference on Sampling Theory and Applications (SampTA), pp. 152–155 (2017)
14. Giraud, M., Groult, R., Leguy, E., Levé, F.: Computational fugue analysis. Comput. Music. J. **39**(2), 77–96 (2015)
15. de Haas, W.B., Wiering, F., Veltkamp, R.C.: A geometrical distance measure for determining the similarity of musical harmony. Int. J. Multimed. Inf. Retrieval **2**(3), 189–202 (2013)
16. Hanna, P., Robine, M., Rocher, T.: An alignment based system for chord sequence retrieval. In: Proceedings of the 9th ACM/IEEE-CS Joint Conference on Digital Libraries, pp. 101–104 (2009)
17. Harte, C., Sandler, M.B., Abdallah, S.A., Gómez, E.: Symbolic representation of musical chords: a proposed syntax for text annotations. In: ISMIR, vol. 5, pp. 66–71 (2005)
18. Humphrey, E.J., Salamon, J., Nieto, O., Forsyth, J., Bittner, R.M., Bello, J.P.: JAMS: a JSON annotated music specification for reproducible MIR research. In: ISMIR, pp. 591–596 (2014)
19. Karydis, I., Lida Kermanidis, K., Sioutas, S., Iliadis, L.: Comparing content and context based similarity for musical data. Neurocomputing **107**, 69–76 (2013). Timely Neural Networks Applications in Engineering
20. Knees, P., Schedl, M.: A survey of music similarity and recommendation from music context data. ACM Trans. Multimedia Comput. Commun. Appl. **10**(1), 1–21 (2013)
21. Kowald, D., Schedl, M., Lex, E.: The unfairness of popularity bias in music recommendation: a reproducibility study. In: Jose, J.M., et al. (eds.) ECIR 2020. LNCS, vol. 12036, pp. 35–42. Springer, Cham (2020). https://doi.org/10.1007/978-3-030-45442-5_5
22. Laurier, C., Grivolla, J., Herrera, P.: Multimodal music mood classification using audio and lyrics. In: 2008 Seventh International Conference on Machine Learning and Applications, pp. 688–693 (2008)

23. Lerdahl, F.: Tonal pitch space. Music Percept.: Interdisc. J. **5**(3), 315–349 (1988)
24. Li, P.C., Su, L., Yang, Y.H., Su, A.W.Y.: Analysis of expressive musical terms in violin using score-informed and expression-based audio features. In: International Society for Music Information Retrieval Conference (2015)
25. Madjiheurem, S., Qu, L., Walder, C.: Chord2vec: learning musical chord embeddings. In: Proceedings of the Constructive Machine Learning Workshop at 30th Conference on Neural Information Processing Systems (NIPS2016), Barcelona, Spain (2016)
26. McFee, B., Barrington, L., Lanckriet, G.: Learning content similarity for music recommendation. IEEE Trans. Audio Speech Lang. Process. **20**(8), 2207–2218 (2012)
27. Medina, R., Smith, L., Wagner, D.: Content-based indexing of musical scores. In: Proceedings of the 2003 Joint Conference on Digital Libraries, pp. 18–26 (2003)
28. Mehrotra, R.: Algorithmic balancing of familiarity, similarity, & discovery in music recommendations. In: Proceedings of the 30th ACM International Conference on Information & Knowledge Management, CIKM 2021, pp. 3996–4005. Association for Computing Machinery, New York (2021)
29. Müller, M.: Fundamentals of Music Processing: Audio, Analysis, Algorithms, Applications, vol. 5. Springer, Heidelberg (2015). https://doi.org/10.1007/978-3-319-21945-5
30. Orio, N., Rodà, A.: A measure of melodic similarity based on a graph representation of the music structure. In: Hirata, K., Tzanetakis, G., Yoshii, K. (eds.) Proceedings of the 10th International Society for Music Information Retrieval Conference, ISMIR 2009, Kobe International Conference Center, Kobe, Japan, 26–30 October 2009, pp. 543–548. International Society for Music Information Retrieval (2009)
31. Sakoe, H., Chiba, S.: Dynamic programming algorithm optimization for spoken word recognition. IEEE Trans. Acoust. Speech Signal Process. **26**(1), 43–49 (1978)
32. Sheikh Fathollahi, M., Razzazi, F.: Music similarity measurement and recommendation system using convolutional neural networks. Int. J. Multimed. Inf. Retrieval **10**(1), 43–53 (2021)
33. Simonetta, F., Ntalampiras, S., Avanzini, F.: Multimodal music information processing and retrieval: Survey and future challenges. In: 2019 International Workshop on Multilayer Music Representation and Processing (MMRP), pp. 10–18 (2019)
34. Suyoto, I.S.H., Uitdenbogerd, A.L., Scholer, F.: Searching musical audio using symbolic queries. IEEE Trans. Audio Speech Lang. Process. **16**(2), 372–381 (2008)
35. Tan, H.H., Herremans, D.: Music fadernets: controllable music generation based on high-level features via low-level feature modelling. In: Cumming, J., et al. (eds.) Proceedings of the 21th International Society for Music Information Retrieval Conference, ISMIR 2020, Montreal, Canada, 11–16 October 2020, pp. 109–116 (2020)
36. Velardo, V., Vallati, M., Jan, S.: Symbolic melodic similarity: state of the art and future challenges. Comput. Music. J. **40**(2), 70–83 (2016)
37. Vinet, H.: The representation levels of music information. In: Wiil, U.K. (ed.) CMMR 2003. LNCS, vol. 2771, pp. 193–209. Springer, Heidelberg (2004). https://doi.org/10.1007/978-3-540-39900-1_17
38. Wiggins, G., Miranda, E., Smaill, A., Harris, M.: A framework for the evaluation of music representation systems. Comput. Music. J. **17**(3), 31–42 (1993)
39. Zheng, E., Moh, M., Moh, T.S.: Music genre classification: a n-gram based musicological approach. In: 2017 IEEE 7th International Advance Computing Conference (IACC), pp. 671–677 (2017)

Semantic Parsing for Knowledge Graph Question Answering with Large Language Models

Debayan Banerjee[✉] [iD]

Language Technology Group, Universität Hamburg, Hamburg, Germany
debayan.banerjee@uni-hamburg.de

Abstract. This thesis explores the topic of Knowledge Graph Question Answering with a special emphasis on semantic parsing approaches, incorporating pre-trained text-to-text language models. We use the text generation ability of these models to convert natural language questions to logical forms. We test whether correct logical forms are being generated, and if not, how to mitigate the failure cases. As a second step, we try to make the same models generate additional information to aid the process of grounding of the logical forms to entities, relations and literals in the Knowledge Graph. In experiments conducted so far, we see encouraging results on both generation of base logical forms, and grounding them to the KG elements. At the same time, we discover failure cases prompting directions in future work (The author considers himself a 'middle-stage' Ph.D. candidate).

1 Introduction

A Knowledge Graph (KG) [21,32] is an information store where data is stored in the form of node-edge-node triples. Nodes represent entities and edges represent relationships between these entities. The aim of Knowledge Graph Question Answering (KGQA) [18] is to produce answers from this KG given an input question in natural language, e.g., `Where did Einstein receive his bachelor degree?`. Usually, the first steps in KGQA are to perform Entity and Relation Linking (EL, RL) where mention spans, e.g., `Einstein` representing the name of a person, place, etc., are linked to a KG node and the relationship of the entity to the potential answer in the KG is extracted, e.g., `educated at`.

Some KGQA systems [9,33] attempt to fetch the answer based on the results of the two steps above, which typically ends up being another entity (node) in the graph. However, for more complex questions, such as count queries or min/max aggregate queries (e.g.: `How many institutions did Einstein study in?`) the answer does not lie in a node or edge in the graph, but instead, a formal query or logical form must be generated. The task of generating a formal query is also known as *semantic parsing*, also the focus of this proposal.

Semantic parsing in KGQA is challenging mainly due to two factors: schema-level complexity and fact-level complexity. The schema of a modern KG is

C. Pesquita et al. (Eds.): ESWC 2023, LNCS 13998, pp. 234–243, 2023.
https://doi.org/10.1007/978-3-031-43458-7_42

diverse. For example, Freebase [6] has over 8K schema items in total (6K relations and 2K types), while a relational database usually comprises dozens of schema items only (i.e., table names and column headers). Hence, learning an alignment between natural language and the schema is much more challenging in KGQA. Moreover, fact-level information (i.e., contents in the KG) plays a vital role in KGQA. Consequently, generating logical forms that can ground to non-empty answers from the KG, i.e., faithful to the KG, requires incorporating fact-level information. In addition, the graph structure of KB facts leads to an enormous search space due to combinatorial explosion, rendering generating faithful queries even more challenging.

A large body of work exists on the topics of entity and relation linking for KGs [13,30]. Similarly, significant literature exists around non-KG semantic parsing (e.g.: text-to-SQL) [27]. There is prior work [14,40,42] that explores the topic of KGQA semantic parsing using encoder-decoder models, that comprises of LSTMs [17], Transformers [37], and pre-trained language models (PLMs) based on the Transformer architecture [11].

However the role of text-to-text large language models (T2TLMs) like T5 [29] and BART [23] remains under-investigated [15]. *This gap motivates us to pursue further research in this direction* (Fig. 1).

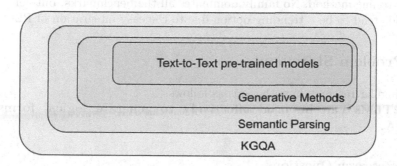

Fig. 1. Situating the topic of this proposal in the KGQA landscape.

2   States of the Art/Related Work

There are three widely followed approaches for semantic parsing approaches for KGQA: *ranking methods, coarse-to-fine methods, and generation methods.* Ranking methods [1,4,39,41] first enumerate candidate queries from the KG and semantic parsing then relies on computing the matching score for each candidate-question pair. Coarse-to-fine methods [5,10,34,42] first generate query skeletons and then ground the skeletons to the KG with admissible schema items. Generation methods [2,19,20,28] which have emerged more recently, typically use a form of Natural Language Generation (NLG) from large language models to

Table 1. Best-published results on KGQA benchmarks.

Dataset	Top-1 F1	Family
COMPLEXWEBQ	70.0 [10]	Coarse-to-fine
LC-QUAD	75.0 [41]	Ranking
GRAILQA	74.4 [39]	Ranking
KQA PRO	90.6 [23]	Generation
WEBQSP	76.5 [8]	Generation
GRAPHQ	31.8 [16]	Generation

produce token-by-token a base logical form. The logical form is often grounded to the KG via constrained decoding, and thus dynamically reduce the search space.

In Table 1, we present the F1-scores and the corresponding family of best-performing models on KGQA benchmarks. On KQA-PRO [7], WEBQSP [3], and GRAPHQ [31], the state-of-the-art models are based on generation, while ranking methods achieve the best results on LC-QUAD [36] and GRAILQA [14] and the best performance on COMPLEXWEBQ [35] is obtained by the coarse-to-fine method. No family dominates all the benchmarks, but generation methods tend to be a trending option due to the easy integration of PLMs.

3   Problem Statement

Our singular research hypothesis is as follows:

T2TLMs can be used effectively to generate logical forms for KGQA.

3.1   Research Questions

RQ 1: Can T2TLMs generate correct logical form structure?

Given the question:
Is it true that an Olympic-size swimming pool's operating temperature is equal to 22.4?
the correct logical form structure for SPARQL would be:

```
ASK WHERE {
          ENT1 REL1 ?obj
          filter ( ?obj = LIT1 )
}
```

The query above depicts a skeleton of the correct SPARQL query, with place-holders instead of grounded entity, relations or literals. The placeholders are ENT1, REL1 and LIT1.

RQ 2: Can T2TLMs aid in grounding of logical forms to the KG?

For the same question, a grounded query is as follows:

```
ASK WHERE { wd:Q2084454 wdt:P5066 ?obj
            filter(?obj = 22.4)
}
```

The query above is a valid and grounded SPARQL query on the Wikidata KG. `wd:Q2084454` is the entity ID for `Olympic-size swimming pool` while `wdt:P5066` is the relation ID for `operating temperature`. The placeholders have been replaced with proper entity and relation IDs, and the correct literal has been extracted from the input question and copied into the literal place-holder. Executing it provides a valid and correct response. Can T2TLMs aid in grounding of skeleton logical forms to KGs?

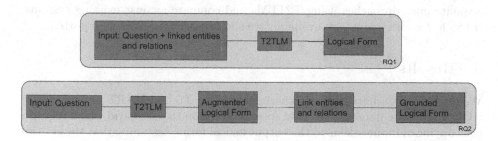

Fig. 2. RQs 1 and 2 depicted visually.

4   Research Methodology and Approach

To test our hypothesis, we require datasets that contain mappings from questions in natural language to corresponding logical forms. Since our focus is on KGQA, these logical forms must be grounded in KGs. Additionally, since our experiments involve large language models, we observed that small datasets are not suitable for our experiments. On an average, we tend to focus on datasets which have more than 5,000 questions. Apart from the datasets mentioned in Table 1, we also test on LC-QuAD 2.0 [12]. For models, we primarily test on T5 and BART, which are the two most popular T2TLMs. We plan to fine-tune and prompt-tune [22] the models on the datasets of our choice, and evaluate their performance on tasks related to RQ1 and RQ2.

5   Evaluation/Evaluation Plan

For RQ1, we need to evaluate whether our models produce the correct logical forms. The two popular methods to evaluate this are the exact-match metric (whether the generated query matches the gold query exactly) and BLEU score [24]. There are several different variants of BLEU in use, however the general method is to measures how many n-grams in the reference sentence are reproduced by the candidate sentence. This value is reduced to a precision in the range of 0–1. BLEU is generally used to evaluate machine translations, however for the task of semantic parsing to logical forms, it has the obvious shortcoming that since it does not take into consideration the word ordering on the output, a logical form which is syntactically incorrect may still produce a high BLEU score. The best metric for use of evaluation of semantic parsing to logical forms remains an open question.

For RQ2, since we expect our models to produce grounded queries instead of mere logical forms, we can additionally evaluate using execution-based metrics such as F1-score.

Our approach to evaluate will be to first find existing semantic parsing and KGQA systems which have a working demo or code available. We will then evaluate our approaches using T2TLMs and compare against existing systems. If too few such systems are available, we shall resort to results as reported.

6   Results

We performed an initial set of experiments using T5 and BART on the task of KGQA semantic parsing, and paid special attention to a scenario which requires the copying of input tokens to the output logical form. Assuming that the entities and relations have been linked before-hand, one may modify the original input question to:

Is it true that an Olympic-size swimming pool's operating temperature is equal to 22.4 ? [SEP] wd:Q2084454 Olympic-size swimming pool [SEP] wdt:P5066 operating temperature

Here, we append the input question with linked entities and relations and also their corresponding labels. The task for the model is to produce the correct logical form. This addresses **RQ1** and we found that T5 outperforms existing approaches on LC-QuAD and LC-QuAD 2.0 datasets, while BART lags behind [2].

In additional experiments for **RQ1**, we found that both for prompt-tuned [22] and fine-tuned T2TLMs, choosing an alternate output vocabulary for the logical-form improves semantic parsing performance. The usual logical-form vocabulary is distinct from human vocabulary. T2TLMs are pre-trained for human language tasks, and hence the logical-form vocabulary may appear alien to it. This work is currently under review.

For **RQ2**, we used T5 to generate not just the logical forms, but also entity and relation labels. As input we provided only the question. Additionally, we trained T5 jointly to produce truncated graph embeddings for each entity. In effect, we generate *augmented logical forms* (Fig. 2). We use the generated augmented logical forms to ground the queries to a KG. We found that such a setup produces strong performance on LC-QuAD 2.0 and SimpleQuestions. This work is currently under review.

During our experiments we realised that T2TLMs have some common short-comings for semantic parsing tasks. They are unable to perform compositional generalisation, handles special tokens, and have a limited ability to generate embeddings. Moreover, existing KGQA datasets are based on the three popular KGs, namely Freebase, DBpedia [21] and Wikidata [38]. T2TLMs are pre-trained on large corpus which is of similar nature as the sources from which these KGs are derived, and hence, a new dataset which belongs to different domain was required, which would remove the natural advantage for T2TLMs of having seen much of the information at a pre-training stage. As a result, we produced a new dataset consisting of 10,000 question-query pairs on a scholarly KG, which provides T2TLMs with specific challenges for KGQA and semantic parsing. This addresses **RQ1** and **RQ2**, and is currently under review.

7 Conclusions/Lessons Learned

In our initial experiments we found that T2TLMs are a potent tool for the task of KGQA semantic parsing. The natural advantage of using them is that they are easily available, well maintained and require minimal initial setup before being put to use. Through this thesis, our aim is to provide strategies to researchers on how to mitigate some of the pitfalls of using T2TLMs on the semantic parsing task, and push accuracy further when starting from a vanilla T2TLM.

At the PhD symposium, I look forward to receiving feedback from mentors on the overall structure of the thesis. In paper submissions so far, I have had trouble convincing reviewers about the quality of my evaluations. There is an evaluation crisis [26] in our field, because several older versions of KGs are not publicly available any more, neither are working versions of KGQA systems, making replication next-to-impossible. Another aspect I am concerned about is whether the current thesis contains enough substance for publication. It is, for example, possible to compare semantic parsing approaches to the SQL parsing community, or work on more popular problems like compositional generalisation [25].

Acknowledgements. I would like to thank my co-supervisors Chris Biemann and Ricardo Usbeck for their valuable guidance and feedback in the drafting of this document.

References

1. Abujabal, A., Yahya, M., Riedewald, M., Weikum, G.: Automated template generation for question answering over knowledge graphs. In: WWW 2017, International World Wide Web Conferences Steering Committee, Republic and Canton of Geneva, CHE, pp. 1191–1200 (2017). https://doi.org/10.1145/3038912.3052583

2. Banerjee, D., Nair, P.A., Kaur, J.N., Usbeck, R., Biemann, C.: Modern baselines for SPARQL semantic parsing. In: SIGIR 2022, pp. 2260–2265. Association for Computing Machinery, New York (2022). https://doi.org/10.1145/3477495.3531841

3. Berant, J., Chou, A., Frostig, R., Liang, P.: Semantic parsing on Freebase from question-answer pairs. In: Proceedings of the 2013 Conference on Empirical Methods in Natural Language Processing, pp. 1533–1544. Association for Computational Linguistics, Seattle (2013). https://aclanthology.org/D13-1160

4. Berant, J., Liang, P.: Semantic parsing via paraphrasing. In: Proceedings of the 52nd Annual Meeting of the Association for Computational Linguistics (Volume 1: Long Papers), pp. 1415–1425. Association for Computational Linguistics, Baltimore (2014). https://aclanthology.org/P14-1133

5. Bhutani, N., Zheng, X., Jagadish, H.V.: Learning to answer complex questions over knowledge bases with query composition. In: Proceedings of the 28th ACM International Conference on Information and Knowledge Management, CIKM 2019, pp. 739–748. Association for Computing Machinery, New York (2019). https://doi.org/10.1145/3357384.3358033

6. Bollacker, K., Evans, C., Paritosh, P., Sturge, T., Taylor, J.: Freebase: a collaboratively created graph database for structuring human knowledge. In: Proceedings of the 2008 ACM SIGMOD International Conference on Management of Data. ACM (2008)

7. Cao, S., et al.: KQA pro: a dataset with explicit compositional programs for complex question answering over knowledge base. In: Proceedings of the 60th Annual Meeting of the Association for Computational Linguistics (Volume 1: Long Papers), pp. 6101–6119. Association for Computational Linguistics, Dublin (2022). https://aclanthology.org/2022.acl-long.422

8. Cao, S., et al.: Program transfer for answering complex questions over knowledge bases. In: Proceedings of the 60th Annual Meeting of the Association for Computational Linguistics (Volume 1: Long Papers), pp. 8128–8140. Association for Computational Linguistics, Dublin (2022). https://aclanthology.org/2022.acl-long.559

9. Christmann, P., Saha Roy, R., Weikum, G.: Beyond NED: fast and effective search space reduction for complex question answering over knowledge bases. In: Proceedings of the Fifteenth ACM International Conference on Web Search and Data Mining, WSDM 2022, pp. 172–180. Association for Computing Machinery, New York (2022). https://doi.org/10.1145/3488560.3498488

10. Das, R., et al.: Case-based reasoning for natural language queries over knowledge bases. In: Proceedings of the 2021 Conference on Empirical Methods in Natural Language Processing, pp. 9594–9611. Association for Computational Linguistics, Online and Punta Cana (2021). https://aclanthology.org/2021.emnlp-main.755

11. Devlin, J., Chang, M.W., Lee, K., Toutanova, K.: BERT: pre-training of deep bidirectional transformers for language understanding. In: Proceedings of the 2019 Conference of the North American Chapter of the Association for Computational Linguistics: Human Language Technologies, Volume 1 (Long and Short Papers), pp. 4171–4186. Association for Computational Linguistics, Minneapolis (2019). https://aclanthology.org/N19-1423

12. Dubey, M., Banerjee, D., Abdelkawi, A., Lehmann, J.: LC-QuAD 2.0: a large dataset for complex question answering over Wikidata and DBpedia. In: Ghidini, C., et al. (eds.) ISWC 2019. LNCS, vol. 11779, pp. 69–78. Springer, Cham (2019). https://doi.org/10.1007/978-3-030-30796-7_5

13. Dubey, M., Banerjee, D., Chaudhuri, D., Lehmann, J.: EARL: joint entity and relation linking for question answering over knowledge graphs. In: Vrandečić, D., et al. (eds.) ISWC 2018. LNCS, vol. 11136, pp. 108–126. Springer, Cham (2018). https://doi.org/10.1007/978-3-030-00671-6_7
14. Gu, Y., et al.: Beyond I.I.D.: three levels of generalization for question answering on knowledge bases. In: WWW 2021, pp. 3477–3488. Association for Computing Machinery, New York (2021). https://doi.org/10.1145/3442381.3449992
15. Gu, Y., Pahuja, V., Cheng, G., Su, Y.: Knowledge base question answering: a semantic parsing perspective (2022). https://arxiv.org/abs/2209.04994
16. Gu, Y., Su, Y.: ArcaneQA: dynamic program induction and contextualized encoding for knowledge base question answering. In: Proceedings of the 29th International Conference on Computational Linguistics, pp. 1718–1731. International Committee on Computational Linguistics, Gyeongju (2022). https://aclanthology.org/2022.coling-1.148
17. Hochreiter, S., Schmidhuber, J.: Long short-term memory. Neural Comput. **9**(8), 1735–1780 (1997)
18. Lan, Y., He, G., Jiang, J., Jiang, J., Zhao, W.X., Wen, J.R.: A survey on complex knowledge base question answering: methods, challenges and solutions. In: Zhou, Z.H. (ed.) Proceedings of the Thirtieth International Joint Conference on Artificial Intelligence, IJCAI-21, pp. 4483–4491. International Joint Conferences on Artificial Intelligence Organization (2021). https://doi.org/10.24963/ijcai.2021/611. Survey Track
19. Lan, Y., Jiang, J.: Query graph generation for answering multi-hop complex questions from knowledge bases. In: Proceedings of the 58th Annual Meeting of the Association for Computational Linguistics, pp. 969–974. Association for Computational Linguistics, Online (2020). https://aclanthology.org/2020.acl-main.91
20. Lan, Y., Wang, S., Jiang, J.: Multi-hop knowledge base question answering with an iterative sequence matching model. In: 2019 IEEE International Conference on Data Mining (ICDM), pp. 359–368 (2019). https://doi.org/10.1109/ICDM.2019.00046
21. Lehmann, J., et al.: DBpedia - a large-scale, multilingual knowledge base extracted from Wikipedia. Semant. Web J. **6**(2), 167–195 (2015)
22. Lester, B., Al-Rfou, R., Constant, N.: The power of scale for parameter-efficient prompt tuning. In: Proceedings of the 2021 Conference on Empirical Methods in Natural Language Processing, pp. 3045–3059. Association for Computational Linguistics, Online and Punta Cana (2021). https://aclanthology.org/2021.emnlp-main.243
23. Lewis, M., et al.: BART: denoising sequence-to-sequence pre-training for natural language generation, translation, and comprehension. In: Proceedings of the 58th Annual Meeting of the Association for Computational Linguistics, pp. 7871–7880. Association for Computational Linguistics, Online (2020). https://aclanthology.org/2020.acl-main.703
24. Papineni, K., Roukos, S., Ward, T., Zhu, W.J.: BLEU: a method for automatic evaluation of machine translation. In: Proceedings of the 40th Annual Meeting of the Association for Computational Linguistics, pp. 311–318. Association for Computational Linguistics, Philadelphia (2002). https://aclanthology.org/P02-1040
25. Patel, A., Bhattamishra, S., Blunsom, P., Goyal, N.: Revisiting the compositional generalization abilities of neural sequence models. In: Proceedings of the 60th Annual Meeting of the Association for Computational Linguistics (Volume 2: Short Papers), pp. 424–434. Association for Computational Linguistics, Dublin (2022). https://aclanthology.org/2022.acl-short.46

26. Perevalov, A., Yan, X., Kovriguina, L., Jiang, L., Both, A., Usbeck, R.: Knowledge graph question answering leaderboard: a community resource to prevent a replication crisis. In: Proceedings of the Thirteenth Language Resources and Evaluation Conference, pp. 2998–3007. European Language Resources Association, Marseille (2022). https://aclanthology.org/2022.lrec-1.321

27. Qin, B., et al.: A survey on text-to-SQL parsing: concepts, methods, and future directions (2022). https://arxiv.org/abs/2208.13629

28. Qiu, Y., et al.: Hierarchical query graph generation for complex question answering over knowledge graph. In: Proceedings of the 29th ACM International Conference on Information and Knowledge Management, CIKM 2020, pp. 1285–1294. Association for Computing Machinery, New York (2020). https://doi.org/10.1145/3340531.3411888

29. Raffel, C., et al.: Exploring the limits of transfer learning with a unified text-to-text transformer. J. Mach. Learn. Res. **21**(140), 1–67 (2020). http://jmlr.org/papers/v21/20-074.html

30. Sevgili, Ö., Shelmanov, A., Arkhipov, M., Panchenko, A., Biemann, C.: Neural entity linking: a survey of models based on deep learning. Semant. Web **13**, 527–570 (2022). https://doi.org/10.3233/SW-222986

31. Su, Y., et al.: On generating characteristic-rich question sets for QA evaluation. In: Proceedings of the 2016 Conference on Empirical Methods in Natural Language Processing, pp. 562–572. Association for Computational Linguistics, Austin (2016). https://aclanthology.org/D16-1054

32. Suchanek, F.M., Kasneci, G., Weikum, G.: YAGO: a core of semantic knowledge. In: WWW 2007, pp. 697–706. Association for Computing Machinery, New York (2007). https://doi.org/10.1145/1242572.1242667

33. Sun, H., Dhingra, B., Zaheer, M., Mazaitis, K., Salakhutdinov, R., Cohen, W.: Open domain question answering using early fusion of knowledge bases and text. In: Proceedings of the 2018 Conference on Empirical Methods in Natural Language Processing, pp. 4231–4242. Association for Computational Linguistics, Brussels (2018). https://aclanthology.org/D18-1455

34. Sun, Y., Zhang, L., Cheng, G., Qu, Y.: SPARQA: skeleton-based semantic parsing for complex questions over knowledge bases (2020). https://arxiv.org/abs/2003.13956

35. Talmor, A., Berant, J.: The web as a knowledge-base for answering complex questions. In: Proceedings of the 2018 Conference of the North American Chapter of the Association for Computational Linguistics: Human Language Technologies, Volume 1 (Long Papers), pp. 641–651. Association for Computational Linguistics, New Orleans (2018). https://aclanthology.org/N18-1059

36. Trivedi, P., Maheshwari, G., Dubey, M., Lehmann, J.: LC-QuAD: a corpus for complex question answering over knowledge graphs. In: d'Amato, C., et al. (eds.) ISWC 2017. LNCS, vol. 10588, pp. 210–218. Springer, Cham (2017). https://doi.org/10.1007/978-3-319-68204-4_22

37. Vaswani, A., et al.: Attention is all you need. In: Advances in Neural Information Processing Systems, vol. 30. Curran Associates, Inc. (2017). https://proceedings.neurips.cc/paper/2017/file/3f5ee243547dee91fbd053c1c4a845aa-Paper.pdf

38. Vrandečić, D., Krötzsch, M.: Wikidata: a free collaborative knowledgebase. Commun. ACM **57**(10), 78–85 (2014). https://doi.org/10.1145/2629489

39. Ye, X., Yavuz, S., Hashimoto, K., Zhou, Y., Xiong, C.: RNG-KBQA: generation augmented iterative ranking for knowledge base question answering. In: Proceedings of the 60th Annual Meeting of the Association for Computational Linguistics

(Volume 1: Long Papers), pp. 6032–6043. Association for Computational Linguistics, Dublin (2022). https://aclanthology.org/2022.acl-long.417

40. Yin, X., Gromann, D., Rudolph, S.: Neural machine translating from natural language to SPARQL. Futur. Gener. Comput. Syst. **117**, 510–519 (2021). https://doi.org/10.1016/j.future.2020.12.013

41. Zafar, H., Napolitano, G., Lehmann, J.: Formal query generation for question answering over knowledge bases. In: Gangemi, A., et al. (eds.) ESWC 2018. LNCS, vol. 10843, pp. 714–728. Springer, Cham (2018). https://doi.org/10.1007/978-3-319-93417-4_46

42. Zhang, H., Cai, J., Xu, J., Wang, J.: Complex question decomposition for semantic parsing. In: Proceedings of the 57th Annual Meeting of the Association for Computational Linguistics, pp. 4477–4486. Association for Computational Linguistics, Florence (2019). https://aclanthology.org/P19-1440

Semantic and Efficient Symbolic Learning over Knowledge Graphs

Disha Purohit[1,2(✉)] ⓘ

[1] Leibniz Universität Hannover, Hannover, Germany
d.purohit@stud.uni-hannover.de
[2] TIB Leibniz Information Centre for Science and Technology, Hannover, Germany

Abstract. In recent years, the rise of large Knowledge Graphs (KGs), which capture knowledge in machine-driven formats, has arisen broadly. KGs are the convergence of data and knowledge, and may be incomplete due to the Open World Assumption (OWA). Inductive Logic Programming (ILP) is a popular traditional approach for mining logical rules to complete the KGs. ILP approaches derive logical rules from ground facts in knowledge bases. Deducing new information or adding missing information to the KGs, identifying potential errors, and understanding the data more substantially can be accomplished by mining logical rules. Inference can be used to deduce new facts and complete KGs. To discover meaningful insights, traditional rule mining approaches first ignore axiomatic systems defining the semantics of the predicates and classes available in KGs. Second, most rule miners measure the impact of mined rules in terms of correlation rather than causation, and they are overwhelmed by the volume of data. Finally, existing frameworks implement blocking methods that require the processing of complete KGs to generate the mined rules. In this Ph.D. proposal, an outline of a rule-mining model explicitly tailored to mine Horn rules encapsulating semantics on top of KGs is reported. Additionally, the rule-mining approach is based on reliably estimating the cause-effect relationships and discovering new facts in the KGs considering data and metadata. Our approach follows an iterative process to inductively mine rules incorporating semantics to enhance completeness. Our experimental results suggest that by combining entailment regimes and querying KGs on demand, our approach outperforms the state-of-the-art in terms of accuracy. A publicly available Jupyter notebook that executes a demonstration is available (https://mybinder.org/v2/gh/SDM-TIB/DIGGER-ESWC2023Demo/HEAD?labpath=Mining%20Symbolic%20Rules%20To%20Explain%20Lung%20Cancer%20Treatments.ipynb).

Keywords: Rule Mining · Causality · KGs · RDFS · OWL

Category: Middle Stage Ph.D.

1   Introduction

Knowledge Graphs (KGs) encode real-world knowledge as factual statements; nodes represent entities and edges define relationships between the entities. KGs are often created from heterogeneous sources that can be highly diverse in terms of structure and granularity [11]. Existing KGs cover many different domains in order to serve the research and industrial communities[1]. Numerous contributions in the Semantic Web community have addressed the open research challenge of mining Horn rules from ground statements.

Knowledge Discovery in Databases (KDD) is defined as the extraction of potentially useful information from a large volume of data, where the information is implicit. *Association rule mining* [2] is one of the most popular methods of mining rules in the relational domain. Various other approaches [3,9,16] also mine rules based on the co-occurrence of items present in the relational databases. For example, rules like "If a client bought beer and wine, she/he also bought aspirin" can be uncovered using association rule mining. The ratio of instances where beer and wine were purchased along with aspirin corresponds to the rule's confidence. Rule mining over relational databases follows the Closed World Assumption (CWA), i.e., it cannot predict items that are not present in a database.

Inductive Logic Programming (ILP) is used in semantic rule mining to extract information in a machine-readable format from Knowledge Bases (KBs). Existing ILP approaches derive logical rules from KBs. Due to the large volume of data and frequent assumption of incomplete data, rule mining over KBs is challenging and dedicated techniques have been proposed to address these issues. Exemplary rule mining approaches (e.g., AMIE [8], AnyBURL [14], AMIE+ [6], and [7,17]) are devised to operate under KBs that consider OWA. However, these approaches are still not tailored to deal with KGs encompassing semantics. Additionally, to mine rules, large KBs must be downloaded in a local system, and the computation of the mining process is done in a blocking fashion, i.e., all the data need to be uploaded/processed to produce results rather than continuously generating rules; thus, negatively affecting scalability in rule mining processes.

Humans are able to infer knowledge from data based on a set of general rules or by knowing the context of available data. This knowledge inferred by humans can be referred to as 'commonsense knowledge, or 'domain knowledge'. For instance, a KB contains a fact that Y has a father X. Then, humans can easily infer that the gender of X is "male" and that Y is the child of X. On the contrary, machines do not have any prior knowledge or information to make inferences over the provided data. Deductive methods are used to infer new facts known as *entailed facts* from existing facts in knowledge graphs using a set of rules often referred to as *entailment regimes*. Further, these entailed facts are used by *Inductive methods* to derive new logical rules. Inductive knowledge is knowledge acquired by generalizing patterns from a given set of input

---

[1] The terms Knowledge Bases (KBs) and Knowledge Graphs (KGs) are used interchangeably.

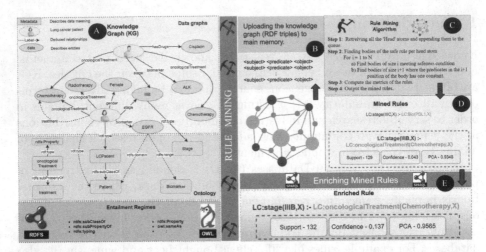

Fig. 1. Motivating Example: Usage of a KG comprising ontologies and their entailment regimes to be considered during rule mining. Naive approaches perform rule mining on graphs uploaded in the main memory. SPARQL queries and entailment regimes empower the semantics of KGs, enriching the mined rules.

observations. Mining Horn rules is conducted using inductive learning to create a symbolic model, i.e., a set of rules or axioms. Entailment regimes describe the relationship between the statements that are true when one statement locally follows from one or more statements [4]. Machines can apply deductions on top of data graphs and by applying entailment regimes efficiently.

The term *Ontology* refers to the concrete and more formal representation of the data present in data graphs. The *Web Ontology Language* [10] and *RDFS* [5] are the two most popular ontology languages recommended by W3C and compatible with RDF graphs. Facts in KGs are usually divided into *A-Box* and *T-Box*. The *A-Box* facts are all the instances of a KG that represent the data graph. Complementary, *T-Box* includes the definition of classes, properties, and hierarchies, which represent the ontological part of KGs. We focus on both *A-Box* and *T-Box* to mine rules that consider the semantics of a KG. Horn clauses are expressed in *IF-THEN-* style consequences over KG predicates. Our preliminary results reveal the key role of semantics in the accuracy of rule mining systems.

1.1 Motivating Example

Our work is motivated by the lack of exploitation of semantics in rule mining approaches over KGs. Nevertheless, state-of-the-art techniques provide rules that are mined over data graphs; ignoring the semantics and meaning of the entities in KGs. The goal of this work is to mine rules from which true missing facts can be predicted; completing, thus, KGs with accurate predictions which take into account KGs and entailment regimes. Figure 1 depicts, with a motivating example, the challenges present in a rule mining process over KGs. Input from the KG is collected Ⓐ, representing lung cancer patients and all the related information about those patients, i.e., gender, age, cancer stage, oncological treatment, and mutations. The ontology layer in the KG represents the unified schema of the lung cancer KG. The entailment regime layer shows the RDFS and OWL entailment regimes. Further, Ⓑ shows that for the execution of the rule mining algorithm, the state-of-the-art techniques require input in the form of RDF triples, i.e., ⟨subject, predicate, object⟩. For instance, ⟨2842697, smokingHabit, CurrentSmoker⟩, ⟨2842697, stage, IVB⟩, and ⟨2842697, gender, Male⟩ are uploaded to a local system. This poses one of the limitations of naive approaches (AMIE [8], AnyBURL [14]) impacting scalability to large KGs.

Ⓒ shows the implementation of rule mining algorithm. Rule mining algorithms (AMIE [8] and AnyBURL [14]) implement *blocking* processes, i.e., to mine rules all the data needs to be uploaded. This type of algorithm lacks the accessibility of KGs via Web interfaces, e.g., SPARQL endpoints, which cannot be utilized unless downloaded locally. Our approach overcomes the limitation of scalability by taking as input the SPARQL endpoints and queries to traverse the KGs. For example, Ⓓ shows that the mined rules generated from the above-mentioned algorithm: LC:stage(IIIB, X) ⇒ LC:oncologicalTreatment(Chemotherapy, X), clearly states that the metadata encoded in the KGs ontology is not considered, i.e., ⟨oncologicalTreatment, rdfs:subPropertyOf, treatment⟩.

The rules mined by the naive approaches demonstrate that the lung cancer patient in stage *IIIB* is more likely to receive oncological treatment *Chemotherapy*. Ⓔ illustrates the process of enrichment of the mined rules by applying the entailment regimes to the above mined rules. This step helps to derive new insights from the KGs. In contrast to naive approaches, our approach considers rdfs:subPropertyOf entailment regime, and as observed the metrics *Support*, *Confidence* and *PCA Confidence* increases; new facts were inferred, and added to the KGs that lead to the increased metrics values.

Contributions: A rule mining system that is inherently designed to work under the OWA and is efficient enough to handle KGs is proposed in this Ph.D. proposal. More specifically, the following are the contributions of this proposal:

1. Rule mining system devised for KGs empowered with semantics.
2. Novel query and mining techniques to improve scalability, and generate rules iteratively while avoiding blocking data processing.
3. 3to enhance meaningful insights.

2 State of the Art

Rule mining methods have gained considerable attention for the past few years, but the existing methods are based on mostly association rule mining [2] or inductive logic programming. This section covers the state-of-the-art techniques for KGs, that perform rule mining over observational data and knowledge bases.

2.1 Mining Rules in Relational Databases

Association rule mining (ARM) is a rule mining approach in the relational domain, and it is implemented on the closed world assumption (CWA). Association rule mining aims to recognize patterns and concurrent occurrences in the database. It discovers relationships among the entities present in the database. Apriori algorithm [18] is a well-known association rule mining [2] approach. It shows how frequently the item appears within the database. Association rule mines frequent patterns of data occurring, using the criteria 'support' and 'confidence' as metrics. It is used in the well-known 'Market Basket analysis' [12]. The mined rules are of the form *wine, beer* $\implies$ *aspirin*, implying that people who purchased wine and beer also purchased aspirin. However, these are not the kinds of rules we aim to discover in this paper. We intend to mine Horn rules. In the work, [1] association rules and frequency analysis are used to identify and classify common misuse patterns for relations over DBpedia. In contrast to our work, this approach mines association rules based on the co-occurrence of values rather than logical rules. Secondly, correlation is a statistical measure that describes the magnitude and direction of a relationship between two or more variables. A correlation between variables, on the other hand, does not imply that a change in one variable is the cause of a change in the values of the other variable. Causation denotes that one event is the result of the other event's occurrence, i.e., causal relationships among events. In this work, we aim to mine rules that encode cause-effect relationships.

2.2 Mining Rules in Knowledge Graphs

AMIE [8] is a rule-mining approach that follows Inductive Logic Programming (ILP) and aims to mine logical rules. When dealing with an incomplete KG, it is not immediately clear how to define negative edges. A common heuristic for a KG is to use a *Partial Completeness Assumption (PCA)*, i.e., a negative edge should be true if it is derived from a Horn clause that partially defines its completeness. AMIE mines rules on large KBs by reducing the search space. The logical rules mined by AMIE are in the form of Horn clauses. AMIE uses several metrics to prune the rules obtained by mining in order to avoid the generation of an exponential amount of irrelevant rules. Various metrics are used to evaluate the quality of rules mined by AMIE, *Head Coverage* that measures the ratio of known true facts that are implied by the rule. *Std Confidence* of the rule is the ratio of all its predictions that are present in the KGs. Lastly, in order to generate heuristic-based negative edges in the KBs, AMIE operates under *PCA*. Different versions of AMIE were AMIE+ [6] and AMIE3 [13]. The newer versions of AMIE claim that it speeds up the process of mining rules even faster. AMIE3 integrates new pruning strategies and many more advancements. However, AMIE lacks scalability as it follows a blocking approach to produce results. *(AnyBURL)* [14] learns logical rules. They focus on a path ranking algorithm that helps them to learn a subset of the rules. Similar to AMIE, they also mine negative edges in order to better complete the knowledge graphs. In contrast to AMIE, AnyBURL learns rules from knowledge graphs from the bottom up, whereas AMIE mines rule from the top down. Above discussed approaches are not tailored to deal with large knowledge graphs with semantics under the Open World Assumption. In contrast to our approach, the process of mining rules with AMIE [8] and AnyBURL [14] follows a blocking process, impacting scalability. Furthermore, by ignoring the semantics of KGs, these techniques fall short of generating more meaningful rules.

In some of the closely related work, Simonne et al. [17] mine two types of differential causal rules, gradual and categorical rules. Gradual rules deal with mining rules over numerical values or entities and categorical rules deal with categorical values. For example, the number of treatments received by cancer patients comes under gradual rules and the type of treatments are classified into categorical rules. Another contribution of this paper is to use a community detection algorithm to compute the similarity between the units of interest. Also, they have defined a metric called *Causal ratio* which is inspired by the odds ratio to evaluate the potential causal rules. Discovering causality in knowledge graphs is a wide area of research performed scarcely. Traditional approaches attempt to detect causal relationships between variables by implementing a probabilistic relational model using Bayesian networks [15] following Judea Pearl's approach. Our approach, in contrast, considers entailment regimes in addition to the semantics from *OWL* ontology to infer new facts and enhance the discovered rules. Furthermore, the aforementioned techniques are not scalable.

3   Problem Statement and Contributions

The goal of rule mining is to identify new rules that entail a high ratio of positive edges from other positive edges, but a low ratio of negative edges from positive edges. This Ph.D. proposal addresses the problem of mining logical rules over KGs with semantics. Our main research objective is to mine rules over large KGs and also incorporate methods to further work on the federation of KGs. Concretely, we aim at encoding richer semantic knowledge from the KGs to mine more meaningful rules. As a result, our goal is to design a scalable approach to mine logical rules which also demonstrates cause-effect relationships.

3.1   Preliminaries

Knowledge Graphs is defined as $G = (V, E, L)$ is a directed edge-labeled graph as defined in [11]. **Horn Rules** A mined rule is a Horn clause of the form: *Body* $\implies$ *Head*, where *Body* is a conjunction of predicate facts; *Head* is a predicate fact. All the variables in *Head* are terms of at least one predicate fact in the *Body*, and every two predicate facts in *Body* share at least one variable. **Partial Completeness Assumption (PCA)** is defined as $G = (V, E, L)$ is a directed edge-labeled graph, the set of *heuristic-based negative edges hE-* in G is to consider as a negative edge, every edge (s, p, o') not in E, but that (s,p,o)

Fig. 2. Research Pipeline: Figure demonstrates the pipeline of steps followed to build a rule mining system. Related research questions are also added.

belongs to E. That is $hE- = (s, p, o')|(s, p, o') \notin E$ and $(s, p, o) \in E$. PCA assumes that heuristic-based negative edges are possible incomplete edges.

Our approach performs task-agnostic mining, which means that it has been generalized to be interoperable across multiple systems, and the goal is to make *true predictions* that can potentially complete the missing relationships in large *incomplete KGs* under *Partial Completeness Assumption (PCA)*. Later these mined rules can be used to identify the causal relationship being observed between the nodes or by the rules mined. These would be termed 'Causal Rules' with added semantics to the Horn rules. Similar to the logical rules mined by AMIE and generating negative edges, we would also like to use the *PCA Confidence* measure to identify the potential incompleteness and predict true positives to complete the KG. Also, *Causal Ratio* metric will be used in order to discover potential causal rules mined over the KGs. To begin with the entailment regimes, we would be taking into consideration `rdfs:subClassOf`, `rdfs:subPropertyOf`, `rdfs:property`, `typing` and `owl:sameAs` as mentioned in the motivating example 1. Later this can be extended with all the entailment available to enhance the power of KGs. Our approach will also follow the incremental approach to generate rules incrementally, which makes it more efficient. This process will interleave the generation of mined rules with the retrieval of data from the KGs via queries executed over SPARQL endpoints.

Research Questions: Our approach aims to improve the rule mining process to answer the following research questions by ensuring KG completion and mining rules efficiently: **RQ1)** What is the impact of injecting entailment regimes to enrich the mined rules? **RQ2)** How can scalability be achieved in large KGs? **RQ3)** Can knowledge extracted from KGs help in identifying causality relationships to enhance explainability?

4   Research Methodology and Approach

Let us briefly discuss the methodology followed in our approach, as illustrated in Fig. 2. In order to further enhance the traditional techniques and optimally mine causal rules, we will fully exploit the benefits of KGs and semantics. To begin, injecting entailment regimes will aid deductive methods in making inferences over KGs. This will answer the **RQ1)**. Inductively mining rules incrementally by avoiding the blocking process will suffice the **RQ1** and **RQ2)**. Traditional approaches executed over a KG upload the RDF triple files in main memory, impacting scalability to large KGs. Therefore, our approach will access SPARQL endpoints and execute queries to traverse the KGs which in turn will help to implement a more scalable algorithm to efficiently mine causal rules. To reduce the search space, our approach would consider the subset of the KG as per the user's interest. Furthermore, more enriched rules will be extracted over the subset of KG by later discovering causal rules that will answer **RQ3)**.

5   Evaluation/Evaluation Plan

The evaluation is performed on the real-world KGs in the biomedical area. We have started our evaluation of the lung cancer KG from P4-LUCAT[2]. The evaluation strategy for our approach in all the steps mentioned in Fig. 2 is to measure efficiency in terms of the time it takes our rule mining approach to mine rules efficiently. In the later phase, our approach will incrementally mine rules and produce output to improve scalability. Rules will be generated based on the user's request, such as if the user requests rules with a higher *PCA Confidence* or any other conditions. These conditions will be taken into account when producing rules in order to save time, making our rule mining approach more scalable and accurate. Furthermore, by keeping humans in the loop, we will evaluate the causal rules generated by our approach. Domain experts in the biomedical domain will be validating the rules produced by our approach to check if they comply with the clinical guidelines and help in identifying causality.

6   Results So Far

We describe the outcomes of evaluating these methods on a KG comprising synthetic lung cancer patients generated from the biomedical KG discussed in the previous section. This initial study aims at reporting the impact of injecting entailment regimes on the KGs to answer our **RQ1)**. The preliminary results are being evaluated on two lung cancer KGs in order to compare them to state-of-the-art methods. The *Lung Cancer (LC) KG* comprises the characteristics of synthetic lung cancer patients (i.e., `identifier`, `gender`, `age`, `biomarker`). Entailment regimes are considered as described in Fig. 1 on the LC KG.

As the motivating example 1 states, enriching the mined rule aids in the extraction of new insights from the KGs. In contrast to naive approaches, our approach takes `rdfs:subPropertyOf` into account for the experiments in the current example. This yields higher metrics values and demonstrates potential true predictions. For example, higher *Inferred PCA Confidence* of a rule quantifies the KG's partial completion by identifying more productive rules.

Observed Results and Discussion. Figure 3a describes the LC KG without inference and after the materialization of the deductive closure of the entailment

---

[2] EraMed project https://p4-lucat.eu/.

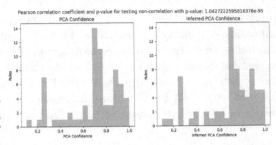

Lung Cancer KG	#T	#E	#P
Without Inference	23,773	1522	20
With Inference	31,932	1668	20

(a) The Lung Cancer (LC) KG Statistics. **#T** Number of Triples, **#E** Number of Entities, and **#P** Number of Predicates.

(b) **PCA Confidence:** Understanding the distribution of the PCA Confidence metric over KGs on how frequently each value occurs.

Fig. 3. Initial Results. (a) depicts statistics of the benchmark used to perform the experiments (b) shows the experimental results of the probability of the correlation between *PCA Confidence* and *Inferred PCA Confidence*. It is represented by the p-value which states that the metrics are statistically significant.

regimes. The same number of rules (10,766 rules) were mined from versions of the LC KG, however, the scores of the mined rules have changed. Figure 3b exhibits the null hypothesis test performed to guarantee statistical independence between *PCA Confidence* and *Inferred PCA Confidence* metrics. When semantics are incorporated, the observed difference in the frequency distribution of metrics reveals the potential completion of KGs with true predictions. The results of our approach are publicly available on GitHub[3].

7   Conclusions/Lessons Learned

We propose a rule mining algorithm for mining causal rules from KGs. Our approach mine rules over both *A-Box* and *T-Box* of the KGs and promises scalability by implementing operators that enable the continuous generation of mined rules. Our initial framework exploits the semantics of the KGs and puts into perspective their relevance during a mining process. Our initial results indicate that these semantic-based mined rules are informative in domains such as healthcare, e.g., to understand how treatments have been prescribed and their relationships with existing medical guidelines. The lessons learned by reviewing the literature on semantic symbolic learning over KGs assisted us in recognizing the benefits and drawbacks of current approaches. This enabled us to improve rule mining systems by effectively utilizing KG semantics for better refinement and completion of KGs. The next steps in this Ph.D. work will be to refine the initial prototype in order to make the rule mining process more scalable and to polish it in order to make better predictions with higher scalability and accuracy.

---

[3] https://github.com/SDM-TIB/Symbolic_Learning_over_KGs.

Acknowledgements. I would like to express my special thanks to my supervisor Prof. Dr. Maria-Esther Vidal for all her guidance and feedback. This work has been supported by the project TrustKG-Transforming Data in Trustable Insights with grant P99/2020 and the EraMed project P4-LUCAT (GA No. 53000015).

References

1. Abedjan, Z., Lorey, J., Naumann, F.: Reconciling ontologies and the web of data. In: ACM CIKM 2012 (2012). https://doi.org/10.1145/2396761.2398467
2. Agrawal, R., Imieliński, T., Swami, A.: Mining association rules between sets of items in large databases. In: ACM SIGMOD (1993). https://doi.org/10.1145/170035.170072
3. Agrawal, R., Imieliński, T., Swami, A.: Mining association rules between sets of items in large databases. SIGMOD Rec. (1993). https://doi.org/10.1145/170036.170072
4. Beall, J., Restall, G., Sagi, G.: Logical consequence. In: The Stanford Encyclopedia of Philosophy (2019)
5. Brickley, D., Guha, R.V.: RDF schema 1.1. W3C recommendation. World Wide Web Consortium (2014)
6. Galárraga, L., Teflioudi, C., Hose, K., Suchanek, F.: Fast rule mining in ontological knowledge bases with AMIE+. VLDB J. (2015). https://hal-imt.archives-ouvertes.fr/hal-01699866
7. Galárraga, L.A., Preda, N., Suchanek, F.M.: Mining rules to align knowledge bases. In: Automated Knowledge Base Construction (2013). https://doi.org/10.1145/2509558.2509566
8. Galárraga, L., Teflioudi, C., Hose, K., Suchanek, F.: AMIE: association rule mining under incomplete evidence in ontological knowledge bases. In: WWW 2013 (2013). https://doi.org/10.1145/2488388.2488425
9. Han, J., et al.: DBMiner: a system for data mining in relational databases and data warehouses. In: CASCON Conference (1997)
10. Hitzler, P., Krötzsch, M., Parsia, B., Patel-Schneider, P.F., Rudolph, S.: OWL 2 Web Ontology Language Primer, 2nd edn. W3C Recommendation, World Wide Web Consortium (2012)
11. Hogan, A., et al.: Knowledge Graphs (2021). https://doi.org/10.2200/S01125ED1V01Y202109DSK022
12. Kaur, M., Kang, S.: Market basket analysis: identify the changing trends of market data using association rule mining. Procedia Comput. Sci. (2016). https://doi.org/10.1016/j.procs.2016.05.180
13. Lajus, J., Galárraga, L., Suchanek, F.: Fast and exact rule mining with AMIE 3. In: Harth, A., et al. (eds.) The Semantic Web (2020)
14. Meilicke, C., Chekol, M.W., Ruffinelli, D., Stuckenschmidt, H.: Anytime bottom-up rule learning for knowledge graph completion. In: IJCAI-19 (2019). https://doi.org/10.24963/ijcai.2019/435
15. Munch, M., Dibie-Barthelemy, J., Manfredotti, C., Wuillemin, P.H.: Towards interactive causal relation discovery driven by an ontology (2018)
16. Sarawagi, S., Thomas, S., Agrawal, R.: Integrating association rule mining with relational database systems: alternatives and implications. SIGMOD Rec. (1998). https://doi.org/10.1145/276305.276335

17. Simonne, L., Pernelle, N., Saïs, F., Thomopoulos, R.: Differential causal rules mining in knowledge graphs. In: ACM KCAP (2021). https://doi.org/10.1145/3460210.3493584
18. Toivonen, H.: Apriori algorithm. In: Sammut, C., Webb, G.I. (eds.) Encyclopedia of Machine Learning and Data Mining (2017). https://doi.org/10.1007/978-1-4899-7687-1_27

Query Answering over the Polymorphic Web of Data

Cosimo Gregucci(✉)

University of Stuttgart, Stuttgart, Germany
cosimo.gregucci@ipvs.uni-stuttgart.de

Abstract. Knowledge graphs are a versatile means to gather Semantic Web data and are typically stored and queried with the W3C standards, RDF and SPARQL. Despite the significant progress made in query processing, predicting plausible answers in presence of missing facts remains a challenge. This aspect has been tackled by proposing methods to predict links and solve queries in some reduced fragments of SPARQL. Thus far, I have explored two parallel directions for this thesis. First, I study how to use knowledge graph embedding methods to predict missing facts. In particular, I explore how to combine different knowledge graph embedding methods to improve the quality of the predictions. Second, I study how to connect techniques to query knowledge graphs from these two research areas, namely database query processing, and graph learning. The former techniques provide actual answers of a query, while the latter provide plausible ones. My hypothesis is that I can define a common query interface, based on SPARQL, to provide answers from these polymorphic data sources. To this end, I propose an extension for SPARQL, called polymorphic SPARQL.

Keywords: link prediction · ensemble · query answering · polymorphic

1 Introduction

The emergence of large knowledge graphs (KGs) stored and queried using the W3C standards RDF [5], and SPARQL [9], has encouraged many researchers to improve query processing over KGs [10]. SPARQL is a database query language and, as such, the result of a SPARQL query over a given dataset is defined based on the data that is in the dataset. Thus, given that knowledge graphs are known to be incomplete, in presence of missing links, some answers might not be retrieved by the SPARQL engine.

Such aspect has been addressed by the graph learning community, who identify two problems: 1) predicting missing links, which is known as *link prediction*, and 2) predicting plausible answers of first-order logic query, which is known as *complex query answering*.

C. Gregucci—Category: Early Stage PhD.

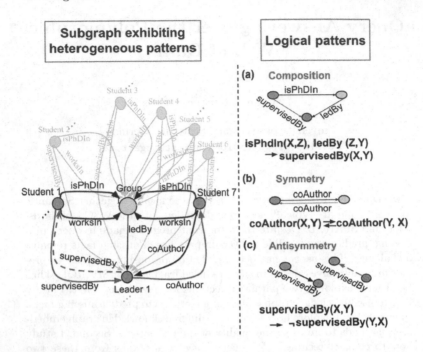

Fig. 1. A sub-graph that exhibits heterogeneous relational patterns [15].

According to the graph learning community, a KG is a triple $(\mathcal{V}, \mathcal{R}, \mathcal{E})$, where $\mathcal{V}$ and $\mathcal{R}$ are two finite sets, whose elements are called *entities* and *relation names*, and $\mathcal{E}$ is a subset of $\mathcal{V} \times \mathcal{R} \times \mathcal{V}$ that represent *relationships between entities*. Relationships are triples (h, r, t) where h and t are called the head and the tail entities.

Like complex query answering, link prediction can be seen as answering first-order logic queries. Indeed, the link prediction problems of finding sensible tails for a given pair of head and relation name, and finding sensible heads for a given pair of relation name and tail, denoted $(h, r, ?t)$ or $(?h, r, t)$, correspond to the respective first order queries $(x).r(h, x)$ and $(x).r(x, t)$. Since SPARQL has the same expressive power as relational calculus [1], a safe subset of first-order logic queries, link prediction and complex query answering methods can be used to return plausible SPARQL answers.

Knowledge graph embeddings (KGEs) are a prominent approach for both problems, link prediction [3,18,20], and complex query answering [11,16,17]. Relations in the graph may follow patterns (Fig. 1) that can be learned. For example, some relations might be symmetric and others might be hierarchical. However, the existing approaches have two limitations:

L1. The learning capability of different knowledge graph embedding methods varies for each pattern and, so far, no single method can learn all patterns equally well (see Table 1).

Table 1. Specification of query representation of baseline and state of the art KGE models and respective pattern modeling and inference abilities. ∘ is element-wise complex product together with relation normalization. S = Symmetry, A = Antisymmetry, I = Inversion, C = Composition, H = Hierarchy

Model	Query	Embeddings	S	A	I	C	H
TransE [3]	$q = h + r$	$q, h, r \in \mathbb{R}^d$	×	✓ − 0	✓ − 0	✓ − 0	×
RotatE [18]	$q = h \circ r$	$q, h, r \in \mathbb{C}^d$	✓ − 2	✓ − 2	✓ − 2	✓ − 2	×
ComplEx [20]	$q = h \times r$	$q, h, r \in \mathbb{C}^d$	✓ − 2	✓ − 2	✓ − 2	×	×
DistMult [28]	$q = h \cdot r$	$q, h, r \in \mathbb{R}^d$	✓ − 0	×	×	×	×
RefH [4]	$q = Ref(\theta_r)h$	$q, h \in \mathbb{H}^d$	✓ − 0	×	×	×	✓ − 0

L2. Both complex query answering and link prediction methods only support a limited subset of SPARQL. Indeed, existing link prediction methods are restricted to the atomic queries $(x).r(h, x)$ and $(x).r(x, t)$, and complex query answering methods are restricted to queries with constants (called *anchors*), returning a single variable, or having no cycles.

In this thesis, I address these two limitations. Regarding **L1**, I developed a method to combine different knowledge graph embedding methods using attention, and showed that the combined method can outperform the individual ones. I published a paper [7] showing these results, and I am currently working on improvements to this idea. Regarding **L2**, I am studying how to integrate SPARQL services with link prediction services to return both, actual answers from explicit links and plausible answers from predicted links. According to [16] completing the knowledge graph with the *predicted* links before executing queries would result in a graph that is too dense, thus I plan to retrieve the predictions at query runtime. Moreover, by completing the graph, the predicted links would be indistinguishable from the actual ones. To this end, I will define a common interface, I called *polymorphic SPARQL (p-SPARQL)*, on top of both interfaces.

2   Related Work

This section presents the work related to limitations **L1** and **L2**.

2.1   Combination of Knowledge Graph Embeddings

Xu et al. [27] show that the combination of multiple runs of low-dimensional embedding models can outperform the corresponding individual high-dimensional embedding model. Unlike my approach [7], they do not combine different methods to combine the different learning capabilities.

Most methods combining different KGEs train models separately and then combine their scoring function [13,21,23,24]. Unlike these approaches, my approach combines the multiple vector representations of a query and uses attention to select, for each query, the best suited representations.

I combine multiple vector representations to increase the learning capabilities of individual methods. Another way to increase the learning capability of a method is to embed queries into spaces that combine different geometrical spaces. For example, Gu et al. [8] combines Hyperbolic, Spherical, and Euclidean spaces, and UltraE [25] uses an Ultra-hyperbolic manifold, which generalizes Hyperbolic and Spherical manifolds allowing to simultaneous embed multiple distinct hierarchical relations and non-hierarchical ones in a single *heterogeneous* geometric space. So far, I have studied how to combine query vectors rather than geometric spaces [7]. My proposed method combines vectors in Euclidean space, and then projects them to non-Euclidean manifolds to learn hierarchical relations; it is not limited to a single geometry, and I will adapt it to combine vector representations beyond the Euclidean space.

2.2   Including Link Prediction in SPARQL Queries

Complex Query Answering. Most approaches for complex query answering map queries into probability distributions [17], or regions [11,16] in the vector space. They map first-order logic queries to directed acyclic graphs (DAGs). They are also called *dependency graphs*, and their nodes are the constants and variables in the query. For each atom $r(u,v)$ a directed edge between u and v with label r is in the dependency graph. The direction of each edge is chosen conveniently to guarantee that the dependency graph have a unique sink node(see Fig. 2). The dependency graph is used to define the operations that are performed to get to the representation of the sink.

As we already mentioned, existing query answering methods do not support every first-order query, even for reduced first-order logic fragments, such as conjunctive queries.

The limitations are that queries must return a single variable (which is the sink), have no cycles, and all local sources (i.e., nodes with no entering edges) are constants. The following conjunctive query violates all these conditions, and hence cannot be solved by the existing methods: $(x,y).\exists z\exists u(p(x,y) \wedge q(y,z) \wedge r(z,x) \wedge s(u,x))$. Unlike the existing methods, the interface I will define, called p-SPARQL, will support all basic graph patterns by combining standard SPARQL interfaces with link-prediction services.

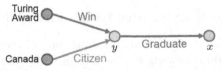

$$(x).(\exists y.(\mathsf{Win}(\mathsf{TuringAdward}, y) \wedge \mathsf{Citizen}(\mathsf{Canada}, y) \wedge \mathsf{Graduate}(y, x))$$

Fig. 2. Dependency graph of a first-order query asking *"Where did Canadian citizens with Turing Award graduate?"* [16].

Including Similarity Metrics in SPARQL Query. Several works propose extending SPARQL with similarity functions [12,14].

However, the aforementioned approaches compute similarity among entities, while in link prediction a similarity metric is computed to match a query to a candidate answer.

3 Problem Statement and Contributions

In this thesis I will study 1) how to combine knowledge graph embeddings, and 2) how to include link prediction in SPARQL queries.

How to Combine Knowledge Graph Embeddings. In this thesis, I study how to improve the link-prediction task by combining query vectors, computed with different KGE methods.

Let $\mathbb{M}$ be a set of several existing KGE methods such as TransE [3], RotatE [18], ComplEx [20], DistMult [28], AttE [4]. For each query $q = (h,r,?)$, let the *query representation set* be $\mathcal{Q} = \{q_m \mid q_m = g_r^m(h), m \in \mathbb{M}\}$ where $q_m = g_r^m(h)$ is the query representation for the method m. For example, TransE defines $q_{\text{TransE}} = g_r^{\text{TransE}}(h) = h + r$. Our problem is thus to find a function g_Θ such that the combined method m_C performs better than each method $m \in \mathbb{M}$ separately. I can define a combined query q_C, as a function of the query vectors q_m, $q_C = g_\Theta(q_{\text{TransE}}, \ldots, q_{\text{AttE}})$, where g_Θ is a combination function and Θ is a vector of parameters for the function.

Hypothesis 1. The query vectors can be combined using a relation-specific attention mechanism, where the best-performing models should have the most importance.

The related research questions are:

RQ1. Is attention able to give more importance to the best-performing models?
RQ2. Is the combined model able to outperform the single models in the link prediction task?

How to Include Link Prediction in SPARQL Query. In this thesis, we will address the problem of how to compute plausible answers for SPARQL having, as input, a SPARQL service s and a link-prediction service m, both defined over the same knowledge graph G.

For convenience, I will focus on the SPARQL fragment consisting of basic graph patterns whose entities and relation names occur in G, and no variables are allowed in predicate position. This SPARQL fragment corresponds to conjunctive queries, that is, first-order logic queries $(x_1, \ldots, x_j).(\exists y_1 \cdots \exists y_z.\varphi)$ where φ is a conjunction of atoms $(p_1(u_1, v_1) \wedge \cdots \wedge p_n(u_n, v_n))$, variables $x_1, \ldots, x_j, y_1, \ldots, y_z$ are the variables occurring in φ, and sets $\{x_1, \ldots, x_j\}$ and $\{y_1, \ldots, y_z\}$ are disjoint. As we already pointed out, link-prediction and complex query answering methods can be used to provide plausible answers to a restricted set of these queries.

Given a conjunctive query q^C, we can evaluate q^C in service s to obtain a set, $[\![q^C]\!]_s$, containing all mappings $\mu = (x_1 \mapsto a_1, \ldots, x_n \mapsto a_n)$ that are answers to q^C in G. We will write $\mu_{x \mapsto a}$ to denote a mapping $\{x \mapsto a\}$. On the other hand, a query q^C cannot be evaluated at the link prediction service m.

However, if we consider q^C to be composed by a set of atomic queries q of the form $(x).r(h, x)$ and $(x).r(x, t)$, then, when considering each atomic query q separately, it is possible to directly evaluate q in m. In this case, the result is a set of pairs $(\mu_{x \mapsto u}, \tau_{\mu_{x \mapsto u}})$ where u is an entity of graph G, and τ_u is a score given to mapping $\mu_{x \mapsto u}$.

If we now want to evaluate the atomic query q in both services, m, and s, we will notice a difference in the form of the answers: the service s returns set of answers, while the service m returns a set of pairs.

In a high level, our problem is how to define a sensible semantics that extends the SPARQL semantics to incorporate scores to the answers. To define such extended semantics, called p-SPARQL, desiderata must consider, for example, that every answer $\mu \in [\![q]\!]_s$ must have the higher possible score, since we know that μ is an actual answer. Otherwise, if $\mu \notin [\![q]\!]_s$, it should have a lower score that accounts for the plausibility of the answer.

Returning scores for all possible mappings is impractical in SPARQL because datasets are huge. Instead, given a number $k \geq 0$, we can define a service, called $s+k$, that returns a set, called $[\![q]\!]_{s+k}$, of pairs (μ, τ_μ) where τ_μ is the score given to mapping μ, and $[\![q]\!]_{s+k}$ contains all mappings $\mu \in [\![q]\!]_s$ plus the top k scored answers according to the p-SPARQL semantics I will propose.

When it is possible to evaluate q directly at both services, the definition of $[\![q]\!]_{s+k}$ is trivial: return all answers of $[\![q]\!]_s$ (assigning them the highest score) plus the top k results given by m. In the other cases, the problem is more complex. For example, if query q is $(x, y).p(x, y)$ then we cannot use directly service m because m does not support query q. Instead, we can iterate over every entity h in graph G to answer query $(y).p(h, y)$ to get the scores of solutions $\mu_{y \mapsto t} \in [\![(y).p(h, y)]\!]_{s+k}$. Similarly, we can compute the scores of solutions $\mu_{x \mapsto h} \in [\![(x).p(x, t)]\!]_{s+k}$. This observation leads to the following hypothesis:

Hypothesis 2. The score for a mapping μ can be computed as the combination of the scores of its individual mappings $\mu_{variable \mapsto entity}$.

Hypothesis 3. We can define an efficient algorithm that does not require computing the score of every mapping $\mu_{variable \mapsto entity}$.

For example, given a query $(x, y).(r(x, y) \wedge p(y, c))$, the score of a mapping $\mu = \{x \mapsto a, y \mapsto b\}$ depend on the scores given by m to mappings $\mu_{x \mapsto a}$ and $\mu_{y \mapsto b}$ for the respective queries $(x).r(x, b)$, $(y).p(a, y)$, and $(y).p(y, c)$. If mapping $\mu_{x \mapsto a}$ has a low score, it may not be worth to compute the score of mapping $\mu_{y \mapsto b}$ because the score of the combined mapping μ will anyway be low.

RQ3. How can we combine the scores given to mappings by the link prediction service to obtain sensible scores for the combined mappings?

RQ4. How can we return the answers $\mu \in [\![q]\!]_{s+k}$ efficiently?

4   Research Methodology and Approach

In this section, I describe the approach I am following for solving the problems identified in the previous section.

Combination of Query Vectors. I already mention that a KG can follow different patterns, as shown in Fig. 1, and that different KGE methods cannot learn all patterns equally well. Table 1 shows the patterns that a KGE method can learn, along with the number of constraints that it has to impose to do so, for each dimension. For example, RotatE defines transformations as rotations $g_r^{\text{RotatE}}(h) = h \circ r$ in Complex space. In this way, RotatE can enforce both $h \circ r = t, t \circ r = h$ if $r^2 = 1$, and thus, requires two constraints $r \neq -1$ and $r \neq 1$ to express antisymmetrical relations. However, TransE can model anti-symmetric patterns naturally, without imposing any constraint, but it is not able to learn symmetrical patterns.

In [7], we showed that an attention-based combination of KGEs can exploit the advantages of each KGE method used in the combination. The combined query representation is defined as $q_C = \sum \alpha_i \mathbf{q}_i$, where each weight α_i can be computed by using an attention mechanism [4]:

$$\alpha_i = \frac{\exp(g(\mathbf{w}\mathbf{q}_i))}{\sum_j \exp(g(\mathbf{w}\mathbf{q}_j))},$$

where i and j identify models in $\mathbb{M}$, and $g(x) = \mathbf{w}x$ is a function with trainable parameter $\mathbf{w}$. This version of our method is called Spherical Embedding with Attention (SEA).

A variant of this method, called Spherical Embedding with Pointcaré Attention (SEPA), projects the combined query q_C to a non-Euclidean manifold, i.e. the Poincaré ball, via the exponential map $q_C^{\mathcal{M}} = \exp_0(q_C)$. The score function is $score(q, a) = d(q_C^{\mathcal{M}} \oplus r, a)$, where $q_C^{\mathcal{M}}, r, a$ are points on a manifold $\mathcal{M}$, $\exp_0(.)$ is the exponential map from origin, and $\oplus$ is Mobius addition.

In future work, we plan to combine various manifolds besides combining the query vectors in knowledge graph embedding.

Including Link Prediction in SPARQL. Regarding **RQ3**, if a query involves more than one literal, then it may involve the scores given to more than one fact. If the score of a mapping μ reflects a probability, then we should consider this as the joint probability given to the facts involved into this mapping μ. For example, if $\mu = \{x \mapsto a, y \mapsto b\}$, and the query q is $(x, y).(p(x, y) \wedge r(y, c))$, then the score of μ for query q must reflect the probability of $p(a, b) \wedge p(b, c)$, which is the joint probability of the links $p(a, b)$ and $p(b, c)$. The computation of this joint probability from the marginal probabilities of these links depends on the conditional probabilities between these links, which are related to the scores of mappings μ and $\mu_{y \mapsto b}$ for the queries $(x, y).p(x, y)$ and $(y).r(y, c)$. Assuming independence between the links, we can simplify the score definition. However, this assumption may not capture some patterns satisfied by relations in the graph. Moreover, it could also be possible to use other frameworks for combining scores, such as using t-norm fuzzy logics.

Regarding **RQ4**, if we know that the top k predicted answers have a score over a certain threshold, then we can discard mappings μ such that we can infer that the score of μ is below the threshold. Indeed, if scores are probabilities (where a score 1 is given to actual links), and a marginal probability is below the threshold, then we can infer that the joint probability is also below the threshold. To use this idea, we can index the top answers for queries of the form $(x).\exists y.p(x, y)$ and $(y).\exists x.p(x, y)$ for each relation name p in graph G.

5   Evaluation Plan

In this section, I will describe the benchmarks and the metrics that I will use for evaluating the proposed solutions.

Combination of Query Vectors. In [7], I used the following standard benchmarks for the evaluation:

- **Wordnet:** WN18RR [6] is a subset of WN18, which contains a mixture of symmetric and antisymmetric as relational patterns, and hierarchical structural patterns. WN18RR contains 11 relations, 86,835 training triples, and 40,943 entities. Compared to the other datasets in KGE literature, WN18RR is considered sparse;
- **FreeBase:** FB15k-237 [19] is the subset of FB15k from removing leakage of inverse relations [6]. FB15k-237 is less sparse than WN18RR and mainly contains composition patterns. It contains 237 relations, 272,115 triples, and 14,541 entities.
- **NELL:** NELL-995 [26] contains 75,492 entities and 200 relations, having ~22% hierarchical relations. I use a subset of NELL-995 with 100% hierarchy, created in [2].

I use the popular ranking metrics [22] namely Mean Reciprocal Rank (MRR), and Hits@k, k = 1, 3, 10. For future works, we plan to use a similar set of datasets and metrics.

Including Link Prediction in SPARQL Queries. Regarding **RQ3**, I plan to evaluate our method using the same datasets used by existing complex query answering methods [11,16], which are created from the ones showed in Sect. 5 and using ranking-based metrics. Besides, I plan to create an additional dataset composed of general BGP queries, which cannot be answered by existing complex query answering methods. I also plan to evaluate our method with SPARQL query performance benchmarks, after adapting them to the link prediction setting. Regarding **RQ4**, we have two metrics: the execution time of queries, and the space and memory used by p-SPARQL.

6   Results

Our work [7] showed that the approaches described in Sect. 2.1 are able to out-perform the individual models used in the combination. Specifically, the hyperbolic version of our combined model (SEPA) outperforms all baselines in low dimensions while the Euclidean one (SEA) is the best model in high dimensions (**RQ2**). It also showed that the attention mechanism can give more importance to the best models for the specific kind of relation involved in the query (**RQ1**).

7   Conclusions

In this thesis, I want to exploit existing knowledge graph embedding methods, to improve their performance in the link prediction task and enhance their usability.

As a first step, I studied how to combine existing KGE methods to improve their performance in link prediction task, which was shown in [7]. Our approach facilitates the combination of the query representations from a wide range of popular knowledge graph embedding models. In future work, we will combine various manifolds besides combining query embeddings. Additionally, the proposed approach could be applied to other tasks, e.g., use an attention mechanism to combine different multi-hop queries [16,17].

The second step of this thesis will be to bridge between the two research areas of database query processing and machine learning, by proposing p-SPARQL, which integrates link prediction within SPARQL queries. This would allow using link prediction within more complex queries, enhancing their usability.

Acknowledgments. This PhD is part of the KnowGraphs project, receiving funding in the European Union's Horizon 2020 research and innovation program under the Marie Skłodowska-Curie grant (agreement No: 860801). Furthermore, I would like to thank my supervisor Prof. Dr. Steffen Staab, and my co-supervisors Dr. Daniel Hernández and Mojtaba Nayyeri for their continuous support.

References

1. Angles, R., Gutierrez, C.: The expressive power of SPARQL. In: Sheth, A., et al. (eds.) ISWC 2008. LNCS, vol. 5318, pp. 114–129. Springer, Heidelberg (2008). https://doi.org/10.1007/978-3-540-88564-1_8
2. Balazevic, I., Allen, C., Hospedales, T.: Multi-relational poincaré graph embeddings. In: NeurIPS, vol. 32, pp. 4463–4473 (2019)
3. Bordes, A., Usunier, N., Garcia-Duran, A., Weston, J., Yakhnenko, O.: Translating embeddings for modeling multi-relational data. In: Advances in Neural Information Processing Systems, vol. 26 (2013)
4. Chami, I., Wolf, A., Juan, D.C., Sala, F., Ravi, S., Ré, C.: Low-dimensional hyperbolic knowledge graph embeddings. In: Proceedings of the 58th Annual Meeting of the Association for Computational Linguistics, pp. 6901–6914 (2020)
5. Cyganiak, R., Wood, D., Lanthaler, M.: RDF 1.1 concepts and abstract syntax. Technical report, W3C Recommendation (2014)

6. Dettmers, T., Minervini, P., Stenetorp, P., Riedel, S.: Convolutional 2D knowledge graph embeddings. In: AAAI (2018)
7. Gregucci, C., Nayyeri, M., Hernández, D., Staab, S.: Link prediction with attention applied on multiple knowledge graph embedding models. In: ACM WebConf (2023)
8. Gu, A., Sala, F., Gunel, B., Ré, C.: Learning mixed-curvature representations in product spaces. In: International Conference on Learning Representations (2018)
9. Harris, S., Seaborne, A.: SPARQL 1.1 query language. Technical report, W3C Recommendation (2013)
10. Hogan, A., et al.: Knowledge graphs. ACM Comput. Surv. (CSUR) **54**(4), 1–37 (2021)
11. Huang, Z., Chiang, M.F., Lee, W.C.: LINE: logical query reasoning over hierarchical knowledge graphs. In: Proceedings of the 28th ACM SIGKDD, pp. 615–625 (2022)
12. Kiefer, C., Bernstein, A., Stocker, M.: The fundamentals of iSPARQL: a virtual triple approach for similarity-based semantic web tasks. In: Aberer, K., et al. (eds.) ASWC/ISWC -2007. LNCS, vol. 4825, pp. 295–309. Springer, Heidelberg (2007). https://doi.org/10.1007/978-3-540-76298-0_22
13. Krompaß, D., Tresp, V.: Ensemble solutions for link-prediction in knowledge graphs. In: Proceedings of the 2nd Workshop on Linked Data for Knowledge Discovery, Porto, Portugal, pp. 1–10 (2015)
14. Kulmanov, M., et al.: Vec2SPARQL: integrating SPARQL queries and knowledge graph embeddings. bioRxiv, p. 463778 (2018)
15. Nayyeri, M., Vahdati, S., Sallinger, E., Alam, M.M., Yazdi, H.S., Lehmann, J.: Pattern-aware and noise-resilient embedding models. In: Hiemstra, D., Moens, M.-F., Mothe, J., Perego, R., Potthast, M., Sebastiani, F. (eds.) ECIR 2021. LNCS, vol. 12656, pp. 483–496. Springer, Cham (2021). https://doi.org/10.1007/978-3-030-72113-8_32
16. Ren, H., Hu, W., Leskovec, J.: Query2box: Reasoning over knowledge graphs in vector space using box embeddings. In: ICLR 2020 (2020)
17. Ren, H., Leskovec, J.: Beta embeddings for multi-hop logical reasoning in knowledge graphs. In: NeurIPS, vol. 33, pp. 19716–19726 (2020)
18. Sun, Z., Deng, Z., Nie, J., Tang, J.: RotatE: knowledge graph embedding by relational rotation in complex space. In: ICLR 2019, New Orleans, LA, USA (2019)
19. Toutanova, K., Chen, D.: Observed versus latent features for knowledge base and text inference. In: Proceedings of the 3rd Workshop on Continuous Vector Space Models and Their Compositionality, pp. 57–66 (2015)
20. Trouillon, T., Welbl, J., Riedel, S., Gaussier, É., Bouchard, G.: Complex embeddings for simple link prediction. In: ICML (2016)
21. Wang, K., Liu, Y., Ma, Q., Sheng, Q.Z.: MulDE: multi-teacher knowledge distillation for low-dimensional knowledge graph embeddings. In: ACM WebConf (2021)
22. Wang, Q., Mao, Z., Wang, B., Guo, L.: Knowledge graph embedding: a survey of approaches and applications. IEEE Trans. Knowl. Data Eng. **29**(12), 2724–2743 (2017)
23. Wang, Y., Gemulla, R., Li, H.: On multi-relational link prediction with bilinear models. In: AAAI (2018)
24. Wang, Y., Chen, Y., Zhang, Z., Wang, T.: A probabilistic ensemble approach for knowledge graph embedding. Neurocomputing **500**, 1041–1051 (2022)
25. Xiong, B., et al.: Ultrahyperbolic knowledge graph embeddings. In: ACM SIGKDD (2022)
26. Xiong, W., Hoang, T., Wang, W.Y.: DeepPath: a reinforcement learning method for knowledge graph reasoning. In: EMNLP (2017)

27. Xu, C., Nayyeri, M., Vahdati, S., Lehmann, J.: Multiple run ensemble learning with low-dimensional knowledge graph embeddings. In: IJCNN (2021)
28. Yang, B., Yih, W., He, X., Gao, J., Deng, L.: Embedding entities and relations for learning and inference in knowledge bases. In: ICLR (2015)

Optimisation of Link Traversal Query Processing over Distributed Linked Data through Adaptive Techniques

Jonni Hanski[✉]

IDLab, Department of Electronics and Information Systems, Ghent University - imec,
Ghent, Belgium
jonni.hanski@ugent.be

Abstract. An increasing amount of distributed Linked Data is being
made available at different locations, with varying formats, structures,
interfaces and availability. Making use of that data through declarative
query languages such as SPARQL requires query engines capable of executing queries over it. Efficiently executing queries over the data requires
efficient query plans, yet prior access to the information for producing
such plans may not be possible due to the distributed and dynamic
nature of the data. Furthermore, the inability to be aware of all data
sources at a given time, following links to discover data in the form of
link traversal may be needed. Consequently, query planning and optimisation may need to be performed with limited information, and the initial
plan may no longer be optimal. Discovering additional information and
data sources during query execution and adjusting the execution based
on such discoveries using adaptive query processing techniques therefore could help perform queries more efficiently. The aim of this work
is to explore a variety of existing or potential new techniques and their
combinations for query-relevant information acquisition and query plan
adaptation within the context of distributed Linked Data. Already prior
results from multiple studies have demonstrated the benefits of various
such techniques within or beyond Linked Data and Link Traversal Query
Processing, and this work seeks to build upon such results to realise the
benefits of various techniques in practice to tackle performance-related
challenges.

Keywords: Link Traversal Query Processing · Adaptive Query
Processing

1 Introduction

An increasing amount of data [28] is being made available on the Web following
the Linked Data principles [13,14]. The data is distributed for a variety of reasons ranging from availability and performance [5] to privacy and personal data
management [39]. Making use of that data via abstraction layers in the form of

C. Pesquita et al. (Eds.): ESWC 2023, LNCS 13998, pp. 266–276, 2023.
https://doi.org/10.1007/978-3-031-43458-7_45

query languages such as SPARQL [1] requires query engines capable of executing declarative queries over distributed Linked Data.

However, without knowledge of all data sources beforehand, approaches such as Link Traversal Query Processing (LTQP) [21–23,35] that rely on the Linked Data principles are needed to discover data sources relevant for answering a given query. Additionally, studies have drawn attention to the variance in the reliability [3], availability [37], contents [28], access options [28] and transfer rates [9] of distributed Linked Data sources, as well as the volume of the data [9]. Such variance results in a variety of challenges such as result completeness when querying a potentially infinite Web of Linked Data [23], as well as a number of query planning challenges with cardinality and selectivity estimation [27] and potential order-dependent selectivities within the data [17].

While some studies have demonstrated the limited impact of local result construction within LTQP scenarios [25], others [24,35] have demonstrated how, even in a distributed environment with network latency, the query plan plays a vital role in efficient data access, depending on the use case. Unfortunately, the traditional optimise-then-execute approach relies on pre-computed statistics to provide sufficient information for producing an optimal query plan, and such an approach may produce sub-optimal plans in more dynamic environments or with limited information available [18], resulting in inefficient data access during query execution.

Within the context of distributed Linked Data, collecting and maintaining sufficient up-to-date information may not be feasible due to the variance described earlier, and some information such as data transfer rates, latencies or source availability may not be possible to know beforehand. Furthermore, within access controlled distributed environments such as Solid [39], the data and the information about it may vary depending on the access rights at the time of execution, and the owners of the data may modify it or change access permissons to it at any time. Maintaining up-to-date privacy-preserving aggregations or precomputed results on top of such data therefore requires further investigation, but through data discovery via link traversal, it will be possible to access the up-to-date data itself at any given time while respecting the data owner's access control policies.

Addressing the problems of query planning with initially missing information or statistics, unexpected correlations, unpredictable transfer rates and dynamically changing data, the concept of Adaptive Query Processing (AQP) has been introduced as a category of techniques to adapt query execution as new information becomes available [18]. Building on prior work, I will seek to apply such techniques and explore new ones to enable more efficient use of LTQP over distributed Linked Data.

Following this introduction, Sect. 2 seeks to provide a brief overview of AQP, LTQP and other existing work, upon which the problem statement is built in Sect. 3. The research methodology is outlined in Sect. 4, evaluation plan in Sect. 5, preliminary results are described in Sect. 6 and conclusions in Sect. 7.

2   State of the Art

The concept of Adaptive Query Processing (AQP) involves the adaptation of query execution based on runtime feedback, in an effort to find an execution plan that is well-suited to runtime conditions [18]. Such feedback could include, for example, information about the data being queried over [17], network latency [36], source availability [3] or quality-of-service metrics [29]. To achieve this adaptivity, a query engine can interleave planning and execution as opposed to first planning and then executing with no interleaving [18]. For implementing such feedback and adaptivity, the concept of an adaptivity loop [18] has been identified, described as having four phases [18], with a total of five when considering pre-plan optimisation [29]:

1. **Plan pre-optimisation** based on information available at the time.
2. **Runtime monitoring** of parameters relevant to the goals of the system, and collection of metrics relevant for the analysis of the current plan and execution.
3. **Plan analysis**, to evaluate whether the goals are being met and if anything should be changed, and to determine whether re-optimisation should be done, taking into consideration the cost of re-optimisation and plan migration.
4. **Plan re-optimisation**, to find the next optimal plan, taking into consideration the techniques available for adjusting the plan and the points of it they allow modifications at, such as materialisation points or scheduling of operations.
5. **Actuation**, to implement the necessary changes from re-optimisation, including the migration of accumulated state inside various operators such as joins.

The remainder of this section will provide a brief overview of LTQP, dataset information acquisition methods and techniques in AQP.

2.1   Link Traversal Query Processing

Within the distributed Web of Linked Data [13,14], knowing all relevant data sources or their supported access methods beforehand may not be possible. Furthermore, initiatives such as Solid [39] seek to distribute data into personal storages with access control [15], making available and accessible data dependent on current access permissions. Tackling some of the challenges, Link Traversal Query Processing (LTQP) [21–23,35] offers a query execution paradigm that relies on only the basic Linked Data principles, by following links during query execution to discover data to query over. Unfortunately, such an approach, in addition to posing limitations with result completeness [23], also relies on some form of heuristics [21] or guidance [35] to efficiently discover relevant data through chains of links, as opposed to following all links in an arbitrary order. With no information on the data necessarily being queried over available beforehand in LTQP, producing optimal query plans prior to query execution becomes potentially infeasible, calling for adaptive approaches to adjust the execution as data is discovered.

2.2   Dataset Information Discovery

With query planning taking advantage of information on the data to produce
optimal query plans [18], queries over distributed Linked Data benefiting from
information on data location [5], and with LTQP benefiting from guidance in
selecting links to follow [35], acquiring such information is needed for the purposes of evaluating whether one query plan or execution approach is closer to
optimal than another one, or if one data source or link should be prioritised
over another. Various approaches have been investigated for making information
about datasets available:

- **Dataset summaries**, such as Vocabulary of Interlinked Datasets (VoID) [8]
  for describing the access methods or structural information such as the total
  number of triples, distinct subjects, occurrences of predicates and similar.
- **Characteristics sets** [30] for estimating the cardinalities of large numbers
  of joins in bottom-up query processing, with techniqus for sample-based characteristics estimation [26] for datasets.
- **Approximate Membership Functions (AMFs)** [38], such as Prefix-
  Partitioned Bloom Filters (PPBFs) [5] and the extended Semantically Partitioned Bloom Filters (SPBFs) [7], already applied to reduce access to datasets
  known to not contain data relevant for answering a query [7,34].
- **Locational Indexing** [5,6], for efficiently locating data relevant for answering a query in a distributed environment.
- **Shape Trees** [31], **Solid Type Index** [42] or other techniques of summarising locations of data within a data source, to help efficiently locate relevant
  data.

2.3   Query Adaptation Techniques

Through adaptation of the query execution, advantage can be taken of newfound
information. While the techniques proposed for implementing adaptivity differ
in their level of interleaving between query execution, plan exploration and plan
modification, two main approaches have been identified [18]:

- **Inter-query adaptivity** as the adaptation of subsequent query executions.
  While such an approach could be a natural next step for systems following
  the optimise-then-execute paradigm, imposing limited runtime overhead, it
  may prove insufficient or of limited benefit in environments where subsequent
  queries have little in common, or where the costs of operations or the characteristics of the data change frequently.
- **Intra-query adaptivity**, where the execution of a query is adapted on-
  the-fly during execution, calling for techniques that can accommodate such
  adaptation at runtime. This will also be the main focus of this work.

While different categorisations exist [2,27,29] for implementations of intra-
query adaptivity, five major approaches could be identified across them as a
compromise:

- **Operator-internal** techniques, using the implementation of a logical operator to achieve adaptivity, without requiring changes to the logical query plan. Techniques such as Symmetric Hash Join (SHJ) [28,41], XJoin [36], MJoin [19] and Adaptive Group Join (agjoin) [3] could fit this category.
- **Data partitioning** techniques, to process different parts of the data differently in a fully pipelined environment, effectively applying different query plans on them, such as on a tuple level. Techniques such as Eddies [2,12], State Modules (SteMs) [32] and STAIR [17] could fit this category.
- **Plan partitioning** techniques, to alter the plan at blocking operators or materialisation points, to delegate subplan selection from planning to execution phase, if sufficient information to select one is unavailable prior to execution [16].
- **Scheduling-based** methods, attempting to hide delays or produce results faster by rescheduling parts of the logical query plan based on intermediate results or unexpected delays. Techniques such as query plan scrambling [9] could fall within this category.
- **Redundant-computation** methods, to execute multiple plans simultaneously until the best-performing one is found and the others are terminated [11].

3   Problem Statement and Contributions

Building upon the existing work in Sect. 2, this thesis will aim to overcome the challenges of traditional query processing outlined in Sect. 1 through the use of adaptive techniques to achieve efficient Link Traversal Query Processing over dynamic distributed Linked Data with no prior knowledge of the data available prior to execution, while also being able to take advantage of any information made available through dataset descriptions. The research questions of this work are the following:

- **Question 1:** Assuming no prior knowledge about the data being queried over, how and what type of information can be discovered during query execution?
- **Question 2:** Taking advantage of newfound information during query execution, what type of new or existing techniques and approaches improve the query execution?
- **Question 3:** What kind of impact can be achieved through the various techniques? How do they affect the execution of the query, on their own or combined?

These research questions have inspired the following hypotheses:

- **Hypothesis 1:** It is possible to obtain sufficient information during query execution to produce an improved version of the initial plan. On average, it will take less time to migrate to the new plan and execute it than it would to finish with the initial one.

- **Hypothesis 2:** The execution time can be reduced by an order of magnitude by introducing a minimal amount of information about the data, for example approximate cardinality estimates.
- **Hypothesis 3:** The information used to guide query planning need not be accurate, as long as it is a step towards more accurate information compared to having no information available at all. That is, Hypothesis 2 holds even with inaccurate information.
- **Hypothesis 4:** Through the use of information available on the data being queried over, together with techniques in adapting the query execution, results can be produced not only faster overall, but also at a more stable rate over the execution of the query. That is, the delay between subsequent results remains, on average, constant. Without the techniques applied, this is expected to not be the case.

The base assumption behind the hypotheses is that, without any prior knowledge of the data, the query engine will produce sub-optimal query plans with trivial errors such as inefficient join orders. Thus, provided but a mere inkling of information slightly indicative of the correct direction, the engine shall already succeed in avoiding such trivial errors and perform an order of magnitude faster. Additionally, applying adaptive techniques should help alleviate any issues within a distributed environment and provide more efficient access to relevant data, helping the engine produce results both faster and at a more constant rate over the duration of the execution.

4   Research Methodology and Approach

Following Sect. 3 and Sect. 1, the aim of this work is to build upon existing research to enable efficient querying with LTQP over distributed Linked Data in practice with no prior knowledge available. This is to be achieved by applying techniques for discovering information about datasets at runtime, together with those for adapting the query plan to take advantage of that information.

The approach will involve the following steps, with prototype implementations and their evaluation outlined in further detail later in Sect. 5, as the overall evaluation revolves around them:

1. **Review of techniques and approaches**, to discover existing ones using publications freely available online. This is to include publications both within and beyond the context of LTQP or distributed Linked Data, as deemed relevant, to discover also techniques not previously applied to LTQP, if any. For example, there may be techniques in querying over traditional relational databases or streams that could be of interest. Furthermore, standards, standards drafts and prototype implementations involving techniques of interest are to be considered.
2. **Identification of approaches of interest**, both existing and novel new ones as they are dicovered, and their **prototype implementations**. The aim is to establish an understanding of applying such techniques in practice.

3. **Evaluation of the techniques** based on their prototype implementations, to establish an understanding of the impact they have on their own and in combination with each other.
4. **Summarisation of results** throughout the process as they are discovered, to contribute to the field of Semantic Web research by providing insights into adaptive LTQP over distributed Linked Data.

The value of the research is to be found in the exploration of a variety of AQP techniques within LTQP over distributed Linked Data in particular. Such investigation has been deemed interesting in existing work [35]. The contributions of this work should help take the next steps towards the use of LTQP in practice, by providing meaningful results and reusable implementations for practical applications.

5 Evaluation Plan

For evaluating the elements of this work, various techniques will be applied through prototype implementations that are evaluated both on their own when possible and in combination with each other as deemed appropriate:

- **Prototype implementations** will be built upon a modular open-source SPARQL query engine [33]. Such a query engine has previously been used [35] in LTQP for evaluating approaches, and should therefore prove adequate for this purpose.
- **Evaluation** will be done using established benchmarking datasets such as the LDBC Social Network Benchmark [10,20], having also been previously adapted for and used with LTQP [35] within the context of Solid [39]. Other benchmarks or reproducible real world datasets will also be considered as deemed interesting, assuming they can be adapted for use with Linked Data.

Drawing inspiration from existing work on LTQP, Linked Data and AQP, metrics such as the following are to be considered to understand the impact of the techniques:

- **Result completeness**, to ensure fair evaluation between techniques, should they produce different results. While not expected, this will be controlled.
- **Number of network requests** done by the query engine to produce a set of results. Existing work has demonstrated how the same set of results can be produced with fewer network requests using specific techniques [34,38].
- **Server and client load**, in the form of processor and memory utilisation. Existing work has demonstrated how decreases in resource consumption on one side can be attained at the expense of the other side [40], and therefore any tests should take into consideration both sides.
- **Delay before initial query results**, as some techniques or implementations may result in delays prior to producing initial results [34].
- **Rate of producing results**, to determine how different techniques affect the intervals between intermediary results or the total execution time.

The last two metrics can be explored via the diefficiency [4] approach, designed to help measure the efficiency of a query engine over time. Such a technique should prove interesting to compare the impact of various techniques over time, and has also been previously applied [35] within the context of LTQP.

Through the observation of these metrics, it should be possible to confirm or reject specific instantiations of the hypotheses presented in Sect. 3.

6   Preliminary Results

Thus far, preliminary results from an initial review of approaches are available, laying the foundation upon which to build the rest of the work. While an overview of the those results has been outlined in Sect. 1 and Sect. 2, the aim is to produce a comprehensive summary at a later stage. Envisioned immediate future work includes the use of some adaptations of Prefix-Partitioned Bloom Filters (PPBFs) [5] within the context of LTQP and Solid, as well as exploratory prototyping with an Eddies-inspired query engine architecture. Additionally, experiments are ongoing on the use of VoID [8] descriptions of datasets for join order optimisation, with mixed initial results using a two-phase join ordering methodology of initial zero-knowledge order followed by order based on initial information.

7   Conclusions

Through the application of dataset information discovery and AQP techniques, I aim to enable efficient LTQP over distributed Linked Data, without relying on pre-made indexes or summaries, although such indexes and summaries will still provide added value for query processing. This will ultimately enable more efficient use of resources throughout the Web of Linked Data, while also making the data more accessible.

Acknowledgements. The research for this work has been supported by SolidLab Vlaanderen (Flemish Government, EWI and RRF project VV023/10).

References

1. SPARQL 1.1 overview. W3c recommendation, W3C (2013). https://www.w3.org/TR/sparql11-overview/
2. Acosta, M., Vidal, M.-E.: Networks of linked data eddies: an adaptive web query processing engine for RDF data. In: Arenas, M., et al. (eds.) ISWC 2015, Part I. LNCS, vol. 9366, pp. 111–127. Springer, Cham (2015). https://doi.org/10.1007/978-3-319-25007-6_7
3. Acosta, M., Vidal, M.-E., Lampo, T., Castillo, J., Ruckhaus, E.: ANAPSID: an adaptive query processing engine for SPARQL endpoints. In: Aroyo, L., et al. (eds.) ISWC 2011, Part I. LNCS, vol. 7031, pp. 18–34. Springer, Heidelberg (2011). https://doi.org/10.1007/978-3-642-25073-6_2

4. Acosta, M., Vidal, M.-E., Sure-Vetter, Y.: Diefficiency metrics: measuring the continuous efficiency of query processing approaches. In: d'Amato, C., Fernandez, M., Tamma, V., Lecue, F., Cudré-Mauroux, P., Sequeda, J., Lange, C., Heflin, J. (eds.) ISWC 2017, Part II. LNCS, vol. 10588, pp. 3–19. Springer, Cham (2017). https://doi.org/10.1007/978-3-319-68204-4_1

5. Aebeloe, C., Montoya, G., Hose, K.: Decentralized indexing over a network of RDF peers. In: Ghidini, C., et al. (eds.) ISWC 2019, Part I. LNCS, vol. 11778, pp. 3–20. Springer, Cham (2019). https://doi.org/10.1007/978-3-030-30793-6_1

6. Aebeloe, C., Montoya, G., Hose, K.: ColChain: collaborative linked data networks. In: Proceedings of the Web Conference 2021, pp. 1385–1396 (2021)

7. Aebeloe, C., Montoya, G., Hose, K.: The lothbrok approach for SPARQL query optimization over decentralized knowledge graphs. arXiv preprint arXiv:2208.14692 (2022)

8. Alexander, K., Cyganiak, R., Hausenblas, M., Zhao, J.: Describing linked datasets with the void vocabulary (2011). https://www.w3.org/TR/void/

9. Amsaleg, L., Tomasic, A., Franklin, M., Urhan, T.: Scrambling query plans to cope with unexpected delays. In: Fourth International Conference on Parallel and Distributed Information Systems, pp. 208–219 (1996). https://doi.org/10.1109/PDIS.1996.568681

10. Angles, R., et al.: The LDBC social network benchmark. arXiv preprint arXiv:2001.02299 (2020)

11. Antoshenkov, G., Ziauddin, M.: Query processing and optimization in oracle RDB. VLDB J. **5**, 229–237 (1996)

12. Avnur, R., Hellerstein, J.M.: Eddies: continuously adaptive query processing. In: Proceedings of the 2000 ACM SIGMOD International Conference on Management of Data, pp. 261–272 (2000)

13. Berners-Lee, T.: Design issues: linked data (2000). https://www.w3.org/DesignIssues/LinkedData.html

14. Berners-Lee, T., Hendler, J., Lassila, O., et al.: The semantic web. Sci. Am. **284**(5), 28–37 (2001)

15. Capadisli, S., Berners-Lee, T.: Web access control (2022). https://solidproject.org/TR/wac

16. Cole, R.L., Graefe, G.: Optimization of dynamic query evaluation plans. In: Proceedings of the 1994 ACM SIGMOD International Conference on Management of Data, pp. 150–160 (1994)

17. Deshpande, A., Hellerstein, J.M., et al.: Lifting the burden of history from adaptive query processing. In: VLDB, pp. 948–959 (2004)

18. Deshpande, A., Ives, Z., Raman, V.: Adaptive query processing. Found. Trends Databases **1**, 1–140 (2007). https://doi.org/10.1561/1900000001

19. Ding, L., Rundensteiner, E.A., Heineman, G.T.: MJoin: a metadata-aware stream join operator. In: Proceedings of the 2nd International Workshop on Distributed Event-Based Systems, pp. 1–8 (2003)

20. Erling, O., et al.: The LDBC social network benchmark: Interactive workload. In: Proceedings of the 2015 ACM SIGMOD International Conference on Management of Data, pp. 619–630 (2015)

21. Hartig, O.: Zero-knowledge query planning for an iterator implementation of link traversal based query execution. In: Antoniou, G., et al. (eds.) ESWC 2011, Part I. LNCS, vol. 6643, pp. 154–169. Springer, Heidelberg (2011). https://doi.org/10.1007/978-3-642-21034-1_11

22. Hartig, O.: Linked data query processing based on link traversal (2014)

23. Hartig, O., Freytag, J.C.: Foundations of traversal based query execution over linked data. In: Proceedings of the 23rd ACM Conference on Hypertext and Social Media, pp. 43–52 (2012)
24. Hartig, O., Heese, R.: The SPARQL query graph model for query optimization. The Semantic Web: Research and Applications, pp. 564–578 (2007)
25. Hartig, O., Özsu, M.T.: Walking without a map: optimizing response times of traversal-based linked data queries (extended version) (2016)
26. Heling, L., Acosta, M.: Estimating characteristic sets for RDF dataset profiles based on sampling. In: Harth, A., et al. (eds.) ESWC 2020. LNCS, vol. 12123, pp. 157–175. Springer, Cham (2020). https://doi.org/10.1007/978-3-030-49461-2_10
27. Ives, Z.G., Halevy, A.Y., Weld, D.S.: Adapting to source properties in processing data integration queries. In: Proceedings of the 2004 ACM SIGMOD International Conference on Management of Data, SIGMOD 2004, pp. 395–406 (2004). https://doi.org/10.1145/1007568.1007613
28. Ladwig, G., Tran, T.: Linked data query processing strategies. In: Patel-Schneider, P.F., et al. (eds.) ISWC 2010. LNCS, vol. 6496, pp. 453–469. Springer, Heidelberg (2010). https://doi.org/10.1007/978-3-642-17746-0_29
29. Liu, M.: Cost-based efficient adaptive query processing for data streams. Ph.D. thesis, University of Pennsylvania (2012)
30. Neumann, T., Moerkotte, G.: Characteristic sets: accurate cardinality estimation for RDF queries with multiple joins. In: 2011 IEEE 27th International Conference on Data Engineering, pp. 984–994 (2011)
31. Prud'hommeaux, E., Bingham, J.: Shape trees specification. W3c editor's draft, W3C (2020). https://shapetrees.org/TR/specification/
32. Raman, V., Deshpande, A., Hellerstein, J.M.: Using state modules for adaptive query processing. In: Proceedings 19th International Conference on Data Engineering, pp. 353–364 (2003)
33. Taelman, R., Van Herwegen, J., Vander Sande, M., Verborgh, R.: Comunica: a modular SPARQL query engine for the web. In: Vrandečić, D., et al. (eds.) ISWC 2018. LNCS, vol. 11137, pp. 239–255. Springer, Cham (2018). https://doi.org/10.1007/978-3-030-00668-6_15, https://comunica.github.io/Article-ISWC2018-Resource/
34. Taelman, R., Van Herwegen, J., Vander Sande, M., Verborgh, R.: Optimizing approximate membership metadata in triple pattern fragments for clients and servers. In: SSWS2020, vol. 2757, pp. 1–16 (2020)
35. Taelman, R., Verborgh, R.: Evaluation of link traversal query execution over decentralized environments with structural assumptions (2023). https://doi.org/10.48550/ARXIV.2302.06933, https://arxiv.org/abs/2302.06933
36. Urhan, T., Franklin, M.J.: XJoin: a reactively-scheduled pipelined join operator (2000)
37. Vandenbussche, P.Y., Umbrich, J., Matteis, L., Hogan, A., Buil-Aranda, C.: SPARQLES: monitoring public SPARQL endpoints. Semant. Web 8(6), 1049–1065 (2017)
38. Vander Sande, M., Verborgh, R., Van Herwegen, J., Mannens, E., Van de Walle, R.: Opportunistic linked data querying through approximate membership metadata. In: Arenas, M., et al. (eds.) ISWC 2015, Part I. LNCS, vol. 9366, pp. 92–110. Springer, Cham (2015). https://doi.org/10.1007/978-3-319-25007-6_6
39. Verborgh, R.: Re-decentralizing the Web, for good this time. In: Seneviratne, O., Hendler, J. (eds.) Linking the World's Information: A Collection of Essays on the Work of Sir Tim Berners-Lee. ACM (2022). https://ruben.verborgh.org/articles/redecentralizing-the-web/

40. Verborgh, R., et al.: Triple pattern fragments: a low-cost knowledge graph interface for the web. J. Web Semant. **37**, 184–206 (2016)
41. Wilschut, A.N., Apers, P.M.: Dataflow query execution in a parallel main-memory environment. Distrib. Parallel Databases **1**, 103–128 (1993)
42. Zagidulin, D., Sambra, A., Carvalho, M., Pavlik, E.: Solid application data discovery (2022). https://github.com/solid/solid/blob/main/proposals/data-discovery.md

Formalizing Stream Reasoning
for a Decentralized Semantic Web

Mathijs van Noort[✉][iD]

Ghent University, Technologiepark-Zwijnaarde 126, 9052 Ghent, Belgium
Mathijs.vanNoort@UGent.be

Abstract. Decentralized storage of data is gaining increased attention as a means to preserve privacy and ownership over personal data. Simultaneously, the share of streaming data on the Web and other applications, e.g. Internet of Things, continues to grow. The large, uncoordinated amount of data streams within these applications requires methods that can coordinate them, especially when a central authority is lacking. We aim to perform said coordination via stream reasoning, using rules and facts to combine and derive information. Decentralized networks, however, present new problems for stream reasoning not yet (fully) addressed in the literature. This includes added expressivity for network heterogeneity, cross-storage referencing and schema variation, out-of-order arrival of data and variance in the representation of time. We aim to propose theoretical solutions that address challenges on temporal expressivity within the network, on out-of-order processing and on the alignment of temporal ontologies. Ultimately, this research aims to provide a solid formal basis for the processing of unbounded streaming data across different data vaults.

Keywords: Decentralized Data Processing · Stream Reasoning · Formal Language

1 Introduction

Recent years have seen increased attention towards decentralized systems, in particular a possible decentralization of the existing Web ecosystem [28]. By decentralizing data and putting access control in the hands of the end-user, rising topics, such as data silos, data ethics and data legislation, can be tackled from a fundamentally different angle. SOLID [29] positions itself as a set of specifications for design of personal data vaults and their content, in which each user, i.e. the vault owner, determines who gets access to which data. Standards set by SOLID are based on existing Semantic Web standards and make explicit use of Linked Data. By providing an alternative for the current centralization of data, the SOLID initiative opens up the possibility of a shift in data storage and processing from centralized to decentralized. Both governmental and industrial

M. van Noort—Early Stage Ph.D.

actors have expressed interested in this novel technology and have committed to development of large-scale applications including healthcare and employment domains [7,10].

Following these developments, derivation of meaningful insights requires the processing of data distributed over a large amount of (relatively) small, decentralized data vaults. This poses distinct technical challenges. When end-users have control over data in their own data vault, those users will naturally publish and handle their data in different ways, interpret the same information differently and express that information in ways that make the most sense for them personally. To deal with this heterogeneity in data, Solid uses Semantic Web specifications to make this difference in meaning explicit. The contents of a SOLID vault consists of documents of Linked Data for which ontologies are used to express the metadata of these documents and data, indicating how it should be interpreted by processing applications. Additionally, one vault can refer to information inside other vaults, leading to cross-storage referencing of information. As in a decentralized environment each vault owner can use their preferred ontologies to express these semantics, Semantic Web reasoning techniques are required to align these schemas and thus meaningfully combine data from multiple data pods.

Within this ecosystem of decentralized data vaults, we turn our attention towards one type of data, being streaming data. Streaming data is the continuous flow of real-time information. The continuous nature of this stream of data implies collected data will never be 'complete' and is unbounded, thus at no point in time can one claim to have collected all data. Streaming data has become omnipresent. As expressed by IDC, the portion of real-time data is expected to climb to 30% of the global datasphere by 2025 [15]. It can be found in Internet of Things (IoT), on social media platforms, stock markets, video games and many others. In most uses cases, streaming data is characterized by a high velocity, where data arrival oftentimes invalidates previous data. This rapid turnover demands frameworks that can express the temporal aspects of the data and techniques that can process said data as efficiently as possible. These challenges related to streaming data are not tied to specific applications, but are inherent to data streams and processing thereof. The research field that addresses how to reason upon heterogeneous data streams, as well as their representation, abstraction and integration in applications, is referred to as *stream reasoning* (SR) [8,9,14].

In a decentralized environment, dealing with streaming data becomes even more challenging. As discussed earlier, users retain a high degree of freedom in their choice to store, publish and semantically annotate their data. Specifically for streaming data, users may employ different notions and structures when it comes to expressing temporal information. A multitude of Temporal Logics (TLs) and temporal processing techniques, called stream reasoning, have emerged to handle various needs of ontology designers and users with respect to temporal expressivity [9]. In a decentralized environment, these different ontology designs are allowed to coexist and are not subjected to design constraints issued by a central authority. In the example given by Fig. 1, vault B uses an ontology (depicted as graph) different from the ones used in vaults A and C. In order to facilitate information exchange within peer-to-peer networks, these different temporal semantics need to be aligned to avoid conflicts or miscommunication. As the temporal semantics employed within a data vault can change over time, (re)alignment also needs to be flexible enough to handle such changes. We identify this alignment of different temporal semantics across data vaults as our first challenge, the challenge of (A) *time-oriented schema alignment*.

In order to perform such time-oriented schema alignment, we aim to design sets of mappings between different temporal schemas. These mappings must therefore take into account the time at which information holds, as well as the 'source' of the information, i.e. the vault. To facilitate these mappings, we aim to identify a logic framework that can capture various different temporal schemas (and hence semantics). This framework thus needs to have a high expressivity. Our second challenge is therefore the search for (B) *a formal logic framework for decentralized stream reasoning*. This includes exploring the applicability of existing frameworks to streaming data in a decentralized system, as well as the development of a novel framework that aims to better suit the new system's needs if no existing framework covers all needs.

Lastly, the velocity of data arrival in the personal vault may differ drastically between streams due to factors such as data vault transmission rates, server location with respect to the data source, bandwidth availability and others. Due to different arrival frequencies, data may not arrive in a chronological order in the vault. An example is given in Fig. 1, where vaults A and B each start an identical stopwatch simultaneously and transmit its advancement to a third vault C. A delay on connection A-C leads to double the transmission time compared to connection B-C, leading to an order of arrival that differs from the true order of events. Applications performing real-time processing of the data in vault C, will thus be faced with out-of-order arrival of data. Additional techniques are required to restore order to the incoming data or new techniques are needed. Our challenge consists of designing (C) *algorithms for out-of-order processing* that make optimal use of the decentralized architecture.

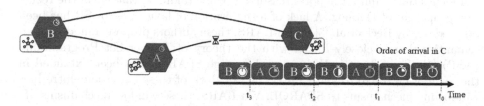

Fig. 1. An example decentralized network with out-of-order arrival in C when A and B start transmitting stopwatch times simultaneously to C, with a delay over the connection A-C. In addition, the ontologies of A and C differ from B's.

To solve the above elaborated three challenges, my Ph.D. research will mainly focus on theoretic, logic-based aspects of reasoning on streaming data in an environment of decentralized data storage – in short decentralized stream reasoning[1]. I will thereby aim to (i) design a logic framework that will serve as a formal basis for a high-level declarative language for decentralized SR, (ii) provide a set of algorithms to tackle challenges in stream processing specific to the decentralized setting, (iii) provide proofs of the theoretical properties of proposed framework and algorithms, and (iv) explore incremental and caching approaches for real-time continuous schema alignment. With the proper expressivity and techniques at their disposal, developers are equipped to maximally leverage the potential of the decentralized Web. The abstract nature of the research aims to provide a theoretic fundament upon which virtually any application domain can function.

2   State of the Art

Based on the identified challenges, three areas of related research are elaborated.

2.1   Formalism for Decentralized Stream Reasoning

Multiple research domains have developed methods for handling streaming data. The ambition of an abstract basis for reasoning, and in particular SR, has been pursued in multiple directions. DLs have been extended to accommodate for SR, resulting in Linear Temporal Logic (LTL), Metric Temporal Logic (MTL) and others, at times grouped under the term Temporal Description Logics (TDL) [12]. The temporal expressivity for each of these TDLs differs due to different choices in semantics. Recent advancements aim to further extend the expressivity. In the work of Gutiérrez-Basulto et al. [12], aspects of LTL and MTL are taken to provide a layer of abstraction that merges qualitative constraints (e.g. event A happens before/after event B) and an explicit quantification of time to obtain a more potent logic for temporal reasoning. Temporal Logics have also been incorporated in rule languages, for example DatalogMTL [30] adds temporal operators from MTL into Datalog, enabling DatalogMTL to address challenges that require temporal reasoning, while taking advantage of the recursive properties of Datalog. A lack of formalisation of languages for SR has been pointed out by Beck et al. [5]. With LARS, these authors propose a model-based semantics that is closely linked with the theory of Answer Set Programming (ASP) [5]. The Semantic Web query language SPARQL has been extended in the form of C-SPARQL and CQELS [4,17]. Both of these extensions introduce windowing mechanisms to SPARQL. Via LARS, these window mechanisms are given a formal basis. A formal basis allows us to analyse theoretical properties, such as model checking and satisfiability. LARS programs can also be seen as a generalization of answer set programs [5]. The close link between LARS and ASP

---

[1] 'decentralized' refers to the manner in which data is stored. No preliminary assumptions are made regarding the execution of the reasoning itself.

semantics allows for cross-analysis and comparison between the two frameworks. Eiter et al. [11] adapted the LARS framework to suit networks with distributed decision-making components. The networks with distributed reasoning considered by Eiter et al. [11] share similarities to the networks of decentralized data storage considered in Sect. 1. The methods for stratification of the reasoning process can serve as inspiration for similar processing methods in the decentralized storage network.

2.2 Decentralized Time Semantics

As mentioned in Sect. 1, out-of-order arrival of data raises questions on timing of processing, especially when delay times are variable across streams and hard to predict. Results can be invalidated by arrival of 'late' data or may require incremental updates. Akidau et al. [1] provide a layer of abstraction for streaming and batch data as part of the Dataflow model. Analogously, Apache Flink merges batch processing, continuous streams and real-time analytics under a single stream processing model [6]. The Open Data Fabric, introduced in Mikhtoniuk and Yalcin [20] makes explicit use of Apache Flink to demonstrate its potential as decentralized exchange protocol for structured data. Both Dataflow and Apache Flink rely on watermarks to monitor divergence of event time and processing time and to (re)introduce order in case of out-of-order arrival. The added complexity of using watermarks is minimal in settings with limited distributed computing and homogeneous delays on data arrival. Watermarks, however, are used in conjunction with windowing [2]. The use of windowing, however, prevents continuous semantics. Current SR languages do not yet offer solutions that are able to preserve continuous semantics [26]. Lastly, LDQL provides semantics that allow link traversal in a Web of Linked Data for querying [13]. Semantics of link patterns allow for evaluation of data distributed over multiple documents. It is therefore suited to capture knowledge distributed over data vaults.

Internet of Things (IoT) systems face similar problems as systems on a decentralized Semantic Web. The issue of timing alignment noted in Marinier et al. [19] and Tu et al. [27] shows a resemblance to the out-of-order processing problem we aim to address. From the perspective of a processing agent, disparity in data generation rate of the various IoT sources and network heterogeneity on the decentralized Semantic Web induce similar patterns of out-of-order data. The decentralized Semantic Web, however, requires peer-to-peer communication, compared to IoT systems where there is often one 'authoritative' processing agent (or multiple). This authoritative figure can impose some uniformity, whereas in decentralized environment no such figure exists. This lack of a single authority has implications for the ways in which problems, such as alignment, can be solved. Nonetheless, research in the field of IoT that addresses timing alignment may serve as a starting point for solutions in a decentralized SR contexts. Our interest goes out to the ISDI architecture proposed by Tu et al. [27], as it addresses both out-of-order data as well as data integration from multiple sources, akin to our problem of real-time schema alignment.

2.3 Time-Oriented Schema Alignment

In order to express temporal information, either in absolute terms or in relative to other pieces of information, existing ontologies have seen temporal extensions [21,32] and newly developed ontologies have incorporated temporal aspects directly [18]. Specifically for OWL, Abir et al. [32]introduces methodology for creating and updating ontology as well as ontology instances. Furthermore, Krieg-Brückner et al. [16] details how Generic Ontology Design Patterns (GODPs) can be employed to introduce time into previously atemporal ontologies. Work on schema alignment specifically geared towards time and temporal concepts were not discovered during exploratory research. Alternatively, recent survey works on ontology alignment, such as Ardjani et al. [3], may serve as a starting point for the development of tailored alignment techniques.

3 Problem Statement

The current state-of-the-art on SR focuses mainly on centralized systems. The overall objective of my research is to provide a formal basis for SR in decentralized systems. The research questions below each aim to support different aspects of this decentralized SR.

RQ-I **Declarative language for stream reasoning in a decentralized environment.** Decentralized data storage complicates tasks of data retrieval and processing that befall query engines and reasoning agents. Our attention goes out to three factors; (a) variation in data due to different schemas, (b) heterogeneity between vaults in data generation speed and (c) cross-storage referencing of information. Starting from logic languages and frameworks underpinning existing declarative languages, can the ones addressing these factors separately be combined into a single logic language that address all three factors, satisfying challenge (B) considered above? Can a declarative language be constructed that is sufficiently high-level, to hide system complexity and process details from the end-user? Lastly, can the semantics be formalized to ensure a uniform interpretation of the language in case of a multi-agent network?

RQ-II **Decentralized time semantics and out-of-order processing.** Given challenge (C) of processing streaming data in a decentralized environment, what heuristics can be *constructed* in order to process data that arrives out-of-order? How can results be updated when data arrives 'late', or how do previous results need to be invalidated?

RQ-III **Formal proof of the functionality of language and algorithms designed.** Is the language for decentralised time semantics sound and complete? If not, do there exist fragments of the language that meet these criteria? Can the correctness of the algorithm(s) be guaranteed? What are the theoretical time and memory complexities of the algorithms? In contrast to the other RQ's, RQ-III does not address a specific challenge stated in Sect. 1, but rather serves to verify the validity of the answers to RQ-I and RQ-II, thus implicitly supporting challenges (B) and (C).

RQ-IV **Time-oriented schema alignment.** As data providers are free to choose in what schema their data is stored, a reasoning process over a decentralized network of data providers is inevitably confronted with different semantics and representations of time. In the interest of the time-oriented schema alignment of challenge (A), how can different time schemas be aligned in real-time fashion, with minimal delay towards network users? Can the most common schemas on the Web be aligned to allow for reasoning on all available data? If a temporal logic framework can serve as a layer of abstraction over different schemas, how do different schemas then map to said abstraction layer?

4   Research Methodology

To ensure our envisioned new formalism builds upon the existing research, I aim to analyze the existing work on formalisms for SR, as elaborated in Sect. 2, via the format of a survey paper. This survey paper should provide insight into the expressivity of current formalisms, as well as missing links with respect to their usability in a decentralized environment.

The research done in the context of this survey paper aims to serve as a gateway towards tackling the challenge of RQ-I. The construction of the new framework is divided in multiple components. First, a fitting selection of temporal semantics must be assessed. Point-based, interval-based, answer set and other semantics each have distinct properties, degrees of complexity and influence data on a different level. The choice of temporal operators within those semantics also strongly influences the kind of temporal relations that can be expressed. The first task thus encompasses selection of semantics that meets the expressivity needs covered in RQ-I. Second, the formalism needs to capture chosen semantics in the appropriate mathematical structures, i.e. terms, formulae, models etc. Lastly, entailment regimes for resulting formulae need to be defined intuitively yet unambiguously. In these three components, a high degree of mathematical rigor is crucial. It serves to formally document semantics, as to allow interoperability between agents, and to enable the proofs pledged by RQ-III.

Regarding the design of algorithms for out-of-order processing and decentralized time semantics (RQ-II), the primary focus goes out to the development of heuristics. Due to the high volatility of the data and their high degree of unpredictability, rapid approximations made by heuristics are preferable from a practical perspective. The algorithms should make optimal use of the semantics defined through RQ-I. By exploiting the increased expressivity, the algorithms should aim to strike a balance between the accuracy of the answer and the computational power it requires. As the increased volatility and the data distribution encumber the direct application of watermarks, an adaption or generalization of watermarking offer an opportunity for novel out-of-order processing techniques. The design of the algorithms is performed in alternating fashion with the correctness proofs of RQ-III, in a 'check-and-improve' iterative fashion.

On RQ-III, existing results on soundness and completeness of languages are leveraged maximally in order to prove the sound- and completeness of the decentralized time semantics given by RQ-I. This includes the direct application of existing theoretical results, the translation of (fragments of) the new language into a language with documented results and the recuperation of proof methodology. An analogous methodology will be applied for the proofs regarding the algorithms considered in RQ-II. In cases where no existing results on soundness and completeness can be leveraged, conventional methods in the analysis of correctness and complexity will be enlisted. The ultimate approach for RQ-III is evidently heavily reliant on the outcomes of RQ-I and RQ-II.

As schema alignment is a broad research topic, we aim to limit the topic of schema alignment in this thesis to alignment of temporal concepts. We aim to identify possible areas of conflict, e.g. discrete vs. continuous time and interval- vs. point-based semantics, and aim to utilize the framework from RQ-I to construct mappings between the various semantics. By using said framework as a 'turntable' between semantics, discrepancies in expressivity can be exposed and investigated.

5   Evaluation Plan

The results of this research will primarily be evaluated through the analysis of theoretical properties. In essence, the evaluation of RQ-I and RQ-II is in part incorporated in the RQ-III. The proofs on soundness and completeness of the proposed framework (RQ-I) aim to support the suitability of the framework and to verify the quality. In order to assess usability of the framework – or fragments thereof –, we will determine the decidability (or undecidability) of the system.

Analogously for the proofs concerning the algorithms of RQ-II, the (partial) correctness assesses their usability. The time and memory complexities of the algorithms serve as metrics to gauge their competitiveness w.r.t. existing algorithms for centralized systems as well as their applicability in real-life use cases. In addition to these theoretical results, the algorithms will be implemented as part of larger use cases in an e-health context, using the datasets and ontologies provided by the DAHCC project [24].

The techniques for real-time schema alignment will be evaluated in terms of data processing time and required computational power. Possible benchmarks to consider include those adopted by the Ontology Alignment Evaluation Initiative [31], in which case the exact benchmark will be identified among those available at the time of evaluation, taking into account the relative niche of the application domain (streaming data in Linked Data networks with decentralized data storage) Geared toward the SOLID environment, the SolidBench [25] benchmark simulates a social network environment in which we can evaluate the schema alignment techniques. The suitability of each of the benchmarks above will need to to be investigated further.

6   Preliminary Results

I commenced the research of my Ph.D. on decentralized stream reasoning in September 2022. The results thus far are hence limited. They can be divided into two main areas. On the one hand, preparatory work on the survey paper has led to a temporary selection of 13 papers between the years 2018 and 2022 that fall within our scope of SR formalisms. As the field of SR is relatively young [22], inclusion of sources from the domains of ASP and IoT is taken into consideration. Among the sources gathered to date, there are none who address the topic of decentralized data storage explicitly. Expectation is to progress towards publication in a fitting peer-reviewed journal by the end of 2023.

On the other hand, some exploratory work has focused on evaluation of temporal operators. I have obtained first results on defining relations between various temporal logic operators currently in use in the literature. These results focus on rewriting operators expressing statements such as '... happened (at least) once before', '... will always be true in the future' ($\diamondsuit$ and $\boxplus$ resp.) and others in function of each other without reliance on a negation operator. As a result, this work aims to provide a minimal set of temporal operators that retains temporal expressivity in negation-less logic frameworks (or fragments thereof) compared to frameworks with negation. These negation-less frameworks can be used to model languages such as RDF and Datalog, which have only limited support for negation (e.g. stratification). The results also streamline new proofs as they only need to cover a smaller set of operators. This scopes within RQ-I as a means of exploratory research, as well as within RQ-III as provision of potential auxiliary lemmas for the intended proofs. These results are currently being bundled for submission to the Conference on Principles of Knowledge Representation and Reasoning [23].

7   Conclusions

In the above, I outlined the research plan for my Ph.D. where I aim to provide a formal basis for SR in a Semantic Web environment with decentralized data storage. Via the four research questions, I identified specific challenges within the environment and delimited the manner in which this thesis aims to address these challenges. The state-of-the-art presented in Sect. 2 covers relevant research, listing work from within the fields of Semantic Web and stream reasoning as well as several works, taken from other research fields, that address similar challenges.

As this thesis focuses heavily on the theoretical aspects, future work will be on the implementation and empirical evaluation of the outcome of this research. This also includes enlisting the theory in more use cases, preferably covering a wide variety of application domains.

Acknowledgements. This research is funded by the FWO Project FRACTION (Nr. G086822N). I thank my supervisors Pieter Bonte (UGent) and Femke Ongenae (UGent) for the feedback and comments on the paper. I thank Maarten Vandenbrande (UGent) for the shared discussions.

References

1. Akidau, T., et al.: The dataflow model: a practical approach to balancing correctness, latency, and cost in massive-scale, unbounded, out-of-order data processing. Proc. VLDB Endow. **8**(12), 1792–1803 (2015)
2. Akidau, T., et al.: Streaming Systems: The What, Where, When, and How of Large-Scale Data Processing. O'Reilly Media, Inc. (2018)
3. Ardjani, F., et al.: Ontology-alignment techniques: survey and analysis. Int. J. Mod. Educ. Comput. Sci. **7**(11), 67 (2015)
4. Barbieri, D., et al.: C-SPARQL: a continuous query language for RDF data streams. Int. J. Semant. Comput. **4**, 3–25 (2010)
5. Beck, H., et al.: LARS: a logic-based framework for analytic reasoning over streams. Artif. Intell. **261**, 16–70 (2018)
6. Carbone, P., et al.: Apache Flink^{TM}: stream and batch processing in a single engine. Bull. Tech. Committee Data Eng. **38**(4), 28–38 (2015)
7. Cellan-Jones, R.: NHS data: can web creator Sir Tim Berners-Lee fix it? BBC News (2020). https://www.bbc.com/news/technology-54871705
8. Della Valle, E., et al.: It's a streaming world! reasoning upon rapidly changing information. IEEE Intell. Syst. **24**(6), 83–89 (2009)
9. Dell'Aglio, D., et al.: Stream reasoning: a survey and outlook. Data Sci. **1**(1–2), 59–83 (2017)
10. Digitaal Vlaanderen: Solid ecosysteem (2020). https://overheid.vlaanderen.be/informatie-vlaanderen/ontdek-onze-producten-en-diensten/solid-ecosysteem
11. Eiter, T., et al.: A distributed approach to LARS stream reasoning (system paper). Theory Pract. Logic Program. **19**, 974–989 (2019)
12. Gutierrez-Basulto, V., et al.: On metric temporal description logics. In: ECAI 2016: 22nd European Conference on Artificial Intelligence, vol. 285, pp. 837–845. IOS Press (2016)
13. Hartig, O., Pérez, J.: LDQL: a query language for the web of linked data. J. Web Semant. **41**, 9–29 (2016)
14. Hirzel, M., et al.: Stream processing languages in the big data era. ACM SIGMOD Rec. **47**(2), 29–40 (2018)
15. IDC: IDC Futurescape outlines the impact "digital supremacy" will have on enterprise transformation and the IT industry (2019). https://www.idc.com/getdoc.jsp?containerId=prUS45613519
16. Krieg-Brückner, B., et al.: Generic ontology design patterns: roles and change over time. arXiv preprint arXiv:2011.09353 (2020)
17. Le-Phuoc, D., Dao-Tran, M., Xavier Parreira, J., Hauswirth, M.: A native and adaptive approach for unified processing of linked streams and linked data. In: Aroyo, L., et al. (eds.) ISWC 2011, Part I. LNCS, vol. 7031, pp. 370–388. Springer, Heidelberg (2011). https://doi.org/10.1007/978-3-642-25073-6_24
18. Madkour, M., et al.: Temporal data representation, normalization, extraction, and reasoning: a review from clinical domain. Comput. Methods Programs Biomed. **128**, 52–68 (2016)
19. Marinier, P., et al.: Maintaining time alignment with multiple uplink carriers (2015). US Patent 8,934,459
20. Mikhtoniuk, S., Yalcin, O.N.: Open data fabric: a decentralized data exchange and transformation protocol with complete reproducibility and provenance. arXiv e-prints pp. arXiv-2111 (2021)

21. Milea, V., et al.: tOWL: a temporal web ontology language. IEEE Trans. Syst. Man Cybern. Part B **42**(1), 268–281 (2011)
22. Pacenza, F.: Reasoning in highly reactive environments. arXiv e-prints arXiv:1909.08260 (Sep 2019)
23. Principles of Knowledge Representation and Reasoning Inc: KR2023 - KR Conference (2023). https://kr.org/KR2023/
24. Steenwinckel, B., et al.: Data analytics for health and connected care: ontology, knowledge graph and applications. In: Tsanas, A., Triantafyllidis, A. (eds) PH 2022. LNICST, vol. 488, pp. 344–360. Springer, Cham (2022). https://doi.org/10.1007/978-3-031-34586-9_23, https://dahcc.idlab.ugent.be
25. Taelman, R.: Solidbench (2023). https://github.com/SolidBench/SolidBench.js
26. Tommasini, R., Sakr, S., Balduini, M., Della Valle, E.: Tutorial: an outlook to declarative languages for big steaming data (2019)
27. Tu, D.Q., et al.: IoT streaming data integration from multiple sources. Computing **102**(10), 2299–2329 (2020)
28. Verborgh, R.: Re-decentralizing the Web, for good this time. In: Linking the World's Information: A Collection of Essays on the Work of Sir Tim Berners-Lee. ACM (2022). https://ruben.verborgh.org/articles/redecentralizing-the-web/
29. W3C Solid Community Group of the W3C: Solid technical reports (2020). https://solidproject.org/TR/
30. Wałęga, P.A., et al.: Reasoning over streaming data in metric temporal datalog. In: Proceedings of the AAAI Conference on Artificial Intelligence, vol. 33, no. 1, pp. 3092–3099 (2019)
31. Zamazal, O.: A survey of ontology benchmarks for semantic web ontology tools. Int. J. Semant. Web Inf. Syst. **16**(1), 47–68 (2020)
32. Zekri, A., et al.: τOWL: a systematic approach to temporal versioning of semantic web ontologies. J. Data Semant. **5**(3), 141–163 (2016)

A Distributed and Parallel Processing Framework for Knowledge Graph OLAP

Bashar Ahmad$^{(\boxtimes)}$ (iD)

Johannes Kepler University Linz, Altenberger Str. 69, 4040 Linz, Austria
ahmad@dke.uni-linz.ac.at

Abstract. Business intelligence and analytics refers to the ensemble of tools and techniques that allow organizations to obtain insights from big data for better decision making. Knowledge graphs are increasingly being established as a central data hub and prime source for BI and analytics. In the context of BI and analytics, KGs may be used for various analytical tasks; the integration of data and metadata in a KG potentially facilitates interpretation of analysis results. Knowledge Graph OLAP (KG-OLAP) adapts the concept of online analytical processing (OLAP) from multidimensional data analysis for the processing of KGs for analytical purposes. The current KG-OLAP implementation is a monolithic system, which greatly inhibits scalability. We propose a research plan for the development of a framework for distributed and parallel data processing for KG-OLAP over big data. In particular, we propose a framework for KG-OLAP over big data based on the data lakehouse architecture, which leverages existing frameworks for parallel and distributed data processing. We are currently at an early stage of our research.

Keywords: business intelligence · analytics · big data · online analytical processing

1 Introduction

Business intelligence (BI) and analytics refers to the ensemble of tools and techniques that allow organizations to obtain insights from *big data* for better decision making. Big Data, in turn, refers to large and complex datasets that cannot be directly processed using monolithic (traditional) data processing systems [20]. The main characteristics of big data are referred to as the *five Vs* [20]: volume, velocity, variety, variability, and value. Volume refers the large amount of data being created. Velocity refers to how fast new data is being generated. Variety refers to the different formats of the generated data. Variability indicates that data may be interpreted differently depending on the source. Finally, value refers to the capability of turning the data into real value. Among those, volume, velocity, and variety are arguably the central characteristics, which are also referred to as the *three Vs* of big data [16].

The concept of *knowledge graph* (KG), with its origins in knowledge representation and reasoning, is increasingly being established as a central data

C. Pesquita et al. (Eds.): ESWC 2023, LNCS 13998, pp. 288–297, 2023.
https://doi.org/10.1007/978-3-031-43458-7_47

hub and a prime source for BI and analytics. A KG organizes knowledge about real-world entities, including their relationships, using a flexible, graph-based representation [11,13]. A KG is often constructed from a wide variety of potentially large-scale sources [11,13]. A KG typically comprises both terminological (ontological) and assertional (instance) knowledge. In other terms, a KG stores data and metadata in an integrated fashion. In the context of BI and analytics, KGs may be used for various analytical tasks, including link prediction, symbolic learning [11] and machine learning [28]; the integration of data and metadata in a KG potentially facilitates interpretation of analysis results.

Knowledge Graph OLAP (KG-OLAP) adapts the concept of *online analytical processing* (OLAP) from multidimensional data analysis for the processing of KGs for analytical purposes [24]. KG-OLAP organizes KGs into different, hierarchically structured contexts—the KG-OLAP cube. Each cell of the cube constitutes a context for KG statements. KG-OLAP then allows for two types of operations: contextual and graph operations. The current KG-OLAP implementation is a monolithic system, which greatly inhibits scalability: As the KG grows the system will start suffering from performance issues.

In this paper, we propose a research plan for the development of a framework for distributed and parallel data processing for KG-OLAP over big data. Such a framework must be able to ingest large volumes of data arriving at high velocity from a variety of sources. The framework must further allow for the extraction of KGs from the ingested data and the efficient use of the extracted KGs for analytical purposes. In particular, we propose a framework for KG-OLAP over big data based on the *data lakehouse* architecture [3], which leverages existing frameworks for parallel and distributed data processing, e.g., Apache Spark and Apache Kafka.

We are currently at an *early stage* of our research. We have surveyed the relevant state of the art and identified the main research objectives. We have obtained preliminary results regarding the design and implementation of a data lakehouse for KG-OLAP, which supports ingestion of large volumes of a variety of source data arriving at high velocity. More research needs to be done regarding efficient use of KGs extracted from the ingested data.

The remainder of this paper is organized as follows. In Sect. 2 we review the state of the art. In Sect. 3 we state the problem to be solved and describe the contributions of our research. In Sect. 4 we present the research methodology and approach. In Sect. 5 we discuss evaluation of our research. In Sect. 6 we present preliminary results. We conclude the paper with Sect. 7.

2   State of the Art

KGs are a form of structured representation of real-world knowledge and facts. A KG consists of entities (real-world objects), relationships between entities, and semantic descriptions of entities and relationships [11,13]. A KG is frequently presented as factual triple using RDF (Resource Description Framework) but it can also be represented as directed graphs with nodes as entities and edges as relations [13]. Some modern graph database system uses Labeled Property Graphs (LGP) to represent graphs [11], a graph property is a "directed multi-graphs where the nodes and edges may be associated with a set of key-value pairs properties" [10]. Knowledge-aware models benefit from Knowledge Graphs representation characteristics such as the integration of heterogeneous information, rich ontologies, and semantics. Many real-world applications, such as Google's knowledge Graph, took advantage of Knowledge Graphs and have shown a strong capacity to provide efficient services [13]. Several fields of research have emerge on the topic of KG, including Knowledge Representation Learning, Knowledge Acquisition, Temporal Knowledge Graphs, and Knowledge-Aware Applications [13]. KG analytics refers to application of analytics algorithm to KG in order to gain insights and discover connections, several type of analytics can be applied, for instance centrality analysis, community analysis, graph summarization, and etc. [11]. Big Knowledge (BK) refers to massive sets of knowledge, the most important properties of BK (referred to as 5 MC) are: Massive knowledge elements (MC1), massive well-connectedness between knowledge elements (MC2), massive clean data resources (MC3), massive cases (MC4), and massive confidence (MC5) [18]. According to Lu et al. [17], any BK that has at least 100 000 concepts, 10 million entities, and millions to billions of facts, with at least a 90% precision, is considered a BKG.

OLAP refers to the mining or extracting of information or knowledge from a large amount of data and it can work on any kind of data [29]. In OLAP, a multidimensional data set is the unit of data consisting of dimensions and measures of a certain members [29]. Contextualized KG refers to a KG in which the entities are enriched with context metadata such as time and location [24]. The multidimensional hierarchical nature of context offers significant similarities of the multidimensional model of OLAP.

SANSA is a scalable semantic analytics stack used to process large scale RDF data and provide a unified framework for KG based application [12]. The Databricks Lakehouse Platform provides an online platform for data engineering using elements of data warehouses such as governance and performance [5]. Stardog is an enterprise knowledge graph platform that can model complex relationships against data that is wide and big and perform graphs operations [26]. Heaven Ape (or HAPE) is a programmable big knowledge graph platform to support the creation, management, and operation of large to massive scale knowledge graphs. [17]. Kona et al. [15] describe a method to use KG to add a semantic data layer for Databricks using Databricks Data Lakehouse platform [5] and Stardog [26]. The Lakehouse platform offers a multi-cloud platform for data analytics artificial intelligence and the Stardog platform offers knowledge graph capabilities to model complex relationships against large dataset. The resulted hybrid is a system which has the data warehouse/lakehouse analytics capabilities and knowledge graph representation capabilities for reasoning and complex analytics. Gassauer-Fleissner et al. [9] refer to another use case, where Amazon EKS and Graph database are used to create a knowledge graph based system to analyze big data for financial crime discovery. Trinity [25] is a distributed graph engine built on top of distributed memory storage (memory cloud). Trinity aim to perform online and offline queries efficiently by addressing random data access issue using cloud based memory infrastructure. The article shows that using distributed infrastructure technologies, trinity is able to serve variety of queries efficiently and in reasonable time.

Recently, we have seen many advancements in the fields of cloud computing. Microservice is defined to be an independently deployed architectural components that are used for the development of distributed applications, they are small in size as they implement a single responsibility [7]. Containerization enables running applications isolated with their dependencies in their own containers [21]. Containers are more lightweight and faster than virtual machines (VM) because containers provide virtualization at the operating system level instead of fully virtualizing the physical server. Kubernetes is an orchestration platform for deploying containerized large software. Docker and Kubernetes complement each other. Docker is responsible for lower-level tasks, where Kubernetes responsible for higher-level tasks [22].

3   Problem Statement and Contributions

In general, the proposed research will investigate the use of KGs as the basis for BI and analytics. Effective BI and analytics must be able to efficiently handle large volumes of a variety of data arriving at high velocity—the key characteristics (3 Vs) of *big data*. Therefore, employing KGs for analytical purposes requires a corresponding processing framework that must be able to handle big data as the source for the KGs. We identify the following requirements for a processing framework that leverages KGs for BI and analytics.

1. The framework shall be able to ingest large amounts of a wide variety of source data arriving at high velocity.
2. The framework shall allow for the extraction of KGs from the ingested source data.
3. The framework shall be able to efficiently process the extracted KGs for analytical purposes.

KG-OLAP [24] provides a conceptual fundamental for leveraging KGs for BI and analytics, comprising a multidimensional data model and query operations for working with KGs, but the existing monolithic, SPARQL-based implementation of KG-OLAP cannot cope with big data. The monolithic KG-OLAP implementation is limited regarding how large the dataset can grow for the system to be still able to answer queries with reasonable response time. The monolithic KG-OLAP implementation could be scaled vertically to some extent, by adding more memory and processing capacity to the server, which is expensive and inefficient. Regarding horizontal scaling, while independent instances of the monolithic KG-OLAP implementation could run on separate server nodes, with each instance handling a KG of a certain size, such replication of a monolithic architecture would require appropriate coordination.

3.1 Hypotheses

Based on the previous observations, we can formulate the following hypotheses.

- **H1**. The concepts of distributed and parallel processing, recent advancements in cloud-native technologies, and microservice architecture will allow for the development of a scalable end-to-end framework for managing big KGs for analytical purposes.
- **H2**. Traditional data warehouse architectures are too rigid for handling big KGs. The data lakehouse may be a suitable architecture for BI and analytics over big KGs, providing flexibility, support for larger datasets, and advanced analytical capabilities, coupled with the data governance features of a data warehouse.
- **H3**. Many analytical tasks require only a subset of the available data or require the data in aggregate form, so it would be redundant to load a single big KG for every analytical tasks. On-demand extraction of KGs based on a subset of the data or aggregating the available data which is much smaller the entire KG, and faster to process and analyze.

3.2 Research Questions

The main research question is, given the main three characteristics of Big data, volume, variety and velocity, how to use KG for BI and analytics over Big data? The hypotheses can be broken down into the following research questions, which we will address in our research.

- **RQ1**. How can we use concepts of distributed and parallel processing to achieve high rates for data ingestion to cope with the characteristics of big data?
- **RQ2**. How can we use concepts of distributed and parallel processing to efficiently extract KGs from the ingested data?
- **RQ3**. How can we efficiently use the extracted KGs for BI and analytics?
- **RQ4**. Is it possible to adapt the concepts of data warehouse and data lakehouse to design and implement a big KG management system that can handle large KGs for analytical purposes?

We propose a distributed and parallel processing framework for KG-OLAP that overcomes the limitations of a monolithic implementation. We will completely redesign the KG-OLAP implementation to support distributed and scalable computation technologies. We will introduce the concept of a virtual KG to allow for flexible distribution of the KG on multiple nodes. In this context, a virtual KG is a single, large KG that exists at the logical level but only parts of which are materialized on different nodes. Those partial KGs are generated on demand, with structure and contents depending on the analytics task at hand.

4 Research Methodology and Approach

The first step, is to redesign the architecture of the KG-OLAP monolithic implementation to allow for distributed and parallel processing. From the problem definition, we identified two functions, data ingestion and querying. In original implementation, the data are being fed directly to a graph database after batch processing the data to include the desired contextual information. Queries are written in SPARQL in the form of OLAP-style operations [24]. The whole system is running as one unit. In the proposed new architecture, we extract each functionality (data ingestion and querying) as their own domains and defined the communication input/output of the system so each component can run independently.

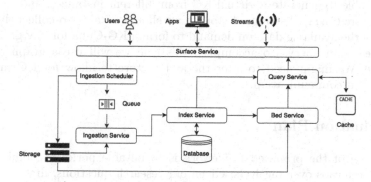

Fig. 1. Proposed data lakehouse architecture for KG-OLAP.

Figure 1 shows the proposed architecture for the framework. The system provides one external contact point to the framework by implementing a REST API interface—the *surface*. Depending on the API being called, either data ingestion or querying, the path of execution is selected. In case of data ingestion, the uploaded data are stored using the distributed storage system, then the request is passed to the *ingestion scheduler*, based on the content of data ingestion request a task will be created and pushed to the *queue*, eventually an *ingestion instance* will pick up the task, the *ingestion instance* will analyze the uploaded data, and create an index using the *index service*. At this point the framework is aware of the ingested data and all information regarding its context (dimensionality) has been indexed by the system.

In case of query, the REST API will forward the query request to the *query service* where the query is parsed and all the contexts and aggregations required to build a KG-OLAP cube are determined. The framework allows to cache previously fetched contexts for performance optimization, if a context does not exist in the cache or if it is expired the *query service* will request the *bed service* to fetch it, using the *index service*, the *bed service* will determine the location of the data to build certain contexts and fetch them from the storage. Finally, aggregation is applied (according to the query) and the resulted KG-OLAP cube is sent back to the user via the *surface service*. It should be noted that much of the proposed architecture has already been implemented (REST interface, ingestion scheduler, storage service, ingestion service, and index service). Since we are using a microservice architecture we were able to deploy and test the finished services using Docker and Kubernetes. This approach gave us the advantage of being able to verify that we are accomplishing our goals as we move along.

The next step is to define a mechanism for multiple instances of the framework to communicate and be able to discover and form *virtual KGs*. In each instance, the index service provides a repository of dataset metadata, which we use to form KG-OLAP cubes on demand. We also employ the metadata to form a meta KG of the existing dataset, Using methods of context matching [27] we should be able to generate a virtual KG from different instances, and since the data are stored using distributed storage we should be able to collect different portions of the available data on demand to form a KG-Cube for any given task as specified by a query. To accomplish this goal we will use a graph reasoning engine. We might need to alter the architecture to allow for KG instance discovery and communication.

5   Evaluation Plan

The purpose of the proposed framework is to be able perform complex data analytics scenarios over big KGs. Given our research questions, first we intend to validate that the framework is able ingest a vast amounts of data as quickly and efficiently as possible (RQ1), second we want to verify that framework is able to scale as ingestion loads increases (RQ2), finally, we would like evaluate the framework ability to answer BI and analytics query efficiently and in reasonable time (RQ3 and RQ4). For the purpose of our evaluation we will focus on the original three Vs of big data: volume, velocity, and variety [16]. Although there have been multiple variants of Vs introduced in the literature and industry [20], the three Vs are arguably the essential characteristics for any dataset to be categorized as big data. The are other Vs (for example veracity and value) are very significant and they have a great impact when performing analytics tasks, however, for our immediate research goal and since at the moment we are using generated data. In the future, and once we acquire real data we will definitely consider the other Vs in our evaluation.

We plan to evaluate the system using realistic datasets for real-world use cases involving large amounts of data. At the current stage, we focus on a use case from air traffic management (ATM) [24], with synthetic sample data following the Aeronautical Information Exchange Model (AIXM) [2]. We employ a tool for the generation of AIXM sample data [1]. We currently only use XML data but we plan to extend support to other data formats to satisfy the *variety* characteristic of big data. We also want to evaluate the system on use cases in the manufacturing domain—we are currently exchanging ideas with a large manufacturing company (Welser Profile) from Lower Austria, who intend to base their analytics endeavours on KGs.

For evaluation purposes, we have designed and implemented a client application that feeds large amounts of AIXM data to the system though the REST interface, which allows to evaluate data ingestion capabilities and show that the framework can cope with high velocity data arrival. Evaluation will consist of taking measurements of how fast the framework ingests the arriving data and the amount of data ingested per second under different scaling configurations to show how the framework reacts to different loads. Other system metrics such as CPU usage, memory usage, disk I/O, and network I/O will also be relevant.

Having ingested a sufficiently large amount of data, the second step would be to design queries to evaluate the framework capabilities of creating various kinds of KGs on demand to address different analytical tasks, for the purpose of the evaluation we will take the following factors into consideration when designing the queries, size of the resulted KG, and complexity of the query. We intend to show that the framework can extract KGs of different sizes in a reasonable amount of time, and demonstrate contextual and graph operation of the queries. We will also verify the queries performance under various data loads. Finally, we intend to demonstrate the concept of virtual KG by querying KGs consisting of data from multiple instances.

6   Preliminary Results

We are at early stages of the implementation, only few parts of the envisioned system are implemented. In this section, we present the preliminary results of the current implementation. To evaluate the system we constructed a Kubernetes cluster consisting of nine nodes using the K3S Kubernetes distribution [14]. Each node is a virtual machine that has eight cores, 16 GiB RAM, and 50 GiB disk space. For the index service we set up a Cassandra cluster [4] consisting of three nodes. For file ingestion we set up an ElasticMQ [8] cluster with one node. All services are implemented using Python [23] and deployed as Docker [6] containers. For distributed storage we set up a MinIO server—a distributed storage system similar to Amazon S3 buckets [19]. For the presented evaluation we used an AIXM dataset containing information corresponding to 82 125 contexts and 1 943 625 statements. We used three different scaling configurations consisting of two, four, and eight instances, respectively, and for every configuration we ran the experiment three times.

We notice from the result of our experiments (Fig. 2) that as we scale up the number of instances, the amount of data ingested per second increased: 10 MBit/s for two nodes, 20 MBit/s for four nodes, and 35 MBit/s for eight nodes. We also notice a decrease in time required to ingest the whole dataset. These results demonstrate that the system design exhibits the desired behavior that as we scale up, the system is able to process more ingestion requests simultaneously.

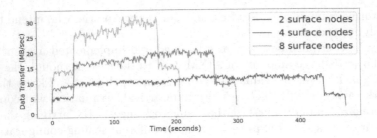

Fig. 2. Data ingestion rate

7   Conclusions

In this paper we proposed a research plan for the development of a distributed and parallel processing framework for Knowledge Graph OLAP that is able to cope with big data. The proposed framework will allow to perform data analytics over big data, with knowledge graphs as the central repository. In particular, the proposed framework will apply the data lakehouse architecture to knowledge graph analytics. In this paper we reviewed the state of the art and related work, identified the problem, described the proposed solution, proposed an evaluation plan, and described preliminary results.

Acknowledgements. The author thanks his advisor Dr. Christoph Schuetz for the suggestions and feedback.

References

1. Ahmad, B.: Aixm Generator (2023). https://github.com/basharah/aixm-gen
2. AIXM: Aeronautical Information Exchange Model (2019). https://www.aixm.aero
3. Armbrust, M., Zaharia, M., Ghodsi, A., Xin, R.: Lakehouse: a new generation of open platforms that unify data warehousing and advanced analytics. In: 11th Conference on Innovative Data Systems Research (CIDR 2021) (2021). http://cidrdb.org/cidr2021/papers/cidr2021_paper17.pdf
4. Cassandra, A.: Cassandra. https://cassandra.apache.org. Accessed 01 Feb 2023
5. Databricks: The Databricks Lakehouse Platform. https://www.databricks.com/product/data-lakehouse. Accessed 14 Feb 2023
6. Docker: Docker. https://www.docker.com. Accessed 01 Feb 2023
7. Dragoni, N., Lanese, I., Larsen, S.T., Mazzara, M., Mustafin, R., Safina, L.: Microservices: how to make your application scale. In: Petrenko, A.K., Voronkov, A. (eds.) PSI 2017. LNCS, vol. 10742, pp. 95–104. Springer, Cham (2018). https://doi.org/10.1007/978-3-319-74313-4_8
8. ElasticMQ: Elasticmq. https://github.com/softwaremill/elasticmq. Accessed 01 Feb 2023
9. Gassauer-Fleissner, S., Shabat, Z.B.: Financial crime discovery using amazon EKS and graph databases. Tech. Rep. Amazon (2022). https://aws.amazon.com/blogs/architecture/financial-crime-discovery-using-amazon-eks-and-graph-databases/

10. Hartig, O.: Foundations to query labeled property graphs using sparql. In: SEM4TRA-AMAR@SEMANTiCS (2019)
11. Hogan, A., et al.: Knowledge graphs. ACM Comput. Surv. **54**(4) (2021). https://doi.org/10.1145/3447772
12. Janev, V., Graux, D., Jabeen, H., Sallinger, E.: Knowledge Graphs and Big Data Processing (2020). https://doi.org/10.1007/978-3-030-53199-7
13. Ji, S., Pan, S., Cambria, E., Marttinen, P., Philip, S.Y.: A survey on knowledge graphs: representation, acquisition, and applications. IEEE Trans. Neural Netw. Learn. Syst. **33**(2), 494–514 (2021)
14. K3s: K3s lightwight kubernetes. https://k3s.io/. Accessed 01 Feb 2023
15. Kona, P., Wallace, A.: Using a knowledge graph to power a semantic data layer for databricks. https://www.databricks.com/blog/2022/06/17/using-a-knowledge-graph-to-power-a-semantic-data-layer-for-databricks.html. Accessed 14 Feb 2023
16. Laney, D.: 3D data management: controlling data volume, velocity, and variety. Tech. rep., META Group (2001). http://blogs.gartner.com/doug-laney/files/2012/01/ad949-3D-Data-Management-Controlling-Data-Volume-Velocity-and-Variety.pdf
17. Lu, R., et al.: Hape: a programmable big knowledge graph platform. Inf. Sci. **509**, 87–103 (2020). https://doi.org/10.1016/j.ins.2019.08.051
18. Lu, R., Jin, X., Zhang, S., Qiu, M., Wu, X.: A study on big knowledge and its engineering issues. IEEE Trans. Knowl. Data Eng. **31**(9), 1630–1644 (2018)
19. MinIO: Minio - multi-cloud object storage. https://min.io/. Accessed 01 Feb 2023
20. Nguyen, T.L.: A framework for five big vs of big data and organizational culture in firms. In: 2018 IEEE International Conference on Big Data (Big Data), pp. 5411–5413 (2018). https://doi.org/10.1109/BigData.2018.8622377
21. Pahl, C., Brogi, A., Soldani, J., Jamshidi, P.: Cloud container technologies: a state-of-the-art review. IEEE Trans. Cloud Comput. **7**(3), 677–692 (2019)
22. Poulton, N., Joglekar, P.: The Kubernetes Book. Leanpub (2023)
23. Python: Python. https://www.python.org/. Accessed 01 Feb 2023
24. Schuetz, C.G., Bozzato, L., Neumayr, B., Schrefl, M., Serafini, L.: Knowledge graph OLAP: a multidimensional model and query operations for contextualized knowledge graphs. Semantic Web **12**(4), 649–683 (2021)
25. Shao, B., Wang, H., Li, Y.: Trinity: a distributed graph engine on a memory cloud, pp. 505–516 (2013). https://doi.org/10.1145/2463676.2467799
26. Stardog: Stardog - the enterprise knowldge graph platform. https://www.stardog.com/. Accessed 14 Feb 2023
27. Tasnim, M., Collarana, D., Graux, D., Vidal, M.-E.: Chapter 8 context-based entity matching for big data. In: Janev, V., Graux, D., Jabeen, H., Sallinger, E. (eds.) Knowledge Graphs and Big Data Processing. LNCS, vol. 12072, pp. 122–146. Springer, Cham (2020). https://doi.org/10.1007/978-3-030-53199-7_8
28. Tiddi, I., Schlobach, S.: Knowledge graphs as tools for explainable machine learning: a survey. Artif. Intell. **302**, 103627 (2022). https://doi.org/10.1016/j.artint.2021.103627
29. Zhenyuan, W., Haiyan, H.: Olap technology and its business application. In: 2010 Second WRI Global Congress on Intelligent Systems, vol. 2, pp. 92–95 (2010)

Ontology-Compliant Knowledge Graphs

Zhangcheng Qiang[✉][iD]

School of Computing, Australian National University, 108 North Road, Acton,
Canberra, ACT 2601, Australia
qzc438@gmail.com

Abstract. Ontologies can act as a schema for constructing knowledge
graphs (KGs), offering explainability, interoperability, and reusability.
We explore *ontology-compliant* KGs, aiming to build both internal and
external ontology compliance. We discuss key tasks in ontology compliance and introduce our novel term-matching algorithms. We also propose
a *pattern-based compliance* approach and novel compliance metrics. The
building sector is a case study to test the validity of ontology-compliant
KGs. We recommend using ontology-compliant KGs to pursue automatic
matching, alignment, and harmonisation of heterogeneous KGs.

Keywords: Ontology · Knowledge Graphs · Matching and Alignment

1 Introduction and Motivation

An ontology is typically used as the backbone for constructing a KG, building so-called *ontology-based KGs*. In this setting, the ontology and the KG are
often treated as independent functional components. An ontology provides a
knowledge-oriented graph schema (i.e., TBox), whereas a KG represents the
corresponding data-driven instances (i.e., ABox). With the proliferation of KGs
in real-world applications, problems arise when data in the KG is generated
for different user requirements. The ontology is likely to be incompatible with
the data in the KG because ABox assertions may extend or be incomplete with
respect to the ontology. While ABox contents can be adapted to suit a TBox, for
interoperability amongst independent TBoxes, an ABox that is compatible with
a number of TBoxes may be needed. Such overarching TBoxes should support
conversion and exchange for cross-KG harvesting and federated searches.

Figure 1 illustrates three types of non-compliance between KG and its ontology. (1) The ABox in the KG only covers a small amount of TBox terminologies, and its ontology has many unused classes and properties. (2) The ABox
in the KG contains more information than the TBox terminologies, and many
terms in the KG cannot find appropriate classes and properties in its ontology. (3) In a combination of (1) and (2), the ABox in the KG and the TBox
in the ontology are mismatched and overlapped on both sides. Many application tasks, for example, KG embedding and ontology learning, are hampered

Category: Early Stage PhD.

C. Pesquita et al. (Eds.): ESWC 2023, LNCS 13998, pp. 298–309, 2023.
https://doi.org/10.1007/978-3-031-43458-7_48

by non-compliance between KG and its ontology. When using KG embedding for ontology-based KGs, unused classes and properties in the ontology are noisy data. This results in inaccurate embeddings for KG terms. Ontology learning is the task of using KG to infer ontology classes and properties. KG data is diverse in nature; thus, the new ontology classes and properties learnt from KG can be different according to KG instances. These task-specific ontology classes and properties may violate the FAIR (i.e., Findability, Accessibility, Interoperability, and Reusability) principle and can be challenging to map and integrate into the original ontology.

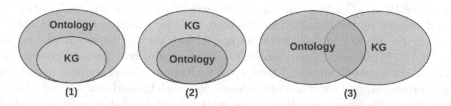

Fig. 1. Non-compliance between KG and its ontology.

Current work mainly focuses on either schema matching (i.e., TBox-TBox compliance) or instance matching (i.e., ABox-ABox compliance). TBox-ABox compliance is underexplored. While it is questionable whether the TBox is always compliant with the ABox, ontology-based KGs assume they are compliant by nature (excluding or ignoring the three types of non-compliance). For this reason, there is rarely a compliance check in popular KG and ontology modelling libraries or editors (e.g., RDFLib [2], Protégé [11], and TopBraid Composer [16]). Even within the Ontology Alignment Evaluation Initiative (OAEI) [12], to the best of our knowledge, we cannot find tools available to track these mismatches and overlaps between ABox in the KG and TBox in its corresponding ontology.

2 State of the Art

Ontology-Based KGs describe the traditional design for using ontologies with KGs, whereby the ontology serves as the schema for the KGs. KGs are generated using the classes and properties pre-defined in the ontology. In this setting, ontology-based KGs assume the ontology has established well-defined concepts, taxonomies, relationships, and domain axioms. Compared with ontology-less KGs, ontology-based KGs provide more formal representations for data understanding, organisation, and integration. They also enable improved logical reasoning, empowered reuse, and enhanced interoperability between different downstream applications. However, a complete ontology is almost impossible. Ontology is built on the Open World Assumption (OWA). We cannot assume an ontology has captured all domain concepts because the absence of concepts is not non-existence (i.e., these concepts may exist in other ontologies). A "well-defined" ontology also requires solid verification and validation. There is no gold standard for dealing with individual differences among opposing viewpoints.

Ontology-Aware KGs follow a reverse way of using ontologies with KGs. Conceptual components learnt from KGs are used to build or evolve the original ontology. The paradigm of ontology-aware KGs assumes the KG data is noiseless. There are two directions for constructing ontology-aware KGs. (1) Ontology reshaping is applied to data in the KG only covers part of the concepts in the ontology. The goal of ontology reshaping is to create a data-oriented local schemata that preserves the domain ontology knowledge while removing unused nodes [18,19]. (2) Ontology enrichment is used where data exists in the KG that is not covered by the ontology. In this case, the new concepts and relationships learnt from the KG are registered as new classes and properties in the ontology [9,17]. While ontology-aware KGs achieve partial compliance between the KG and its ontology, they still have some limitations. Concepts that have been locally reshaped and redefined are task-specific, with limited sharing and reusing capabilities. Moreover, ontology-aware KGs cannot track the poly-ontological representation of KGs as they only match one KG to its corresponding ontology.

3   Problem Statement and Contributions

In the real world, KGs and ontologies are mostly incomplete. Neither ontology-based KGs nor ontology-aware KGs could fully handle the compliance issue between KGs and ontologies. We plan to propose **Ontology-Compliant KGs** to fill this gap. "Compliant" here has two aspects: (1) The terms used in KG are in line with the definition provided by the ontology. Mismatched terms in the KG are replaced with the most relevant classes and properties defined in the original ontology. (2) The size of the ontology complies with the information coverage of the KG. There are no unused classes or properties. In this work, we also extend this definition to be ontology compliant across KGs. Joint learning, vector embedding methods, and pattern-based engineering concepts are employed to achieve the goal of both internal and external compliance between KGs and ontologies. Figure 2 shows the difference between ontology-compliant KGs and the other two types of ontology-related KGs. While ontology-based and ontology-aware KGs only consider a one-way connection, in ontology-compliant KGs, the link between ontology and KG is bidirectional and can be bridged by their patterns (details are described in Sect. 6).

Hypothesis. Ontology-compliant KGs have the following unique features:

> **H1.** Given an ontology and a baseline KG, ontology-compliant KGs can eliminate the unused classes and properties in the ontology and reduce misdefined terms in the KG (interpreted as Ontology Compliance *within* KG).
> **H2.** Given a set of ontologies and a baseline KG, ontology-compliant KGs allow automatic transmission from one schema to another (interpreted as Ontology Compliance *over* KGs).

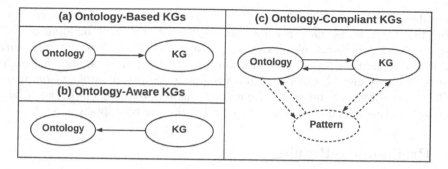

Fig. 2. The difference between ontology-compliant KGs and the other two types.

H3. Given a set of ontologies and a baseline KG, ontology-compliant KGs allow different ontology fragment representations via a pattern-based approach. These ontology fragments are provided with multiple criteria for integration, evaluation, and selection (interpreted as *Pattern-based* Compliance).

Research Questions. We formulate the related research questions:

RQ1 (wrt H1). How to reconstruct ontology-based KGs into ontology-compliant KGs, while retaining critical information and primary inference capability but eliminating unused nodes and reducing misdefined nodes?

RQ2 (wrt H2). How to enable schema-free KGs that can be compliant with multiple ontologies, using the ontology-compliant KGs to automate and optimise the ontology alignment and matching process?

RQ3 (wrt H3). How to select the most compliant set of ontology fragments for KGs? How to capture the different ontology fragment representations using a pattern-based approach, and evaluate them according to sound criteria from different useful perspectives?

4   Research Methodology and Approach

Details of preliminary results based on the research methodology and approach are described in Sect. 6. This PhD aims to define a generalised approach to constructing ontology-compliant KGs. We propose to classify three stages of compliance in ontology-compliant KGs, namely (1) Ontology Compliance *within* KG, (2) Ontology Compliance *over* KGs, and (3) *Pattern-Based* Compliance. In each stage, we intend to address the hypothesis and its related research question. The "building domain" is selected as a case study. We design, implement, and evaluate our matching algorithms, and analyse their matching performance in terms of different building use cases and various application-level tasks.

5   Evaluation Plan: A Case Study in the Building Sector

In the context of Industry 5.0 and the Internet of Things (IoT), digitisation and automation are becoming emerging research areas in the building sector. While a number of building and building-related ontologies have been developed, data interoperability issues have become more apparent. Different building ontologies are developed and maintained by different institutions. These ontologies are modelled at multiple levels of abstraction for various purposes, and their definitions are frequently competing and overlapping. Proposed ontology-compliant KGs would potentially help with the unified vision of building ontologies, where the data in this domain has complexity and variety in concepts and relations.

6   Preliminary Results

6.1 Ontology Compliance Within KG.
A KG and its ontology share all terms and topology. However, the concepts and properties defined in KG and ontology can be mismatched due to human errors, design choices, or changes in newer versions. Figure 3 shows different types of node matching in a snippet of an air handling unit (AHU) system represented by a KG and its ontology Brick Schema [1] (abbr. "Brick"). The concepts with green colours are KG classes, while the concepts with yellow colours are ontology classes. Different matching types and their examples are shown in the table below. These also applied to the property matching between KG and its ontology. We design Algorithm 1 for building ontology compliance within KG. It has two phases: (1) Entity Alignment and (2) Ontology Reconstruction. We first find non-compliant terms in the KG and replace them with the most relevant classes and properties in the original ontology, assigning a confidence score for each replacement. Then, we find all the related triples (including constraints and axioms) and restore the ontology hierarchies.

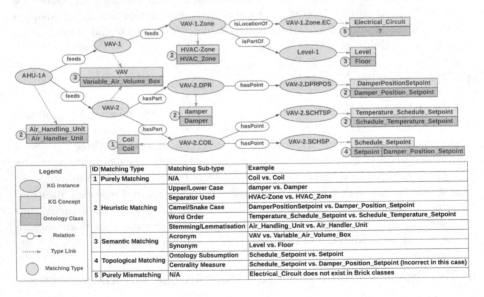

Fig. 3. An example of ontology compliance within KG.

Algorithm 1. Building Ontology Compliance within KG

Input: Ontology-based KG, Ontology $Onto$
Output: Reshaped Onto $Onto_{RE}$, Confidence μ
  /* **Phase 1: Entity Alignment** */
  /* Find all terms in KG */
  Concept Set Con_S, Relation Set $Rel\_S \leftarrow \varnothing$
  $Con\_S, Rel\_S \leftarrow findConceptAndRelation(KG)$
  /* Find all classes and properties in Onto */
  Class Set Cls_S, Property Set $Pro\_S \leftarrow \varnothing$
  $Cls\_S, Pro\_S \leftarrow findClassAndProperty(Onto)$
  /* Divide each naming into a keyword set */
  $Con\_S, Rel\_S \leftarrow findKwd(Con\_S, Rel\_S)$
  $Cls\_S, Pro\_S \leftarrow findKwd(Cls\_S, Pro\_S)$
  /* Match classes between KG and Onto */
  for $i \in Con\_S$ do
    for $j \in Cls\_S$ do
      if $purelyMatching(i, j) \neq \varnothing$ then
        $\mu_i \leftarrow 1$
      else if $heuristicMatching(i, j) \neq \varnothing$
      then
        $\mu_i \leftarrow LevenshteinDistance$
        $Con\_S \rightarrow i \wedge Con\_S \leftarrow j$
      else if $semanticMatching(i, j) \neq \varnothing$
      then
        $\mu_i \leftarrow Similarity$
        $Con\_S \rightarrow i \wedge Con\_S \leftarrow j$
      else if $topologicalMatching(i, j) \neq \varnothing$
      then

        $\mu_i \leftarrow Accuracy$
        $Con\_S \rightarrow i \wedge Con\_S \leftarrow j$
      end if
    end for
  end for
  /* Match properties between KG and Onto */
  for $k \in Rel\_S$ do
    for $l \in Pro\_S$ do
      /* Corresponding procedure applies to
      Rel_S and Pro_S */
    end for
  end for
  /* Calculate total confidence */
  Total Confidence $\mu \leftarrow \varnothing$
  $\mu \leftarrow Avarage(\mu_1, ..., \mu_i, \mu_1, ..., \mu_k)$
  /* **Phase 2: Ontology Reconstruction** */
  /* Find super-classes */
  $Onto\_RE$ Class Set $RE\_Cls\_S \leftarrow \varnothing$
  $RE\_Cls\_S \leftarrow findSuperClasses(Con\_S)$
  /* Find super-properties */
  $Onto\_RE$ Property Set $RE\_Pro\_S \leftarrow \varnothing$
  $RE\_Pro\_S \leftarrow findSuperProperties(Rel\_S)$
  /* Restore reshaped ontology */
  Reshaped Ontology $Onto_{RE} \leftarrow \varnothing$
  $Onto_{RE} \leftarrow findTriples(RE\_Cls\_S, RE\_Pro\_S)$

  return $Onto_{RE}, \mu$

Evaluation. The preliminary experiment uses the sample example from the Brick Schema official website. We synthesise a number of mismatched classes and properties with different types. The results in Table 1 show that reshaped ontologies can significantly reduce the original ontology size and increase the number of used and matched classes. We can also observe a trade-off between the confidence score and the level of matching applied. The confidence score slightly decreases when the level of matching increases. A potential reason is that Level 3 and Level 4 use learning-based approaches. While they are more powerful at discovering more pairs of matches, the confidence level of the matching accuracy highly depends on the models and methods used.

Table 1. Evaluation of algorithm for building ontology compliance within KG.

Type of Ontology and Matching Level	Used Entity	Matching Rate	Confidence
Original Ontology and Matching Lv. 1	0.52%	46.15%	100.00%
Reshaped Ontology and Matching Lv. 1	30.00%	46.15%	100.00%
Reshaped Ontology and Matching Lv. 2	38.46%	76.92%	97.50%
Reshaped Ontology and Matching Lv. 3	42.31%	84.62%	88.00%
Reshaped Ontology and Matching Lv. 4	46.15%	92.31%	78.33%

6.2 Ontology Compliance over KGs. It is often the case that a KG may be restructured to comply with one of several different ontologies, while preserving the KG's intended information content, as illustrated in Fig. 4.

The key task is ontology alignment and matching. Embedding-based methods are prevalent for exploring the potential matching in graphs due to their conceptual simplicity and computational operability. However, there are several challenges when applying the embedding methods to ontology alignment and matching. Firstly, not all the classes and properties from the original ontology are useful for KG instance embedding. The unused classes and properties could be noise for matching. Secondly, the respective KGs have no connection with each other. Embedding methods are based on random sampling, meaning the vector only represents the relative position of the nodes, and the vector number sets can be different. If two graphs are not tightly connected, the embedding results are most likely to be incorrect. Thirdly, the majority of the embedding methods are targeting graphs without schema. They focus more on topological matching rather than lexicographic matching. We employ our findings from ontology-compliant within KG to address the first challenge, and use their compliance as an intermediate link to connect two graphs - the second challenge, and facilitate lexicographical order - the third challenge. We design Algorithm 2 for building ontology compliance over KGs. It has three phases: (1) Build ontology compliance within each KG, (2) Match terms across ontologies, and (3) Match overlapping terms. Phases 1 and 2 also reuse the Algorithm 1.

Evaluation. The preliminary experiment is set to predict the similarity of two overlapping properties, brick:hasPoint in Brick Schema [1] (abbr. "Brick") and core:hasCapability in RealEstateCore [8] (abbr. "RECore"). The ground truth is that the meanings of these two properties are very similar. Their different names are due to their different views on how building points are embedded in the building. brick:hasPoint states that the building points are the measurable data points installed in the building, whereas core:hasCapability stands for the

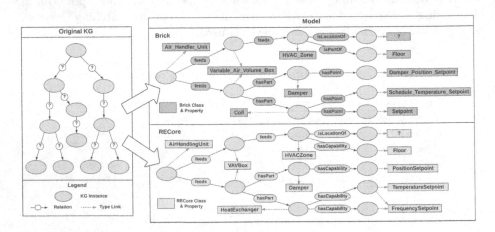

Fig. 4. An example of ontology compliance over KGs.

Algorithm 2. Building Ontology Compliance over KGs

Input: KG_1 and related ontology $Onto_1$,
KG_2 and related ontology $Onto_2$
Output: Matching Set $Match\_S(Onto_1, Onto_2)$,
Confidence Set $\mu(\mu_{within}, \mu_{over})$
/* **Phase 1: Compliance within KG** */
$Onto_{RE_1}, \mu_1 = withinComp(KG_1, Onto_1)$
$Onto_{RE_2}, \mu_2 = withinComp(KG_2, Onto_2)$
$\mu_{within} \leftarrow \mu_1, \mu_2$
/* **Phase 2: Match terms across Onto** */
/* Create matching set */
Matching Set $Match\_S(Onto_1, Onto_2) \leftarrow \varnothing$
/* Follow same procedure in Algorithm 1 */
for $i \in Con\_Onto_{RE_1}, k \in Rel\_KG_1$ **do**
   for $j \in Con\_Onto_{RE_2}, l \in Rel\_KG_2$ **do**
      $Match\_S(Onto_1, Onto_2), \mu_{cmatch} \leftarrow$
      Matched Con & Rel, $\mu_{over} \leftarrow \mu_{cmatch}$
   end for
end for
/* **Phase 3: Match overlapping terms** */
/* Set a vector space */
Vector space $VecSpace \leftarrow \varnothing$
/* Put KGs and Onto_RE */
for $i \in KG_1, Onto_{RE_1}, KG_2, Onto_{RE_2}$ **do**

$VecSpace \leftarrow i$
end for
/* Put matched Onto set to build links */
$VecSpace \leftarrow Match\_S(Onto_1, Onto_2)$
/* Define embedding model */
Embedding Model $Model \leftarrow X2Vec.train()$
/* Define vector set */
Vector Set $Vec\_S \leftarrow Model.getEmbeddings()$
/* Add predict match for overlapping */
Predict Match $P \leftarrow \varnothing$
for Unmatched $U \notin Match\_S(Onto_1, Onto_2)$
do
   $P, \mu_{overlap} \leftarrow Vec\_S.getMostSimilar(U)$
   $Match\_S(Onto_1, Onto_2) \leftarrow (U, P)$
   $\mu_{over} \leftarrow \mu_{overlap}$
end for
/* Summarise total confidence */
Confidence Set $\mu \leftarrow \varnothing$
$\mu \leftarrow \mu_{within}$
$\mu \leftarrow \mu_{over}$

return $Match\_S(Onto_1, Onto_2)$,
$\mu(\mu_{within}, \mu_{over})$

---

building points are the capabilities provided by the building to produce and ingest data. We employ three different vector embedding models to evaluate the top-k searches. Exp.1 uses the traditional KG embedding without ontology compliance, and Exp.2 uses our proposed compliance algorithm. Table 2 shows the results of the comparison in a test run. We can see Exp.2 outperforms Exp.1 in all three sample embedding models, particularly in top-1 and top-3 searches.

6.3 Pattern-Based Compliance. Ontology can be decomposed into smaller ontology fragments. For example, the concepts defined in Brick Schema (abbr. "Brick") can be decomposed into three high-level abstraction fragments: Spaces (i.e., brick:Location), Building Equipment and Systems (i.e., brick:Equipment and brick:System), and Building Points (i.e., brick:Point). For each fragment, they can be replaced with the same concepts defined in other building ontologies, such as RealEstateCore [8] (abbr. "RECore") and Project Haystack [10] (abbr. "Haystack"), or building-related domain ontologies, such as BOT [14] for spatial information, SAREF [4] for equipment and systems, and SSN [3]/SOSA [7] for building points. Figure 5 demonstrates an example of KG represented by different combinations of building and related domain ontologies. These new ontology fragments can represent the same information as the original ontology, but they can have different numbers of classes, properties, and hierarchies. If we consider ontology fragments, the problem of ontology compliance becomes more complex.

Table 2. Evaluation of algorithm for building ontology compliance over KGs.

@k	DeepWalk [13]		Node2Vec [6]		Struc2Vec [15]	
	Exp.1	Exp.2	Exp.1	Exp.2	Exp.1	Exp.2
1	0.03 ± 0.17%	25.86 ± 4.48%	0.04 ± 0.20%	15.32 ± 3.70%	96.88 ± 1.52%	99.98 ± 0.14%
3	1.36 ± 1.07%	57.49 ± 4.86%	13.4 ± 3.35%	56.65 ± 5.28%	100 ± 0.00%	100 ± 0.00%
5	7.58 ± 2.57%	75.51 ± 4.17%	66.54 ± 4.85%	84.86 ± 3.63%	100 ± 0.00%	100 ± 0.00%

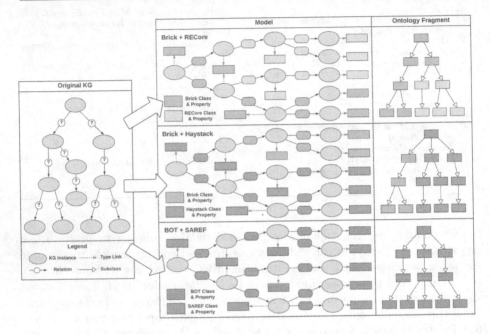

Fig. 5. An example of pattern-based compliance.

Figure 6 shows the architecture of building pattern-based compliance. It has three main components, namely (1) Pattern Cognition, (2) Pattern Recognition, and (3) Pattern Optimisation. The basic idea is to extract the concepts, relationships, and constraints from the ontology-compliant KG. Each of them goes through a learning and matching process to find their patterns. Then, we integrate and align the same or similar patterns, and use these generic patterns to reconstruct new ontology fragments.

Evaluation. Ontology fragments may have different numbers of namespaces, levels of abstraction, concept coverage, depth of the class hierarchy, completeness and expressiveness, and performance metrics. Liebig's law [5] is used for ontology fragment construction, evaluation, and selection. The multi-criteria selection depends on the minimum criteria being satisfied. We also introduce a joint-learning approach to evaluate the performance of ontology fragments. An example is shown in Fig. 7. Ontology Fragment 1, 2, and 3 are generated from the same KG. We fit them into the embedding model and perform the classification task according to the original KG. Based on different levels of abstraction, the

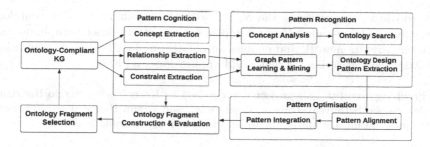

Fig. 6. The architecture of building pattern-based compliance.

classification accuracy of the KG embedding decreases at different rates. Fragment 1 and 2 have higher accuracy in Level 1 and Level 2 abstractions, but they have a significant drop in Level 3. By contrast, Fragment 3 decreases gradually at all levels of abstraction.

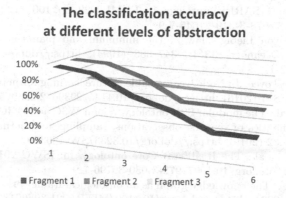

Fig. 7. A joint approach using classification accuracy to evaluate the performance. The fluctuation of each ontology fragment varies at different levels of abstraction.

Results given here may have slight differences across different platforms and library versions. The code implementation is available at https://github.com/qzc438/ontology-compliant-kgs (access will be made available on request).

7   Conclusions

In this paper, we present a new concept of ontology-compliant KGs, showing promising results in matching and aligning ontologies within KG and over KGs. We also illustrate our design for advanced pattern-based compliance. Further work will focus on justifying the results with the capability to allow ontology compliance on large-scale KGs, and implementing pattern-based compliance in a comprehensive framework that enables automatic ontology fragment integration, evaluation, and selection for real-world application-level KGs.

Acknowledgements. This project is supervised by Kerry Taylor, Sergio Rodríguez Méndez, Subbu Sethuvenkatraman, Qing Wang, and Armin Haller. The author also thanks program mentor Maria Maleshkova for providing valuable feedback.

References

1. Balaji, B., et al.: Brick: towards a unified metadata schema for buildings. In: BuildSys 2016, pp. 41–50 (2016). https://doi.org/10.1145/2993422.2993577
2. Boettiger, C.: RDFLib (2018). https://github.com/RDFLib/rdflib
3. Compton, M., et al.: The SSN ontology of the W3C semantic sensor network incubator group. J. Web Semant. **17**, 25–32 (2012). https://doi.org/10.1016/j.websem. 2012.05.003
4. Daniele, L., et al.: Created in close interaction with the industry: the Smart Appliances REFerence (SAREF) ontology. In: FOMI 2022, pp. 100–112 (2015). https:// doi.org/10.1007/978-3-319-21545-7_9
5. de Baar, H.: von Liebig's law of the minimum and plankton ecology (1899–1991). Prog. Oceanogr. **33**(4), 347–386 (1994). https://doi.org/10.1016/0079-6611(94)90022-1
6. Grover, A., Leskovec, J.: Node2vec: scalable feature learning for networks. In: KDD 2016, pp. 855–864 (2016). https://doi.org/10.1145/2939672.2939754
7. Haller, A., et al.: The modular SSN ontology: a joint W3C and OGC standard specifying the semantics of sensors, observations, sampling, and actuation. Semantic Web **10**(1), 9–32 (2019). https://doi.org/10.3233/SW-180320
8. Hammar, K., et al.: The RealEstateCore ontology. In: ISWC 2019, pp. 130–145 (2019). https://doi.org/10.1007/978-3-030-30796-7_9
9. Hurlburt, G.F.: The knowledge graph as an ontological framework. IT Professional **23**(4), 14–18 (2021). https://doi.org/10.1109/MITP.2021.3086918
10. John, J., Gowan, M.: Project haystack data standards. In: Energy and Analytics, pp. 237–243 (2020). https://doi.org/10.1201/9781003151944-16
11. Musen, M.A.: Protégé (2020). https://protege.stanford.edu
12. Ontology Alignment Evaluation Initiative. http://oaei.ontologymatching.org/
13. Perozzi, B., et al.: DeepWalk: online learning of social representations. In: KDD 2014, pp. 701–710 (2014). https://doi.org/10.1145/2623330.2623732
14. Rasmussen, M.H., et al.: BOT: the building topology ontology of the W3C linked building data group. Semantic Web **12**, 143–161 (2021). https://doi.org/10.3233/SW-200385
15. Ribeiro, L.F., et al.: Struc2vec: learning node representations from structural identity. In: KDD 2017, pp. 385–394 (2017). https://doi.org/10.1145/3097983.3098061
16. TopQuadrant Inc: TopBraid Composer (2022). https://www.topquadrant.com
17. Zhao, L., et al.: Learning ontology axioms over knowledge graphs via representation learning. In: ISWC 2019 (Satellites), pp. 57–60 (2019)

18. Zhou, D., et al.: Enhancing knowledge graph generation with ontology reshaping - Bosch case. In: ESWC 2022 (Demos/Industry) (2022). https://doi.org/10.1007/978-3-031-11609-4_45
19. Zhou, D., et al.: Ontology reshaping for knowledge graph construction: applied on Bosch welding case. In: ISWC 2022, pp. 770–790 (2022). https://doi.org/10.1007/978-3-031-19433-7_44

Evaluating Knowledge Graphs
with Hybrid Intelligence

Stefani Tsaneva[1,2]([⊠]) [iD]

[1] Vienna University of Economics and Business, Wien, Austria
[2] TU Wien, Wien, Austria
stefani.tsaneva@wu.ac.at

Abstract. Knowledge graphs (KGs) enable the conceptualization of knowledge about the world in a machine-readable format and serve as a foundation to many advanced intelligent applications, such as conversational agents. Ensuring the correctness and quality of KGs is essential for the prevention of invalid application outputs and biased systems, which can result from incorrectly or incompletely represented information. While certain KG quality issues can be automatically detected, others require human involvement, including the identification of incorrectly modeled statements or the discovery of concepts not compliant with how humans think. Human computation and crowdsourcing (HC&C) techniques have been used as a promising method for outsourcing human-centric tasks to human contributors at a reduced cost. Nevertheless, there is no clear guideline on how human-centric KG evaluations should be prepared and scalable evaluation of large KGs utilizing HC&C techniques alone remains a challenge. In this thesis, we investigate a human-centric KG evaluation approach, relying on hybrid (human-AI) intelligence, which leverages techniques from the semantic web, HC&C and multi-agent systems communities for ensuring an efficiently planned, scalable, well-coordinated, and thus transparent KG evaluation process.

Keywords: Semantic Web · Knowledge Graph Evaluation · Human Computation · Crowdsourcing · Hybrid Intelligence

1 Introduction

Knowledge graphs enable the representation of domain-specific and domain-independent information in a machine-readable format and are commonly used as a backbone to many information systems and advanced intelligence applications, which rely on human knowledge [20]. KGs are often curated by extracting information from semi-structured data sources or through crowdsourcing campaigns. Since an automated extraction of knowledge is rarely impeccable, the quality of the resulting KGs should be evaluated. Moreover, KGs are often reused

Early Stage Ph.D.

and extended over time, thus it is essential to ensure that they remain up-to-date and accurately reflect evolving knowledge through ongoing maintenance [17].

Many quality issues related to knowledge graphs can be automatically detected (e.g., logical inconsistencies), while others require a human-centric evaluation. An example is the identification of concepts not compliant with human cognition, inaccurately represented facts and controversial statements modeled from a single perspective [4,14,23]. The traditional approach for addressing such issues relies on domain-expert-evaluations. However, this is a costly and time-intensive process, particularly when dealing with large KGs.

Human computation (HC), a method of outsourcing unautomatable tasks of a system to human participants, can reduce evaluation costs by replacing domain experts with crowd workers. HC is widely adopted for various tasks in the semantic web (SW) research community [24]. A recent systematic mapping study (SMS) [25] showed that 40% of papers, discussing a human-centric evaluation of SW resources, rely on HC&C methods. For example, HC&C techniques were utilized for verifying large biomedical ontologies [15], and evaluating the quality of linked data as a collaborative effort between experts and the crowd [1]. Yet, several issues in the human-centric KG evaluation domain remain:

P1: Lack of methodology and tools. The SMS [25] highlighted that while human-centric KG evaluation has been abundantly addressed there is currently no standardized methodology and tools supporting the knowledge engineers in the preparations of such evaluations. This results in significant amount of manual efforts for the engineers planing an evaluation campaign.

P2: Scalability Issue. Large KGs present a scalability challenge even for crowd-sourced evaluations. In [21] the authors calculated that applying the crowdsourcing assessment, proposed in [1], would require 3,000 years to validate DBpedia, a large KG curated using automated extraction methods.

P3: Lack of transparency. To ensure a transparent KG evaluation process, especially when both human and AI agents perform the evaluation, the question arises of how such an evaluation approach should be coordinated, so that each evaluation can be traced back to its origin across the process.

In this thesis we aim to establish a typical process of human-centric KG evaluation and implement a tool supporting the preparation of such evaluation campaigns (contribution C1, addressing P1). Additionally, we intend to implement a human-centric knowledge graph evaluation system, relying on hybrid (human-AI) intelligence to enable an efficient evaluation of large KGs (C2,P2). To ensure transparency in the KG evaluation process, we further formalize a coordination framework within the hybrid approach (C3,P3).

To address the outlined objectives we employ a design science methodology [7] and adhere to principles from experimental software engineering [31]. We utilize prior research on hybrid intelligence systems proposed for SW tasks (i.e., ontology alignment [27] and entity linking [3]) and multi-agent system approaches aiming at crowd coordination [5,13]. Moreover, we specify two concrete use cases for the evaluation of the established artifacts, namely evaluating the *Computer Science Ontology* and *WebIsALOD*.

We continue by providing introductory definitions and related work in Sect. 2. The problem statement and a discussion of the formulated research questions follow in Sect. 3. We outline the followed research methodology and the planned evaluation of the proposed approach in Sect. 4 and 5 respectively. Preliminary results are included in Sect. 6 and we conclude with a summary in Sect. 7.

2 Background and Related Work

We start by defining introductory notions in Sect. 2.1, continue with a discussion of related work in the human-centric KG evaluation problem space (Sect. 2.2) and an overview of current approaches in the solution space covering hybrid-intelligence and multi-agent systems (Sect. 2.3).

2.1 Definitions

Knowledge Graph. We refer to the definition of knowledge graphs recently proposed by Hogan et al., which defines a KG as "a graph of data intended to accumulate and convey knowledge of the real world, whose nodes represent entities of interest and whose edges represent potentially different relations between these entities" [8]. This definition is broad and as such also encompass other types of semantic resources, such as ontologies and linked data.

Knowledge Graph Evaluation. In this thesis we view knowledge graph evaluation as the refinement of KGs, defined by Paulheim as the improvement of KGs by means of the identification and correction of errors or by completion of missing information [20].

Human-Centric Knowledge Graph Evaluation. Combining the definition above with Mortensen's argument that "only domain experts can interpret the symbols in an ontology and determine whether they reflect their understanding of the domain." [16], we define human-centric KG evaluation as the *improvement of knowledge graphs by means of dealing with errors which require human judgment to be identified and corrected and the completion of missing information by leveraging human (domain/general) knowledge.*

2.2 State of the Art in Human-Centric Knowledge Graph Evaluation

Evaluating the correctness of KGs has been extensively studied for more than 20 years. McDaniel and Storey [14] reviewed research in ontology assessment from the last 20 years and identified that semantic mistakes cannot (yet) be fully automatically detected. While automatic methods are fast and scalable, they have limitations that require human involvement to be addressed.

Recently, Sabou et al. conducted a systematic mapping study of 100 papers from the last decade (2010–2020) dealing with human-centric evaluation of various semantic resources, corresponding to our definition of KGs [25]. The study showed that human-centric evaluations have been applied in a variety of domains and verification tasks. For instance, Acosta et al. proposed a find-fix-verify workflow for assessing linked data quality issues, where domain experts identify potential errors and crowd workers verify them [1]. Mortensen et al. presented a crowd-based verification of taxonomic relationships from a medical ontology [15], while in [4] crowdsourcing was used to investigate humans' perception on viewpoints and controversial facts modeled in ontologies. Ontology enhancement achieved by crowdsourcing was investigated in [11] and a validation of enriched ontologies was explored in [9].

Several methods have been proposed for the evaluation of SW resources, aligning with our KG definition, such as *linked data triples quality evaluation* through crowdsourcing and the TripleCheckMate tool [12], a *task-based ontology evaluation* methodology [22], and a *Protégé plugin* that outsources certain tasks of the ontology engineering process to games with a purpose or a crowdsourcing platform [30]. Nevertheless, these methods lack important details and have been established in an ad-hoc manner, rather than using a structured approach.

Despite the abundance of human-centric KG evaluation approaches, there is yet no agreed upon methodology for conducting KG evaluation campaigns and no tool supporting the knowledge engineers preparing them. Additionally, current HC&C approaches have limitations when evaluating large KGs, and evaluations are often not transparent. Thus, we next look into approaches of hybrid human-AI and multi-agent systems addressing similar challenges in related fields.

2.3   Related Work on Hybrid-Intelligence and Multi-agent Systems

Hybrid Human-AI Workflows for Semantic Web Tasks. Evaluations performed with human involvement achieve high accuracy, but can become costly when verifying large-scale knowledge graphs. Hybrid human-machine workflows, where automated methods are supplemented by human input when the confidence score is low, have been successfully applied for semi-automatic entity-linking [3] and ontology alignment [27] tasks. Nevertheless, such a hybrid solution has not yet been approached for the human-centric evaluation of KGs.

Coordination in Human-AI Collaborations. Workflow coordination known from crowd coordination theory is mainly focused on the self-organization of the crowd, while the coordination of hybrid systems has different requirements. Previous studies [2,10] have identified that methods known from multi-agent systems (MAS) can be utilized to solve crowd coordination challenges.

There has been limited research on how MAS methods can be used to coordinate a hybrid process including both human agents and algorithms. It has been shown that MAS algorithms can support and improve the performance of crowd workers in tasks such as constraint satisfaction problems [13]. Additionally, the combination of crowdsourcing and MAS has been investigated in a sustainable transportation use case, where best route calculations guide delivery drivers [5]. Yet, there has not been an investigation of how MAS can be used to support KG evaluation campaigns and their transparency.

3 Problem Statement and Contributions

This thesis aims at investigating scalable and transparent evaluation of large knowledge graphs. The following research questions are formulated and their connection to specific challenges and contributions are visualized in Fig. 1:

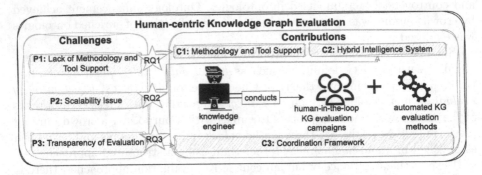

Fig. 1. Challenges in human-centric KG evaluation (P1-P2), formulated research questions (RQ1-RQ3) and expected contributions (C1-C3).

RQ1. *What is a typical process of human-centric knowledge graphs evaluation?*

Currently, the process of managing a (large-scale) KG evaluation campaign involving human participants requires high efforts of the knowledge engineer conducting the evaluation (P1 in Fig. 1) as a result of a lack of clear design guidance (e.g., how to manage the qualification of the participants or how to display the KG segments to the evaluators) and missing methodology (i.e., what part of the evaluation should be designed at which stage). To minimize the organizational efforts of knowledge engineers, clear steps to be followed should be outlined and a tool supporting this methodology should be implemented (C1 in Fig. 1).

RQ2. *How can hybrid intelligence be applied for achieving a scalable human-centric knowledge graph evaluation process?*

Large KGs pose a challenge for current human-centric evaluation approaches (P2 in Fig. 1). This thesis will investigate how the strengths of state-of-the art algorithms and human-in-the-loop approaches can be combined to reduce human efforts and costs of human-centric KG evaluations to ensure a scalable solution. We will explore methods, reducing the tasks assigned to human participants (e.g., graph-based defect candidate detection, link prediction), and requirements (e.g., possible human-AI interaction workflows) for an efficient hybrid intelligence system by looking at concrete KG evaluation use cases. The investigations performed will lead to the implementation of a hybrid intelligence system for human-centric KG evaluation (C2 in Fig. 1).

RQ3. How can a human-AI knowledge graph evaluation campaign be coordinated to ensure a transparent evaluation process?

A hybrid human-machine framework requires the coordination of complex workflows between human and machine (algorithmic) agents. A clear transparent process should be followed for delegating the tasks and coordinating them between all agents to ensure the traceability of potential mistakes for the ease of their correction (P3 in Fig. 1). The process should also allow for information of the evaluation to be saved so that in case a re-evaluation is needed, e.g., after a KG modification, only these KG elements are verified that are affected by the implemented changes. Therefore, the result of RQ3 would be a coordination framework for human-centric KG evaluations (C3 in Fig. 1).

4 Research Methodology and Approach

In this thesis, we follow the *design science methodology* for information systems research [7] to establish the following information artifacts: a set of task design guidelines for human-centric KG evaluation tasks (C1); a methodology and tool support for carrying out human-centric KG evaluation campaigns (C1); a hybrid intelligence system for conducting KG evaluation studies (C2); and a coordination framework for hybrid intelligence KG evaluations (C3).

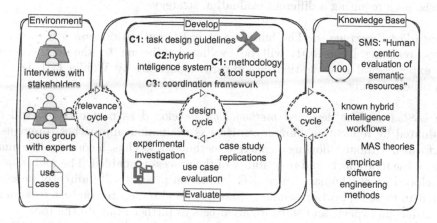

Fig. 2. An overview of the design-science-based methodology followed in this thesis.

Figure 2 visualizes how the relevance, rigor and design cycles are addressed. By involving key stakeholders in need of such artifacts (i.e., knowledge engineers) and focusing on two concrete use cases we address the *relevance cycle* of the design science methodology. We ensure the rigor cycle by incorporating knowledge from existing literature, among others, the results of a large scale SMS [25], developed workflows for hybrid intelligent systems, methods from MAS, and empirical principles of software engineering followed in the planned evaluations.

The artifacts resulting from the investigation of each research question will rely on (several) *evaluation cycles* as described in Sect. 5. We plan two evaluation use cases, which allow us to test the hybrid system for e.g., evaluating the correctness of hierarchical relations, in both a domain-specific and a general setting:

Evaluating the Computer Science Ontology (CSO). CSO structures computer science knowledge extracted automatically from 16 M publications [18] and enables novel scientometrics tasks such as identifying research communities [19] and forecasting research trends [26]. Its current verification relies on domain experts, who search through the CSO Portal, rate topics and relations as (in)correct, and provide alternative viewpoints, aggregated by an editorial team.

Evaluating WebIsALOD. WebIsALOD is a large KG containing 400 M hypernymy relations, automatically extracted from the CommonCrawl web corpus, describing generic knowledge [6]. The current verification of the resource relies on machine learning models trained with a set of 500 relations, validated by crowd workers, to determine confidence scores related to relation correctness.

5   Evaluation Plan

Several information systems artifacts are to be developed in the course of this thesis, each requiring a different evaluation strategy.

Controlled Experiments. The human-centric KG evaluation *task design guidelines*, resulting from RQ1, will be evaluated adhering to the methodology for experimental investigation in software engineering by Wohlin [31], i.e., by hypothesis testing.

Case Studies. The designed *methodology*, developed as part of RQ1, will be evaluated by replicating human-centric KG evaluation approaches, previously performed without following a concrete methodology. Thus, a comparative analysis of the time efforts and re-usability of the process is enabled. The *tool support* developed for the human-centric KG evaluation process will indirectly be evaluated in these replication studies. However, we also plan to conduct *interviews* with domain experts and software architects to further evaluate the tool.

For the evaluation of the *hybrid intelligence system*, designed as part of RQ2, we will apply the system in the concrete use case of the Computer Science Ontology. We plan to organize an evaluation with computer science researchers, where one control group will use the CSO Portal as a baseline and the other(s) the implemented hybrid system. The evaluation will consist in assessing differences in terms of the quantity and range of identified defects and viewpoints as well as the time needed to perform the evaluation.

Lastly, to evaluate the *coordination framework* (RQ3) for the hybrid intelligence system we plan an active-learning evaluation approach of WebIsALOD. We will test different strategies to select tasks to be sent to human agents (e.g., based on confidence scores, outlier detection, etc.). Verified items will be used to update the classification model and the evaluation will consist in iterating through the process until no significant improvements in the classification accuracy are observed when refining the model. Additionally, the transparency of the framework will be evaluated along several dimensions such as understandability, conciseness, provenance, etc.

6   Preliminary Results

HC&C Methods for Ontology Verification. As an entry point to this thesis, human-centric tasks and their solution was investigated in parallel to the conducted SMS [25]. In [29], we proposed a HC solution for the verification of ontology restrictions by means of universal and existential quantifiers and reported on a controlled experiment to study two core task design aspects: (i) the formalism to represent ontology axioms in the HC task and (2) participant qualification testing. We found that visual axiom representation and prior knowledge of ontology restriction models lead to best results while prior modeling knowledge reduces the evaluation times. In a future publication, we will discuss how the qualification test was set up and propose implementation guidelines that could be used for ontology-related tasks, contributing to answering RQ1.

HERO - A Human-Centric Ontology Evaluation PROcess. RQ1 was also partially addressed in [28] where we formalized a process for conducting human-centric ontology evaluation. In addition, an initial framework was developed to support this process by (semi-)automating a portion of the activities. HERO is a process model for human-centric KG evaluation, targeted toward micro-tasking environments such as crowdsourcing platforms and focusing on batch-style evaluations. At a high-level the process and its activities can be structured into the stages of preparation, execution and follow-up. The process was derived by analyzing steps discussed in literature, semi-structured interviews with experts and an expert focus group discussion. For the evaluation, we replicated our previous manual evaluation approach from [29] with the support of the HERO artifacts and compared the time effort in both approaches. We found that HERO could decrease manual effort up to 88% for the preparation activities involved in human-centric ontology evaluation campaigns. In [28] we focused on describing the process that knowledge engineers follow when conducting human-centric evaluation, while in a future publication the implemented tool will be discussed in detail.

7   Summary

Knowledge graphs are used as a skeleton of many AI applications having high impact on human society. Since automated methods have their limitations, human involvement is a requirement for the evaluation of KGs. Assessing and improving low-quality KGs deals with incorrectly modeled information, and can thus prevent biased and discriminating systems resulting from knowledge graph quality issues. The proposed hybrid intelligence approach would enable human-centric KG evaluation of large-scale KGs, which are a problem for currently available evaluation methods. By providing a transparent evaluation process, bias sources can easily be identified and corrected, and the overall quality of the KG, and the system using it, can be improved. The outlined work holds the potential to bring novel contributions that can impact not only the SW, HC&C, and MAS communities, but also offer valuable insights for human-AI collaborations across various domains.

Acknowledgments. I would like to thank my supervisor, Prof. Marta Sabou, for her valuable advice, expert insights and guidance. The work presented in this paper is partly supported by the FWF HOnEst project (V 754-N).

References

1. Acosta, M., Zaveri, A., Simperl, E., Kontokostas, D., Auer, S., Lehmann, J.: Crowd-sourcing linked data quality assessment. In: Alani, H., et al. (eds.) ISWC 2013. LNCS, vol. 8219, pp. 260–276. Springer, Heidelberg (2013). https://doi.org/10.1007/978-3-642-41338-4_17
2. Das, R., Vukovic, M.: Emerging theories and models of human computation systems: a brief survey. In: Proceedings of the 2nd International Workshop on Ubiquitous Crowdsourcing, pp. 1–4 (2011)
3. Demartini, G., Difallah, D.E., Cudré-Mauroux, P.: Zencrowd: leveraging probabilistic reasoning and crowdsourcing techniques for large-scale entity linking. In: Proceedings of the 21st International Conference on World Wide Web, pp. 469–478 (2012)
4. Erez, E.S., Zhitomirsky-Geffet, M., Bar-Ilan, J.: Subjective vs. objective evaluation of ontological statements with crowdsourcing. In: Proceedings of the Association for Information Science and Technology, pp. 1–4 (2015)
5. Giret, A., Carrascosa, C., Julian, V., Rebollo, M., Botti, V.: A crowdsourcing approach for sustainable last mile delivery. Sustainability 10(12), 4563 (2018)
6. Hertling, S., Paulheim, H.: WebIsALOD: providing hypernymy relations extracted from the web as linked open data. In: d'Amato, C., et al. (eds.) ISWC 2017. LNCS, vol. 10588, pp. 111–119. Springer, Cham (2017). https://doi.org/10.1007/978-3-319-68204-4_11
7. Hevner, A.R., March, S.T., Park, J., Ram, S.: Design science in information systems research. In: MIS Quarterly, pp. 75–105 (2004)
8. Hogan, A., et al.: Knowledge graphs. ACM Comput. Surv. 54(4), 1–37 (2021)
9. Iyer, V., Sanagavarapu, L.M., Raghu Reddy, Y.: A framework for syntactic and semantic quality evaluation of ontologies. In: International Conference on Secure Knowledge Management in Artificial Intelligence Era, pp. 73–93. Springer, Cham (2021). https://doi.org/10.1007/978-3-030-97532-6_5
10. Jiang, J., et al.: Understanding crowdsourcing systems from a multiagent perspective and approach. ACM Trans. Autonom. Adapt. Syst. 13(2), 1–32 (2018)
11. Kiptoo, C.C.: Ontology enhancement using crowdsourcing: a conceptual architecture. Int. J. Crowd Sci. (2020)

12. Kontokostas, D., Zaveri, A., Auer, S., Lehmann, J.: Triplecheckmate: a tool for crowdsourcing the quality assessment of linked data. Commun. Comput. Inf. Sci. **394**, 265–272 (2013)
13. Mao, A., Parkes, D.C., Procaccia, A.D., Zhang, H.: Human computation and multiagent systems: an algorithmic perspective. In: Proceedings of the 25th AAAI Conference on Artificial Intelligence. Citeseer (2011)
14. McDaniel, M., Storey, V.C.: Evaluating domain ontologies: clarification, classification, and challenges. ACM Comp. Surv. **52**(4), 1–44 (2019)
15. Mortensen, J.M., et al.: Using the wisdom of the crowds to find critical errors in biomedical ontologies: a study of SNOMED CT. J. Am. Med. Inf. Assoc. **22**(3), 640–648 (2015)
16. Mortensen, J.M., et al.: Is the crowd better as an assistant or a replacement in ontology engineering? An exploration through the lens of the gene ontology. J. Biomed. Inf. **60**, 199–209 (2016)
17. Nishioka, C., Scherp, A.: Analysing the evolution of knowledge graphs for the purpose of change verification. In: IEEE 12th International Conference on Semantic Computing, pp. 25–32. IEEE (2018)
18. Osborne, F., Motta, E.: Klink-2: integrating multiple web sources to generate semantic topic networks. In: Arenas, M., et al. (eds.) ISWC 2015. LNCS, vol. 9366, pp. 408–424. Springer, Cham (2015). https://doi.org/10.1007/978-3-319-25007-6_24
19. Osborne, F., Scavo, G., Motta, E.: Identifying diachronic topic-based research communities by clustering shared research trajectories. In: Presutti, V., d'Amato, C., Gandon, F., d'Aquin, M., Staab, S., Tordai, A. (eds.) ESWC 2014. LNCS, vol. 8465, pp. 114–129. Springer, Cham (2014). https://doi.org/10.1007/978-3-319-07443-6_9
20. Paulheim, H.: Knowledge graph refinement: a survey of approaches and evaluation methods. Semantic Web J. **8**(3), 489–508 (2017)
21. Paulheim, H., Bizer, C.: Improving the quality of linked data using statistical distributions. Int. J. Semantic Web Inf. Syst. **10**(2), 63–86 (2014)
22. Pittet, P., Barthélémy, J.: Exploiting users' feedbacks: towards a task-based evaluation of application ontologies throughout their lifecycle. In: International Conference on Knowledge Engineering and Ontology Development, vol. 2 (2015)
23. Poveda-Villalón, M., Gómez-Pérez, A., Suárez-Figueroa, M.C.: Oops!(ontology pitfall scanner!): an on-line tool for ontology evaluation. Int. J. Semantic Web Inf. Syst. **10**(2), 7–34 (2014)
24. Sabou, M., Aroyo, L., Bontcheva, K., Bozzon, A., Qarout, R.K.: Semantic web and human computation: the status of an emerging field. Semantic Web J. **9**(3), 291–302 (2018)
25. Sabou, M., Fernandez, M., Poveda-Villalón, M., Suárez-Figueroa, M.C., Tsaneva, S.: Human-centric evaluation of semantic resources: a systematic mapping study. In preparation
26. Salatino, A.A., Osborne, F., Motta, E.: Augur: forecasting the emergence of new research topics. In: Proceedings of the 18th ACM/IEEE on Joint Conference on Digital Libraries, pp. 303–312 (2018)
27. Sarasua, C., Simperl, E., Noy, N.F.: CROWDMAP: crowdsourcing ontology alignment with microtasks. In: Cudré-Mauroux, P., et al. (eds.) ISWC 2012. LNCS, vol. 7649, pp. 525–541. Springer, Heidelberg (2012). https://doi.org/10.1007/978-3-642-35176-1_33

28. Tsaneva, S., Käsznar, K., Sabou, M.: Human-centric ontology evaluation: process and tool support. In: International Conference on Knowledge Engineering and Knowledge Management, pp. 182–197. Springer, Cham (2022). https://doi.org/10.1007/978-3-031-17105-5_14
29. Tsaneva, S., Sabou, M.: A human computation approach for ontology restrictions verification. In: AAAI Conference on Human Computation and Crowdsourcing (2021). www.humancomputation.com/2021/assets/wips_demos/HCOMP_2021_paper_90.pdf
30. Wohlgenannt, G., Sabou, M., Hanika, F.: Crowd-based ontology engineering with the ucomp protégé plugin. Semantic Web **7**(4), 379–398 (2016)
31. Wohlin, C., Runeson, P., Höst, M., Ohlsson, M.C., Regnell, B., Wesslén, A.: Experimentation in Software Engineering. Springer, Heidelberg (2012). https://doi.org/10.1007/978-3-642-29044-2

Exploiting Semantics for Explaining Link Prediction Over Knowledge Graphs

Yashrajsinh Chudasama[1,2](✉) [iD]

[1] Leibniz University, Hannover, Germany
[2] TIB Leibniz Information Centre for Science and Technology, Hannover, Germany
yashrajsinh.chudasama@stud.uni-hannover.de

Abstract. The use of Symbolic and sub-symbolic AI techniques on Knowledge Graphs (*KGs*) has shown significant progress in several applications. However, many of these methods remain opaque, and the decision-making process behind them can be perplexing. This can result in a lack of trust and reliability in the overall framework. While various explainable frameworks have been proposed to address these issues, do not always provide a complete understanding and may raise privacy concerns as sensitive data may be revealed during the explanation process. In contrast, our proposed approach leverages the semantics of *KGs* and causal relationships to enhance explainability while still maintaining a high level of trust and reliability. By focusing on XAI for link prediction models and considering entailment regimes (e.g., `rdfs:subPropertyOf`), the approach can provide more comprehensive and accurate explanations. Moreover, the use of symbolic reasoning allows for more transparent and interpretable explanations. The preliminary results show that our approach is capable of exploiting the semantics of an entity in *KG* and enhancing the explanations. Henceforth, more work needs to be conducted, to fully comprehend all impacting factors and to identify the most relevant explanations of the machine learning models over *KGs*.

Keywords: Knowledge Graphs · Link Prediction · Explainability

1 Introduction

Recent advances in Artificial Intelligence (AI) have already started to impact our daily lives in terms of intelligence, and demonstrated their success in forecasting machine learning problems (e.g., disease diagnosis [9]). Explainability refers to the degree to which humans can understand the decisions made by computational frameworks. Extracting explanations is crucial, particularly because they are often obscure, and the explainability of the outcomes is partially achieved. Explainable predictive models have rapidly become a pertinent problem [4] in data management. Various approaches [6,11] attempt to understand the algorithmic decisions made by machine learning models, but they are unable to capture the insights of the model behavior to translate them into the domain.

Category: Early Stage Ph.D.

© The Author(s), under exclusive license to Springer Nature Switzerland AG 2023
C. Pesquita et al. (Eds.): ESWC 2023, LNCS 13998, pp. 321–330, 2023.
https://doi.org/10.1007/978-3-031-43458-7_50

KGs are data structures that encode data and knowledge together with domain ontologies representing real-world information, where entities like Louis XIV and Marie Theresa are linked via directed edges denoted by binary relationships forming triples called facts, i.e., ⟨Louis XIV, spouse, Marie Theresa⟩.

In recent years, *KGs* have been built in various domains, and have led to a broad range of applications, including Knowledge Graph Completion (*KGC*) [1], or Query Processing [12]. *KGC* can discover new knowledge based on existing ones and check knowledge consistency. It is an appealing research topic that is important for completing and cleaning up *KGs*.

KGs represent knowledge in the form of factual statements of the form ⟨head entity, relation, tail entity⟩, shortened as ⟨e_h, r, e_t⟩. In the literature about *Knowledge Graph Embeddings (KGE)*, these notations are used to represent the facts in *KG*. *KGE* models, e.g., TransE, learn latent representations of entities and relations in continuous vector spaces, called embeddings, to preserve the *KG* structure. The most common learning methods for *KGC* are link predictions or triple classifications tasks based on a *KGE* model. Link Prediction (LP) confronts the issue of incompleteness by analyzing the already known facts to deduce new missing facts. For example, knowing the facts ⟨Louis XIV, hasChild, Wessex⟩ and ⟨Wessex, hasMother, Marie Theresa⟩, a LP model could predict ⟨Louis XIV, spouse, Marie Theresa⟩. However, these latent vector representations of the entities and the relations are not self-explainable, and an evaluation of the inductive abilities is still an open research issue.

Recently, the problem of explainable methods for link prediction has received attention [13,15]. Following the taxonomy by Rossi et al. [13] the *necessary* and *sufficient* explanations can be seen as either the set of facts in absence of which the link prediction model would not be able to yield the prediction; or a set of facts if given to an entity would lead the model to yield that prediction. For instance, given a tail prediction ⟨Berlin, country, Germany⟩, the facts about head entity Berlin: ⟨Berlin, capital, Germany⟩, and ⟨Berlin, located, Germany⟩ if removed from the training facts, leads the model to change the predicted tail. Thus, these facts were the necessary for the model to predict the correct tail entity, i.e., Germany with relation country. In *sufficient* explanation scenario, for example, when explaining the tail prediction ⟨Berlin, country, Germany⟩, identifying all the training facts about Berlin, if given to any head entity in the training facts, can lead the model to predict their country as Germany. For instance, adding the fact ⟨Washington D.C., capital, Germany⟩ to the training model is enough to yield the predicted country for Washington D.C. to be Germany. One of the crucial tasks for embedding-based explanation is efficiently learning and extracting explanations not only considering the data graphs, but also the meaning of the data given an ontology. When there are more triples or relations to consider, embedding-based reasoning is more effective.

SHACL[1] (the Shapes Constraint Language) is the W3C recommendation for defining integrity constraints over knowledge graphs. To trace and enhance the explanation for the predictive models built over data collected from *KGs*, our

---

[1] https://www.w3.org/TR/2017/REC-shacl-20170720/.

approach **InterpretME**[2,3] relies on a symbolic system, currently, this system validates integrity constraints that provide a meaningful description of an entity of a prediction model. The current version of **InterpretME** is customized for supervised machine learning models (e.g., Decision Trees), embedding models (e.g., TransE), and interpretable tools (e.g., LIME [11]). In this proposal, the approach of **InterpretME** is introduced to fill the gap towards the application of LP Explainability over the *KGs*. The preliminary results of the research reveal the key role of Semantic Web technologies in explainable AI and demonstrate the importance of considering entailment regimes for the extraction of explanations.

1.1 Motivating Example

The motivation of our work originates from the lack of explainability methods with machine learning models over *KGs*. Although state-of-art techniques provide automated machine-learning pipelines, they are unable to generate human- and machine-readable decisions to assist users and enhance their efficiency. In this proposal, explainability over the link prediction tasks is considered as an application. This task can be subdivided into a tail prediction task, which predicts the most plausible tail e_t and a head prediction task that predicts the most plausible head e_h. Figure 1 depicts a naive approach that explains a link prediction task, i.e., ⟨lc:2304772, lc:hasBio, ?⟩; the expected tail to be inferred is lc:PDL1. Embedding models (e.g., TransE) for link prediction (e.g., tail prediction) are utilized; they are executed on top of facts in data graphs.

Figure 1 illustrates the explanations based on link prediction tasks considering the RDF graph: **i)** as factual statements and, **ii)** with the meaning of an entity (i.e., rdf:type, rdfs:domain, rdfs:subPropertyOf). An input is collected from an **RDF** *KG* accessible via SPARQL endpoint, that integrates data about lung cancer patients. An RDF graph includes features describing the main characteristics of a lung cancer patient, i.e., patient identifier (a.k.a. LC_ID), gender, age, smoking habits, and lung cancer biomarkers. The predictive task is a link prediction of a tail entity into a low dimensional latent vector space to predict new infer facts about the patient by considering the neighborhood.

InterpretME resorts to Pykeen optimizer recommendations for hyperparameter optimization in the *KGE* models. Further, in the naive approach, the explainable tool Kelpie [13] is utilized to provide local interpretations of each patient in the training triples. Kelpie yields the relevant facts, by worsening or improving the scores of prediction, categorizing them into two categories *necessary* and *sufficient*. The terms *necessary* and *sufficient* are complementary to each other. Figure 1 depicts an exemplar entity where Kelpie determines the most plausible explanations based on facts for the tail prediction task ⟨lc:2304772, lc:hasBio, lc:PDL1⟩ and generates the necessary explanations of a particular tail prediction are: ⟨lc:2304772, lc:hasSmokingHabit, lc:PreviousSmoker⟩, ⟨lc:2304772, lc:age, "OLDER"⟩. The naive approach

---

[2] https://github.com/SDM-TIB/InterpretME.
[3] https://github.com/SDM-TIB/InterpretME_Demo_ESWC2023.

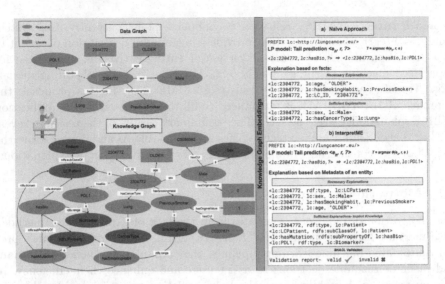

Fig. 1. Motivating Example. Explainable link prediction. a) Naive Approaches show facts with the head entity which leads to the particular prediction of a tail entity with *hasBio*. b) InterpretME depicts facts with the head entity and implicit knowledge which lead to the tail entity with *hasBio* and also provides SHACL validation reports.

outcomes allow for understanding the quality of the implemented framework. Although our user would have been able to understand the explanations generated by Kelpie, this user would need to trace these results back to the original data attributes to discover, for instance, whether the reported patient lc:2304772 violates the domain integrity constraints or not. In contrast, **InterpetME** yields the explanations of the link prediction model based on the facts, implicit knowledge (e.g., rdfs:subClassOf, rdfs:subPropertyOf) and SHACL constraints to ensure the trustability of RDF data and predictions are consistent with the domain constraints.

2   State of the Art

The necessity of automated machine learning frameworks with assistance has gained tremendous popularity in various domains. Amongst the explainability over the *KGs*, the works most related to ours form four main categorizations: *XAI, Link Prediction, SHACL Validation, and Causal Models.*

XAI Frameworks. Within the Explainable AI community, there has been a surge of research on explainability techniques. These techniques are of two main categories: 1) Intrinsic, and 2) Post-hoc explainability. Intrinsic explainability refers to the machine learning models that are considered explainable due to their simple structure, e.g., decision trees. Post-hoc explainability embodies the fully trained black-box models, thus, trying to explain and justify the logic behind the model outputs. The advantage of such techniques is that they are model-agnostic (i.e., the explanations can be generated across any models); LIME [11] is one of the exemplary post-hoc explainable methods. LIME aims to approximate any data-driven algorithm, with a local interpretable model to explain each instance prediction. Such techniques started showing major growth in many domains (e.g., Biomedical). However, this *saliency* explanations are human intuition matching techniques for entities and cannot be translated into a domain application. Our approach overcomes these limitations and provides fine-grained explanations linked to the entities in the *KGs*.

Link Prediction. *KGE* encodes the structure of triples in a KG, and can thus be used to perform link predictions, i.e., inferring the missing facts. Borrego et al. [3] propose a *KGC* approach using a set of neighborhood-aware features. However, the problem of learning embeddings for *KGs* has gained considerable attention, and only a few works address the explainability issues in link prediction over *KGs*. Zhang et al. [15] introduce a method of data poisoning; given a prediction $\langle e_h, r, e_t \rangle$, this data poisoning method identifies facts that, if are removed or added to training samples, they make worse the scoring function $\phi(e_h, r, e_t)$. Rossi et al. [13] propose the Kelpie framework, which explains the predicted links based on embedding via *necessary* and *sufficient* explanations. Rossi et al. state that the Kelpie framework computes the subset of training triples which can be seen as either the set of triples in addition or removal of which the model would yield that prediction. This framework is based on the aforementioned Post-hoc explainability. Nonetheless, these methods still lack in considering the semantic meaning of an entity and properties in a *KG*. Our approach aims at explaining the predictions based on the entailment regimes.

SHACL Validation. Explainability refers to the ability to interpret, understand and provide justifications for the decisions made by the machine learning models. In the context of *KGs*, SHACL validations are used to justify the machine learning model's prediction. Hence, defining the constraints on the structure and the data in the knowledge graph, SHACL is used to ensure that the predictions made by the link prediction model are consistent with the constraints and can provide justification for the predictions. The proposed approach relies on Trav-SHACL [5], Figuera et al. describe the capability of validating the shape schema against a SPARQL endpoint and scales better compared to other baseline approaches. Rohde et al. [12] report the perception of incorporating the SHACL validation result into SPARQL query answers by running the validation during the query processing. These validation results can provide one more layer of explainability. Thus, SHACL is more evident for enabling explainable AI in the context of *KGs*, provides validation, and explain the predictions.

Causal Models. A growing literature on causal models for the explainability of black-box models emphasizes that explanation is a normative goal that relates to real-world relationships (cause-effect) [2]. Pearl et al. [10] describe the essential role of the causal models via seven pillars which are beyond the reach of current machine learning models. In some recent work on the relational database,

Salimi et al. [14] propose a declarative language, $CARL$ which represents complex causal models using Horn clauses and constructs a unit table specific to the query and implements a causal model to identify the impact of treatment variable. In some of the closely related work, Huang [8] proposes $CareKG$, a causal query framework over the KGs to analyze the impact of treatment variables on the outcome and defines the aggregation function for multiple treatment variables. However, these approaches describe the formalism for the causal model but do not explain "*Why this particular decision?*" and also ignores the meaning of an entity in KG. To our best knowledge, none applied causality to provide more expressive explanations over KGs. Henceforth, one research focus of the proposal is to connect explainability and cause-effect analysis over KGs, so that the framework can provide more accurate explanations for its predictions and will greatly impact the Semantic Web community.

3   Problem Statement

Consider an RDF knowledge graph KG (ζ, R, G), defined as a directed edge labeled graph such that each node $e \in \zeta$ represents an entity, each $r \in R$ represents a unique relation, and each directed edge $\langle e_h, r, e_t \rangle \in G$ represents a fact about the head entity e_h. Given a tail prediction[4]. $\langle e_h, r, ? \rangle$ where e_h is the head entity, r is the relation between entities, and $\langle e_h, r, e_t \rangle \notin G$, the aim is to find a set of most plausible entities e_t by inferring new facts based on the existing relations and entities in G and provides an interpretable set of facts $T = \{(e_h, r, e) | e \in \zeta\}$ which lead the black-box model to predict new facts. Unlike the previous method uses a fact-based approach to provide explanations. Our approach considers entailment regimes (i.e., RDFS and OWL) over KGs and causal relations; scalability is also one of our goals.

   In contrast to baselines, the goal is to develop a framework that can be qualitatively and quantitatively evaluated for the explainability of machine learning models over KGs. To this end, we evaluate our approach by answering the following research questions: **RQ1)** What is the impact of integrating machine learning frameworks with KGs to enhance explainability? **RQ2)** To what extent do the extracted explanations comply with the predictions? **RQ3)** What is the impact of injecting RDFS and OWL axioms in the explanations over the KGs? With the above research questions, we aim to contribute to the Semantic Web and AI communities and develop a generalized framework that leverages black-box models to provide meaningful post-hoc explanations on top of the knowledge graphs. The expected contributions of this doctoral proposal are: 1) A novel framework to integrate machine learning methods and KG; 2) Explainability with the exploitation of the semantics of an entity in KG; 3) Exploitation of cause-effect relationships to empower the explanations; 4) Formalism for the metrics to evaluate the explanations and enhance the efficiency.

---

[4] Analogously Head prediction $\langle ?, r, e_t \rangle$.

4   Research Methodology

The research methodology for this Ph.D. proposal refers to a structured, conceptual, analysis of the Semantic Web Technologies applied to the research problem of explainability. The **RQ3)** is still an open problem, the first step focuses on the integration of ontology and entailment regimes, i.e., RDFS and OWL. For instance, extracting the explanations of tail prediction shown in Fig. 1, the baseline ignores the ontology in their approach. Considering this metadata of the entity, we aim to enhance the explainability of a model's prediction. The second step involves logical reasoning over the *KG*, considering the most implicit facts, and adding those facts to any other training entities would enhance the tail rank for that particular entity. This shows the impact of implicit knowledge in explainability (**RQ3)**. Our goal is not to limit the approach to RDFS entailment but also to extend it to OWL entailment in the next steps of the Ph.D.

The third step aims at integrating the machine learning frameworks with *KGs* to provide more insights into explainability (**RQ1)**. Three main components were identified for the implementation of explainable driven frameworks over *KG*: collecting valid data, training the model, and creating the explanations. The data collected from the RDF graph, given to any machine learning model needs to be valid, so our approach first implements the SHACL constraints to assure validity. One technique would be adapting SPARQL queries over an RDF graph, to avoid inconsistencies in the data given to the predictive model and the second technique will be reasoning via SPARQL queries to retrieve the implicit knowledge of a particular prediction. In the end, our approach will generate a knowledge graph comprising all the traced metadata collected during a data-driven pipeline followed during the resolution of a prediction task.

LIME [11] and Kelpie [13] can be the basis for providing feature contributions and fact-based explanations. **RQ2)** still remains a complex challenge. For instance, consider explainability task when integrated with *KGs* generates a huge search space for selecting a particular feature or a fact which leads the model to predict. Henceforth, the main aim of **RQ2)** is to provide valid scalable and trustable explanations. To tackle **RQ2)**, the implementation of an algorithm that optimally prunes the search space of valid explanations will be accomplished in the subsequent phases of this Ph.D. proposal. The fourth step includes the exploitation of causal relationships between the entities and provides more insights into the extraction of explanations. The last step integrates all the components and implements a fully-fledged framework compatible with domain agnostic.

5   Evaluation Plan

The previous section outlines the benefit of integrating knowledge-driven frameworks with explainable frameworks. Indeed **RQ1)** is a non-trivial research question, it might be complicated to evaluate a framework as a complete end-to-end task. However, the aim of **RQ1)** will be to integrate the symbolic system with sub-symbolic approaches. The creation of the possible set of explanations **RQ2)** can be decomposed into two categories: SHACL validation result, then building the possible explanation set. To evaluate the effectiveness of explanations, metrics like `Mean Reciprocal Rank (MRR)` or `Hits@k` will be utilized.

Indeed, for the evaluation of predictive models, i.e., supervised learning, metrics like Accuracy, Precision, or Recall are computed. To explain predictive models, LIME [11] would be a better option to have an idea of influential features for a particular prediction. In the end, the aim will be to build a knowledge graph with all the characteristics traced in the predictive task (i.e., features, prediction probabilities, etc.) to enhance the explainability of the particular entity. The techniques to evaluate the framework with axioms injection **RQ3)**, would be challenging to provide new insights. **RQ3)** will also attempt to define and formalize the metrics quantifying the enhanced performance of explainability.

We aim to evaluate **InterpretME** on top of the following *KGs*: 1) *ImProVIT*[5] to explain the link prediction task about the impact of the immune system over the response of Hepatitis B and Influenza vaccines; 2) *CLARIFY*[6] to define machine learning models to predict biomarkers of a lung cancer patient and generate explanations. In these tasks, the components of InterpretME will be evaluated and implemented to provide explainability over *KGs*; assist the domain experts to have more insights into the predictive task.

6   Results so Far

We have analyzed the state of the art and the challenges to achieve explainability in prediction models. As a first result, we have developed **InterpretME**, a tool describes in a *KG* the outcomes and interpretations of a predictive method. In this section, we report on our initial assessment of **InterpretME** in the explainability of link prediction (Fig. 2). The *French Royalty KG* [7] depicts the information about each person in the French royal family.

Explainability over French Royalty KG.[7] The link predictive task is to determine whether a member of the French royalty has a spouse. For instance, let us consider the tail prediction of a french royal member ⟨dbo:Charles the Simple, dbo:hasSpouse, dbo:Yes⟩ over *French Royalty KG*[8]. The evaluation of the *LP* model obtained respectively with `TransE` is reported. Here, the *necessary* explanations are analogous to the state-of-the-art approaches with the removal of combination facts. *Sufficient* explanations are given based on axioms injected, showing how to improve the predictions by adding implicit knowledge to any random entities in the training. Removing only the most important fact about the `dbo:Charles the Simple` will likely not change the prediction because it

---

[5] German Funded project https://www.tib.eu/en/research-development/project-overview/project-summary/improvit.

[6] EU H2020 Funded project https://www.clarify2020.eu/.

[7] https://github.com/SDM-TIB/LinkPrediction_Explanations_over_KGs.

[8] https://labs.tib.eu/sdm/InterpretME-og/sparql.

LP model	Hits@1	MRR	Score	rank
Necessary	0.07	-0.02	-5.84	1
Sufficient	0.093	0.39	-7.47	3

(a) Link Prediction(LP) model performance

InterpretME	ΔHits@1	ΔMRR	Score	rank
Necessary	-0.023	-0.02	**-7.47**	3
Sufficient	0.10	0.0052	**-6.06**	1

(b) Evalution of InterpretME explanations

Fig. 2. Initial Results. Figure 2a shows the evaluation of link prediction model performed over French Royalty KG. Figure 2b indicates the effectiveness of removing or adding the combination of facts. The values in *bold* indicate the change in the metrics. For *necessary*, score and tail rank are worsened, and conversely for *sufficient* got improved. We report the efficacy of explanations as the difference of Hits@1 and MRR on the particular tail prediction i.e., ΔHits@1 and ΔMRR. For necessary, more negative values $\Rightarrow$ higher efficacy and, sufficient, more positive values $\Rightarrow$ higher efficacy.

is still supported by other facts. Hence, **InterpetME** identifies the *necessary* explanations, removing the combination of facts featuring e_h, i.e., *Charles the Simple has child Gisela of France and has a spouse Frederuna* leads to worsens ϕ. The score reduced drastically to 7.47 and the tail rank from 1 to 3.

Sufficient scenario, **InterpretME** utilizes the implicit knowledge encoded in an ontology of the *KG* using entailment regimes, i.e., *subClassOf*, *domain*, *subPropertyOf*. For instance, using ontology about *dbo:Charles the Simple*, the implicit facts obtained: $\langle$dbo:marriedTo, rdfs:subPropertyOf, dbo:spouse$\rangle$, and $\langle$dbo:child, rdfs:domain,dbo:Person$\rangle$ added to the entities improve the *score* and the *tail rank* change from 3 to 1. For instance, assume the fact: $\langle$dbo:Charles the Simple, dbo:marriedTo, dbo:Eadgifu of Wessex$\rangle$, with the entailment regime *subPropertyOf*. As a result, we can infer: $\langle$dbo:Charles the Simple, dbo:spouse, dbo:Eadgifu of Wessex$\rangle$. Since the original model was not able to infer the correct tail, their Hits@1 and MRR are more likely to be null. The re-trained should infer the correct predict tail, i.e., dbo:Yes. Thus, adding the implicit fact improves the prediction of an entity. The variation observed in the Hits@1 and MRR are reported. As the *KG* is limited to some instances, the neighborhood of that particular member is less. Lastly, the SHACL validation results are used to provide one more layer of explainability and to justify the model's outcome. Here, SHACL constraint explains a dbo:Person link satisfying the domain constraints about a member having a child or spouse. For instance, the tail prediction $\langle$dbo:Charles the Simple, dbo:hasSpouse, dbo:Yes$\rangle$, the head entity satisfies the constraint having a child. The initial results are prominent to address the **RQ3)** and more refined results will be achieved in the next steps of this doctoral work.

7   Conclusions and Lessons Learned

This proposal introduces and formalizes the problem of explainability which can be particularly useful for explaining the Link Prediction model over *KGs*. In state-of-art approaches, we have explored different techniques for extracting explanations, including *LIME* and *Kelpie*. We found that each of these techniques has strengths and weaknesses depending on the application domain. One area for improvement is to prune the search space for explanations, and the techniques for handling the SPARQL queries and entailment regimes. The aim was to see the impact of considering the axioms in the explainability of a Link Prediction model. The proposal identifies the challenges for developing a framework with exploiting semantics over the *KGs* to show more expressiveness in the explainability. We expect that the proposed research will make contributions to the development of a more robust explainable framework over *KGs*.

The next task for my Ph.D. will be to improvise the proposed approach for enhancing the explainability of the machine learning models over the *KGs*. The future work will be about the execution of a fully fledge explainable framework, like searching relevant entailment regimes or important characteristics of an entity. Moreover, the presented research plan involves the cause-effect relations between entities. Henceforth, future work will also be on such causal relations.

Acknowledgements. I express my special thanks to my supervisor Prof. Dr. Maria-Esther Vidal her guidance and support. This work is funded by TrustKG-Transforming Data in Trustable Insights with grant P99/2020.

References

1. Akrami, F., Saeef, M.S., Zhang, Q., Hu, W., Li, C.: Realistic re-evaluation of knowledge graph completion methods: an experimental study. In: SIGMOD (2020)
2. Beckers, S.: Causal explanations and XAI. CLeaR (2022)
3. Borrego, A., Ayala, D., Hernández, I., Rivero, C.R., Ruiz, D.: Cafe: knowledge graph completion using neighborhood-aware features. In: IFAC (2021)
4. De Bie, T., De Raedt, L., Hern_'andez-Orallo, J., Hoos, H.H., Smyth, P., Williams, C.K.I.: Automating data science. In: CACM (2022)
5. Figuera, M., Rohde, P.D., Vidal, M.E.: Trav-shacl: efficiently validating networks of shacl constraints. In: WWW (2021)
6. Guidotti, R., Monreale, A., Ruggieri, S., Turini, F., Giannotti, F., Pedreschi, D.: A survey of methods for explaining black box models. ACM Comput. Surv. (2018)
7. Halliwell, N., Gandon, F., Lecue, F.: User scored evaluation of non-unique explanations for relational graph convolutional network link prediction on knowledge graphs. In: K-CAP. ACM (2021)
8. Huang, H.: Causal relationship over knowledge graphs. In: CIKM (2022)
9. Myszczynska, M., et al.: Applications of machine learning to diagnosis and treatment of neurodegenerative diseases. Nat. Rev. Neurol. (2020)
10. Pearl, J.: Theoretical impediments to machine learning with seven sparks from the causal revolution. In: WSDM (2018)
11. Ribeiro, M.T., Singh, S., Guestrin, C.: "Why should i trust you?": explaining the predictions of any classifier. In: SIGKDD (2016)
12. Rohde, P.D.: SHACL constraint validation during SPARQL query processing. In: VLDB PhD Workshop (2021)
13. Rossi, A., Firmani, D., Merialdo, P., Teofili, T.: Explaining link prediction systems based on knowledge graph embeddings. In: SIGMOD (2022)
14. Salimi, B., Parikh, H., Kayali, M., Getoor, L., Roy, S., Suciu, D.: Causal relational learning. In: SIGMOD (2020)
15. Zhang, H., et al.: Data poisoning attack against knowledge graph embedding. In: IJCAI (2019)

A Window into the Multiple Views of Linked Data

Sitt Min Oo[(✉)][iD]

IDLab, Department of Electronics and Information Systems,
Ghent University – imec, Technologiepark-Zwijnaarde 122, 9052 Ghent, Belgium
x.sittminoo@ugent.be

Abstract. RDF mapping engines enable access to existing heterogeneous data sources as RDF Knowledge Graph (KG). However, these mapping engines have two challenges: i) processing streaming data sources with changing velocity efficiently, ii) and providing a rich variety in the format of the generated KG output. To tackle these challenges, I carry out my research in 3 steps. I will first design a highly scalable data stream mapping solution to handle dynamic velocity of streaming data sources. Preliminary results indicate that our stream mapping solution outperforms state of the art engines with lower latency, constant memory usage, and higher throughput. I will then refine this architecture in a task-based fashion, aiming to be a common architecture for any kind of mapping. Finally, I will utilize the common modular mapping architecture and extend it with a component to derive an intermediate representation of the data mapping process, enabling heterogeneous to heterogeneous data mapping. The combined solution will provide a highly scalable heterogeneous to heterogeneous data stream mapping engine, enabling us to have multiple views of the underlying KG.

Keywords: RML · Knowledge Graph Generation · Mapping Engine

1 Introduction

Knowledge Graph (KG) adoption is further intensified by technologies such as Solid [20], which decouples data from applications. This decoupling requires integrating heterogeneous data from different organizations and applications, which is seamlessly achieved with KGs [11].

KG data is represented in various formats such as those compliant with the Resource Definition Framework (RDF). These formats are required to facilitate data sharing in the form of a decentralized database. To use data from multiple heterogeneous data sources, mapping engines could be used to convert existing data to RDF data in a shape as required by the different applications.

However, current mapping engines are incapable of dealing with the following two characteristics of data: i) the **velocity** of streaming data sources, ii) and the **variety** in the KG output of these engines. The mapping engines cannot handle

© The Author(s), under exclusive license to Springer Nature Switzerland AG 2023
C. Pesquita et al. (Eds.): ESWC 2023, LNCS 13998, pp. 331–340, 2023.
https://doi.org/10.1007/978-3-031-43458-7_51

the dynamic velocity (i.e., variable data velocity with respect to time) of streaming data sources efficiently. Furthermore, the mapping engines are designed to generate RDF data adhering to a single shape from heterogeneous data sources; there is no variation in the output. Finally, research on mapping engines is slowed down as they have redundant implementations due to the lack of a common, reusable, and modular components.

In this PhD thesis, I aim to provide a scalable heterogeneous to heterogeneous mapping engine. This is done in 3 steps: i) an RDF mapping solution to handle dynamic velocity, ii) a common modular architecture for mapping engines, and iii) an intermediate data mapping representation that can be used to achieve full heterogeneous to heterogeneous mapping.

2   State of the Art

After discussing mapping languages (Sect. 2.1) and mapping engines (Sect. 2.2) for mapping heterogeneous data to RDF data, I will elaborate and discuss optimization techniques employed for batch processing (Sect. 2.3).

2.1   Languages for Mapping Heterogeneous Data

Several mapping languages exist for mapping heterogeneous data into RDF data [18]. Depending on the extensibility of the mapping language, data processing operations such as joins and data transformations are supported.

Languages such as R2RML [5], and its extensions such as RML [7] use Turtle syntax to write mapping rules. Extensions such as alignment to FnO [6] and Logical Target [19] are applied to RML to enable data transformations on the input, and describe how and where the output should be generated respectively.

Languages such as SPARQL-Generate [15] and Facade-X [4] extend SPARQL, while others such as ShExML [9] are based on ShEx. SPARQL-Generate and Facade-X rely on the underlying SPARQL engine for joins and data transformations. ShExML uses custom definitions to describe how to iterate over the data sources, process them, and join the iterated data items.

2.2   Mapping Engines

Mapping engines generate RDF data and store it in a specific document or (triple) store [18]. The existing generation approaches could be further categorized into two groups based on its processing type: i) *batch processing* and ii) *stream processing*.

Batch processing engines work with inputs based on the assumption that the data is finite and bounded. RML's reference implementation RMLMapperis one example of a batch processing mapping engine.

Stream processing engines have to work with data which are potentially *unbounded* and *infinite in size* [14]. For example, a temperature sensor monitoring a building's ambient temperature will keep generating data as long as they are powered. Mapping engines handling streaming data sources include SPARQL-Generate [15], Chimera [2], and RMLStreamer [10].

2.3   Optimization Techniques

In recent years, optimization of the mapping processes with batch processing has been the focus of research in KG generation [18], to either speed up the execution time, lower the memory footprint, or remove duplicates from the output.

Morph-KGC is a batch processing implementation that focuses on the *optimization of the mapping rules* in the mapping document through *partitioning* [1]. SDM-RDFizer employs *specialized data structures* to eliminate duplicates and empty values, and optimize joins [12].

The application of arbitrary functions during the mapping process – e.g. via FnO [6] – also presents opportunities for optimization as they bring processing overhead. FunMap [13] reduces the aforementioned processing overhead through eager execution of function rules, storing the function-applied results in an intermediate dataset before proceeding with the mapping rules.

The aforementioned optimization approaches are implemented in monolithic engines without the capability to integrate different optimizations from each other due to the **lack of a modular architecture**.

To the best of our knowledge, stream processing optimizations techniques are not actively researched unlike batch processing optimization techniques for KG generation. Approaches such as SPARQL-Generate [15] process streaming input data, without detailing generalizable optimizations.

3   Problem Statements and Contributions

I will focus on the two major drawbacks in the current state of the art mapping engines: i) inefficient handling of streaming data with dynamic **velocity**, and ii) lack of **variety** in the output data serialization by only serializing in RDF.

On the one hand, the velocity of streaming data can vary over time. For example, a temperature sensor might have an emission rate of 1 Hz under default conditions which can increase to 100 Hz in an event of a fire disaster to provide more accurate measurements. If there are multiple sensors feeding the data to the mapping engine, this can become the bottleneck of the mapping process if the engines are not scalable, leading to significantly increased latency. Thus, mapping engines handling streaming data sources must be able to deal with such a burst in data velocity.

On the other hand, there are numerous mapping solutions which output only *RDF* serializations, leading to a lack of variety in data being generated. In the context of web applications, current web applications utilizing a KG must communicate in RDF compliant formats with the servers hosting the KG. A mapping solution from heterogeneous to *heterogeneous* data would increase KG adoption, for example, by acting as a data translation layer between the server and the clients.

3.1   Inefficient Handling of Streaming Heterogeneous Data

The first problem I identified is the mapping engines' inability to handle streaming heterogeneous data efficiently. Mapping engines, working with data streams, must take into account that the data stream can change in velocity over time. This might have a performance impact if these engines cannot handle a sudden and large change in velocity. Complexity increases if the mapping engines have to join multiple data streams of different velocity. This leads us to our first Research Question (RQ).

RQ 1: What is an efficient architecture for mapping heterogeneous data streams which change in velocity over time, especially when joining data streams of different velocity in a distributed and parallel environment?

H: A task-based granular architecture with the ability to join two data streams of different velocity using a dynamic windowing algorithm would enable efficient mapping of heterogeneous data streams to RDF in terms of latency, memory, and CPU usage.

Contribution: A parallel and scalable stream processing architecture for mapping heterogeneous data to RDF data, which is able to efficiently process multiple data streams, with changing velocity, and also bounded datasets.

3.2   Lack of Variety in Output

Current state of the art stream mapping engines only map from heterogeneous data to RDF data. This leads to the problem that the underlying KG can only be viewed in a specific RDF shape: supporting multiple views is currently only possible by setting up multiple parallel mapping processes, inhibiting potential optimization opportunities. It can be serialized in multiple ways (JSON-LD, Turtle, etc.), but the shape remains the same. We do not have the ability to construct multiple views of the underlying KG for the client. Combined with Problem 3.1, this leads us to the following RQ:

RQ 2: How can we scale heterogeneous to heterogeneous stream mapping engines to support the complete decoupling of data and applications?

H: We can extend existing heterogeneous to RDF data mapping engines by modularizing them into granular operators, and devising an intermediate representation for the mapping process. The intermediate representation makes the mapping process independent from any source or target formats and languages.

Contribution: A modular heterogeneous to heterogeneous streaming data mapping engine. Using this engine, we can support generating multiple views simultaneously on top of the same source data. Not only would we be able to generate multiple RDF views, but also non-RDF views, achieving full heterogeneous to heterogeneous mapping.

I broke down RQ 2 into following subproblems with respective sub RQs. The combined solution from the subproblems provides the answer to heterogeneous to heterogeneous mapping.

Subproblem 1: Modular Architecture. There is no modular mapping architecture from which existing research is built upon. Hence, existing mapping engines have redundant implementations and their optimizations can not be easily integrated with each other. Furthermore, it is difficult to integrate state of the art mapping approaches and optimizations in existing mapping engines due to the complex and engine-specific architecture they are presented in.

RQ 2.1: Which components do we need to modularize the materialization process of mapping heterogeneous data to RDF data sufficiently to support existing optimization approaches?

H: Through generalizing the optimization approaches for the mapping engines, we find the set of components which enable mapping engines to be configured with granular optimizations and thus modularizing the materialization process of mapping heterogeneous data to RDF data.

Contribution: A modular heterogeneous to RDF mapping architecture that efficiently processes data streams by integrating existing optimizations.

Subproblem 2: Heterogeneous to Heterogeneous Mapping. Mapping from heterogeneous to heterogeneous data requires metadata on the target data structure and data format.

Current mapping engines derive the target RDF data structure from the mapping document defined in the mapping language of their choice. However, it is currently unknown how to incorporate the desired output *heterogeneous* data format and structure.

RQ 2.2: How do we incorporate the desired heterogeneous data structure in the mapping process to enable heterogeneous to heterogeneous data mapping?

H: The modular architecture, from Sub Problem 1, extended with a component to derive the intermediate representation of the data mapping process, has all necessary information on the output data structure to enable mapping from heterogeneous data to heterogeneous data.

Contribution: An intermediate representation to describe the mapping process from heterogeneous to heterogeneous data.

4   Research Methodology and Approach

Stream Mapping Engine. I conduct an in depth study of state of the art mapping engines and their mapping processes. The mapping processes – broken down into clearly defined tasks – are used in my architecture design as granular task-based components. I review data processing paradigms and best practices to design the streaming architecture, and put additional focus on the component that joins multiple data sources with dynamic velocity. Existing stream joining techniques utilizing windows (a temporary buffer of an incoming data stream) are studied to choose the window type on which the dynamic window is built upon. I study congestion control techniques from networking as possible references to implement the dynamically adjusting window. The dynamically adjusting window enables us to deal with sudden changes in data velocity, and mitigate the resulting *congestion* effects such as high latency and low throughput.

Modular Mapping Architecture. I conduct a systematic survey of optimization techniques in mapping engines to analyze the impact of individual optimization techniques. For individual analysis of optimizations, I extend the aforementioned modular architecture to enable isolation of every optimization techniques, and investigate their impact on the different stages of the mapping workflow. Through the comparison of the different combinations of optimization techniques, I want to investigate if having a modular architecture for mapping engine results in a similar or better performance than state of the art mapping engines, with significant improvements in flexibility.

Heterogeneous to Heterogeneous Mapping. I extend the previously developed modular architecture to map heterogeneous to heterogeneous data. I investigate the execution graph of the modular architecture and state of the art techniques for Intermediate Representation (IR) generation. From the execution graph of the modular architecture, I will apply IR generation techniques for data mapping. The generated IR will contain all necessary metadata on the data structures and formats for mapping from heterogeneous to heterogeneous data.

5   Evaluation

Stream Mapping Engine. To evaluate my stream mapping engine, I need to consider the context in which the stream mapping engine is expected to be deployed. The stream mapping engine is located at the boundary of two domains: traditional stream processing for the data stream input that it consumes, and RDF stream processing for the output RDF stream that it produces. Thus, benchmark approaches from the domain of traditional stream processing and RDF stream processing are combined: i) the benchmark architecture from RSPLab [17], ii) the workload design to emulate dynamic streaming characteristics from Open Stream Processing Benchmark [8], and iii) the measurement strategies from Karimov et al [14]. As input for the evaluation, I will use real-world (logged) sensor data. This ensures that the data characteristics reflect with real-world data expected to be processed by a stream mapping engine.

The following metrics are measured to evaluate the performance of the stream mapping engine:

a) **Event-time latency (ms)** is measured to avoid the effect of coordinated occlusion [14], where queuing time is ignored, by also taking into account the queuing time of the records inside the engine. The output generation latency should be kept low if the stream processing engines are to process real-time data streams and match the velocity of the data stream.

b) **Throughput (records/s)** with increasing data velocity. I aim to find the *sustainable throughput* [14] which is the highest throughput an engine could sustain without increasing latency due to back-pressure.

c) **CPU and the peak memory usage** to evaluate the efficiency of the engine resource usage while dealing with varying input data stream velocity.

These are the core metrics I will use throughout my PhD to evaluate the subsequent implementations, since they are common metrics to evaluate stream processing engine.

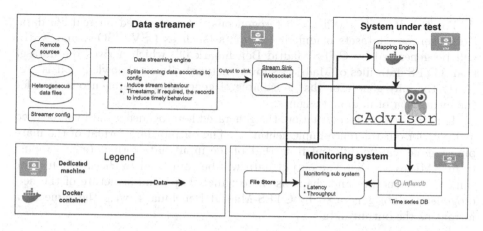

Fig. 1. Benchmark architecture to evaluate the different engines, inspired by RSPLab.

The benchmark architecture is inspired by RSPLab [17] with a modification to include a custom data streaming component (Fig. 1). I isolate the different benchmark components (e.g. the measurement component from the System Under Test (SUT)) to reduce the influence of the benchmark components on the engines during the evaluation process.

The dataset for the evaluation is the time annotated traffic sensor data from the Netherlands provided by NDW (Nationale Databank Wegverkeers-gegevens)[1], which is also used in Open Stream Processing Benchmark [8]. The traffic sensor data set has high duplicates, time characteristics and relationship between multiple sensors. This enables us to evaluate the mapping engine derived from the modular architecture for duplicate removal, ability to deal with data velocity through replaying the time series dataset, and joins or even functions to transform relationships between the different sensors.

Modular Mapping Architecture. A combination of current state of the art optimization techniques, implemented using the modular architecture, will be evaluated using the same evaluation benchmark architecture as above. This allows me to find the best combination based on the aforementioned evaluation metrics, and also to analyze the impact of individual optimization techniques.

The implementation will be evaluated for performance against the state of the art monolithic engines with the same feature set. The performance of the modular architecture should be similar to the target engine but very flexible to be extended with extra optimization components.

Heterogeneous to Heterogeneous Mapping. For the heterogeneous to heterogeneous mapping contribution, I will evaluate the reference implementation of intermediate representation for correctness.

---

[1] NDW: http://www.ndw.nu.

For the dataset, I will use heterogeneous datasets based on real-life data. Heterogeneous datasets of different formats (such as CSV, JSON, and XML) will be generated by GTFS-Madrid Benchmark [3], which derives the dataset from GTFS data files of Madrid's subway network. To my knowledge, it is currently the only generator that is capable of generating heterogeneous data for the evaluation of mapping engines.

For the correctness evaluation, the generated heterogeneous data will be used as input for our reference implementation. The output data format of the mapping engine will be different from that of the input data format (e.g. mapping from XML to JSON). The output data will be compared to check if it has the same data structure and shape as the original shape and structure of the heterogeneous data generated by GTFS-Madrid Benchmark, with the same data format as the output data.

6   Intermediate Results

I developed RMLStreamer-SISO: a streaming mapping engine published at ISWC 2022[2]. The paper, "RMLStreamer-SISO: an RDF stream generator from heterogeneous data" [16], introduces RMLStreamer-SISO as a scalable stream mapping engine that is able to efficiently process data streams with varying velocity.

To develop RMLStreamer-SISO's architecture, I considered the dataflow architecture paradigm of existing stream processing engines, such as Apache Flink[3], with a task-based architecture and incorporated it in our stream mapping engine. To enable joining of multiple streaming data sources with dynamic velocity, I took inspiration from congestion control algorithms such as additive-increase, multiplicative decrease algorithm of TCP congestion control. This enabled RMLStremaer-SISO to be capable of joining multiple heterogeneous data streams with dynamic velocity by relying on a dynamic windowing algorithm, where the window changes its size based on the incoming data velocities.

I showed that the approach of a task-based architecture for mapping streaming data sources is scalable in terms of the volume, increasing velocity, and dynamic velocity of the input data streams. It outperforms state of the art streaming mapping engines by achieving millisecond latency, constant memory usage for all workloads, and sustainable throughput of around 70,000 records/s [16]. This answers our RQ 1 on efficient mapping of streaming heterogeneous data to RDF data, and confirmed our hypothesis.

The task-based architecture from RMLStreamer-SISO is the starting point for developing a modular mapping architecture, in which multiple optimizations can be independently evaluated. I identified following most common components of the mapping process through studying the architecture of the state of the art mapping engines: a) Mapping language interpretation, b) Source iterator, c) Windowing, d) Transformation, e) RDF Mapping, and f) Serialization.

---

[2] RMLStreamer-SISO: https://github.com/RMLio/RMLStreamer/releases/tag/v2.3.0.
[3] Apache Flink:https://flink.apache.org/.

I also identified different optimization techniques employed by state of the art mapping engines. These techniques have been categorized according to the different mapping stages they are applied on: a) Language interpretation stage, b) Pre-mapping stage right before the data records are mapped, and c) Mapping stage while the data records are being mapped.

7 Conclusion and Lessons Learned

This thesis contributes to the KG generation community by enabling highly scalable and efficient heterogeneous to heterogeneous streaming data mapping. Preliminary results already show that having a task-based architecture enables an efficient and scalable stream mapping engine. This architecture has the potential to be extended to be modular where users could integrate the only specific stages of the mapping process to create their custom mapping engine.

Current optimization research is slowed down due to overlapping feature implementation even though the focus of the research is on just a specific stage of the mapping process. Researchers would greatly benefit from a modular architecture where they could build their own mapping engine by utilizing the common components of the modular architecture. The benefits are: a) a faster research speed on mapping engines, b) higher quality research by allowing researchers to focus only on the components that matter, and c) fairer comparisons during the evaluation of optimization approaches based on a modular common architecture.

On the industry side, integrating this engine into KG ecosystems such as Solid can increase its uptake, as KG application developers can keep using existing data format standards when communicating with KG servers, without needing to dedicate time to learn RDF graph technologies.

References

1. Arenas-Guerrero, J., Chaves-Fraga, D., Toledo, J., Pérez, M.S., Corcho, O.: Morph-KGC: scalable knowledge graph materialization with mapping partitions. Semantic Web 1–20 (2022). https://doi.org/10.3233/sw-223135
2. Belcao, M., Falzone, E., Bionda, E., Valle, E.D.: Chimera: a bridge between big data analytics and semantic technologies. In: The Semantic Web (ISWC 2021), pp. 463–479 (2021)
3. Chaves-Fraga, D., Priyatna, F., Cimmino, A., Toledo, J., Ruckhaus, E., Corcho, O.: Gtfs-madrid-bench: a benchmark for virtual knowledge graph access in the transport domain. J. Web Semant. 65, 100596 (2020)
4. Daga, E., Asprino, L., Mulholland, P., Gangemi, A.: Facade-X: an opinionated approach to SPARQL anything. In: Further with Knowledge Graphs - 17th International Conference on Semantic Systems, vol. 53, pp. 58–73 (2021)
5. Das, S., Sundara, S., Cyganiak, R.: R2RML: RDB to RDF mapping language. In: Working Group Recommendation, World Wide Web Consortium (W3C) (2012). http://www.w3.org/TR/r2rml/
6. De Meester, B., Seymoens, T., Dimou, A., Verborgh, R.: Implementation-independent function reuse. Futur. Gener. Comput. Syst. 110, 946–959 (2020). https://doi.org/10.1016/j.future.2019.10.006

7. Dimou, A., Vander Sande, M., Colpaert, P., Verborgh, R., Mannens, E., Van de Walle, R.: RML: a generic language for integrated RDF mappings of heterogeneous data. In: 7th Workshop on Linked Data on the Web, vol. 1184 (2014)
8. van Dongen, G., Van den Poel, D.: Evaluation of stream processing frameworks. IEEE Trans. Parallel Distrib. Syst. **31**(8), 1845–1858 (2020). https://doi.org/10.1109/TPDS.2020.2978480
9. García-González, H., Boneva, I., Staworko, S., Labra-Gayo, J.E., Lovelle, J.M.C.: ShExML: improving the usability of heterogeneous data mapping languages for first-time users. PeerJ Comput. Sci. **6** (2020)
10. Haesendonck, G., Maroy, W., Heyvaert, P., Verborgh, R., Dimou, A.: Parallel RDF generation from heterogeneous big data. In: International Workshop on Semantic Big Data, no. 1 (2019). https://doi.org/10.1145/3323878.3325802
11. Hogan, A., et al.: Knowledge graphs. ACM Comput. Surv. **54**(4), 1–37 (2021). https://doi.org/10.1145/3447772
12. Iglesias, E., Vidal, M., Jozashoori, S., Collarana, D., Chaves-Fraga, D.: Empowering the SDM-RDFizer tool for scaling up to complex knowledge graph creation pipelines. Semantic Web J. (2022)
13. Jozashoori, S., Chaves-Fraga, D., Iglesias, E., Vidal, M.E., Corcho, O.: Funmap: efficient execution of functional mappings for knowledge graph creation. In: International Semantic Web Conference, pp. 276–293 (2020)
14. Karimov, J., Rabl, T., Katsifodimos, A., Samarev, R., Heiskanen, H., Markl, V.: Benchmarking distributed stream data processing systems. In: IEEE 34th International Conference on Data Engineering (ICDE) (2018). https://doi.org/10.1109/icde.2018.00169
15. Lefrançois, M., Zimmermann, A., Bakerally, N.: A SPARQL extension for generating RDF from heterogeneous formats. In: The Semantic Web 14th International Conference, ESWC, pp. 35–50 (2017). https://doi.org/10.1007/978-3-319-58068-5_3
16. Oo, S.M., Haesendonck, G., De Meester, B., Dimou, A.: RMLStreamer-SISO: an RDF stream generator from streaming heterogeneous data. In: The Semantic Web (ISWC 2022), pp. 697–713 (2022). https://doi.org/10.1007/978-3-031-19433-7_40
17. Tommasini, R., Della Valle, E., Mauri, A., Brambilla, M.: Rsplab: rdf stream processing benchmarking made easy. In: The Semantic Web (ISWC 2017), pp. 202–209 (2017). https://doi.org/10.1007/978-3-319-68204-4_21
18. Van Assche, D., Delva, T., Haesendonck, G., Heyvaert, P., De Meester, B., Dimou, A.: Declarative RDF graph generation from heterogeneous (semi-)structured data: a systematic literature review. J. Web Semant. (2022). https://doi.org/10.1016/j.websem.2022.100753
19. Van Assche, D., et al.: Leveraging Web of Things W3C Recommendations for Knowledge Graphs Generation, pp. 337–352 (2021). https://doi.org/10.1007/978-3-030-74296-6_26
20. Verstraete, M., Verbrugge, S., Colle, D.: Solid: enabler of decentralized, digital platforms ecosystems (2022)

Author Index

C. Pesquita et al. (Eds.): ESWC 2023, LNCS 13998, pp. 341–342, 2023.
https://doi.org/10.1007/978-3-031-43458-7

Printed in the United States
by Baker & Taylor Publisher Services

Printed in the United States
by Baker & Taylor Publisher Services